By 1850 Herman Melville's first two books, *Typee* and *Omoo,* had made him a reputation as an entertaining writer on travel. Because reviewers of his succeeding books tended to approach them from that point of view, a work such as *Moby Dick* was praised almost solely for its novelty and realism. Despite the protests of ardent but obscure admirers, later critics classed him as a writer of sea stories, on a par with Richard Henry Dana and James Fenimore Cooper. The other facets of his writing were either ignored or dismissed as "metaphysical extravagance," "difficult and sometimes repulsive."

Melville remained a lesser novelist until the 1920's, when a sudden revival reversed earlier opinion. One critic described his reaction to *Moby Dick* as "incoherent rapture." Such enthusiasm gave way to a steadily growing academic appreciation, and by 1938 Melville's place as a major author was ensured. Since then, a new generation of scholars has done exhaustive research on Melville himself and applied it to his work. Recent criticism has also drawn such books as *Clarel, Pierre,* and *The Confidence-Man* out of their former obscurity.

The Recognition of Herman Melville is a collection of important American and British reviews and critical essays that have appeared since the publication of *Typee* in 1846. It presents in chronological order the basic documents, nowhere else anthologized, on Melville's reception and gradual acceptance. Each piece is representative of the literary opinions of its time. More than that, each piece is also representative of the underlying attitudes that formed the literary opinions of its time. The book is thus a survey of more than one hundred years of literary criticism, a review of reviews, as well as a documentation of Melville's erratic and long-delayed recognition.

The Recognition of Herman Melville

Herman Melville as a young man.
Painting by Asa W. Twitchell

The Recognition of HERMAN MELVILLE

Selected Criticism Since 1846

Edited by
HERSHEL PARKER

Ann Arbor
THE UNIVERSITY OF MICHIGAN PRESS

Preface

In the last fifty years Melville has been called both a minor contemporary of Cooper and the greatest American writer. In his own time the reversals in his fame were equally dramatic. His first book, *Typee* (1846), was a popular success, though it outraged the Protestant Missions. With *Omoo, Redburn,* and *White-Jacket* Melville enhanced his reputation here and in England as a "modernised DeFoe" and a successor to Smollett, though the Rabelaisian form of *Mardi* baffled its few readers. Perceptive critics hailed the Shakespearean power of *Moby-Dick,* though dissenters attacked the Carlylean rhetoric and called the book and the author mad. *Pierre* (1852), an experimental psychological novel, met universal hostility, and Melville's stunning achievements in *The Piazza Tales* and *The Confidence-Man* were unrecognized by even friendly critics. After 1857 Melville published no fiction at all, and only four volumes of poetry, all "eminently adapted for unpopularity." Known until his death in 1891 as the author of *Typee* and *Omoo,* and known during the Melville revival of the 1920's as the author of *Moby-Dick,* Melville only now begins to receive recognition commensurate with his achievements not only in *Moby-Dick* but also in *Pierre, The Piazza Tales, The Confidence-Man, Clarel,* and the posthumously published *Billy Budd, Sailor.*

    This book brings together the criticism essential for understanding Melville's gradual recognition. The first section, "Reviews and Early Appraisals, 1846–1876," reprints the significant portions of the handful of early British and American essays which surveyed Melville's achievement at midcareer. It also reprints or quotes from dozens of representative contemporary reviews, including many famous—and notorious—ones. Among them are a clerical attack on *Typee,* the Boston *Post*'s review of *Mardi* (more alluded to than read), the review of *White-Jacket* in the New York *Albion* (which may have provoked Melville's appeal in *Moby-Dick* to the Spirit of Equality for justification against "all mortal critics"), the splendid newly discovered review of *Moby-Dick* in *The Spirit of the Times,* Melville's friend Evert A. Duyckinck's condemnation of *Pierre,* three reviews of *The Confidence-Man,* and all four serious reviews of *Clarel.* Enough reviews are included to characterize the critical reception of all of Melville's books through *Clarel* and to show how valid was Melville's fear that he would be a victim of the popularity of *Typee* and go down to posterity "as a 'man who lived among the cannibals'!" and wrote " 'Pedee' 'Hullabaloo' & 'Pog-Dog.' " Enough are included to illustrate tragically the critics' opposition to Melville's attempts to write what he felt "most moved to write" and to account for his gradual withdrawal from writing for publication.

Most of these early reviews and essays will reward the reader who approaches them to learn something of nineteenth-century periodical criticism rather than to reproach the reviewers for cruelty to Melville. Even so much-maligned an "attack" as the *Post* review of *Mardi* will be found to contain a fascinating attempt to define the special quality of Melville's "commingled fact and fiction."

There are no selections for 1877–83, when Melville was only perfunctorily mentioned in textbooks, encyclopedias, magazines, and newspapers. The second section, "Academic Neglect and Prophecies of Renown, 1884–1912," covers the period of Melville's near-oblivion in America and his growing recognition in England by a few literary men. Apparently, his books were passed lovingly from friend to friend among groups of English writers. Michael Sadlier saw Charles Reade's extensively marked copy of *Moby-Dick* (or was it *The Whale?*), and Reade was a friend of Robert Buchanan, whose high tribute to Melville in 1885 is reprinted here. James Thomson introduced John W. Barrs to Melville, and Barrs's friend Henry S. Salt "was brought into touch with Herman Melville" through his biography of Thomson. Salt then introduced *Moby-Dick* to William Morris, who began quoting it with "huge gusto and delight." The leading critics of America's age of gentility were not fitted to appreciate Melville, but by the 1890's a few Americans were enthusiastic about *Moby-Dick* as well as *Typee* and *Omoo* and were beginning to communicate their excitement to their friends.

And Frank Jewett Mather said of his experience in the first two decades of this century that "extraordinary persons on both sides the seas" were drawn together by discovering their mutual love of Melville—during the years that the Boston-oriented American textbook industry was ignoring Melville altogether or assigning him a place somewhat lower than Simms, not to mention Cooper. In the selections given here for 1884–1912 there is tremendous tension between the brave words of the Melville enthusiasts and the cautious words of the academicians—both those who, unaware of the current attempts at reevaluation, assigned him a niche with the minor fiction writers, and their more alert colleagues, who uneasily tried to explain away the curiously recurrent interest.

At last, in 1917, the tension began to be resolved when Carl Van Doren's four-page essay in a major new literary history, the *Cambridge History of American Literature*, provided the general assessment Melville awaited. Van Doren concluded his essay with the most memorable single line of all twentieth-century Melville criticism: "Of late his fame has shown a tendency to revive." Published accounts have not revealed the extent to which Van Doren himself was responsible for the revival. It was Van Doren, from his office at *The Nation*, who solicited Raymond Weaver's article on Melville's centennial and who stimulated the researches that led to Weaver's *Herman Melville: Mariner and Mystic* (1921), the first biography of Melville. Years later, assembling the memorabilia of his early Melville investigations, Weaver attached this fascinating explanatory note to a letter from Van Doren on 1 July 1919 regarding Weaver's forthcoming article on Melville. It is published here for the first time with the kind permission of Columbia University, holder of the Raymond Weaver Papers:

> Some days previous we had been seated beside each other at an English Department Dinner [at Columbia].— It was this that started it all. He had said to me: "You know, there will soon be a centenary of Herman Melville. He was a wonderful old boy—and I'd like to do him myself. But if you'd try him, I'm willing."
>
> I knew almost nothing of Melville—beyond the fact that Brander Matthews had mentioned him in course [*sic*]. I'd begun *Typee*—and stopped at the beginning. So, with Carl

Van Doren's offer, being unhampered with information, I fell in with his request. I thought: "I'll read a few South Sea travel books, examine Melville's official biographies, and turn out an adequate article." The following day, I visited Columbia library, to find books and books by Melville—an indecent spawning—and no "official" biographies at all. So I consulted Poole's Index—to learn, by the references, that Melville had started off well enough, but went wrong, some how—living to an incredible forty years of sedulous obscurity.

I read him—with gaping wonderment and incredulity. I also bought him. A first edition of *Moby-Dick*, in 1918, could be had for less than a dollar. I picked up easily enough a complete set of him. Duplicates, when they were offered me as pleading gifts, I charitably bought: in my excitement they seemed incredibly inexpensive gifts of an excitement I feared to credit, to unconverted friends. *Moby-Dick*'s that now are unpurchasable at $200 I scorned at the piracy of anything over a dollar. Evidently, I did not view Melville as an *investment*. He was an excitement, rather—a kind of indulgent madness vastly interesting to myself, but not trusted to wholesale consumption.

Despite centennial essays like Weaver's and, especially, Frank Jewett Mather's superb essay, Americans were slow to respond, and throughout the 1920's they responded almost solely to *Moby-Dick*. In 1921 for *The American Novel* Carl Van Doren qualified his former conclusion about Melville's reviving fame:

> Of late years, however, his fame shows a tendency to re-vive, perhaps more considerably in England than in Amer-ica. Barrie's Captain Hook is confessedly derived from Melville; John Masefield has said that *Moby Dick* speaks the whole secret of the sea; Lady Sybil Scott admitted passages from Melville to *The Book of the Sea*, which, though verse for the most part, she could not think com-plete without Defoe, Melville, and Joseph Conrad. And while Melville at home has had somewhat slighter praise, an acquaintance with his work is a sign by which it may be learned whether any given American knows the litera-ture of his country.

Melville's English admirers just after the centennial were un-

doubtedly more enthusiastic than the Americans. Viola Mey-
nell in her essay in the *Dublin Review* (1920) confronted the
problem of conveying her full sense of Melville's power without
appearing to speak lightly:

> Perhaps that praise had better not be too much obtruded
> which might be of a kind to provoke contention, for it
> chances that to the present writer Herman Melville satisfies
> not only every judgment but every inmost preference; so
> that it seems as if no greatness that has ever been surpasses
> his greatness.

H. M. Tomlinson, who was the colleague on the London *Nation*
mentioned in the Wayfarer's deposition (printed in this section), became perhaps the most generous of Melville's English
admirers in the 1920's. In the London *Athenaeum* (7 April 1923,
when he could already be retrospective about the revival),
Tomlinson wrote that *Moby-Dick* "is an immense experience in
one's reading life. Incoherent rapture is its first fruits." And
he added:

> When I began to read it, I did not believe it. That first
> chapter was too good to be true. Books beginning at that
> elevation cannot be maintained there except by magicians;
> and how often do we meet writers of that kind? Moreover,
> I had come to it late, for I had ridiculed at least one rare
> and exciting rumor about it.

At the same time that many readers were discovering
Moby-Dick in the 1920's, Melville frequently served as ammu-
nition for critical attacks on contemporary values. As Michael P.
Zimmerman showed in his *Herman Melville in the 1920's* (1963),
Raymond Weaver's biography was, like Van Wyck Brooks's *The
Ordeal of Mark Twain*, a contribution to the postwar Menck-
ensque criticism of America—it was "a dark melodrama in which
a doomed American writer wars with his puritanical and con-
formist age." And the Melville presented by Lewis Mumford's
biography in 1929, Zimmerman observes, "was meant to be an
exemplar for those Americans in 1929 who, as Mumford saw
them, had given over their lives to the meaningless accumulation
of material goods and the single-minded pursuit of a successful
career. . . ." Mumford relied on Weaver's inaccurate study for
his information about Melville's life and made sweeping psycho-

logical deductions on the basis of factual mistakes. But Mumford is a brilliant critic, and his biography, more than Weaver's, opened to new readers not only *Moby-Dick* but also many of Melville's lesser-known works.

The writing on Melville increased so much during the revival that section three (1917–32) does not include all the major essays, as the first two sections did, but only representative pieces. Most important is Mather's centennial essay, the first comprehensive essay on all of Melville's works and the fruit of long devotion to Melville, but this section also contains samples from the new researchers like Weaver, a typical "appreciation," Arnold Bennett's minority report on *Pierre*, and the most notable European essay on Melville during the revival, that by Cesare Pavese.

Throughout the 1920's there were warnings that the enthusiasm for Melville was exaggerated and that he would eventually be assigned to a respectable place on the shelf of minor American fiction. In the early 1930's some editors of American textbooks began quietly to omit from their revised editions the Melville selections dutifully inserted during the 1920's. Ludwig Lewisohn in *Expression in America* (1932) announced baldly: "It will be seen at once that I consider the recent reëstimate of Melville to have somewhat overshot the mark," and he denounced the younger generation of Melville enthusiasts as "both deceived and self-deceived." In a more temperate survey in *A History of American Letters* (1936), Walter F. Taylor concluded that two influences (early twentieth-century interest in the South Seas, and the modern mind's approval of Melville as a "thinker whose cynical bitterness matches its own mood of postwar disillusion") "have led to an exaggerated estimate of Melville's greatness, which in all probability cannot be maintained." But Taylor concluded that it would be hard to name any writer except Conrad "who can take rank with Melville as a writer of the sea."

There was a strong rival tendency in other anthologies and histories to discuss Melville at length, and to discuss works other than *Typee, Omoo,* and *Moby-Dick*. Percy H. Boynton, a scholar who had not responded to the first impulses of the revival, opened his essay in *Literature and American Life* (1936) with an especially apt quotation—not from *Moby-Dick* but from *The Encantadas:*

> If you seek to ascend Rock Rondondo, take the following prescription. Go three voyages round the world as a main-royal-man of the tallest frigate that floats; then serve a year or two apprenticeship to the guides who conduct strangers up the Peak of Teneriffe; and as many more respectively to a rope dancer, an Indian juggler, and a chamois. This done, come and be rewarded by the view from our tower. How we get there, we alone know. If we sought to tell others, what the wiser were they? Suffice it, that here at the summit you and I stand. Does any balloonist, does the outlooking man in the moon, take a broader view of space? Much thus, one fancies, looks the universe from Milton's celestial battlements.

"It was," Boynton said, "Melville's comment to those who care to reach his vantage point and share his view." In his attempt to reach this vantage point Boynton by the mid-1930's had pondered over *Pierre* and even *Clarel.*

It was Willard Thorp who in 1938 established Melville as a major American writer to be studied in all American colleges. His Introduction to the Melville volume in the popular American Writers Series contained the best brief biographical account yet written (indeed, the best until Leon Howard's University of Minnesota pamphlet on Melville was published in 1961) as well as what remains the best brief survey of Melville's social and political views. Thorp's whole Introduction helped to end the period when one could safely write biographical essays on Melville without attention to factual evidence and write literary criticism without attention to all of Melville's works. The selection from Thorp's Introduction reprinted here, "The Trilogy," was the most intensive literary analysis of Melville yet written, and it fittingly begins the fourth section of this book.

This section, "Academic Recognition: 1938 to the Present," cannot claim to be as comprehensive as the first three sections, but much of the best of recent criticism appears here. That most extraordinary phenomenon of Melville scholarship, the group of Yale graduate students who did dissertations under Stanley T. Williams in the 1940's and early 1950's, is represented by selections from Merton M. Sealts, Jr., Nathalia Wright, William H. Gilman, and Walter Bezanson. It represents, through Sealts's article, a dozen cogent and slightly incredulous studies of Melville's private allegorizing in the mid-1850's and typifies, through the same article, the recent shift of attention to the tales, especially *The Piazza Tales*. It represents Leon Howard, the author of the standard biography (1951), by his first serious article on Melville. It provides an example of recent source studies, Millicent Bell's graceful article on "Jonah Historically Regarded." (One indefatigable source hunter not included is Howard P. Vincent, whose *The Trying-Out of MOBY-DICK* is available in paperback, and whose study of the composition of *White-Jacket* is forthcoming.) It includes a chapter from Warner Berthoff's well-balanced study of Melville's craft as a writer. Several fine recent dissertations are represented by a section from the Introduction of Walker Cowen's mammoth unpublished 1965 Harvard dissertation, which reproduces and analyzes all of Melville's known marginalia, and by a comprehensive essay by John D. Seelye—an outgrowth of his recent dissertation on Melville's irony that is to serve as the Introduction to his booklength study.

One special area of the recognition of Herman Melville cannot be represented in this anthology, and perhaps not in any anthology—the uses of Melville by other writers, both in their works and in their lives. It may be that Melville is finally being "recognized" most profoundly by his fellow writers—by Hart Crane, Conrad Aiken, Malcolm Lowry, William Faulkner, Charles Olson, Ralph Ellison, Robert Lowell. That sort of recognition Melville would have understood and exulted in, for he was a master "recognizer" of great writers—of Rabelais, Milton, Sterne, Byron, Carlyle, Arnold; and only in the writings of a handful of Melville's fellow immortals is Shakespeare as profoundly recognized as in *Moby-Dick*.

A NOTE: This anthology follows the original reviews and essays in anomalies and occasional outright misspellings (like Stubbs for Stubb), but it corrects typographical errors that the authors could not have written (like Hantia for Hautia). Errors of fact have not been corrected, or even pointed out, but erroneous biographical paragraphs have been omitted from several of the essays, with the omissions indicated.

Contents

Reviews and Early Appraisals: 1846–76

Academic Neglect and Prophecies of Renown: 1884–1912

The Melville Revival: 1917–32

Academic Recognition: 1938–67

Contents

My peace and my supper are my reward, my dear Hawthorne. So your joy-giving and exultation-breeding letter is not my reward for my ditcher's work with that book, but is the good goddess's bonus over and above what was stipulated for—for not one man in five cycles, who is wise, will expect appreciative recognition from his fellows, or any one of them.

From Melville's reply to Hawthorne's letter about *Moby-Dick* (17? November 1851).

Reviews and
Early Appraisals:
1846-76

MARGARET FULLER [1810–50], transcendentalist, social reformer, and editor of the *Dial,* from December 1844 until August 1846 was the literary critic for Horace Greeley's New York *Tribune.* She had a formidable reputation as a critic.

Review of *Typee*

Attributed to MARGARET FULLER

"Typee" would seem, also, [like another book being reviewed] to be the record of imaginary adventures by some one who had visited those regions. But it is a very entertaining and pleasing narrative, and the Happy Valley of the gentle cannibals compares very well with the best contrivances of the learned Dr. Johnson to produce similar impressions. Of the power of this writer to make pretty and spirited pictures as well [as] of his quick and arch manner generally, a happy specimen may be seen in the account of the savage climbing the cocoa-tree, p. 273, vol. 2d. Many of the observations and narratives we suppose to be strictly correct. Is the account given of the result of the missionary enterprises in the Sandwich Islands of this number? We suppose so from what we have heard in other ways. With a view to ascertaining the truth, it would be well if the sewing societies, now engaged in providing funds for such enterprises [,] would read the particulars, [which] they will find in this book beginning p. 249, vol. 2d, and make inquiries in consequence before going on with their efforts. Generally, the sewing societies of the country villages will find this the very book they wish to have read while assembled at their work. Othello's hairbreadth 'scapes were nothing to those by this hero in the descent of the cataracts, and many a Desdemona might seriously incline her ear to the descriptions of the lovely Fay-a-way.

New York *Tribune,* 4 April 1846.

Review of *Typee*

ANONYMOUS

We were not disposed at first to say any thing against this volume. The rather free and easy style in which it is written, and the sort of clever-heartedness that seemed indicative of the author's disposition, made us suppose that whatever errors of fact the book contained were probably unintentional, and that its statements with some allowance might be received. On reading farther, however, we entirely changed our views; for it is difficult to believe that the author was not actuated, either by a perverse spirit of intentional misrepresentation, or that he is not utterly incapable, from moral obtuseness, of an accurate statement. If we were to sum up the author's mind, gathered from his whole book, we should say he was one who had first been fretted out of good humor by civilized life; that he had then become a wanderer until he had forgotten his ill nature, and also the advantages of civilization; that he had then chanced to be thrown, for a while, on the Sandwich Islands, where he perhaps came into uncomfortable collision with the civil authority, which engendered a special prejudice against those who were striving to civilize those islands; that he had then been wandering two or three years longer in various parts of the earth, till what he remembered of the Islands of the Pacific had become a sort of confused mass in his own brain; after which he came to this country, and sat down to write a book. These facts seem to be scattered along through the volume. This moral obtuseness appears, whenever there is an opportunity for exhibiting a correct spirit. No opportunity slips by for giving a glowing description of savage life, and for launching quips and small anathemas against civilization. For missionaries and missionary labor,—except in *general,*—he has a special abhorrence. The cause of Missions is a good thing—except where it raises man from cannibalism to civilization. If he meets a native female Islander, she is a goddess;—if a missionary's wife, she is a blowzy looking, red-faced, fat oppressor of the poor native—reducing him to the station of drudge. All statements made by

The New Englander, Vol. 4 (July 1846) 449–50.

missionaries are, with slight exceptions, infinitely exaggerated; and those whose money is asked for the blessed work of sending men to elevate the character of the savage, had best be careful that their money does not go into other channels. The vices of savages are much overdrawn; and for the vices that do exist, their counterpart, or what is worse, is found every where in Christian nations. Of truths of general history he seems to know nothing. The fact of the depopulation of the Sandwich Islands, seems to him to be something new; and this is specially brought about by the efforts of missionaries and their hypocrisy. The fact that wherever civilization comes in contact with savage life, there the savage wastes away; or at least that this has been so, wherever the Saxon stock comes into contact with it; he never thought of;—and now for the first time seeing the fact he gives his own crude explanation of it, and would have the world then receive his volume as a work of authority. Now justice to the cause of truth demands that *we* say, that whosoever shall read this book, and its statements touching the Islands of the Pacific, should ask themselves a moment as to the capability of a man to give an accurate statement of moral facts, when, according to his own showing, he has not been in a course of life calculated greatly to improve his moral eyesight. They should think who and what is writing, when such facts are recorded; and then, though they may not think the writer *intends* to misrepresent, they will at least be prepared to resist the false impressions, which a book with such statements is most certain to produce. The book is not without literary merit. It is a very companionable one. As a specimen of the lighter writing of the day, it is entitled to notice. But as to the writer's ability to treat on some of the matters of his volume, it would rank well with Joseph Smith's competency to give an exegetical work on the book of Genesis, or Bishop Southgate's to pronounce on the authenticity of an ancient MS. among the Armenians of Turkey.

BY HERMAN MELVILLE.

TYPEE.

One Volume, 12mo, Muslin, 87½ cents ; Paper, 75 cents.

"Why I never chanced upon Mr. Melville's work before, is one of the inscrutable mysteries of my fate. While luxuriating in its perusal, I looked back upon myself in my ante-Typee-cal existence, with positive commiseration. There are those, I am aware, who doubt the authenticity of this charming narrative. 'Oh, ye of little faith!' I have a solemn conviction of its truth—a pertinacious belief in the entire work—an humble, unquestioning reliance on the word of the narrator."—*Correspondence of* "GRACE GREENWOOD" *to the Home Journal.*

Chateaubriand's Atala is of no softer or more romantic tone—Anacharsis scarce presents us with images more classically exquisite.—*New York Mirror.*

Typee is a happy hit, whichever way you look at it—whether as travels, romance, poetry, or humor. The *bonhommie* of the book is remarkable. It appears as genial and natural as the spontaneous fruits of the island.—*Morning News.*

The air of freshness and romance which characterizes Typee, gives it the appearance of an improved edition of our old favorites, Peter Wilkins and Gulliver.—*Richmond Republican.*

A charming book—full of talent, composed with singular elegance, and as musical as Washington Irving's Columbus —*Western Continent.*

Enviable Herman! A happier dog it is impossible to imagine than Herman in the Typee valley.—*London Times.*

Some of these pictures but require us to call the savages celestials, to have supposed Mr. Melville to have dropped from the clouds, and to fancy some Ovidian grace added to the narrative in order to become scenes of classic mythology.—*London Spectator.*

Such is life in the valley of the Typees ; and surely Rasselas, if he had had the good luck to stumble on it, would not have gone further in his search after happiness.—*Douglas Jerrold's Magazine.*

The whole narrative is most simple, most affecting, and most romantic. Ah ! thou gentle and too enchanting Fayaway, what has become of thee?—*Lon. Gent's. Mag.*

Since the joyous moment when we first read Robinson Crusoe, and believed it all, and wondered all the more because we believed, we have not met with so bewitching a work as this narrative of Herman Melville's.—*London John Bull.*

A book full of fresh and richly-colored matter.—*London Athenæum.*

This is really a very curious book. The happy valley of our dear Rasselas was not a more romantic or enchanting scene.—*London Examiner.*

This is a most entertaining and refreshing book. The writer, though filling the post of a common sailor, is certainly no common man.—*London Critic.*

The style is racy and pointed, and there is a romantic interest thrown around the adventure, which to most readers will be highly charming.—*American Review.*

It bears the unexhausted characteristics of talent.—*National Intelligencer.*

The story is eventful—wonderful ; some of the deeds performed by the author and his companion almost surpass belief.—*Cincinnati Herald.*

Harper & Brothers, Publishers, New York.

The Harper & Brothers Advertisement for *Typee*

BY HERMAN MELVILLE.

O M O O.

One Volume, 12mo, Muslin, $1 25 ; Paper, $1 00.

After the pungent and admirably written narrative of that accomplished, able sea-man, Herman Melville, few books of the same class but must appear flat and unprofitable. Omoo would have found readers at any time ; and that although twenty publishers had combined with fifty authors to deluge the public with the Pacific Ocean during the five previous years.—*Blackwood's notice of Coulter's Cruise.*

Let Mr. Melville write as much as he will, provided always he writes as well as now, and he shall find us greedy devourers of his productions. He has a rare pen for the delineation of character ; an eye for the humorous and grotesque which is worth a Jew's ; for the description of natural scenery he is not to be beaten, either on this side of the Atlantic or the other. His pencil is most distinct, the coloring beautiful and rich. As for invention, he will bear comparison with the most cunning of the modern French school. * * * At the last page of his second work, Mr. Melville is as fresh and vigorous as at the first line of the book which preceded it. Lkie his reader, he leaves off with an appetite.—*London Times.*

Unlike most sequels, Omoo is equal to its predecessor. The character of the composition is clear, fresh, vivacious, and full of matter.—*London Spectator.*

The adventures are depicted with force and humor.—*London Athenæum.*

Some of the scenes are like cabinet pictures.—*London Critic.*

Written in a style worthy of Philip Quarles or Robinson Crusoe.—*Lon. Lit. Gaz.*

It would be difficult to imagine a man better fitted to describe the impressions such a life and such scenes are calculated to call forth, than the auther of Omoo. Every variety of character, and scene, and incident, he studies and describes with equal gusto.—*London People's Journal.*

A stirring narrative of very pleasant reading. It possesses much of the charm that has made Robinson Crusoe immortal—life-like description. It commands attention, as if old interest were created by the narratives—

> "Of Raleigh, Frobisher, and Drake—
> Adventurous hearts, who bartered bold
> Their English steel for Spanish gold."

The history is one of comparatively new lands and new people. His account of the natives corresponds with that of Kotzebue and others.—*Douglas Jerrold's Paper.*

Mr. Melville has more than sustained his widely-spread reputation in these volumes. Omoo and Typee are actually delightful romances of real life, embellished with powers of description, and a graphic skill of hitting off characters, little inferior to the highest order of novel and romance writers.—*Albion.*

A curious and fascinating narrative.—*Anglo American.*

These volumes contain a vast amount of exceedingly entertaining and interesting matter.—*Philadelphia Courier.*

Omoo is characterized by all the animation, picturesqueness, and felicity of style which commended the author's first writings to a second reading, even after curiosity is satisfied by tracing out the singularity of the story.—*Literary World.*

Harper & Brothers, Publishers, New York.

WILLIAM JERDAN [1782–1869]. The attribution rests on Jerdan's being the editor of the London *Literary Gazette* from 1817 until 1850.

Review of *Mardi: and a Voyage Thither*

Attributed to WILLIAM JERDAN

Our author, it may be remembered, took in many of the knowing ones in his former work; but we fancy the present will puzzle them more. At least it has posed us, and is a 3 vol. metaphor into the applications of which we can only now and then catch a glimpse. It has struck our head like one of those blows which set everything glancing and dancing before your eyes like splintered sunrays; and amid the sparkle and glitter you can discern nothing distinctly. Yet the images are brilliant, and upon the whole you wonder how aught so luminous can be so dark. We never saw a book so like a kaleidoscope. As for giving any idea of it, we have none ourselves. As far as we can make out, Mardi is a group of islands in the Pacific Ocean; perhaps on the way to California! The author is thereabouts, in a good old ship, the captain of which resolves to proceed to Arctic regions, a-whaling; on which our friend resolves to leave, and persuading an ancient tough Skyeman sailor, one Jarl, to accompany him, they cut and run in a boat by night, and trust themselves to the wide expanse of waters, tolerably well provided for a few weeks' chance to fall in with land. Their adventures are superb. The sharks and other fish of the sea are described in the style of Coleridge's *Ancient Mariner. . . .*

The London *Literary Gazette, and Journal of the Belles Lettres,* No. 1679 (24 March 1849) 202–3.

EVERT A. DUYCKINCK [1816–78], prominent New York editor and critic, friend of almost every major American writer of his time, and with his brother GEORGE LONG DUYCKINCK [1823–63] compiler-author of the monumental *Cyclopaedia of American Literature* (2 vols., 1855).

From Mardi

EVERT (AND GEORGE?) DUYCKINCK

It is a critical period in the life of an author, when, having received ample honors for his early productions, having on a first appearance achieved a distinguished reputation, he comes before the public again, after an interval, with a new book. The question of his intellectual stamina is to be decided. It is to be determined by a full and accurate survey, a calculation of bearings and distances, and the relations of the whole heavenly system; whether "the comet of a season" is to assume a steady rank in the great planetary world; whether there is heat as well as light in the brilliant body which has attracted the public gaze. To drop metaphor, Mr. Herman Melville, American sailor, fresh from the Pacific, one summer morning, appears before his countrymen and another great audience in England, in the wondrous tale of "Typee." The narrative is immediately caught up from its freshness, vivacity, the grace of the story, the humor and ease of the style. "A very uncommon common sailor, even for America!" quoth the London Times. Hard working Jerrold laps himself in the Typee Elysium. The venerable old Gentleman's, Sylvanus Urban, older than old Parr, nearing his second centennial, feels youthful blood revive in his veins, even as when he read Rasselas (fresh from the press), and sighs "Ah! thou gentle and too enchanting Fayaway!" Blackwood shrugged his broad Scot shoulders and cried, "There is no Melville! Can such things come out of a forecastle?" At home the wonder was not less and the sale was as great. Poets took up Fayaway and turned capital prose into indifferent verse; the daily newspapers ran out their vocabulary on the spot. The book was "racy"— "exceedingly racy," said the Courier; "readable," said the Morning News; "a charming book," the hundred-eyed Argus. There

New York *Literary World*, Vol. 4 (7 and 14 April 1849) 309–10, 333–36.

was no mistaking the matter. "Typee" was a hit, a palpable hit—and the arrows from that quiver are not exhausted yet. Typee is constantly getting printed and going off in new editions, which it is quite too much trouble to put upon the title page. "Omoo" followed, less unique, but full of entertainment, humor, and character. It was and is successful—as it deserved. The good humor of the "Times" was again poured out in a column or two of that broad sheet, and

> Blackwood murmured soft applause.

But these were books of Travels; and books of Travels, though written in a highly artistic style, will not sustain a great literary reputation. American travellers have frequently written successful Travels. The national quickness of observation coming in contact with new scenes, the freshness of view which belongs to an American in the old world, and the national curiosity at home, have been prolific of popular Tours and Travels. Was there anything more in the author of "Typee"?

That question "MARDI" is to decide.

It is exactly two years since Mr. Melville's last book. The interval has undoubtedly been devoted conscientiously and laboriously to "Mardi," which is not only a very happy, genial production, in the best mood of luxurious invention, but a book of thought, curious thought and reflection. There is "something in it" everywhere. We read on and on for simple amusement; but we find these pictures leave traces on the memory, and are reproduced with our thoughts, pointing many a significant moral.

If we were seeking for comparisons, to give the reader an idea of "Mardi," we should suggest something of Rabelais—but the reader will be better prepared to understand that when he has read the book through.

What is the book? A purely original invention. Says Mr. Melville, in his brief preface:—"Not long ago, having published two narratives of voyages in the Pacific, which, in many quarters, were received with incredulity, the thought occurred to me, of indeed writing a romance of Polynesian adventure, and publishing it as such; to see whether the fiction might not, possibly, be received for a verity: in some degree the reverse of my previous experience. This thought was the germ of others, which have resulted in Mardi." The romance of Polynesian adventure is the romance of real life, human nature in a new setting, the romance of Rasselas, Gaudentio di Lucca, the Voyage of Panurge. . . .

In fact it is beginning to be pretty evident now to the reader that this Mardi into which he has been led, in spite of the glorious feasting, and drinking, and lounging, the eloquent dissertations on Meerschaums and the like, is quite a serious region after all. Indeed is it, for Mardi expands before us from the coral-cinctured isle of summer seas, the reef-girt lagune-watered atoll of Polynesia, with its chieftain palms and Eden gardens, into a wider circuit, broad as that enveloped by old ocean on the wonderous shield of Achilles. The sea has many isles, and the continents are but isles in Mardi—Mardi is the world. Be not surprised then, reader, at finding thyself flitting about, here and there, among its characters, or at seeing thy birthplace and country figured on its ample map. What is this isle of Dominora and its king Bello, of Vivenza, this Porpheero, with its volcanic eruption—marvellously like John Bull, America, and Republican France! Verily his subjects should not be displeased at the portraiture of King Bello—John Bull in Otaheitan guise. . . .

And what of Vivenza? Hope and good cheer, and with fair play all around, some satire.

Vivenza

"In good round truth, and as if an impartialist from Arcturus spoke it, Vivenza was a noble land. Like a young tropic tree she stood, laden down with greenness, myriad blossoms, and the ripened fruit thick-hanging from one bough. She was promising as the morning.

"Or Vivenza might be likened to St. John, feeding on locusts and wild honey, and with prophetic voice, crying to the nations from the wilderness. Or, child-like, standing among the old robed kings and emperors of the Archipelago, Vivenza seemed a young Messiah, to whose discourse the bearded Rabbis bowed.

"So seemed Vivenza in its better aspect. Nevertheless, Vivenza was a braggadocio in Mardi; the only brave one ever known. As an army of spurred and crested roosters, her people chanticleered at the resplendent rising of their sun. For shame, Vivenza! Whence thy undoubted valor? Did ye not bring it with ye from the bold old shores of Dominora, where there is a fulness of it left? What isle but Dominora could have supplied thee with that stiff spine of thine?—That heart of boldest beat? Oh, Vivenza! know that true grandeur is too big for a boast; and nations, as well as men, may be too clever to be great."

Is not this sign of a true manhood, when an American author lifts his voice boldly to tell the truth to his country people? There has been a time when the land could not bear this strong meat, but forsooth must be fed on windy adulation. As she grows stronger, and girts herself for stouter enterprises, she appears less afraid to look at her own faults. This is a good sign! Mardi probes yet deeper.

States and kingdoms, however, do not touch the whole matter yet. The individual world of man, the microcosm, is to be explored and navigated. To this must all true literature come at last. The Poets but begin

in gladness
Whereof in the end comes despondency and sadness.

There is no such thing as trifling in a genuine book. Set even a Thomas Hood, lightest of word-wreathers, down to spin rhymes, and we find ourselves soon caught in a mesh in which the soul is struggling. Most mirthful, most serious of men was Hood. Set a Rabelais upon invention, with the widest range of the earthy, and there will be solemnity enough under his grotesque hood. The irony of Swift, and his persecution of humanity, but prove his love for the race. Is it not significant that our American mariner, beginning with pleasant pictures of his Pacific Ocean, should soon sweep beyond the current of his isles into this world of high discourse: revolving the condition, the duties, the destiny of men? No vagrant lounger, truly, into the booths of literature, where frivolous wit is sold in the fashion of the hour, but a laborious worker, of a rare discipline, on our American book shelves.

Mardi is a species of Utopia—or rather a satiric voyage in which we discover—human nature. There is a world of poetical, thoughtful, ingenious moral writing in it which Emerson would not disclaim—gleams of high-raised fancy, quaint assemblages of facts in the learned spirit of Burton and the Doctor. Mardi exhibits the most various reflection and reading. It is an extraordinary book.

We have indicated but a part of its contents, not the whole. The party embraced on the voyage with King Media include a speculative, moralizing philosopher, Babbalanja, very fond of quoting from the ancient writings of one Bardianna (a species of Herr Teufelsdroch authority, an eloquent author, and quite to the point), and occasionally getting into the regions of the incomprehensible; a youthful poet Yoomy, a fair type of the class, all sensibility and expression; the antiquarian Mohi. As for our unphilosophic friend Jarl, of the first volume, he seems to have not been wanted in this learned company; so he was left behind at one of the islands to be killed off by the natives. The discourse of these parties is generally very poetical, at times quite edifying, excepting when they get into the clouds, attempting to handle the problem of the universe.

Mardi will undoubtedly add to Mr. Melville's reputation. The public will discover in him, at least, a capital essayist, in addition to the fascinating novelist and painter of sea life. In these there can be no question of his powers. We might multiply instances of ingenious thought, raised by a subtle fancy, or point to the slender resources of savage life, upon which he has built up the most varied and probable superstructure of manners and character. But enough. It will be felt that America has gained an author of innate force and steady wing, a man with material and work in him—who has respect for his calling, in company with original powers of a high order; with whom the public, we trust, may walk hand in hand, heart in heart, through many good years of goodly productiveness.

CHARLES GORDON GREENE [1804–86], the editor of the Democratic Boston *Post* from 1831 until 1875, had special reason for being interested in Melville: he had profited from the Jacksonian take-over that turned Melville's grandfather out of the Boston Customs House, and in 1843 and 1844 he had been an associate of Melville's fire-eating Repealer and Polkite brother, Gansevoort Melville.

Review of *Mardi*

CHARLES GORDON GREENE

Mardi: and a Voyage Thither. By Herman Melville. New York: Harper & Brothers. Boston: Redding & Co.—Many a *nine shillings*, we imagine, will be wasted on these two externally handsome volumes. Mr Melville's reputation as a writer of commingled fact and fiction is deservedly high, but we have always thought it not so high as it ought to be. His "Typee" and "Omoo" are much more than graceful, fascinating and vivacious books— they are filled with powerful descriptions, and strongly drawn, well filled and natural characters. His personages purport to be real people, but it is almost needless to say that they must be, in the main, and as much as most fictitious characters are, the mental creations of the author. And it is for this unpretending, homely, real delineation, found in the midst of so much that is wild, light, fanciful and gorgeous, that Mr Melville has not received sufficient praise; and while his productions have been commended quite as much as they deserve to be for the last named attributes, the portions displaying the most genius, tact and knowledge of human nature have usually escaped the general eye, as far at least as the remarks of reviewers are concerned. In his two former books the author under notice is quite worthy of being called a modernised Defoe—much of the strength, homeliness and naturalness of the great original being overlaid with a coating of modern grace and spiritualness. It was with these feelings that we began to read "Mardi," and we have written the preceding sentences, not to raise up that we might the more effectually knock down, but to show that we have a cordial appreciation of Mr Melville's previous writings, and that

Boston *Post,* 18 April 1849.

in commencing the present one, we had no sort of prejudice against it or him.

With these premises, it is almost needless to say that we were disappointed with "Mardi." It is not only inferior to "Typee" and "Omoo," but it is a really poor production. It ought not to make any reputation for its author, or to sell sufficiently well to encourage him to attempt any thing else. "The Voyage Thither" is interesting enough, though even this is almost spoiled by the everlasting assumption of the brilliant, jocose and witty in its style. After the arrival at "Mardi," the book becomes mere *hodge-podge*, reminding us of the *talk* in Rabelais, divested of all its coarseness, and, it may be added, of all its wit and humor. In his preface, Mr Melville intimates, that having previously written truth which was believed to be fiction, he has now attempted a romance "to see whether it might not possibly be received as a verity." We think he need be under no apprehension that the present volumes will be received as gospel—they certainly lack all show of truth or naturalness. He had better stick to his "fact" which is received as "fiction," but which puts money in his purse and wreathes laurels round his head, than fly to "fiction" which is not received at all, as we opine will be the case with "Mardi," in a very short time, and in spite of the all extending and pervading influence of his publisher. We doubt not, however, that the book will sell and be read, for a time, but if the "man who read the Monikins" was one of the greatest curiosities in the land, we think the "man who read Mardi and *liked it*" will be an *unexampled* product of the age—he may be the "coming man," perhaps, spoken of by Punch and the Transcendentalists. We have said that Mardi is *hodge-podge*. It describes adventures in the Polynesian Islands, but lacks incident and meaning. The conversations are like nothing one ever read or heard, and, if they have any significance, are too recondite, at least, for our intelligence to fathom. Sometimes it seems as if the book were a satire upon matters and things in general, but this idea is soon dispersed by the appearance of a mass of downright nonsense. The characters are "legion" and uninteresting—the whole book is not only tedious but unreadable. In a word, "Mardi" greatly resembles Rabelais emasculated of every thing but prosiness and puerility.

GEORGE RIPLEY [1802–80], a leading transcendentalist and an associate of Brook Farm, was a frequent contributor to the *Tribune*. This review is signed "R."

Review of *Mardi*

Attributed to GEORGE RIPLEY

We have seldom found our reading faculty so near exhaustion, or our good nature as critics [*sic*] so severely exercised, as in an attempt to get through this new work by the author of the fascinating "Typee" and "Omoo." If we had never heard of Mr. Melville before, we should soon have laid aside his book, as a monstrous compound of Carlyle, Jean-Paul, and Sterne, with now and then a touch of Ossian thrown in; but remembering our admiration of his former charming productions, we were unable to believe that the two volumes could contain so little of the peculiar excellence of an old favorite, and only mock us with a constant sense of disappointment.

"Typee" and "Omoo" were written under the immediate inspiration of personal experience.—The vivid impressions which the author had received from his residence among those fairy Edens of the Sea had not faded from his mind. He describes what he saw and felt, with the careless hilarity of a sailor, relating a long yarn to his shipmates in the forecastle—he has no airs, but airs from the perfumed islands where he revelled so jubilantly in the wild freedom of nature—he has no reputation to keep from damage, except that of a good fellow who has seen strange things in his day—and he talks on in his riotous, rollicking manner, always saucy, often swaggering, but ever revealing the soul of a poet and the eye of a painter; and accordingly, his books have had a popular run, that might gratify the proudest author in modern literature. They have been read with equal delight by the rough sailor, who had to spell out the words by his dim lantern, and the refined scholar who gladly turned from graver toils to these enchanting scenes—by the lawyer amid waiting clients, the seamstress at her needle, and the mechanic at his bench.

New York *Tribune*, 10 May 1849.

The present work aims at a much higher mark but fails to reach it. It professes to be a work of imagination, founded on Polynesian adventures, and for a portion of the first volume maintains that character with tolerable success. In the description of the escape of the "Ancient Mariner" and himself from the whale ship—their strange voyage in an open boat over a thousand miles of ocean—of their gaining unexpected possession of a new craft, MELVILLE is himself—and this is saying a great deal. There are passages in this part of the work, which, taken as separate pictures, display unrivaled beauty and power—the same simple, unaffected grace—the same deep joy in all the rare and precious things of nature—and the same easy command of forcible, picturesque language, which in his former productions called forth such a gush of admiration, even from the most hide-bound reviewer.

But the scene changes after we arrive at "Mardi" and the main plot of the book (such as it is) begins to open.

We are then presented with a tissue of conceits, fancifully strung about the personages of the tale, expressed in language that is equally intolerable for its affectation and its obscurity. The story has no movement, no proportions, no ultimate end; and unless it is a huge allegory—bits of which peep out here and there—winding its unwieldy length along, like some monster of the deep, no significance or point. We become weary with the shapeless rhapsody, and wonder at the audacity of the writer which could attempt such an experiment with the long suffering of his readers.

We should not think it worth while to express ourselves so unambiguously on the character of this work, if we did not recognize in Mr. MELVILLE a writer not only of rare promise, but of excellent performance. He has failed by leaving his sphere, which is that of graphic, poetical narration, and launching out into the dim, shadowy, spectral, Mardian region of mystic speculation and wizard fancies. . . . Let the author return to the transparent narration of his own adventures, in the pure, imaginative prose, which he handles with such graceful facility, and he will be everywhere welcomed as one of the most delightful of American writers.

WILLIAM ALFRED JONES [1817–1900]. The attribution was first made by Jay Leyda in *The Melville Log*. Jones, a leading writer of periodical criticism in the 1840's, is a major character in Perry Miller's *The Raven and the Whale*.

From Melville's Mardi

Attributed to WILLIAM ALFRED JONES

Mr. Melville has given us in his work a sort of retina picture, or inverted view of the world, under the name of Mardi. The different countries are represented by different islands in the South Sea. Thus Dominora represents England; and the hump-backed King Bello represents the British monarchy, with the load of the national debt. Those who have not looked at the world, and the kingdoms of it, from all Mr. Melville's points of sight, will not recognize his pictures, and will find no buried treasure. It is not strange that many will not accept this work as a fair showing of their world. What is fetor to the author is fragrance to them; and they have never beheld the view that his pencil has delineated. They could not see it if they would—they would not if they could.

The beginning of the book is accepted by most, perhaps all, readers. It is in the style of Omoo and Typee—books that made the multitude crazy with delight. These works were to Mardi as a seven-by-nine sketch of a sylvan lake, with a lone hunter, or a boy fishing, compared with the cartoons of Raphael.

Once upon a time a certain married couple were litigating for divorce. The lady possessed great literary talent, more artistic skill, was highly accomplished, and, in fine, had almost all sorts of ability. We need not describe the husband, only by calling him a gentleman. Having large sympathy for women and wives, we enquired of a friend as to the character of the husband, hinting that we opined he was no better than he should be. Our friend answered: "There is nothing to condemn, only the mistake of marriage. There is incompatibility of character—nothing worse. The husband likes a breeze—the wife gets up a storm; he loves a flute—she wants a full orchestra."

United States Magazine and Democratic Review, Vol. 25 (July 1849) 44–50.

We were reminded of this explanation when we saw those who rejoiced in the flute-like music of Melville's Typee and Omoo, and had not the slightest conception of the meaning of his magnificent orchestra in Mardi. Is it our misfortune, or Sivori's fault, that we do not understand or love the harmonies that he educes with Paganini's bow?

Typee and Omoo were written for the multitude, and consequently had no deep philosophy; and, being a true record of simplistic life, had not high harmonic beauty. They were pictures of earth's loveliest vallies, rich with green fields, and flowers, and golden-fruits, with a warm, mellow light glowing over all. The shadows upon the picture were a gross preponderance of the sensual life, occasionally a dead man's head, and the fact that the author was imprisoned in this lap of beauty. We believe it is not in human nature—we *know* it is not in Yankee human nature—to live in heaven, without liberty to leave any hour in the twenty-four, and a night-key in the bargain to make return equally feasible. So we must confess to the slightest possible prejudice against the Paradise of Typee. But we would give all due credit to books that won the plaudits of the people so widely. Now, every one who had read Typee and Omoo, anxiously expected Mardi—and more, they expected a work of similar character. The man who expects and asks for loaf sugar will not be satisfied with marble, though it be built into a palace.

An honest man who had read Mardi, expecting another and more beautiful Omoo, said to us: "I am disappointed. I feel much as I did, when, a good many years ago, I came a long distance from the country to see an elephant on the stage, at the Chatham Theatre. I went home *sick*, from disappointment, *for he looked just like any other elephant.*"

The fact that Mardi is an allegory that mirrors the world, has thus far escaped the critics, who do notices for the book-table on a large scale. Pilgrim's Progress and Gulliver's Travels were written so long ago, that they seem to have dropped through the meshes of the memory of critics, and they have ceased to think any reproduction or improvement of that sort of thing possible in the future, because they have forgotten its existence in the past. . . .

BY HERMAN MELVILLE.

MARDI.

2 Volumes, 12mo, Muslin, $1 75; Paper, $1 50.

A work such as was never heard of before. You might accumulate upon it all the epithets which Madame de Sevigné affectionated. Fancy Daphnis and Chloe dancing I know not what strange *gavotte* with Aristotle and Spinoza. escorted by Gargantua and Gargamelle. Mardi is the modern political world. This part is the most piquant of the book. The colossal machine invented by Mr. Melville might be compared to the American Panorama now placarded on the walls of London in these terms: "*Gigantic original American Panorama, now on exhibition in the great American Hall; the prodigious moving Panorama of the Gulf of Mexico, the Falls of St. Anthony, and of the Mississippi, covering an extent of canvass four miles long, and representing more than 4000 miles of scenery.*" *Translated from the "Revue de Deux Mondes.*"

From the first chapter of the book to the last, where the hero is swept from our sight in a cloud of spray, the book is a magnificent drama.—*Bentley's Miscellany.*

Mardi is a purely original invention, an extraordinary book. It is a species of Utopia, or, rather, a sea voyage in which we discover human nature. There is a world of poetical, thoughtful, ingenious, moral writing in it, exhibiting the most various reflection and reading. Is it not significant that we should soon be swept beyond the current of the isles into this world of high discourse—revolving the conditions, the duties, and destinies of men?—*New York Literary World.*

Mardi has posed us. It has struck our head like one of those blows which set every thing dancing and glancing before your eyes like splintered sun's rays. The images are brilliant; the adventures superb.—*London Literary Gazette.*

Full of pictures from the under world.—*London Athenæum.*

Mardi is full of all Oriental delights.—*Home Journal.*

The reader who has business in Mardi will find it rich in wisdom and brilliant with beauty. It is a magnificent allegory, wherein the world is seen as in a mirror. The germ of the oak is not more surely hid in the acorn than Melville's fame in this book.—*Chronotype.*

An extraordinary production. Mardi is the world.—*Musical Times.*

There is strange interest, at times replete with power of a peculiar and uncommon kind.—*Blackwood.*

A sort of retina picture, or inverted view of the world, under the name of Mardi. Typee and Omoo are to this work as a seven-by-nine sketch of a sylvan lake with a lone hunter, or a boy fishing, compared with the cartoons of Raphael.—*Dem. Rev.*

A wonderful book; at once enthusiastic and epigrammatic; it burns at one and the same time with an intense and richly colored glow of poetic ardor, and the more glittering, but paler fires of an artful rhetoric.—*London Morning Chronicle.*

Charles Lamb might have imagined such a party as Mr. Melville imagines at Pluto's table—*London Examiner.*

The public will discover in him, at least, a capital essayist, in addition to the fascinating novelist and painter of sea life.—*Literary World.*

Harper & Brothers, Publishers, New York.

The Harper & Brothers Advertisement for *Mardi*

From Mr. Melville's *Redburn*

EVERT (AND GEORGE?) DUYCKINCK

Redburn; his First Voyage: being the Sailor-boy Confessions and Reminiscences of the Son of a Gentleman in the Merchant Service. By Herman Melville. Harper & Brothers.

In our last number we called Mr. Melville the De Foe of the Ocean. It is an honorable distinction, to which we think he is fairly entitled by the life-like portraiture of his characters at sea, the strong relishing style in which his observations are conveyed, the fidelity to nature, and, in the combination of all these, the thorough impression and conviction of reality. The book belongs to the great school of nature. It has no verbosity, no artificiality, no languor; the style is always exactly filled by the thought and material. It has the lights and shades, the mirth and melancholy, the humor and tears of real life.

Redburn's First Voyage is the introduction to sailor-life of a youth brought up on the banks of the Hudson, who quits his home from straitened family circumstances, and not uninfluenced by romantic impulses, for a voyage to Liverpool and back before the mast. . . .

A book of incident and detail cannot be described in an article, but we have suggested to the reader the main outlines of Redburn.

In the filling up there is a simplicity, an ease, which may win the attention of a child, and there is reflection which may stir the profoundest depths of manhood. The talk of the sailors is plain, direct, straightforward; where imagery is employed the figure being vivid and the sense unmistakable. This sailor's use of language, the most in the shortest compass, may be the literary school which has rescued Herman Melville from the dull verbosity of many of his contemporaries. If some of our writers were compelled to utter a few words occasionally through the breathings of a gale of wind it might benefit their style. There is also much sound judgment united with good feeling in "Redburn"—a knowledge of sailor's life unobtrusively conveyed through a narrative which has the force of a life current from the writer's own heart.

New York *Literary World*, Vol. 5 (10 November 1849) 395–97 and (17 November 1849) 418–20.

The Harper & Brothers Advertisement for *Redburn*

From Mr. Melville's White Jacket

EVERT (AND GEORGE?) DUYCKINCK

The keen sense of outward life, mingled with the growing weight of reflection which cheers or burdens the inner man, observable in Mr. Melville's later volumes, keep us company in the present. It is this union of culture and experience, of thought and observation, the sharp breeze of the forecastle alternating with the mellow stillness of the library, books and work imparting to each other mutual life, which distinguishes the narratives of the author of Typee from all other productions of their class. He is not a bookish sailor or a tar among books; each character is separate and perfect in its integrity, but he is all the better sailor for the duty and decision which books teach, all the better reader for the independence and sharpness of observation incidental to the objective life of the sea. It is very seldom that you can get at the latter from this point of view. Your men of choice literature and of educated fancy, your Sternes, Jean Pauls, Southeys, and Longfellows, are not likely to acquire the practical experiences of the tar bucket. The sea of course attracts them with its materials for poetic illustration, but they copy from the descriptions of others. To have the fancy and the fact united is rare in any walk, almost unknown on the sea. Hence to Herman Melville, whose mind swarms with tender, poetic, or humorous fancies, the ship is a new world, now first conquered. No one has so occupied it. Sailors have been described and well described, as sailors, and there has been a deal of brilliant and justly admired nautical writing, from the quarter-deck; but the sailor as a man, seen with a genial philosophy and seen from the forecastle, has been reserved for our author. The effect is novel and startling. It is a new dish *en matelote* brought upon our epicurean over-civilized tables. Is Jack to be recognised, you ask, with all this embroidery of reading and reflection about him and his tarry ways? Yes! for Jack is a man, and his ways, tarry as they are, point as indexes to the universal nature among all surely as any gilded duties or elegances on shore.

New York *Literary World*, Vol. 6 (16 March 1850) 271–72 and (23 March 1850) 297–99.

Mr. Melville is true to his title, the *world* in a man-of-war: there is no difficulty in finding it there; it may be concentrated in less space with fewer subjects. And it is a sound humanitarian lesson which he teaches, or rather that life teaches, which he records. There is no sentimentality, no effort to elevate the "people" or degrade the commodores; his characters are not thrust out of their ordinary positions or range of ideas; he does not sew any finery upon them, but they are all heroes nevertheless, interesting while they are on the stage, one and all, as genuine Shakspearean, that is human personages.

Open the book, this White Jacket, which is simply a clear reflecting mirror, in a quaintly-cased gold frame, of a twelve months' voyage in a United States frigate, of an "ordinary seaman," and see what company you are in.

Here is a fellow with the salt on him. Chaucer could not have seen him with brighter eyes:—

Mad Jack

"The man who was born in a gale! For in some time of tempest—off Cape Horn or Hatteras—*Mad Jack* must have entered the world—such things have been—not with a silver spoon, but with a speaking-trumpet in his mouth; wrapped up in a caul, as in a main-sail—for a charmed life against shipwrecks he bears —and crying, *Luff! luff, you may!—steady!—port! World ho!— here I am! . . .*"

A quaint being with quaint associations,—when his guns are all thrown into the ocean a hundred years hence, he will seem still quainter,—is

Quarter-Gunner Quoin

"Quoin, one of the quarter-gunners, had eyes like a ferret. Quoin was a little old man-of-war's man, hardly five feet high, with a complexion like a gun-shot wound after it is healed. He was indefatigable in attending to his duties; which consisted in taking care of one division of the guns, embracing ten of the aforesaid twenty-four-pounders. Ranged up against the ship's side at regular intervals, they resembled not a little a stud of sable chargers in their stalls. Among this iron stud little Quoin was continually running in and out, currying them down, now and then, with an old rag, or keeping the flies off with a brush.

To Quoin, the honor and dignity of the United States of America seemed indissolubly linked with the keeping his guns unspotted and glossy. . . ."

The Surgeon of the Fleet is a full-length portrait, and minutely described in his grim humors. His appearance was that of a ghoul:—

"He was a small, withered man, nearly, perhaps quite, sixty years of age. His chest was shallow, his shoulders bent, his pantaloons hung round his skeleton legs, and his face was singularly attenuated. In truth, the corporeal vitality of this man seemed, in a good degree, to have died out of him. He walked abroad, a curious patch-work of life and death, with a wig, one glass eye, and a set of false teeth, while his voice was husky and thick; but his mind seemed undebilitated as in youth; it shone out of his remaining eye with basilisk brilliancy."

But we cannot stop at this great portrait-gallery of the man-of-war. They are all there, from the inhabitants of the main-top to the old men of the cock-pit. Truly is it a world, the frigate, with its thousand picked men, the contribution of every state of life, of every stage of civilization, of each profession, of all arts and callings, but—of one sex. And therein is a significant key to the peculiar position of the "Navy" in the affairs of the race. The man-of-war is divorced from civilization,—we will not repeat the stale phrase, from the progress of humanity,—but from humanity itself. *How* thus divorced, through all the windings and intricacies of the artificial system, White Jacket will show.

Herman Melville tests all his characters by their manhood. His book is thoroughly American and democratic. There is no patronage in his exhibition of a sailor, any more than in his portraits of captains and commodores. He gives all fair play in an impartial spirit. There is no railing, no scolding; he never loses his temper when he hits hardest. A quaint, satirical, yet genial humor is his grand destructive weapon. It would be a most dangerous one (for what is there which cannot be shaken with ridicule?), were it not for the poetic element by which it is elevated. Let our author treasure this as his choicest possession, for without it his humor would soon degenerate into a sneer, than which there is nothing sadder, more fatal. In regarding, too, the spirit of things, may he not fall into the error of undervaluing their forms, lest he get into a bewildering, barren, and void scepticism!

We have intimated Herman Melville is a poet, and such he is, though, perhaps, "lacking the accomplishment of verse." Let this old main-mast-man prove it:—

"The *main-mast-man* of the Neversink was a very aged seaman, who well deserved his comfortable berth. He had seen more than half a century of the most active service, and through all had proved himself a good and faithful man. He furnished one of the very rare examples of a sailor in a green old age; for, with most sailors, old age comes in youth, and Hardship and Vice carry them on an early bier to the grave.

"As in the evening of life, and at the close of day, old Abraham sat at the door of his tent, biding his time to die, so sits our old mast-man on the *coat of the mast,* glancing round him with patriarchal benignity. And that mild expression of his sets off very strangely a face that has been burned almost black by the torrid suns that shone fifty years ago—a face that is seamed with three sabre cuts. You would almost think this old mast-man had been blown out of Vesuvius, to look alone at his scarred, blackened forehead, chin, and cheeks. But gaze down into his eye, and though all the snows of Time have drifted higher and higher upon his brow, yet deep down in that eye you behold an infantile, sinless look, the same that answered the glance of this old man's mother when first she cried for the babe to be laid by her side. That look is the fadeless, ever infantile immortality within."

See, too, the forgetive Fallstaffian fancy in such passages as this, his noble Jack Chase's objurgations at a Yankee whaler:—

" 'Why, you limb of Nantucket! you train-oil man! you sea-tallow strainer! you bobber after carrion! do *you* pretend to vilify a man-of-war? Why, you lean rogue, you, a man-of-war is to whalemen, as a metropolis to shire-towns, and sequestered hamlets. *Here's* the place for life and commotion; *here's* the place to be gentlemanly and jolly. And what did you know, you bumpkin! before you came on board this *Andrew Miller?* . . . Bah! you are full of the fore-peak and the forecastle; you are only familiar with Burtons and Billy-tackles; your ambition never mounted above pig-killing! which, in my poor opinion, is the proper phrase for whaling! Topmates! has not this Tubbs here been but a misuser of good oak planks, and a vile desecrator of the thrice holy sea? turning his ship, my hearties! into a fat-kettle, and *the ocean into a whale-pen?* Begone! you graceless, godless knave! pitch him over the top there, White Jacket!' "

There is a fine accumulation of historic recollections in the chapter on the harbor of Rio—the "Bay of all Beauties.". . .

And the whole book is written with this abounding life and freshness—from the first page to the last.

We have but indicated some of its general characteristics. The speciality of the book, its particular treatment of the "service:" its views on the naval reform questions which are now prominently before the public, afford matter for another article. We shall return to "The World in a Man-of-War," in our next.

It is, we should add, a book essentially of personal observation, the author claiming this in the few lines prefixed of preface, in which he refers to 1843 as the date of his "experiences."

———————

WILLIAM YOUNG [1809–88], an English-born journalist, was editor of the New York *Albion* from 1848 until 1867.

Review of *White-Jacket*

Attributed to WILLIAM YOUNG

Two extracts from this book, that appeared lately in our columns, will have prepared readers for a work of rare merit; and a perusal of it entire will fully confirm that impression—at least on the minds of those who do not "hate the sea," and have not very dainty nerves. If you be in either predicament, seek entertainment elsewhere, for herein you will only get such scanty glimpses of land as may be at times seen through the port-holes, and meet with such revelations of inner life on board a frigate as have more truth than poetry to recommend them. As if to certify also that there is no fiction, no allegory, in the startling

New York *Albion*, n.s., Vol. 9 (30 March 1850).

avowal that he here presents to his countrymen, the author conspicuously prefixes to them the following brief but comprehensive "note," bearing date in this city, and in this month of March. . . .

The United States ship *Neversink*, the old Commodore, Captain Claret, Lieutenants Bridewell, Selvagee, and Mad Jack, the Purser, and Dr. Cuticle the surgeon, will probably, by the aid of the above note be recognised as portraits. But be that as it may, they are admirably drawn as types of a class. The object of the book is—or at least the effect must be—to bring to public notice the oppressive rigor of the laws that regulate the American Navy, and the terrible severity with which they are carried into effect. Now in order to do this, Mr. Melville has not peopled his quarter-deck with demons, and his forecastle with angels: he has not made officers and men play the parts respectively of wolves and lambs. His choice, picked men amongst the crew, his "Jack Chases" and two or three more, are exceptions to the general rule; for as a whole his "jovial tars" are, in a moral point of view, as villainous a set of fellows as can well be got together, outside the walls of a penitentiary. . . .

Flogging is anathematised in as plain and emphatic language as man can use, denounced as "religiously, morally, and immutably *wrong*." Almost every occurrence on board the *Neversink* is painfully interwoven with allusions to the "gratings," past, present, or to come. And yet, in spite of this pervading effort to represent things as we fear they too often are, we cannot say that the perusal of White Jacket's narrative induces us to join him in his eloquent cry for the immediate abolition of flogging in the Navy, at all risks and every hazard. Page after page, our indignation has been aroused, and our sense of humanity and justice outraged—not by the fact that flogging is recognised by naval law, but by proofs that punishment is sometimes atrociously converted into torture, and that caprice, malice, or ignorance on the part of irresponsible officers too often renders justice null and void. Curiously enough, though the comments of "Jack" on naval discipline, and other matters pertaining to man-of-war life, are here set down with a remarkable air of truth, we remember no direct testimony that "Jack" himself considered flogging, *per se*, as the most intolerable of his grievances. In so able, so practical, and so large-minded an author as Herman Melville, we scarcely expected to find the "essential dignity of man" and "the spirit of our domestic institutions" lugged in on such a question as this. Is it consistent with the "essential dignity," that one man should sweep the floor of Congress, and another make laws upon it which his democratic countrymen must obey? If the world were big enough, and each man had his desolate island to himself, Robinson Crusoe fashion, we might keep up this pleasant non-committal delusion, but in the "world in a man-of-war," or in the world out of it, this phantom may be left to the Transcendentalists, amongst whom our author is by far too good a fellow to be classed. Ere we leave this part of White Jacket's adventures and opinions, let us moreover acknowledge how candidly he admits, that in English ships of war there is less tyranny than in his own. His words are as follows, and we quote them as a little set-off against the "democratic institutions:" . . . .

We entirely agree with Mr. Melville in his condemnation of many of the internal regulations of ships of war, by which "Jack's" comforts are abridged and his health is injured, without any adequate cause whatever. The bad distribution of sleep and food, by which he is left sixteen consecutive hours without the latter, and never enjoys more than four hours of the former on a stretch, is one of the most crying of these evils; which, however, we have no room to trace. We prefer repeating our unqualified admiration of the touches of humour, pathos, wit, and practical philosophy, with which the lighter portions of White-Jacket are plentifully seasoned. The nautical sketches are unsurpassed, so pleasantly set off as they are, that one almost forgives the writer for taking away so much of the romance of the sea. Our pencil has marked twice as many passages for quotation as we can afford to quote, and so we must needs content ourselves with picking out the shortest. . . .

To curtail it would spoil his description of his own nondescript substitute for a pea-jacket, from which fantastic garment the book takes its title. It gets him into all sorts of scrapes, and will give his readers many a laugh. Nor will the individual portraits fail to do the same, so abounding are they with sly touches of genial humour. . . .

"White Jacket" in its serious portions must draw the attention of serious men. In its lighter pages, it bears those inherent marks of fancy, freshness, and power, which the public has determined to find in every work that bears the name of Herman Melville.

FREDERICK SWARTWOUT COZZENS [1818–69]. Jay Leyda first suggested the attribution to Cozzens, a minor poetaster, essayist, and editor. Perry Miller assumes that the review is by Lewis Gaylord Clark [1808–73], a poet and the editor of *The Knickerbocker* magazine.

Review of *White-Jacket*

Attributed to FREDERICK S. COZZENS

Well, we are glad to find the author of 'Typee' on the right ground at last. When we read his 'Mardi,' or rather *tried* to read it, for we never could get quite through it, we feared that the author had mistaken his bent, like a comic actor with a 'penshong' for tragedy, and that we were thenceforth to hear from him in a pseudo-philosophical *rifacciemento* of CARLYLE and EMERSON. 'Redburn' reässured us; and now comes 'White-Jacket,' to reïnstate the author in the best good-graces of the reading public. Not a page of this last work has escaped us; and so strong was the *continuous* interest which it excited, a quality not always encountered even in the most popular works of our time, that we accomplished its perusal in two 'sittings,' unavoidably protracted, we may remark, for we could not leave the work, while there was yet a page unread. Without the aid of much imagination, but with a daguerreotype-like naturalness of description of all which the writer saw and felt himself, and all which he saw others feel, Mr. MELVILLE has given us a volume which, in its evident truthfulness and accuracy of personal and individual delineation, reminds us continually of that admirable and justly popular work, the '*Two Years Before the Mast*' of the younger DANA. A vein of sly humor percolates through the book; and a sort of unctuous toying with verbal double-meanings, is once in a while to be met with, which go far to indicate, that if the author had lived in the 'City of *Brotherly Love*,' (church-burners, firemen-fighters, assassins, and rowdies, excuse the implied exceptions!) he might, with a little proper instruction, have become as celebrated as 'a Philadelphia lawyer,' that preëminent model of a pun-hunter. We had intended to present several extracts from 'White-Jacket,' which we had pencilled for that purpose in the perusal; but the universal prevalence of the book itself, at this late period, would doubtless make them 'twice-told tales' to the great majority of our readers. We would call especial attention, as a matter of present public interest, to the chapters descriptive of an instance of almost indiscriminate flogging on board a man-of-war, and the consequences of such inconsistent punishment, in the case of each offender. The force of public opinion, and the example of certain humane officers in the highest rank of the American navy, would seem to indicate that the time is not distant when corporeal punishment, if not mainly abolished, will at least be hereafter less frequently resorted to than formerly, and greatly lessened in its severity. The signs of the times would seem to point unerringly to this result.

BY HERMAN MELVILLE.

WHITE-JACKET.

One Volume, 12mo, Paper, $1 00; Muslin, $1 25.

White-Jacket will find (since it deserves to find) many animated and interested readers. Mr. Melville stands as far apart from any past or present marine painter in pen and ink as Turner does from Vandervelde. We can not recall another novelist or sketcher who has given the poetry of the ship, her voyages, and her crew, in a manner at all resembling his.—*London Athenæum.*

The characters brought upon the stage are admirable life-pictures, exhibiting by the magic effect of a few masterly touches each man in the complete individuality of his person and his office, from the commodore, who, as he paces the quarter-deck, covers up his deficiency in the qualities necessary for command by the unblending starchness of official etiquette, down to the meanest specimen of the genus loblolly-boy.—*John Bull.*

Had not Mr. Melville already appeared before the world with productions which, by their powerful energy and general worth, have won both attention and admiration, this work would be sufficient to establish him as a substantial favorite for the future. Whatever he writes upon, he writes on it well, and throughout his pages, open them where you may, will be found, amid a host of beauties and singularities, the strongest evidence of an untiring spirit, great vigor, lofty imagination, and a pure style of writing. The perusal of it has caused us so much real and sterling pleasure, that we feel it a duty we owe both to its author and the public to recommend it to the latter in the strongest manner.—*London Morning Post.*

Many of the wonders of the world of a man-of-war are now revealed to us for the first time. The whole narrative is marked by all the sobriety of truth, and, though enlivened by the sparkling and racy style which characterizes the author in his happiest moments, is full of those details which bear with them the conviction that the scene is sketched from the life.—*London Atlas.*

Varied as are the pictures which Herman Melville here presents to us, the same natural delineation of a master-hand is visible in them all, and few who have followed its momentous career will arrive without regret at the chapter which records "the end of the Jacket."—*London Sun.*

We have called Mr. Melville a common sailor, but he is a very uncommon common sailor, even for America, whose mariners are better educated than our own. His descriptions of scenery are life-like and vigorous, sometimes masterly, and his style throughout is rather that of an educated literary man than of a working seaman.—*London Times.*

Brilliant and dashingly spirited descriptions abound in this volume. It is written in the author's best style; and no modern author ranks higher as a marine painter. The mysteries of life on ship-board are revealed, and the abuses of the service freely commented on.—*Baltimore American.*

It is full of humor and keen satire, and it ought to have a good effect in reforming some of the abuses in our navy.—*Norfolk Democrat.*

Harper & Brothers, Publishers, New York.

The Harper & Brothers Advertisement for *White-Jacket*

Herman Melville's Whale

ANONYMOUS

This sea novel is a singular medley of naval observation, magazine article writing, satiric reflection upon the conventionalisms of civilized life, and rhapsody run mad. So far as the nautical parts are appropriate and unmixed, the portraiture is truthful and interesting. Some of the satire, especially in the early parts, is biting and reckless. The chapter-spinning is various in character; now powerful from the vigorous and fertile fancy of the author, now little more than empty though sounding phrases. The rhapsody belongs to wordmongering where ideas are the staple; where it takes the shape of narrative or dramatic fiction, it is phantasmal—an attempted description of what is impossible in nature and without probability in art; it repels the reader instead of attracting him.

The elements of the story are a South Sea whaling voyage, narrated by Ishmael, one of the crew of the ship Pequod, from Nantucket. Its "probable" portions consist of the usual sea matter in that branch of the industrial marine; embracing the preparations for departure, the voyage, the chase and capture of whale, with the economy of cutting up, &c., and the peculiar discipline of the service. This matter is expanded by a variety of digressions on the nature and characteristics of the sperm whale, the history of the fishery, and similar things, in which a little knowledge is made the excuse for a vast many words. The voyage is introduced by several chapters in which life in American seaports is rather broadly depicted.

The "marvellous" injures the book by disjointing the narrative, as well as by its inherent want of interest, at least as managed by Mr. Melville. In the superstition of some whalers, (grounded upon the malicious foresight which occasionally characterizes the attacks of the sperm fish upon the boats sent to capture it,) there is a *white* whale which possesses supernatural power. To capture or even to hurt it is beyond the art of man; the skill of the whaler is useless; the harpoon does not wound it; it exhibits a contemptuous strategy in its attacks upon the boats

The London *Spectator,* Vol. 24 (25 October 1851) 1026–27.

of its pursuers; and happy is the vessel where only loss of limb, or of a single life, attends its chase. Ahab, the master of the Pequod—a mariner of long experience, stern resolve, and indomitable courage, the high hero of romance, in short, transferred to a whale-ship—has lost his leg in a contest with the white whale. Instead of daunting Ahab, the loss exasperates him; and by long brooding over it his reason becomes shaken. In this condition he undertakes the voyage; making the chase of his fishy antagonist the sole object of his thoughts, and, so far as he can without exciting overt insubordination among his officers, the object of his proceedings.

Such a groundwork is hardly natural enough for a regular-built novel, though it might form a tale, if properly managed. But Mr. Melville's mysteries provoke wonder at the author rather than terror at the creation; the soliloquies and dialogues of Ahab, in which the author attempts delineating the wild imaginings of monomania, and exhibiting some profoundly speculative views of things in general, induce weariness or skipping; while the whole scheme mars, as we have said, the nautical continuity of story—greatly assisted by various chapters of a bookmaking kind.

Perhaps the earliest chapters are the best, although they contain little adventure. Their topics are fresher to English readers than the whale-chase, and they have more direct satire. One of the leading personages in the voyage is Queequeg, a South Sea Islander, that Ishmael falls in with at New Bedford, and with whom he forms a bosom friendship.

"Queequeg was a native of Kokovoko, an island far away to the West and South. It is not down in any map; true places never are.

"While yet a new-hatched savage, running wild about his native woodlands in a grass clout, followed by the nibbling goats, as if he were a green sapling,—even then, in Queequeg's ambitious soul lurked a strong desire to see something more of Christendom than a specimen whaler or two. . . ."

The strongest point of the book is its "characters." Ahab, indeed, is a melodramatic exaggeration, and Ishmael is little more than a mouthpiece; but the harpooners, the mates, and several of the seamen, are truthful portraitures of the sailor as modified by the whaling service. The persons ashore are equally good, though they are soon lost sight of. The two Quaker owners are the author's means for a hit at the religious hypocrisies. Captain Bildad, an old sea-dog, has got rid of everything pertaining to the meeting-house save an occasional "thou" and "thee." Captain Peleg, in American phrase "professes religion." The following extract exhibits the two men when Ishmael is shipped. . . .

It is a canon with some critics that nothing should be introduced into a novel which it is physically impossible for the writer to have known: thus, he must not describe the conversation of miners in a pit if they *all* perish. Mr. Melville hardly steers clear of this rule, and he continually violates another, by beginning in the autobiographical form and changing ad libitum into the narrative. His catastrophe overrides all rule: not only is Ahab, with his boat's-crew, destroyed in his last desperate attack upon the white whale, but the Pequod herself sinks with all on board into the depths of the illimitable ocean. Such is the go-ahead method.

HORACE GREELEY [1811–72], the great editor of the New York *Tribune*, had traveled for the Irishman's issue of Repeal with Gansevoort Melville in 1843, but aptly described Gansevoort's anglophobic speeches of 1844 as full of "gas and glory." He treated Herman Melville with the same friendly incisiveness.

Review of *Moby-Dick*

Attributed to HORACE GREELEY

Everybody has heard of the tradition which is said to prevail among the old salts of Nantucket and New-Bedford, of a ferocious monster of a whale, who is proof against all the arts of harpoonery, and who occasionally amuses himself with swallowing down a boat's crew without winking. The present volume

New York *Daily Tribune*, 22 November 1851.

is a "Whaliad," or the Epic of that veritable old leviathan, who
"esteemeth iron as straw, and laughs at the spear, the dart, and
the habergeon," no one being able to "fill his skin with a barbed
iron, or his head with fish-hooks." Mr. Melville gives us not only
the romance of his history, but a great mass of instruction on
the character and habits of his whole race, with complete details
of the wily stratagems of their pursuers.

The interest of the work pivots on a certain Captain Ahab,
whose enmity to Moby-Dick, the name of the whale-demon,
has been aggravated to monomania. In one rencounter with
this terror of the seas, he suffers a signal defeat; loses a leg in
the contest; gets a fire in his brain; returns home a man with
one idea; feels that he has a mission; that he is predestined to
defy his enemy to mortal strife; devotes himself to the fulfill-
ment of his destiny; with the persistence and cunning of insanity
gets possession of another vessel; ships a weird, supernatural
crew of which Ishmael, the narrator of the story, is a prominent
member; and after a "wild huntsman's chase" through unknown
seas, is the only one who remains to tell the destruction of the
ship and the doomed Captain Ahab by the victorious, indomitable Moby-Dick.

The narrative is constructed in Herman Melville's best manner. It combines the various features which form the chief at-
tractions of his style, and is commendably free from the faults
which we have before had occasion to specify in this powerful
writer. The intensity of the plot is happily relieved by minute
descriptions of the most homely processes of the whale fishery.
We have occasional touches of the subtle mysticism, which is
carried to such an inconvenient excess in Mardi, but it is here
mixed up with so many tangible and odorous realities, that we
always safely alight from the excursion through mid-air upon
the solid deck of the whaler. We are recalled to this world by
the fumes of "oil and blubber," and are made to think more of
the contents of barrels than of allegories. The work is also full
of episodes, descriptive of strange and original phases of character. One of them is given in the commencement of the volume,
showing how "misery makes a man acquainted with strange bed-
fellows." We must pass over this in which the writer relates
his first introduction to Queequeg, a South Sea cannibal, who
was his chum at a sailor boarding house in New-Bedford and

afterward his bosom friend and most devoted confederate. We will make a room for the characteristic chapter, which describes the ripening of their acquaintance into the honeymoon of friendship. . . .

But we must go out to sea with Ishmael, if we would witness his most remarkable exploits. We are now, then, in the midst of things, and with good luck, may soon get a sight of Moby-Dick. Meantime, we may beguile our impatience with the description of a rope on which Melville gives us a touch of his quaint moralizings. . . .

We are now ready to kill our first whale. Here is the transaction in full: "Killing a Whale." . . .

At last, Moby-Dick, the object of such long vigalant, [*sic*] and infuriate search, is discovered. We can only give the report of "The Chase—First Day." . . .

Here we will retire from the chase, which lasts three days, not having a fancy to be in at the death. We part with the adventurous philosophical Ishmael, truly thankful that the whale did not get his head, for which we are indebted for this wildly imaginative and truly thrilling story. We think it the best production which has yet come from that seething brain, and in spite of its lawless flights, which put all regular criticism at defiance, it gives us a higher opinion of the author's originality and power than even the favorite and fragrant first-fruits of his genius, the never-to-be-forgotten Typee.

Melville's Moby Dick; or, The Whale

EVERT (AND GEORGE?) DUYCKINCK

Every reader throughout the United States has probably perused in the newspapers the account of a recent incident in the whale fishery which would stagger the mind by its extent of the marvellous, were it not parallelled by a well known case—

New York *Literary World,* Vol. 9 (15 November 1851) 381–83 and (22 November 1851) 403–4.

that of the Essex of Nantucket, still authenticated by living witnesses. It appears from a narrative published in the *Panama Herald* (an American newspaper in that region, itself one of the wonders of the age!), taken down from the lips of the captain of the vessel, John S. Deblois, that the ship Ann Alexander, of New Bedford, having left that port in June of last year with the usual vicissitudes of Cape Horn service, losing a New Hampshire man overboard in a storm at that point, had entered upon her Pacific hunting-grounds, and in the recent month of August was coursing within a few degrees of the Equator—a well known haunt of the whale. . . .

[A detailed account of the sinking of the *Ann Alexander* by a whale is here omitted.]

By a singular coincidence this extreme adventure is, even to very many of the details, the catastrophe of Mr. Melville's new book, which is a natural-historical, philosophical, romantic account of the person, habits, manners, ideas of the great sperm whale; of his haunts and of his belongings; of his associations with the world of the deep, and of the not less remarkable individuals and combinations of individuals who hunt him on the oceans. Nothing like it has ever before been written of the whale; for no man who has at once seen so much of the actual conflict, and weighed so carefully all that has been recorded on the subject, with equal powers of perception and reflection, has attempted to write at all on it—the labors of Scoresby covering a different and inferior branch of the history. To the popular mind this book of Herman Melville, touching the Leviathan of the deep, is as much of a discovery in Natural History as was the revelation of America by Christopher Columbus in geography. Let any one read this book with the attention which it deserves, and then converse with the best informed of his friends and acquaintances who have not seen it, and he will notice the extent and variety of treatment; while scientific men must admit the original observation and speculation.

Such an infuriated, resolute sperm whale as pursued and destroyed the Ann Alexander is the hero, Moby Dick, of Mr. Melville's book. The vengeance with which he is hunted, which with Capt. Deblois was the incident of a single, though most memorable day, is the leading passion and idea of Captain Ahab of the Pequod for years, and throughout the seas of the world.

Incidentally with this melo-dramatic action and spiritual development of the character of Ahab, is included a full, minute, thorough investigation, and description of the whale and its fishery. Such is a short-hand account of this bulky and multifarious volume.

It opens, after a dedication to Nathaniel Hawthorne, with a preliminary flourish in the style of Carlyle and the "Doctor" of etymology, followed by a hundred or so of extracts of "Old Burton," passages of a quaint and pithy character from Job and King Alfred to Miriam Coffin; in lieu of the old style of Scott, Cooper, and others, of distributing such flourishes about the heads of chapters. Here they are all in a lump, like the grace over the Franklin barrel of pork, and may be taken as a kind of bitters, a whet and fillip to the imagination, exciting it to the curious, ludicrous, sublime traits and contemplations which are to follow.

It is some time after opening with Chapter I. before we get fairly afloat, but the time is very satisfactorily occupied with some very strange, romantic, and, withal, highly humorous adventures at New Bedford and Nantucket. A scene at the Spouter Inn, of the former town, a night in bed with a Pacific Islander, and a mid-ocean adventure subsequently with a Frenchman over some dead whales in the Pacific, treat the reader to a laugh worthy of Smollet. We might perhaps as well introduce this at once. The Pequod, the ship in which the reader embarks from Nantucket, one day meets a French whaler under peculiar circumstances, in a calm, with two carcasses of whales secured to her, which the unadventurous crew had picked up, dead waifs of previous conflicts on the ocean. The Mate, Stubb, had boarded this vessel seeking information for Capt. Ahab, of Moby Dick, and returns to circumvent the ambergris, a product found in the diseased animal. . . .

A difficulty in the estimate of this, in common with one or two other of Mr. Melville's books, occurs from the double character under which they present themselves. In one light they are romantic fictions, in another statements of absolute fact. When to this is added that the romance is made a vehicle of opinion and satire through a more or less opaque allegorical veil, as particularly in the latter half of Mardi, and to some extent in this present volume, the critical difficulty is considerably thickened. It becomes quite impossible to submit such books to a distinct classification as fact, fiction, or essay. Something of a parallel may be found in Jean Paul's German tales, with an admixture of Southey's Doctor. Under these combined influences of personal observation, actual fidelity to local truthfulness in description, a taste for reading and sentiment, a fondness for fanciful analogies, near and remote, a rash daring in speculation, reckless at times of taste and propriety, again refined and eloquent, this volume of Moby Dick may be pronounced a most remarkable sea-dish—an intellectual chowder of romance, philosophy, natural history, fine writing, good feeling, bad sayings —but over which, in spite of all uncertainties, and in spite of the author himself, predominates his keen perceptive faculties, exhibited in vivid narration.

There are evidently two if not three books in Moby Dick rolled into one. Book No. I. we could describe as a thorough exhaustive account admirably given of the great Sperm Whale. The information is minute, brilliantly illustrated, as it should be—the whale himself so generously illuminating the midnight page on which his memoirs are written—has its level passages, its humorous touches, its quaint suggestion, its incident usually picturesque and occasionally sublime. All this is given in the most delightful manner in "The Whale." Book No. 2 is the romance of Captain Ahab, Queequeg, Tashtego, Pip & Co., who are more or less spiritual personages talking and acting differently from the general business run of the conversation on the decks of whalers. They are for the most part very serious people, and seem to be concerned a great deal about the problem of the universe. They are striking characters withal, of the romantic spiritual cast of the German drama; realities of some kinds at bottom, but veiled in all sorts of poetical incidents and expressions. As a bit of German melodrama, with Captain Ahab for the Faust of the quarter-deck, and Queequeg with the crew, for Walpurgis night revellers in the forecastle, it has its strong points, though here the limits as to space and treatment of the stage would improve it. Moby Dick in this view becomes a sort of fishy moralist, a leviathan metaphysician, a folio Ductor Dubitantium, in fact, in the fresh water illustration of Mrs.

Malaprop, "an allegory on the banks of the Nile." After pursuing him in this melancholic company over a few hundred squares of latitude and longitude, we begin to have some faint idea of the association of whaling and lamentation, and why blubber is popularly synonymous with tears.

The intense Captain Ahab is too long drawn out; something more of *him* might, we think, be left to the reader's imagination. The value of this kind of writing can only be through the personal consciousness of the reader, what he brings to the book; and all this is sufficiently evoked by a dramatic trait or suggestion. If we had as much of Hamlet or Macbeth as Mr. Melville gives us of Ahab, we should be tired even of their sublime company. Yet Captain Ahab is a striking conception, firmly planted on the wild deck of the Pequod—a dark disturbed soul arraying itself with every ingenuity of material resources for a conflict at once natural and supernatural in his eye, with the most dangerous extant physical monster of the earth, embodying, in strongly drawn lines of mental association, the vaster moral evil of the world. The pursuit of the White Whale thus interweaves with the literal perils of the fishery—a problem of fate and destiny—to the tragic solution of which Ahab hurries on, amidst the wild stage scenery of the ocean. To this end the motley crew, the air, the sky, the sea, its inhabitants are idealized throughout. It is a noble and praiseworthy conception; and though our sympathies may not always accord with the train of thought, we would caution the reader against a light or hasty condemnation of this part of the work.

Book III., appropriating perhaps a fourth of the volume, is a vein of moralizing, half essay, half rhapsody, in which much refinement and subtlety, and no little poetical feeling, are mingled with quaint conceit and extravagant daring speculation. This is to be taken as in some sense dramatic; the narrator throughout among the personages of the Pequod being one Ishmael, whose wit may be allowed to be against everything on land, as his hand is against everything at sea. This piratical running down of creeds and opinions, the conceited indifferentism of Emerson, or the run-a-muck style of Carlyle is, we will not say dangerous in such cases, for there are various forces at work to meet more powerful onslaught, but it is out of place and uncomfortable. We do not like to see what, under any view, must be to the world the most sacred associations of life violated and defaced.

We call for fair play in this matter. Here is Ishmael, telling the story of this volume, going down on his knees with a cannibal to a piece of wood, in the second story fireplace of a New-Bedford tavern, in the spirit of amiable and transcendent charity, which may be all very well in its way; but why dislodge from heaven, with contumely, "long-pampered Gabriel, Michael and Raphael." Surely Ishmael, who is a scholar, might have spoken respectfully of the Archangel Gabriel, out of consideration, if not for the Bible (which might be asking too much of the school), at least for one John Milton, who wrote Paradise Lost.

Nor is it fair to inveigh against the terrors of priestcraft, which, skilful though it may be in making up its woes, at least seeks to provide a remedy for the evils of the world, and attribute the existence of conscience to "hereditary dyspepsias, nurtured by Ramadans"—and at the same time go about petrifying us with imaginary horrors, and all sorts of gloomy suggestions, all the world through. It is a curious fact that there are no more bilious people in the world, more completely filled with megrims and head shakings, than some of these very people who are constantly inveighing against the religious melancholy of priestcraft.

So much for the consistency of Ishmael—who, if it is the author's object to exhibit the painful contradictions of this self-dependent, self-torturing agency of a mind driven hither and thither as a flame in a whirlwind, is, in a degree, a successful embodiment of opinions, without securing from us, however, much admiration for the result.

With this we make an end of what we have been reluctantly compelled to object to this volume. With far greater pleasure, we acknowledge the acuteness of observation, the freshness of perception, with which the author brings home to us from the deep, "things unattempted yet in prose or rhyme," the weird influences of his ocean scenes, the salient imagination which connects them with the past and distant, the world of books and the life of experience—certain prevalent traits of manly sentiment. These are strong powers with which Mr. Melville wrestles in this book. It would be a great glory to subdue them to the highest uses of fiction. It is still a great honor, among the crowd of successful mediocrities which throng our publishers' counters, and know nothing of divine impulses, to be in the company of these nobler spirits on any terms.

Review of *Moby-Dick*

Attributed to GEORGE RIPLEY

A new work by HERMAN MELVILLE, entitled *Moby Dick; or, The Whale*, has just been issued by Harper and Brothers, which, in point of richness and variety of incident, originality of conception, and splendor of description, surpasses any of the former productions of this highly successful author. *Moby Dick* is the name of an old White Whale; half fish and half devil; the terror of the Nantucket cruisers; the scourge of distant oceans; leading an invulnerable, charmed life; the subject of many grim and ghostly traditions. This huge sea monster has a conflict with one Captain Ahab; the veteran Nantucket salt comes off second best; not only loses a leg in the affray, but receives a twist in the brain; becomes the victim of a deep, cunning monomania; believes himself predestined to take a bloody revenge on his fearful enemy; pursues him with fierce demoniac energy of purpose; and at last perishes in the dreadful fight, just as he deems that he has reached the goal of his frantic passion. On this slight framework, the author has constructed a romance, a tragedy, and a natural history, not without numerous gratuitous suggestions on psychology, ethics, and theology. Beneath the whole story, the subtle, imaginative reader may perhaps find a pregnant allegory, intended to illustrate the mystery of human life. Certain it is that the rapid, pointed hints which are often thrown out, with the keenness and velocity of a harpoon, penetrate deep into the heart of things, showing that the genius of the author for moral analysis is scarcely surpassed by his wizard power of description.

Harper's New Monthly Magazine, Vol. 4 (December 1851) 137.

In the course of the narrative the habits of the whale are fully and ably described. Frequent graphic and instructive sketches of the fishery, of sea-life in a whaling vessel, and of the manners and customs of strange nations are interspersed with excellent artistic effect among the thrilling scenes of the story. The various processes of procuring oil are explained with the minute, painstaking fidelity of a statistical record, contrasting strangely with the weird, phantom-like character of the plot, and of some of the leading personages, who present a no less unearthly appearance than the witches in Macbeth. These sudden and decided transitions form a striking feature of the volume. Difficult of management, in the highest degree, they are wrought with consummate skill. To a less gifted author, they would inevitably have proved fatal. He has not only deftly avoided their dangers, but made them an element of great power. They constantly pique the attention of the reader, keeping curiosity alive, and presenting the combined charm of surprise and alternation.

The introductory chapters of the volume, containing sketches of life in the great marts of Whalingdom, New Bedford and Nantucket, are pervaded with a fine vein of comic humor, and reveal a succession of portraitures, in which the lineaments of nature shine forth, through a good deal of perverse, intentional exaggeration. To many readers, these will prove the most interesting portions of the work. Nothing can be better than the description of the owners of the vessel, Captain Peleg and Captain Bildad, whose acquaintance we make before the commencement of the voyage. The character of Captain Ahab also opens upon us with wonderful power. He exercises a wild, bewildering fascination by his dark and mysterious nature, which is not at all diminished when we obtain a clearer insight into his strange history. Indeed, all the members of the ship's company, the three mates, Starbuck, Stubbs, and Flash, the wild, savage Gay-header, the case-hardened old blacksmith, to say nothing of the pearl of a New Zealand harpooner, the bosom friend of the narrator—all stand before us in the strongest individual relief, presenting a unique picture gallery, which every artist must despair of rivaling.

The plot becomes more intense and tragic, as it approaches toward the denouement. The malicious old Moby Dick, after long cruisings in pursuit of him, is at length discovered. He comes up to the battle, like an army with banners. He seems inspired with the same fierce, inveterate cunning with which Captain Ahab has followed the traces of his mortal foe. The fight is described in letters of blood. It is easy to foresee which will be the victor in such a contest. We need not say that the ill-omened ship is broken in fragments by the wrath of the weltering fiend. Captain Ahab becomes the prey of his intended victim. The crew perish. One alone escapes to tell the tale. Moby Dick disappears unscathed, and for aught we know, is the same "delicate monster," whose power in destroying another ship is just announced from Panama.

WILLIAM T. PORTER [1809–58], the editor of *The Spirit of the Times,* the first American sporting journal. He provided a Northern market for Southwestern humorists such as Thomas Bangs Thorpe and edited collections of their work. His reviews of Melville were uniformly appreciative.

Review of *Moby-Dick*

Attributed to WILLIAM T. PORTER

Our friend Melville's works begin to accumulate. His literary family increases rapidly. He had already a happy and smiling progeny around him, but lo! at the appointed time another child of his brain, with the accustomed signs of the family, claims our attention and regard. We bid the book a hearty welcome. We assure the "happy father" that his "labors of love" are no "love's labor lost."

We confess an admiration for Mr. Melville's books, which, perhaps, spoils us for mere criticism. There are few writers, living or dead, who describe the sea and its adjuncts with such true art, such graphic power, and with such powerfully resulting interest. "Typee," "Omoo," "Redburn," "Mardi," and "White

New York *Spirit of the Times,* December 1851.

Jacket," are equal to anything in the language. They are things of their own. They are results of the youthful experience on the ocean of a man who is at once philosopher, painter, and poet. This is not, perhaps, a very unusual mental combination, but it is not usual to find such a combination "before the mast." So far Mr. Melville's early experiences, though perhaps none of the pleasantest to himself, are infinitely valuable to the world. We say *valuable* with a full knowledge of the terms used; and, not to enter into details, which will be fresh in the memory of most of Mr. Melville's readers, it is sufficient to say that the humanities of the world have been quickened by his works. Who can forget the missionary *exposé*—the practical good sense which pleads for "Poor Jack," or the unsparing but just severity of his delineations of naval abuses, and that crowning disgrace to our navy—flogging? Taken as matters of art these books are amongst the largest and the freshest contributions of original thought and observation which have been presented in many years. Take the majority of modern writers, and it will be admitted that however much they may elaborate and rearrange the stock of ideas pre-existant, there is little added to the "common fund." Philosophers bark at each other—poets sing stereotyped phrases—John Miltons re-appear in innumerable "Pollock's Courses of Time"—novelists and romances [romancers?] stick to the same overdone incidents, careless of the memories of defunct Scotts and Radcliffs, and it is only now and then when genius, by some lucky chance of youth, ploughs deeper into the soil of humanity and nature, that fresher experiences—perhaps at the cost of much individual pain and sorrow—are obtained; and the results are books, such as those of Herman Melville and Charles Dickens. Books which are living pictures, at once of the practical truth, and the ideal amendment: books which mark epochs in literature and art.

It is, however, not with Mr. Melville generally as a writer that we have now to deal, but with "Moby Dick, or The Whale," in particular; and at first let us not forget to say that in "taking titles" no man is more felicitous than our author. Sufficiently dreamy to excite one's curiosity, sufficiently explicit to indicate some main and peculiar feature. "Moby Dick" is perhaps a creation of the brain—"The Whale" a result of experience; and the whole title a fine polished result of both. A title may be a truth or a lie. It may be clap-trap, or true art. A bad book may have a good title, but you will seldom find a good book with an inappropriate name.

"Moby Dick, or The Whale," is all whale. Leviathan is here in full amplitude. Not one of your museum affairs, but the real, living whale, a bona-fide, warm-blooded creature, ransacking the waters from pole to pole. His enormous bulk, his terribly destructive energies, his habits, his food, are all before us. Nay, even his lighter moods are exhibited. We are permitted to see the whale as a lover, a husband, and the head of a family. So to speak, we are made guests at his fire-side; we set our mental legs beneath his mahogany, and become members of his interesting social circle. No book in the world brings together so much whale. We have his history, natural and social, living and dead. But Leviathan's natural history, though undoubtedly valuable to science, is but a part of the book. It is in the personal adventures of his captors, their toils, and alas! not unfrequently their wounds and martyrdom, that our highest interest is excited. This mingling of human adventures with new, startling, and striking objects and pursuits, constitutes one of the chief charms of Mr. Melville's books. His present work is a drama of intense interest. A whale, "Moby Dick"—a dim, gigantic, unconquerable, but terribly destructive being, is one of the persons of the drama. We admit a disposition to be critical on this character. We had doubts as to his admissibility as an actor into dramatic action, and so it would seem had our author, but his chapter, "The Affidavit," disarms us; all improbability or incongruity disappears, and "Moby Dick" becomes a living fact, simply doubtful at first, because he was so new an idea, one of those beings whose whole life, like the Palladius or the Sea-serpent, is a romance, and whose memoirs unvarnished are of themselves a fortune to the first annalist or his publisher.

"Moby Dick, or The Whale," is a "many-sided" book. Mingled with much curious information respecting whales and whaling there is a fine vein of sermonizing, a good deal of keen satire, much humor, and that too of the finest order, and a story of peculiar interest. As a romance its characters are so new and unusual that we doubt not it will excite the ire of critics. It is not tame enough to pass this ordeal safely. Think of a monomaniac whaling captain, who, mutilated on a former voyage by a particular whale, well known for its peculiar bulk, shape, and color—seeks, at the risk of his life and the lives of his crew, to capture and slay this terror of the seas! It is on this idea that the romance hinges. The usual staple of novelists is entirely wanting. We have neither flinty-hearted fathers, designing villains, dark caverns, men in armor, nor anxious lovers. There is not in the book any individual, who, at a certain hour, "might have been seen" ascending hills or descending valleys, as is usual. The thing is entirely new, fresh, often startling, and highly dramatic, and with those even, who, oblivious of other fine matters, scattered with profusest hand, read for the sake of the story, must be exceedingly successful.

Our space will not permit us at present to justify our opinions by long quotations; but, at the risk of doing Mr. Melville injustice by curtailment, let us turn to the chapter headed "The Pequod meets the Rose Bud," p. 447, in which a whaling scene is described with infinite humor. . . .

Did our limits permit we would gladly extract the fine little episode, contained in the chapter called "The Castaway," as a favorable specimen of Mr. Melville's graphic power of description. But we must conclude by strongly recommending "Moby Dick, or The Whale," to all who can appreciate a work of exceeding power, beauty, and genius.

Review of *Pierre*

CHARLES GORDON GREENE

Pierre; or the Ambiguities. By Herman Melville. New York: Harper & Brothers. Boston: Fetridge & Co.—As the writer of the fascinating and *Crusoish* "Typee," Mr Melville has received considerable attention from those whose hard fate it is, to "notice new books"; and as emanating from the writer of "Typee," Mr Melville's subsequent works, ranging from fair to execrable, have been held worthy of lengthy critiques, while critics have

Boston *Post* (4 August 1852).

been at some pains to state, in detail and by means of extracts, their various merits and defects. But we think it full time to stop this mode of treatment. The author of one good book more than offsets the amusement derived from it by the reading public when he produces a score of trashy and crazy volumes; and in the present case, and after the delivery of such stuff as "Mardi" and the "White Whale," [we] are not disposed to stand upon much ceremony. Mr. Melville's latest books, we are pleased to say, fell almost stillborn from the press, and we opened the volume under notice with the hope and almost the expectation that he would not again abuse the great gift of genius that has been bestowed upon him. We hoped and almost expected that he had sown his literary wild oats, and had now come forth, the vivid and brilliant author that he might be, if he chose to criticise himself, and lop off the puerility, conceit, affectation and insanity which he had previously exhibited. But we reckoned without our host. "Pierre; or the Ambiguities" is, perhaps, the craziest fiction extant. It has scenes and descriptions of unmistakeable power. The characters, however false to nature, are painted with a glowing pencil, and many of the thoughts reveal an intellect, the intensity and cultivation of which it is impossible to doubt. But the amount of utter trash in the volume is almost infinite—trash of conception, execution, dialogue and sentiment. Whoever buys the book on the strength of Melville's reputation, will be cheating himself of his money, and we believe we shall *never* see the man who has endured the reading of the whole of it. We give the story of the book in a few sentences. Pierre Glendinning and his proud but loving mother are living together, surrounded by everything the world, intellect, health and affection can bestow. The son is betrothed to a beautiful girl of equal position and fortune, and everything looks brightly as a summer morning. All at once, Pierre learns that his father has left an illegitimate daughter, who is in poverty and obscurity. His conscience calls upon him to befriend and acknowledge her—although, by the way, his proof of the fact that the girl is his father's offspring is just nothing at all. On the other hand, he will not discover to the world or to his mother the error of his (supposed) sainted father, and he adopts the novel expedient of carrying off the girl, and giving out that he has married her. His mother discards him and soon dies of wounded love and pride, and his betrothed is brought to the brink of the grave. She finally recovers somewhat, and strange to say, invites herself to reside with Pierre and his sister, who, as far as the world and herself were concerned, are living as husband and wife. The relatives of Lucy, as a matter of course, try to regain her, and brand Pierre with every bad name possible. The latter finally shoots his cousin who had become the possessor of the family estate and a pretender to the hand of Lucy—is arrested and taken to prison. There he is visited by the two ladies, the sister and the betrothed. Lucy falls dead of a broken heart and Pierre and his sister take poison and also give up the ghost. This tissue of unnatural horrors is diversified a little, by the attempts of the hero to earn his living by authorship, and by the "ambiguous" love between Pierre and his natural sister.

Comment upon the foregoing is needless. But even this string of nonsense is equalled by the nonsense that is strung upon it, in the way of crazy sentiment and exaggerated passion. What the book means, we know not. To save it from almost utter worthlessness, it must be called a prose poem, and even then, it might be supposed to emanate from a lunatic hospital rather than from the quiet retreats of Berkshire. We say it with grief—it is too bad for Mr Melville to abuse his really fine talents as he does. A hundred times better if he kept them in a napkin all his natural life. A thousand times better, had he dropped authorship with "Typee." He would then have been known as the writer of one of the pleasantest books of its class in the English language. As it is, he has produced more and sadder trash than any other man of undoubted ability among us, and the most provoking fact is, that in his bushels of chaff, the "two grains of wheat" are clearly discernible.

Pierre; or, The Ambiguities

EVERT (AND GEORGE?) DUYCKINCK

The purpose of Mr. Melville's story, though vaguely hinted, rather than directly stated, seems to be to illustrate the possible antagonism of a sense of duty, conceived in the heat and impetuosity of youth, to all the recognised laws of social morality; and to exhibit a conflict between the virtues. The hero of the tale is Pierre, a fiery youth full of love and ardor. He is the last of the Glendennings, a family that can boldly face the memory of at least two generations back without blushing, which is a pretty fair title to an American nobility. He is an only son, the pride of his mother and his house, and the expectant heir of its wide domains. A warm affection unites Mrs. Glendenning, an aristocratic dame, and Pierre, and the heart of the proud woman is all content in the responsive love of her son. A certain Lucy Tartan, with all the requisite claims for a novelist's beauty, wins the affection of and in due course of time is betrothed to Pierre. All appears smooth and prosperous to a future of happiness, when a mysterious dark-eyed, dark-haired damsel, Isabel, proves herself to the satisfaction of Pierre, though on testimony that would not pass current in any court of law, to be his sister, the natural child of his father. Here is a sad blot upon the memory of a Glendenning, a living testimony of the sin of one who had been embalmed in the heart of Pierre, as pure and without reproach. Pierre, tortured with this damning fact that pollutes his filial ideal of a virtuous parent, conceives and rightly, that he has two duties to perform: to screen his dead father's memory and give to a living sister her due, a brother's affection. Pierre impetuously decides that the only way of reconciling these two duties is by the expedient of a pretended marriage with Isabel, and thus shield the memory of his father while he protects and unites himself in brotherly affection with his sister.

Mark the tragical result. The proud mother's proudest hopes are blasted by this supposed marriage; she drives Pierre from her house, disinherits him and dies a maniac. Pierre, an outcast, seeks in the company of his sister, his pretended wife, a refuge

New York *Literary World*, Vol. 11 (21 August 1852) 118–20.

with his cousin, a rich denizen of the city, is totally ignored by him and repelled from his door. He is compelled to seek his livelihood with his pen. While he is thus engaged, struggling with poverty and misery, Lucy Tartan, who has survived the first shock from the agony of Pierre's abandonment and supposed marriage, unable to live without Pierre and instinctively justifying his infidelity on a principle, by no means clear to the reader, of abstract faith to her former lover, resolves to live with him, and joins the household of Pierre and Isabel. Lucy is followed to Pierre's dwelling by her brother and Pierre's cousin, who has succeeded Pierre as a suitor of Lucy. They attempt to force Lucy away, but she is rescued by Pierre with the aid of his fellow lodgers. Vengeance is sworn by the brother and cousin. An insulting letter is written to Pierre, denouncing him as a seducer and liar. To add to the agony of Pierre he receives at the same time a letter from his publishers, rejecting his novel. Pierre is outrageous, and arming himself with two pistols, seeks out his cousin, finds him, is struck by him, and in return shoots his cousin doubly dead with the two pistols. He is thrown into prison. He is sought out there by Isabel and Lucy. Lucy learning for the first time, from an agonizing cry of "brother" from Isabel, that she was Pierre's sister and not his wife, swoons away and dies. While Isabel and Pierre, conjointly help themselves in a fraternal way, to a draught of poison that Isabel has concealed upon her person, and they also die— *felo de se.* Nor is this the end of the casualty, the full list of the dead and wounded, for the surviving Tartan family must be necessarily plunged in irretrievable agony, leading to the probable result of some broken and various wounded hearts, on account of the death and supposed dishonor of Lucy.

Mr. Melville may have constructed his story upon some new theory of art to a knowledge of which we have not yet transcended; he evidently has not constructed it according to the established principles of the only theory accepted by us until assured of a better, of one more true and natural than truth and nature themselves, which are the germinal principles of all true art.

The pivot of the story is the pretended marriage of Pierre with his sister, in order to conceal her illegitimacy and protect his father's memory. Pierre, to carry out his purpose, abandons mother, home, his betrothed, all the advantages of his high social position, wealth and its appointments of ease and luxury and respect, and invites poverty, misery, infamy, and death. Apart from the very obvious way of gaining the same object at an infinitely smaller cost, is it natural that a loving youth should cast away the affection of his mother and his betrothed and the attachment of home to hide a dim stain upon his father's memory and to enjoy the love of an equivocal sister? Pierre not only acts thus absurdly, but pretends to act from a sense of duty. He is battling for Truth and Right, and the first thing he does in behalf of Truth is to proclaim to the whole world a falsehood, and the next thing he does is to commit in behalf of Right, a half a dozen most foul wrongs. The combined power of New England transcendentalism and Spanish Jesuitical casuistry could not have more completely befogged nature and truth, than this confounded Pierre has done. It is needless to test minutely the truth and nature of each character. In a word, Pierre is a psychological curiosity, a moral and intellectual phenomenon; Isabel, a lusus naturæ; Lucy, an incomprehensible woman; and the rest not of the earth nor, we may venture to state, of heaven. The object of the author, perhaps, has been, not to delineate life and character as they are or may possibly be, but as they are not and cannot be. We must receive the book, then, as an eccentricity of the imagination.

The most immoral *moral* of the story, if it has any moral at all, seems to be the impracticability of virtue; a leering demoniacal spectre of an idea seems to be peering at us through the dim obscure of this dark book, and mocking us with this dismal falsehood. Mr. Melville's chapter on "Chronometricals and Horologicals," if it has any meaning at all, simply means that virtue and religion are only for gods and not to be attempted by man. But ordinary novel readers will never unkennel this loathsome suggestion. The stagnant pool at the bottom of which it lies, is not too deep for their penetration, but too muddy, foul, and corrupt. If truth is hid in a well, falsehood lies in a quagmire.

We cannot pass without remark, the supersensuousness with which the holy relations of the family are described. Mother and son, brother and sister are sacred facts not to be disturbed by any sacrilegious speculations. Mrs. Glendenning and Pierre, mother and son, call each other brother and sister, and are described with all the coquetry of a lover and mistress. And again, in what we have termed the supersenuousness of description, the horrors of an incestuous relation between Pierre and Isabel seem to be vaguely hinted at.

In commenting upon the vagueness of the book, the uncertainty of its aim, the indefiniteness of its characters, and want of distinctness in its pictures, we are perhaps only proclaiming ourselves as the discoverers of a literary mare's nest; this vagueness, as the title of the "Ambiguities" seems to indicate, having been possibly intended by the author, and the work meant as a problem of impossible solution, to set critics and readers a woolgathering. It is alone intelligible as an unintelligibility.

In illustration of the manner of the book, we give this description of a gloomy apparition of a house, such as it was conjured up by the vague confused memory of Isabel. There is a spectral, ghost-like air about the description, that conveys powerfully to the imagination the intended effect of gloom and remote indistinctness:—

"My first dim life-thoughts cluster round an old, half-ruinous house in some region, for which I now have no chart to seek it out. If such a spot did ever really exist, that too seems to have been withdrawn from all the remainder of the earth. It was a wild, dark house, planted in the midst of a round, cleared, deeply-sloping space, scooped out of the middle of deep stunted pine woods. Ever I shrunk at evening from peeping out of my window, lest the ghostly pines should steal near to me, and reach out their grim arms to snatch me into their horrid shadows. . . ."

All the male characters of the book have a certain robust, animal force and untamed energy, which carry them through their melodramatic parts—no slight duty—with an effect sure to bring down the applause of the excitable and impulsive. Mr. Melville can think clearly, and write with distinctness and force —in a style of simplicity and purity. Why, then, does he allow his mind to run riot amid remote analogies, where the chain of association is invisible to mortal minds? Why does he give us incoherencies of thought, in infelicities of language? Such incoherency as this:—"Love is both Creator's and Saviour's gospel to mankind; a volume bound in rose-leaves, clasped with violets, and by the beaks of humming birds, printed with peach-juice on the leaves of lilies. Endless is the account of love. Time and space cannot contain Love's story. All things that are sweet to see, or taste, or feel, or hear, all these things were made by Love, and none other things were made by Love. Love made not the Arctic zones, but Love is ever reclaiming them. Say, are not the fierce things of this earth daily, hourly going out? Where are now your wolves of Britain? Where in Virginia now find you the panther and the pard? Oh, Love is busy everywhere. Everywhere Love hath Moravian missionaries. No propagandist like to Love. The south wind wooes the barbarous north; on many a distant shore the gentler west wind persuades the arid east. All this earth is Love's affianced; vainly the demon Principle howls to stay the banns." Such infelicities of expression, such unknown words as these, to wit: "human*ness*," "heroic-*ness*," "patriarchal*ness*," "descended*ness*," "flushful*ness*," "ama-ranthi*ness*," "instantaneous*ness*," "leapingly acknowledging," "fateful frame of mind," "protecting*ness*," "young*ness*," "infan-tile*ness*," "visible*ness*," *et id genus omne!*

The author of "Pierre; or, the Ambiguities;" the writer of a mystic romance, in which are conjured up unreal nightmare-conceptions, a confused phantasmagoria of distorted fancies and conceits, ghostly abstractions and fitful shadows, is certainly but a spectre of the substantial author of "Omoo" and "Typee," the jovial and hearty narrator of the traveller's tale of incident and adventure. By what *diablerie,* hocus-pocus, or thimble-rigging, "now you see him and now you don't" process, the transformation has been effected, we are not skilled in necromancy to detect. Nor, if it be a true psychological development, are we sufficiently advanced in transcendentalism to lift ourselves skywards and see clearly the coming light with our heads above the clouds. If this novel indicates a chaotic state of authorship, —and we can distinguish fragmentary elements of beauty—out of which is to rise a future temple of order, grace, and proportion, in which the genius of Mr. Melville is to enshrine itself, we will be happy to worship there; but let its foundation be firmly based on *terra firma*, or, if in the heavens, let us not trust our common sense to the flight of any waxen pinion. We would rejoice to meet Mr. Melville again in the hale company of sturdy sailors, men of flesh and blood, and strengthened by the wholesome air of the outside world, whether it be land-breeze or sea-breeze, listen to his narrative of a traveller's tale, in which he has few equals in power and felicity.

Review of *Pierre*

Attributed to JOHN R. THOMPSON

We know not what evil genius delights in attending the literary movements of all those who have achieved great success in the publication of their first book; but that some such companion all young and successful authors have, is placed beyond dispute by the almost invariable inferiority of their subsequent writings. With strong intellects, there is little danger that the influence of this unhappy minister will be lasting, but with far the greater number it continues until their reputation is wholly gone, or as the phrase runs.—*they have written themselves out.* Mr. Melville would really seem to be one of this class. Few books ever rose so rapidly and deservedly into popular favor as Typee. It came from the press at a time when the public taste wearied and sickened of didactic novels and journals of travel through fields explored many hundred times before. It presented us with fresh and delightful incidents from beyond the seas, over which was thrown an atmosphere soft and glowing as that hung above the youthful lovers in the enchanting story of St. Pierre. In a word, it was a novelty, and a novelty in literature, when it offends not against rule, is always to be commended. But from the time that Typee came from Mr. Melville's portfolio, he seems to have been writing under an unlucky star. The meandering nonsense of Mardi was but ill atoned for even by the capital sea-pieces of Redburn and White Jacket; Moby Dick proved a very tiresome yarn indeed, and as for the Ambiguities, we are compelled to say that it seems to us the most aptly titled volume we have met with for years.

Southern Literary Messenger, Vol. 15 (September 1852) 574–75.

The purpose of the Ambiguities, (if it have any, for none is either avowed or hinted,) we should take to be the illustration of this fact—that it is quite possible for a young and fiery soul, acting strictly from a sense of duty, and being therefore in the right, to erect itself in direct hostility to all the universally-received rules of moral and social order. At all events, such is the course of Pierre the hero of the story, from the opening chapter, without one moment's deviation, down to the "bloody work" of the final catastrophe. And our sympathies are sought to be enlisted with Pierre for the reason that throughout all his follies and crimes, *his sense of duty* struggles with and over-comes every law of religion and morality. It is a battle of the virtues, we are led to think, and the supreme virtue prevails.

To show how curiously Mr. Melville proceeds in his pur-pose, (supposing him to have one,) it will be necessary for us to give some hurried sketch of the story. Pierre, then, the hero, is the sole male representative of the family of Glendinning, a sprig of American Aristocracy, the idol of his proud and accom-plished mother and the plighted lover of Lucy Tartan, who is every thing that she should be, either in or out of a story-book. The course of true love runs without a ripple for these pleasant young people, until one day there appears an obstacle in the person of a fair unknown, with eyes of jet and tress of raven hue, who demonstrates to the entire conviction of Pierre that she is his sister—the illegitimate offspring of the paternal Glen-dinning. To Pierre, then, here was a dreadful disclosure—a bar sinister upon the family escutcheon—an indisputable and living reproach upon the memory of a sainted father. Pierre was there-fore perplexed. How to reconcile the obligation which rested upon him to protect his father's fame with the equally binding obligation to love his newly found sister, was indeed a puzzle, and one which he proceeded to solve in a very extraordinary manner. Pierre affects to marry the darkeyed one, the sister, by name Isabel; by which agreeable device he accomplishes three things—

1st. He drives his mother to the horrors of lunacy, in a par-oxysm of which she dies.

2nd. He brings upon himself and sister penury and anguish, while endeavoring to live by literary labor; and

3rd. He involves in wholesale assassination by pistols, poison and other diabolical means, the rest of the characters, making as much work for the Coroner as the fifth act of Romeo and Juliet, or the terrific melodrama of the Forty Thieves.

This latter state of things is thus brought about. Pierre having been driven off by his relatives, sets up a small establishment of his own. Lucy Tartan, recovering from the earliest burst of grief into which she had been thrown by Pierre's pretended marriage, and still, most unaccountably, clinging to the belief that Pierre is not wholly unfaithful, determines to live in his presence at all hazards. But her brother, and a new suitor to her hand, a cousin of Pierre, attempt to wrest her by violence from Pierre's household. Frustrated in this, they write to Pierre, calling him some rather hard names, such as liar and seducer, whereupon Pierre,—in no very good humor from having received a communication from his publishers, declining to purchase his last novel,—arms himself, seeks his cousin, and kills him several times with two pistols. But Pierre is "no sooner out than taken by the watch" and escorted to jail. Here he is visited by Isabel and Lucy, and the latter discovering that Isabel is the sister and not the mistress of Pierre, there ensues a fainting scene, after which these amiable ladies, for no adequate motive that we can see, proceed to drink each other's healths in prussic acid, though not exactly with the air of Socrates pouring off his hemlock to immortality. Here fitly ends the volume, for surely in its 'shocking department' we have "supped full of horrors," and yet the tragic effect of its perusal does *not* end here, for Lucy's fate, and supposed infamy 'leave to the imagination of the reader' any desired quantity of despair among the surviving relatives.

Such is the outline of the Ambiguities hurriedly given. The observant reader will see at once the absurdity of the principle upon which it has been constructed. Pierre discovers a sister whose very existence is evidence of a father's sin. To treat that sister with kindness and to cover over the father's shame, is without doubt a most laudable thing. But to accomplish it, Pierre is led to do things infinitely worse than it would be to neglect it. He not only acts like a fool in severing the most sacred ties and making the dearest sacrifices to purchase what he might have obtained at a much lighter expense, but he justifies his conduct by a sense of duty, false in the extreme. He

wishes to uphold the just and true, and to do this he commences
by stating a lie—his marriage with Isabel. It is in the cause of
affection and consanguinity that he is content to suffer, and for
this cause, he breaks off the closest and holiest bond that exists
on earth, the bond of filial love, thus causing the mother that
bore him to die a maniac. For every duty he performs, he is
compelled to commit a dozen outrages on the moral sense, and
these are committed without hesitancy or compunction. The
truth is, Mr. Melville's theory is wrong. It should be the object
of fiction to delineate life and character either as it is around
us, or as it ought to be. Now, Pierre never did exist, and it is
very certain that he never ought to exist. Consequently, in the
production of Pierre, Mr. Melville has deviated from the legitimate line of the novelist. But badly as we think of the book as
a work of art, we think infinitely worse of it as to its moral
tendency. We have not space left us to enter upon this view
of the volume, and we must therefore leave it with the remark
that if one does not desire to look at virtue and religion with
the eye of Mephistopheles, or, at least, through a haze of *ambiguous* meaning, in which they may readily be taken for their
opposites, he had better leave "Pierre or the Ambiguities" un-
bought on the shelves of the bookseller.

HENRY F. CHORLEY [1808–72], a reviewer in the London *Athenaeum* from
1833 until 1866. Leslie A. Marchand in *The Athenaeum: A Mirror of Victorian Culture* (Chapel Hill, 1941), identifies him as the author of the
Athenaeum's reviews of *Mardi, White-Jacket,* and *The Whale;* presumably
he was also the author of this review.

Review of *Pierre*

Attributed to HENRY F. CHORLEY

Pierre; or, the Ambiguities. By Herman Melville. Low & Co.

The brilliant success of some recent American fictionists makes us turn with more than common interest to any new work coming from transatlantic authors. This volume is a would-be utterance of 'Young Yankee' sentimentalism:—but beyond that its writer may be a subject of the States, we can discern nothing either American or original in its pages. It reads like an "upsetting" into English of the first novel of a very whimsical and lackadaisical young student at

the U—

niversity of Gottingen.

It is one of the most diffuse doses of transcendentalism offered for a long time to the public. When he sat down to compose it, the author evidently had not determined what he was going to write about. Its plot is amongst the inexplicable "ambiguities" of the book,—the style is a prolonged succession of spasms,— and the characters are a marrowless tribe of phantoms, flitting through dense clouds of transcendental mysticism. "Be sure," said Pope to a young author, "when you have written any passage that you think particularly fine—*to erase it.*" If this precept were applied to 'Pierre; or, the Ambiguities,'—its present form would shrink into almost as many pages as there are now chapters. German literature with its depths and shallows is too keenly appreciated in this country for readers to endure Germanism at second hand. We take up novels to be amused— not bewildered,—in search of pleasure for the mind—not in pursuit of cloudy metaphysics; and it is no refreshment after the daily toils and troubles of life, for a reader to be soused into a torrent rhapsody uttered in defiance of taste and sense.

Love has often driven wise men mad, and the workings of that subtle passion have given rise to many strange effusions even from men of genius:—but what do our readers think of a passage like this?—

London *Athenaeum*, No. 1308 (20 November 1852) 1265–66.

"No Cornwall miner ever sunk so deep a shaft beneath the sea, as Love will sink beneath the floatings of the eyes. Love sees ten million fathoms down, till dazzled by the floor of pearls. The eye is Love's own magic glass, where all things that are not of earth, glide in supernatural light. There are not so many fishes in the sea, as there are sweet images in lovers' eyes. In those miraculous translucencies swim the strange eye-fish with wings, that sometimes leap out, instinct with joy; moist fish-wings wet the lover's cheek. Love's eyes are holy things; therein the mysteries of life are lodged; looking in each other's eyes, lovers see the ultimate secret of the worlds; and with thrills eternally untranslateable, feel that Love is god of all. Man or woman who has never loved, nor once looked deep down into their own lover's eyes, they know not the sweetest and the loftiest religion of this earth. Love is both Creator's and Saviour's gospel to mankind; a volume bound in rose-leaves, clasped with violets, and by the beaks of humming birds printed with peach-juice on the leaves of lilies. Endless is the account of love. Time and space can not contain Love's story. All things that are sweet to see, or taste, or feel, or hear, all these things were made by Love; and none other things were made by Love. Love made not the Arctic zones, but Love is ever reclaiming them. Say, are not the fierce things of this earth daily, hourly going out? Where now are your wolves of Britain? Where in Virginia now, find you the panther and the pard? Oh, Love is busy every where. Everywhere Love hath Moravian missionaries. No Propagandist like to Love. The south wind woos the barbarous north; on many a distant shore the gentler west wind persuades the arid east."

Pierre finds a rocking stone in the woods, and thus apostrophizes.—

"'If the miseries of the undisclosable things in me, shall ever unhorse me from my manhood's seat; if to vow myself all Virtue's and all Truth's, be but to make a trembling, distrusted slave of me; if Life is to prove a burden I cannot bear without ignominious cringings; if indeed our actions are all fore-ordained, and we are Russian serfs to Fate; if invisible devils do titter at us when we most nobly strive; if Life be a cheating dream, and virtue as unmeaning and unsequeled with any blessing as the midnight mirth of wine; if by sacrificing myself for Duty's sake, my own mother re-sacrifices me; if Duty's self be but a bug-bear, and all things are allowable and unpunishable to man;—then do thou, Mute Massiveness, fall on me! Ages thou hast waited; and if these things be thus, then wait no more, for whom better canst thou crush than him who now lies here invoking thee?' A down-darting bird, all song, swiftly lighted on the unmoved and eternally immovable balancings of the Terror Stone, and cheerfully chirped to Pierre. The tree-boughs bent and waved to the rushes of a sudden, balmy wind; and slowly Pierre crawled forth, and stood haughtily upon his feet, as he owed thanks to none, and went his moody way."

That many readers will not follow "the moody way" of Pierre, is in our apprehension not amongst the "ambiguities" of the age. The present chaotic performance has nothing Ameri-can about it, except that it reminds us of a prairie in print,—wanting the flowers and freshness of the savannahs, but almost equally puzzling to find a way through it.

FITZ-JAMES O'BRIEN [1828–62], Irish-born American playwright, drama critic, and short-story writer. He is remembered now as the best writer of horror stories after Poe and before Bierce.

From Our Young Authors—Melville

FITZ-JAMES O'BRIEN

It is no easy matter to pronounce which of Mr. Melville's books is the best. All of them (and he has published a goodly number, for so young an author) have had their own share of success, and their own peculiar merits, always saving and excepting Pierre—wild, inflated, repulsive that it is.

For us there is something very charming about Mardi, all the time fully aware of its sad defects in taste and style. Of course, we give Mr. Melville every credit for his deliberate

Putnam's Monthly, Vol. 1 (February 1853) 155–64.

plagiarisms of old Sir Thomas Browne's gorgeous and metaphorical manner. Affectation upon affectation is scattered recklessly through its pages. Wild similes, cloudy philosophy, all
things turned topsy-turvy, until we seem to feel all earth melting away from beneath our feet, and nothing but Mardi remaining. Reading this wild book, we can imagine ourselves mounted
upon some Tartar steed, golden caparisons clank around our
person, ostrich plumes of driven whiteness hang over our brow,
and cloud our vision with dancing snow. . . .

A greater difference could hardly exist between two men
than between Mr. Mitchell and Mr. Melville, albeit we have
chosen to link them together in our chain. Mitchell writes
essentially from the heart. He is continually gazing inward,
picking up what he finds there, and displaying it with a child-
like, innocent pleasure to the world. From forms, and forms
alone does Melville take his text. He looks out of himself, and
takes a rich outline view of what he sees. He is essentially
exoterical in feeling. Matter is his god. His dreams are material. His philosophy is sensual. Beautiful women, shadowy
lakes, nodding, plumy trees, and succulent banquets, make
Melville's scenery, unless his theme utterly preclude all such.
His language is rich and heavy, with a plating of imagery. He
has a barbaric love of ornament, and does not mind much how
it is put on. Swept away by this sensual longing, he frequently
writes at random. One can see that he uses certain words only
because they roll off the pen lusciously and roundly, just as a
child, who is entirely the sport of sense, grasps at the largest
apple. In Mardi is this peculiarly obvious. A long experience
of the South sea islanders has no doubt induced this. The languages of these groups are singularly mellifluous and resonant,
vowels enter largely into the composition of every word, and
dissyllabled words are rare. Mr. Melville has been attracted by
this. Whenever he can use a word of four syllables where a
monosyllable would answer just as well, he chooses the former.
A certain fulness of style is very attractive. Sir Thomas Browne,
from whom Mr. Melville copies much that is good, is a great
friend of magnificent diction. And his tract on urn burial is as
lofty and poetical as if Memnon's statue chanted it, when the
setting sun fell aslant across the Pyramids. But we find no nonsense in Sir Thomas. In every thing he says there is a deep

meaning, although sometimes an erroneous one. We cannot always say as much for Mr. Melville. In his latest work he transcended even the jargon of Paracelsus and his followers. The Rosetta stone gave up its secret, but we believe that to the end of time Pierre will remain an ambiguity.

Mardi, we believe, is intended to embody all the philosophy of which Mr. Melville is capable, and we have no hesitation in saying that the philosophical parts are the worst. We do not for a moment pretend to say that we understand the system laid down by the author. Whether there be a system in it at all, is at least somewhat problematical, but when Mr. Melville does condescend to be intelligible, what he has to say for himself in the way of philosophy, is so exceedingly stale and trite, that it would be more in place in a school-boy's copy-book, than in a romance otherwise distinguished for splendor of imagery, and richness of diction. The descriptive painting in this wild book is gorgeous and fantastic in the extreme. It is a tapestry of dreams, worked with silken threads, dyed in the ocean of an Eastern sunset. Nothing however strange startles us as we float onwards through this misty panorama. King Media looms out from the canvas, an antique gentleman full of drowsy courtesy. Babbalanja philosophizes over his calabash, or relates the shadowy adventures of shadows in the land of shades. From out the woods, canopied with flowers, that let the daylight in only through courtesy, comes Donjalolo, the Southern Sardanapalus. Women droop over his pale enervate figure, and strive to light its exhausted fires with their burning eyes. He looks up lazily, and opens his small, red mouth to catch a drop of honey that is trembling in the core of some over-hanging flower. Fatigued with this exertion, he sinks back with a sigh into the soft arms interlaced behind. Then comes Hautia, Queen of spells that lie in lilies, and mistress of the music of feet. Around her float flushing nymphs, who love through endless dances, and die in the ecstasy of mingled motion. While far behind, throned in mist, and with one foot dabbling in the great ocean of the Future, stands the lost Yillah; problem of beauty to which there is no solution save through death.

All these characters flit before us in Mardi, and bring with them no consciousness of their unreality and deception. As shadows they come to us, but they are sensual shades. Their

joys thrill through us. When they banquet in drowsy splendor
—when they wander upon beaches of pearls and rubies—when
they wreath their brows with blossoms more fragrant and lus-
cious than the buds that grow in Paradise, our senses twine with
theirs, and we forget every thing, save the vision of their gorgeous pleasures. It is this sensual power that holds the secret
of Mr. Melville's first successes. No matter how unreal the
scenery, if the pleasure be but truly painted, the world will cry
"bravo!" We draw pictures of Gods and Goddesses, and hang
them on our walls, but we take good care to let their divinity
be but nominal. Diana, Juno, Venus, are they known, but they
loom out from the canvas, substantial, unadulterated women.
Seldom does there live an Ixion who loves to embrace clouds.
Call it a cloud if you will, and if it have the appearance of flesh
and blood, the adorer will be satisfied. But we doubt if there
is to be found any man enthusiast enough to clasp a vapor to
his heart, be it schirri-shaped or cumulous, and baptized with
the sweetest name ever breathed from the Attic tongue. Mr.
Melville therefore deals in vapors, but he twines around them
so cunningly all human attributes, and pranks them out so lusciously with all the witcheries of sense, that we forget their
shadowy nomenclatures, and worship the substantial incarnation.

It must not be imagined from this, that Mr. Melville is incapable of dealing with the events of more matter-of-fact life.
He is averse to it, no doubt, and if we may judge by Pierre, is
becoming more averse to it as he grows older. But he sometimes
takes the vulgar monster by the shoulders and wields it finely.
In Omoo, which by the way contains some exceedingly fine
passages, occurs the following account of the attempt of a South
sea savage named Bembo to run the ship ashore on a coral reef,
because he had been insulted by one of the ship's crew is very
graphic. . . .

Typee, the first and most successful of Mr. Melville's books,
commands attention for the clearness of its narrative, the novelty of its scenery, and the simplicity of its style, in which latter
feature it is a wondrous contrast to Mardi, Moby Dick, and
Pierre. . . .

White Jacket is a pure sea-book, but very clever. It is a
clear, quiet picture of life on board of a man-of-war. It has less
of Mr. Melville's faults than almost any of his works, and is

distinguished for clear, wholesome satire, and a manly style. There is a scene describing the amputation of a sailor's leg by a brutal, cold-blooded surgeon, Patella, that Smollett might have painted. We would gladly quote it, but that it rather exceeds the limits usually afforded in an article so short as ours.

There is one chapter in which the hero details the loss of the White Jacket, from wearing which, he and the book take their name, that strikes us as a very fine piece of descriptive writing. We give it entire. . . .

This is fine. We have often met with descriptions, some well painted enough, of dizzy aerial adventures, but never one like this. Our ears tingle as we read it. The air surges around us as we fall from that fearful height. The sea divides, the green mist flashes into a thousand hues, and we sit for an instant a stride of Death's balance. Weight, unutterable weight presses upon our shoulders, and we seem as if about to be crushed into nothingness. Then a sudden change. A revulsion which is accompanied with soft, low music; and we float upwards. We seem gliding through an oiled ocean, so smoothly do we pass. It breaks, it parts above our head. The next moment we shoot out from a cloud of feathers, and are battling with the waves.

In Redburn, we find an account of the death of a sailor, by spontaneous combustion. Well described, poetically described, fraught with none of the revolting scenery which it is so easy to gather round such an end. In the last number of Bleak House, Mr. Dickens has attempted the same thing. He has also performed what he attempted. But, if ever man deserved public prosecution for his writing, he does, for this single passage. A hospital student could not read it without sickening. A ghoul, who had lived all his days upon the festering corruption of the grave-yard, could have written nothing more hideously revolting than the death of Krook. It is as loathsome to read it as to enter one of the charnels in London city. We do not believe that a woman of sensitive nerves could take it up without fainting over the details. For ourselves, we fling the book away, with an anathema on the author that we should be sorry for him to hear.

Mr. Melville does not improve with time. His later books are a decided falling off, and his last scarcely deserves naming; this however we scare believe to be an indication of exhaustion.

Keats says beautifully in his preface to Endymion, that "The imagination of a boy is healthy, and the mature imagination of a man is healthy, but there is a space of life between, in which the soul is in a ferment, the character undecided, the way of life uncertain, the ambition thick-sighted."

Just at present we believe the author of Pierre to be in this state of ferment. Typee, his first book, was healthy; Omoo nearly so; after that came Mardi, with its excusable wildness; then came Moby Dick, and Pierre with its inexcusable insanity. We trust that these rhapsodies will end the interregnum of nonsense to which Keats refers, as forming a portion of every man's life; and that Mr. Melville will write less at random and more at leisure, than of late. Of his last book we would fain not speak, did we not feel that he is just now at that stage of author-life when a little wholesome advice may save him a hundred future follies. When first we read Pierre, we felt a strong inclination to believe the whole thing to be a well-got-up hoax. We remembered having read a novel in six volumes once of the same order, called "The Abbess," in which the stilted style of writing is exposed very funnily; and, as a specimen of unparalleled bombast, we believed it to be unequalled until we met with Pierre. In Mardi there is a strong vein of vague, morphinized poetry, running through the whole book. We do not know what it means from the beginning to the end, but we do not want to know, and accept it as a rhapsody. Babbalanja philosophizing drowsily, or the luxurious sybaritical King Media, lazily listening to the hum of waters, are all shrouded dimly in opiate-fumes, and dream-clouds, and we love them only as sensual shadows. Whatever they say or do; whether they sail in a golden boat, or eat silver fruits, or make pies of emeralds and rubies, or any thing else equally ridiculous, we feel perfectly satisfied that it is all right, because there is no claim made upon our practical belief. But if Mr. Melville had placed Babbalanja and Media and Yoomy in the Fifth Avenue, instead of a longitude and latitude less inland; if we met them in theatres instead of palm groves, and heard Babbalanja lecturing before the Historical Society instead of his dreamy islanders, we should feel naturally rather indignant at such a tax upon our credulity. We would feel inclined to say with the Orientals, that Mr. Melville had been laughing at our beards, and Pacha-like condemn on the instant to a literary bastinado. Now Pierre has all the madness of Mardi, without its vague, dreamy, poetic charm. All Mr. Melville's many affectations of style and thought are here crowded together in a mad mosaic. Talk of Rabelais's word-nonsense! there was always something queer, and odd, and funny, gleaming through his unintelligibility. But Pierre transcends all the nonsense-writing that the world ever beheld.

Thought staggers through each page like one poisoned. Language is drunken and reeling. Style is antipodical, and marches on its head. Then the moral is bad. Conceal it how you will, a revolting picture presents itself. A wretched, cowardly boy for a hero who from some feeling of mad romance, together with a mass of inexplicable reasons which, probably, the author alone fathoms, chooses to live in poverty with his illegitimate sister, whom he passes off to the world as his wife, instead of being respectably married to a legitimate cousin. Everybody is vicious in some way or other. The mother is vicious with pride. Isabel has a cancer of morbid, vicious, minerva-press-romance, eating into her heart. Lucy Tartan is viciously humble, and licks the dust beneath Pierre's feet viciously. Delly Ulver is humanly vicious, and in the rest of the book, whatever of vice is wanting in the remaining characters, is made up by superabundant viciosities of style.

Let Mr. Melville stay his step in time. He totters on the edge of a precipice, over which all his hard-earned fame may tumble with such another weight as Pierre attached to it. He has peculiar talents, which may be turned to rare advantage. Let him diet himself for a year or two on Addison, and avoid Sir Thomas Browne, and there is little doubt but that he will make a notch on the American Pine.

American Authorship

ANONYMOUS ("SIR NATHANIEL")

From No. IV.—Herman Melville

"Omoo," the Rover, keeps up the spirit of "Typee" in a new form. Nothing can be livelier than the sketches of ship and ship's company. "Brave *Little Jule,* plump *Little Jule,*" a very witch at sailing, despite her crazy rigging and rotten bulwarks —blow high, blow low, always ready for the breeze, and making you forget her patched sails and blistered hull when she was dashing the waves from her prow, and prancing, and pawing the sea—flying before the wind—rolling now and then, to be sure, but in very playfulness—with spars erect, looking right up into the wind's eye, the pride of her crew; albeit they had their misgivings that this playful craft, like some vivacious old mortal all at once sinking into a decline, might, some dark night, spring a leak, and carry them all to the bottom. The Captain, or "Miss Guy,"—essentially a cockney, and no more meant for the sea than a hairdresser. The bluff mate, John Jermin, with his squinting eye, and rakishly-twisted nose, and grey ringleted bullet head, and generally pugnacious looks, but with a heart as big as a bullock—obstreperous in his cups, and always for having a fight, but loved as a brother by the very men he flogged, for his irresistibly good-natured way of knocking them down. The ship's carpenter, "Chips," ironically styled "Beauty" on strict *lucus à non lucendo* principles—as ugly in temper as in visage. Bungs, the cooper, a man after a bar-keeper's own heart; who, when he felt, as he said, "just about right," was characterised by a free lurch in his gait, a queer way of hitching up his waistbands, and looking unnecessarily steady at you when speaking. Bembo, the harpooner, a dark, moody savage—none of your effeminate barbarians, but a shaggy-browed, glaring-eyed, crisp-haired fellow, under whose swart, tattooed skin the muscles worked like steel rods. Rope Yarn, or Ropey, the poor distraught land-lubber—a forlorn, stunted, hook-visaged creature, erst a journeyman baker in Holborn, with a soft and underdone heart, whom a kind word

London *New Monthly Magazine,* Vol. 98 (July 1853) 300–308.

made a fool of. And, best of all, Doctor Long Ghost, a six-feet tower of bones, who quotes Virgil, talks of Hobbes, of Malmesbury, and repeats poetry by the canto, especially "Hudibras;" and who sings mellow old songs, in a voice so round and racy, the real juice of sound; and who has seen the world from so many angles, the acute of civilisation and the obtuse of savagedom; and who is as inventive as he is incurable in the matter of practical jokes—all effervescent with animal spirits and tricksy good-humour. Of the Tahiti folks, Captain Bob is an amusing personage, a corpulent giant, of three-alderman-power in gormandising feats, and so are Po-po and his family, and the irreverently-ridiculed court of Queen Pomare. It is uncomfortable to be assured in the preface, that "in every statement connected with missionary operations, a strict adherence to facts has, of course, been scrupulously observed"—and the satirist's rather flippant air in treating this subject makes his protestation not unnecessary, that "nothing but an earnest desire for truth and good has led him to touch upon it at all." Nevertheless, there is mournful emphasis in these revelations of *mickonaree* progress —and too much reason to accept the tenor of his remarks as correct, and to bewail the inapplicability to modern missionaries in general, of Wordsworth's lines—

> Rich conquest waits them:—the tempestuous sea
> Of Ignorance, that ran so rough and high
> These good men humble by a few bare words,
> And calm with awe of God's divinity.

For does not even so unexceptionable a pillar of orthodoxy as Sir Archibald Alison, express doubt as to the promise of Missions, in relation to any but European ethnology? affirming, indeed,* that had Christianity been adapted to man in his rude and primeval state, it would have been revealed at an earlier period, and would have appeared in the age of Moses, not in that of Caesar:—a dogmatic assertion, by the way, highly characteristic of the somewhat peremptory baronet, and not very harmonious, either in letter or spirit, with the broad text on which world-wide missionary enterprise is founded, and for which Sir Archibald must surely have an *ethnic* gloss of his own private interpretation. . . .

* See "Alison's History of Europe" (New Series), vol. i., p. 74.

For so successful a trader in "marine stores" as Mr. Melville, "The Whale" seemed a speculation every way big with promise. From such a master of his harpoon might have been expected a prodigious hit. There was about blubber and spermaceti something unctuously suggestive, with him for whaleman. And his three volumes entitled "The Whale" undoubtedly contain much vigorous description, much wild power, many striking details. But the effect is distressingly marred throughout by an extravagant treatment of the subject. The style is maniacal—mad as a March hare—mowing, gibbering, screaming, like an incurable Bedlamite, reckless of keeper or strait-waistcoat. Now it vaults on stilts, and performs *Bombastes Furioso* with contortions of figure, and straining strides, and swashbuckler fustian, far beyond *Pistol* in that Ancient's happiest mood. Now it is seized with spasms, acute and convulsive enough to excite bewilderment in all beholders. When he pleases, Mr. Melville can be so lucid, straightforward, hearty, and unaffected, and displays so unmistakable a shrewdness, and satirical sense of the ridiculous, that it is hard to suppose that *he* can have indited the rhodomontade to which we allude. Surely the man is a Doppelganger—a dual number incarnate (singular though he be, in and out of all conscience):—surely he is two single gentlemen rolled into one, but retaining their respective idiosyncrasies—the one sensible, sagacious, observant, graphic, and producing admirable matter—the other maundering, drivelling, subject to paroxysms, cramps, and total collapse, and penning exceeding many pages of unaccountable "bosh." So that in tackling every new chapter, one is disposed to question it beforehand, "Under which king, Bezonian?"—the sane or the insane; the constitutional and legitimate, or the absolute and usurping? Writing of Leviathan, he exclaims, "Unconsciously my chirography expands into placard capitals. Give me a condor's quill! Give me Vesuvius' crater for an inkstand! Friends, hold my arms!" Oh that his friends had obeyed that summons! They might have saved society from a huge dose of hyperbolical slang, maudlin sentimentalism, and tragi-comic bubble and squeak. . . .

O author of "Typee" and "Omoo," we admire so cordially the proven capacity of your pen, that we entreat you to doff the "non-natural sense" of your late lucubrations—to put off your worser self—and to do your better, real self, that justice which its "potentiality" deserves.

Review of *Israel Potter*

ANONYMOUS

Mr. Melville's books have been from the outset of his career somewhat singular,—and this is not the least so of the company. Whether Israel Potter belongs to the family of *Mrs. Harris,* or was an actual *bonâ fide* American who took despatches in the heels of his boots to Franklin at Paris, and who sailed with that buccaneer hero, Paul Jones, we confess our inability to decide. Some "Noter" or "Querist," well versed in the minor history of the American War, may perhaps oblige us with the facts, if facts there be. But whether Israel Potter be man or myth, he is here set in a strange framework. Mr. Melville tries for power and commands rhetoric,—but he becomes wilder and wilder, and more and more turgid in each successive book. Take as a specimen, the following passage concerning the Thames, which makes part of his picture of London:—"Hung in long, sepulchral arches of stone, the black, besmoked bridge seemed a huge scarf of crape, festooning the river across. Similar funeral festoons spanned it to the west, while eastward, towards the sea, tiers and tiers of jetty colliers lay moored, side by side, fleets of black swans. The Thames, which far away, among the green fields of Berks, ran clear as a brook, here, polluted by continual vicinity to man, curdled on between rotten wharves, one murky sheet of sewerage. Fretted by the ill-built piers, while it crested and hissed, then shot balefully through the Erebus arches, desperate as the lost souls of the harlots, who, every night, took the same plunge. Meantime, here and there, like awaiting hearses, the coal-scows drifted along, poled broadside, pell-mell to the current."—Benjamin Franklin, it is true, is painted in less peculiar colours than those employed to blacken the "City of Dis." But the philosophical printer, however available for the purposes of such a nice observer and delicate delineator as Mr. Thackeray, retains neither bone, blood, nor muscle when dealt with by such a proficient in the "earthquake" and "alligator" style as Mr. Melville. He is selfish in his prudence, and icy in his calmness, —rather weak and very tiresome. Such, we take it, was not the

London *Athenaeum,* No. 1440 (2 June 1855) 643.

real Franklin. On the other hand, Paul Jones is a melo-dramatic caricature—an impossible mixture of a Bayard and a bully; and in a book were scene-painting has been tried for, we have encountered few scenes less real than the well-known attempt to burn Whitehaven, and the descent on St. Mary's Isle, as told in 'Israel Potter.' Mr. Melville, to conclude, does not improve as an artist,—yet his book, with all its faults, is not a bad shilling's worth for any railway reader, who does not object to small type and a style the glories of which are nebulous.

From A Trio of American Sailor-Authors

ANONYMOUS

America has produced three authors, who, having acquired their knowledge of sea-life in a practical manner, have written either nautical novels or narratives of the highest degree of excellence. We allude to Fenimore Cooper, R. H. Dana, jun., and Herman Melville, each of whom has written at least one book, which is, in our estimation, decidedly A 1. Our task here happily is not to institute a critical comparison of the respective merits of American and English sea-novelists and writers; but we do not hesitate incidentally to admit that, to say the very least, America worthily rivals us in this department of literature. Taking Cooper, for instance, all in all, we question greatly whether any English author excels him as a sea-novelist. Our two best are Marryat and Michael Scott ("Tom Cringle"), but they are in some respects essentially inferior to Cooper; and although they both have very great distinctive merits of their own, in what shall we deliberately pronounce them superior to the great American? Turn to Dana, and where is the English author, living or dead, who has written a book descriptive of real foremast life worthy to be compared with "Two Years before the Mast?" Again, to select only a single work by Herman Melville, where shall we find an English picture of man-of-war life to rival his marvellous "White-Jacket?" Tastes and opinions of course vary, and there may be, and doubtless are, able and intelligent critics who will dissent from our verdict; but we may be permitted to say that we believe very few works of nautical fiction and narrative (by either English or American authors) exist, with which we are not familiar.

Ere proceeding to consider the peculiar and distinguishing excellencies of our three American sailor-authors, we would observe that, as regards sea-novels, not one realises our idea of what this species of literature ought to be. A sea-novel, to which we can appeal as a standard by which to judge the general artistic merits of similar compositions, is yet, and will, we fear, long continue to be, a desideratum. In many so-called naval fictions, two-thirds or more of the scenes are described as occurring on shore, and the actors are more frequently landsmen than sailors; and even in the very best works of the class we find not a few chapters occupied by scenes and characters which have no connexion whatever with the sea. A genuine sea story should be evolved afloat from first to last; its descriptions should be confined to the ocean and its coasts—to ships and their management; its characters should exclusively be seamen (unless a fair heroine be introduced on shipboard); its episodes and all its incidental materials should smack of sea-life and adventure—the land, and all that exclusively pertains thereto, should as much as possible be *sunk* and forgotten! But, it will be asked, has a book of this kind yet been written? No, it has not. And if the most eminent naval novelists have not attempted such a performance, does not that prove that they considered the idea one that could not be practically carried out? So at least it would appear, and very successful nautical writers explicitly give their testimony against our theory. For example, Captain Chamier—whose "Ben Brace," and other nautical novels and narratives are, by the way, very little inferior to Marryat's—in his "Life of a Sailor," makes the following remark:—

"The mere evolutions of a ship, the interior arrangements, the nautical expressions, would soon pall on a landsman. Even Marryat, who wrote, in my opinion, the very best naval novel ever penned, 'The King's Own,' has found it impossible to keep to nautical scenes; and the author of the 'Post Captain,' a most excellent specimen of nautical life, has wisely painted the beauty of Cassandra, and made most of the interesting scenes occur on shore."

We dissent decidedly from much which our gallant friend here maintains. The evolutions of Cooper's ships, and the "nautical expressions" which he puts in the mouths of his characters, do *not* pall; the "King's Own" is *not* the best naval novel that even Marryat himself penned; and as to the "Post Captain," we admit that two or three opening chapters of that very coarsely-written anonymous work are pretty good, but all the rest are unmitigated balderdash; and how it happened that many editions of such a miserable performance found purchasers, is a greater mystery to us than a reel in a bottle was to our venerable great-grandmother. We must not digress further; but we re-iterate our firm belief that a nautical fiction strictly written on the plan we have proposed, if by a man of genius, would not merely be the *facile princeps* of its class of literature, but would delight landsmen as much as seamen, and interest all hands to a greater degree than any work written on the mongrel system of alternately describing life at sea and life on shore, which has hitherto prevailed. . . .

Herman Melville completes our Trio. A friend has informed us that "Herman Melville" is merely a *nom de plume,* and if so, it is only of a piece with the mystification which this remarkable author dearly loves to indulge in from the first page to the last of his works. We think it highly probable that the majority of our readers are only familiar with his earliest books; but as we have read them all carefully (excepting his last production, "Israel Potter," which is said to be mediocre) we shall briefly refer to their subjects seriatim, ere we consider the general characteristics of his style. His first books were "Omoo" and "Typee," which quite startled and puzzled the reading world. The ablest critics were for some time unable to decide whether the first of these vivid pictures of life in the South Sea Islands was to be regarded as a mere dexterous fiction, or as a narrative of real adventures, described in glowing, picturesque, and romantic language; but when the second work appeared, there could no longer exist any doubt, that although the author was intimately acquainted with the Marquesas and other islands, and might introduce real incidents and real characters, yet that fiction so largely entered into the composition of the books, that they could not be regarded as matter-of-fact narratives. Both these works contain a few opening chapters, descriptive of foremast-life in whaling-ships, which are exceedingly interesting and striking.

Melville's next work was entitled "Redburn," and professed to be the autobiographical description of a sailor-boy's first voyage across the Atlantic. It contains some clever chapters, but very much of the matter, especially that portion relative to the adventures of the young sailor in Liverpool, London, &c., is outrageously improbable, and cannot be read either with pleasure or profit. This abortive work—which neither obtained nor deserved much success—was followed by "Mardi; and a Voyage Thither." Here we are once more introduced to the lovely and mysterious isles of the vast Pacific, and their half-civilised, or, in some cases, yet heathen and barbarous aborigines. The reader who takes up the book, and reads the first half of volume one, will be delighted and enthralled by the original and exceedingly powerful pictures of sea-life, of a novel and exciting nature, but woful will be his disappointment as he reads on. We hardly know how to characterise the rest of the book. It consists of the wildest, the most improbable, nay, impossible, series of adventures amongst the natives, which would be little better than insane ravings, were it not that we dimly feel conscious that the writer intended to introduce a species of biting, political satire, under grotesque and incredibly extravagant disguises. Moreover, the language is throughout gorgeously poetical, full of energy, replete with the most beautiful metaphors, and crowded with the most brilliant fancies, and majestic and melodiously sonorous sentences. But all the author's unrivalled powers of diction, all his wealth of fancy, all his exuberance of imagination, all his pathos, vigour, and exquisite graces of style, cannot prevent the judicious reader from laying down the book with a weary sigh, and an inward pang of regret that so much rare and lofty talent has been wilfully wasted on a theme which not anybody can fully understand, and which will inevitably repulse nine readers out of ten, by its total want of human interest and sympathy. It is, in our estimation, one of the saddest, most melancholy, most deplorable, and humiliating perversions of genius of a high order in the English language.

Next in order—if we recollect rightly as to the date of publication—came "White Jacket; or the World in a Man-of-war." This is, in our opinion, his very best work. He states in the preface that he served a year before-the-mast in the United States frigate, Neversink, joining her at a port in the Pacific, where he had been left by—or deserted from, for we do not clearly comprehend which—a whaling-ship, and that the work is the result of his observations on board, &c. We need hardly say that the name Neversink is fictitious, but from various incidental statements we can easily learn that the real name of the frigate is the United States—the very same ship that captured our English frigate Macedonian in the year 1812. The Macedonian, we believe, is yet retained in the American navy. "White Jacket" is the best picture of life-before-the-mast in a ship of war ever yet given to the world. The style is most excellent—occasionally very eccentric and startling, of course, or it would not be Herman Melville's, but invariably energetic, manly, and attractive, and not unfrequently noble, eloquent, and deeply impressive. We could point out a good many instances, however, where the author has borrowed remarkable verbal expressions, and even incidents, from nautical books almost unknown to the general reading public (and this he does without a syllable of acknowledgment). Yet more, there are one or two instances where he describes the frigate as being manœuvred in a way that no practical seaman would commend—indeed, in one case of the kind he writes in such a manner as to shake our confidence in his own practical knowledge of seamanship. We strongly suspect that he can handle a pen much better than a marlingspike—but we may be wrong in our conjecture, and shall be glad if such is the case. At any rate, Herman Melville himself assures us that he has sailed before the mast in whalers, and in a man-of-war, and it is certain that his information on all nautical subjects is most extensive and accurate. Take it all in all, "White Jacket" is an astonishing production, and contains much writing of the highest order.

The last work we have to notice is a large one, entitled "The Whale," and it is quite as eccentric and monstrously extravagant in many of its incidents as even "Mardi;" but it is, nevertheless, a very valuable book, on account of the unparalleled mass of information it contains on the subject of the history and capture of the great and terrible cachalot, or sperm-whale. Melville describes himself as having made more than one cruise in a South-sea-whaler; and supposing this to have been the fact, he must nevertheless have laboriously consulted all the books treating in the remotest degree on the habits, natural history, and mode of capturing this animal, which he could obtain, for such an amazing mass of accurate and curious information on the subject of the sperm-whale as is comprised in his three volumes could be found in no other single work—or perhaps in no half-dozen works—in existence. We say this with the greater confidence, because we have written on the sperm-whale ourselves, and have consequently had occasion to consult the best works in which it is described. Yet the great and undeniable merits of Melville's book are obscured and almost neutralised by the astounding quantity of wild, mad passages and entire chapters with which it is interlarded. Those who have not read the work cannot have any conception of the reckless, inconceivable extravagancies to which we allude. Nevertheless, the work is throughout splendidly written, in a literary sense; and some of the early chapters contain what we know to be most truthful and superlatively-excellent sketches of out-of-the-way life and characters in connexion with the American whaling trade.

To give a fair idea of Herman Melville's powerful and striking style, when he condescends to restrain his exuberant imagination, and to write in what we may call his natural mood, we request the reader's attention to a short extract or two which we select from "White Jacket." We must premise that the frigate is overtaken by an awful gale at midnight, when off "the pitch" of Cape Horn, and is in a position of imminent danger. The boatswain called all hands to take in sail:—

"Springing from our hammocks," says Melville, "we found the frigate leaning over to it so steeply, that it was with difficulty we could climb the ladders leading to the upper deck. Here the scene was awful. The vessel seemed to be sailing on her side. The maindeck guns had several days previously been run in and housed, and the portholes closed; but the lee carronades on the quarterdeck and forecastle were plunging through the sea, which undulated over them in milkwhite billows of foam.

With every lurch to leeward, the yard-arm ends seemed to dip into the sea; while forward, the spray dashed over the bows in cataracts, and drenched the men who were on the foreyard. By this time, the deck was all alive with the whole strength of the ship's company—five hundred men, officers and all—mostly clinging to the weather bulwarks. The occasional phosphorescence of the yeasty sea cast a glare upon their uplifted faces, as a night's fire in a populous city lights up the panic-stricken crowd. . . . The ship's bows were now butting, battering, ramming, and thundering over and upon the head seas, and, with a horrible wallowing sound, our whole hull was rolling in the trough of the foam. The gale came athwart the deck, and every sail seemed bursting with its wild breath. All the quartermasters, and several of the forecastlemen, were swarming round the double-wheel on the quarterdeck. Some were jumping up and down with their hands on the spokes; for the whole helm and galvanised keel *were fiercely feverish with the life imparted to them by the tempest.*"

The words we have italicised strike us as being intensely poetical, and adapted to convey a vividly truthful idea of the state of a ship desperately battling with a powerful gale. We have ourselves repeatedly noted, when at sea during a gale, how "the whole helm" (by which is meant the rudder, tiller, wheel, steering-barrel, &c.) vibrated in such a manner, that one could judge from that alone of the position of the vessel and the manner in which the seas struck her, and also the manner in which she bore herself; and not only did the helm, but also the whole fabric of the ship, feel "fiercely feverish with life," and almost a sentient thing, conscious of her jeopardy, and of the necessity of bravely struggling with the tempest. The lands-man may possibly think we are indulging in wild, fanciful rhapsodies; but we appeal to every seaman who possesses a spark of sensibility and of imagination, and he will tell you that what Melville has asserted, and what we assert, is literally true, but must be *felt* to be understood.

We must give yet another and more characteristic "taste of the quality" of our favourite—for, with all his faults, we can truly say, "Melville, we love thee still!" We will select our final specimen from the last chapter of "White Jacket." When the frigate draws nigh to port, at the expiry of her long three years' cruise, and strikes soundings "by the deep nine!" the seaman-author thus describes the feelings of himself and messmates:—

"It is night. The meagre moon is in her last quarter—that betokens the end of a cruise that is passing. But the stars look forth in their everlasting brightness—and *that* is the everlasting, glorious Future, for ever beyond us. We maintopmen are all aloft in the top; and round our mast we circle, a brother-band, hand-in-hand, all spliced together. We have reefed the last top-sail; trained the last gun; blown the last match; bowed to the last blast; been tranced in the last calm. We have mustered our last round the capstan; been rolled to grog the last time; for the last time swung in our hammocks; for the last time turned out at the sea-gull call of the watch. . . . Hand-in-hand we top-mates stand, rocked in our Pisgah-top. And over the starry waves, and broad out into the blandly blue, boundless night, spiced with strange sweets from the long-sought land—the whole long cruise predestinated ours, though often in tempest time we al-most refused to believe in that far distant shore—"

But here Melville begins to hold forth in his favourite mystical form, and so we shall break off.

Perhaps we have so far indicated our opinion of the merits and demerits of Herman Melville in the course of the foregoing remarks, that it is hardly necessary to state it in a more general way. Yet, in conclusion, we may sum up our estimate of this singular author in a few short sentences. He is a man of genius —and we intend this word to be understood in its fullest literal sense—one of rare qualifications too; and we do not think there is any living author who rivals him in his peculiar powers of describing scenes at sea and sea-life in a manner at once poetical, forcible, accurate, and, above all, original. But it is his *style* that is original rather than his *matter*. He has read prodigiously on all nautical subjects—naval history, narratives of voyages and shipwrecks, fictions, &c.—and he never scruples to deftly avail himself of these stores of information. He undoubtedly is an original thinker, and boldly and unreservedly expresses his opin-ions, often in a way that irresistibly startles and enchains the interest of the reader. He possesses amazing powers of expres-sion—he can be terse, copious, eloquent, brilliant, imaginative, poetical, satirical, pathetic, at will. He is never stupid, never dull; but, alas! he is often mystical and unintelligible—*not* from any inability to express himself, for his writing is pure, manly English, and a child can always understand what he *says*, but the ablest critic cannot always tell what he really *means;* for he at times seems to construct beautiful and melodious sentences only to conceal his thoughts, and irritates his warmest admirers by his provoking, deliberate, wilful indulgence in wild and half-insane conceits and rhapsodies. These observations apply mainly to his latter works, "Mardi" and "The Whale," both of which he seems to have composed in an opium dream; for in no other manner can we understand how they could have been written.

Such is Herman Melville! a man of whom America has reason to be proud, with all his faults; and if he does not eventually rank as one of her greatest giants in literature, it will be owing not to any lack of innate genius, but solely to his own incorrigible perversion of his rare and lofty gifts.

Review of *The Piazza Tales*

ANONYMOUS

For some time the literary world has lost sight of Herman Melville, whose last appearance as an author, in "Pierre or the Ambiguities," was rather an unfortunate one, but he "turns up" once more in "The Piazza Tales" with much of his former freshness and vivacity. Of the series of papers here collected, the preference must be given to the *"Encantadas, or the Enchanted Islands"* in which he conducts us again into that "wild, weird clime, out of space, out of time," which is the scene of his earliest and most popular writings. "The Lightning Rod Man" is a very flat recital which we should never have suspected Melville of producing, had it not been put forth under the sanction of his name.

Southern Literary Messenger, Vol. 22 (June 1856) 480.

Review of *The Piazza Tales*

CHARLES GORDON GREENE

"The Piazza Tales" is Herman Melville's new book, received by P. S. & Co., from Dix & Edwards, New York. It embraces six stories, entitled "The Piazza, Bartleby, Benito Cereno, The Lighning-Rod Man, The Encantadas or Enchanted Islands, and The Bell Tower." All of them are readable and forcibly written tales.

Review of *The Piazza Tales*

ANONYMOUS

That the Americans excel in short tales, the mention of Irving, Poe, Hawthorne, will remind our readers. That Mr. Melville might deserve to be added to the list is also possible; but in these 'Piazza Tales' he gives us merely indications, not fulfilment. Under the idea of being romantic and pictorial in style, he is sometimes barely intelligible; as, for instance, in the following passage, which opens the last Piazza tale, that of 'The Bell Tower':—"In the south of Europe, nigh a once frescoed capital, now with dank mould cankering its bloom, central in a plain, stands what, at distance, seems the black mossed stump of some immeasurable pine, fallen, in forgotten days, with Anak and the Titan. As all along where the pine tree falls, its dissolution leaves a mossy mound—last flung shadow of the perished trunk; never lengthening, never lessening; unsubject to the fleet falsities of the sun; shade immutable, and true gauge which cometh by prostration—so westward from what seems the stump, one steadfast spear of lichened ruin veins the plain. From that tree-top, what birded chimes of silver throats had

Boston *Post*, Vol. XLVIII, No. 133 (4 June 1856).

London *Athenaeum*, No. 1500 (26 July 1856) 929.

rung. A stone pine; a metallic aviary in its crown: the Bell-Tower, built by the great mechanician, the unblest foundling, Bannadonna."—The author who "flames amazement" in the eyes of his readers by putting forth such grand paragraphs as the above must content himself with a very young public. Elder folk, however tolerant of imagery, and alive to the seductions of colour, will be contented with a few such pages and phrases, and lay by the rhapsody and the raving in favour of something more temperate. The legends themselves have a certain wild and ghostly power; but the exaggeration of their teller's manner appears to be on the increase.

———

Review of *The Piazza Tales*

ANONYMOUS

The author of "Typee" and "Omoo" requires none of "the tricks of the trade" to secure a favorable audience for a collection of tales upon which he seems to have lavished even more than his usual care. As criticism is exhausted, and too much eulogy does not suit our taste, we shall confine ourselves as briefly as possible to an enumeration of the dishes, adapted to various palates, and disagreeable to none, which the purchasers of this book will find set forth before them. The book takes its name from the first story of six, which are here re-collected from the magazines in which they originally appeared. They are called respectively "The Piazza," "Bartleby," "Benito Cereno," "The Lightning-rod Man"—a story which excited great attention when originally published in *Putnam's Monthly*—"The Encantadas; or, Enchanted Islands," and the "Bell Tower." All of them exhibit that peculiar richness of language, descriptive vitality, and splendidly sombre imagination which are the author's characteristics. Perhaps the admirers of Edgar Poe will see, or think they see, an imitation of his concentrated gloom in the wild, weird tale, called "Bartleby:" in the "Bell Tower," as well, there

United States Democratic Review, Vol. 38 (September 1856) 172.

is a broad tinge of German mysticism, not free from some resemblance to Poe. As a companion for the sultry summer months,
and a country residence, we can fancy no volume more agreeable: the tales are perfect in themselves, and would each form
the feast of a long summer's noon.

From Our Authors and Authorship:
Melville and Curtis

FITZ-JAMES O'BRIEN

Who can tell how much good Alfred Tennyson gained from that
stout, straightforward, large-hearted paper in which old Christopher North took him so smartly to task for his early follies,
and commended, with such a fond and generous warmth, his immortal gifts—his works of real beauty already achieved? Heaven
send you such a critic of that first book which you now profoundly meditate, dear and aspiring young friend! You will bless
his memory when your laurels are greenest.

If there ever was an author who deserved such a critic, and
needed such an one, alike for praise and blame, it is our old
acquaintance and esteemed prose-poet, Herman Melville.

It is long, now, since we first sailed with Melville to Typee,
but we shall never forget the new sensations of that delectable
voyage. Over silent stretches of the sleeping sea it led us, and
left us on a miraculous shore, to live there a miraculous life.

The tropic island, into whose delicious glades we wandered,
was not, indeed, wholly new to us; for we had been there before,
partly in the way of business, and partly on a pleasure trip,
with Bougainville and La Perouse, with Foster and Cook. But
the manner of our being there was intensely new. It was the
dream of the passionate and despairing lover of "Locksley Hall,"
fulfilled in the spirit of Robinson Crusoe, and with all the "modern improvements." We had, indeed, burst all links of habit,

Putnam's Monthly, Vol. 9 (April 1857) 384–93.

and had wandered to a happy world of most unconventional bliss—to islets favored of heaven.

"Larger constellations burning, mellow moons and happy skies,
  Breadths of tropic shade, and palms in cluster, knots of paradise;
  Never comes the trader, never floats an European flag,
  Slides the bird o'er lustrous woodland, droops the trailer from the crag;
  Droops the heavy-blossomed bower, hangs the heavy fruited tree,
  Summer isles of Eden, lying in dark purple spheres of sea."

Love and balls, the opera and angling, boating and swimming, and the piquant delights of a highly original cuisine were none of them denied to us. Refreshing converse with our fellow-men alternated with the most bracing solitude and the deepest communion with the soul of nature. In fact, we tasted all the most refined pleasures of civilization, in a new and sublimated form, while we exhausted the primæval poetry of savage life. But for the slight and single drawback of cannibalism, making its ugly mouth at our own precious persons, we should never have wished to leave so enchanting a place.

How Mr. Melville contrived to get us thither, we never stopped to think. We accepted his maoris, his palm-trees, his amazing gymnastics, his irresistible Fayaway, and his faithful Toby, as we had accepted the *graundees* of Peter Wilkins, or the Uncases of Cooper.

The book fascinated us with the fascination of genius. We recognized in this new writer a man's large nature, and quick sympathy with all things beautiful and strong—an eye to see, nerves to feel, muscle to achieve, and a heart to dare. Was the charming romance, after all, intended to be a satire upon the world in which we habitually live? Were these strange and beautiful pictures painted to strike us into thought, and develop in us that vague universal conviction of needed and impending change, which now pervades all Christendom, and mingles with the fancies and colors the speech of all who think and feel?

This might or might not have been so. We felt that the writer had purpose enough in him, at all events, and that whatever the origin of this first book might have been, it was but the prelude of a career which could not fail to be, at least, remarkable.

In the matters of style and form, Mr. Melville's first book exhibited a rare degree of ripeness and perfection. It was deformed with ungraceful locutions, it is true, and the simple flow of the narrative was not unbroken in all its course. But what was not to be hoped from a young author who displayed so much native intensity and vigor of speech—such a command of vivid coloring, and such a felicitous touch in his designs.

The promise of "Typee" has been kept, but rather to the ear than to the secret spirit. Mr. Melville has done a great deal since; but he has not yet done the precise things we hoped of him. He has pursued a distinct path with unfaltering steps; he has shown capital qualities, and, above all, the indispensable first qualities of pluck and perseverance. But he has been going wrong, we fear, rather than right, and we wish with all our heart that we could bring him over to our way of thinking.

"Typee" was published, if our memory deceive us not (how can one recall the date of a book, which has numbered, at least, twice as many editions as it has years?) in or about the year 1847; that is just ten years ago, and Mr. Melville has suffered hardly one of these ten years to pass without reminding us agreeably of his existence. "Omoo," "Mardi," "Redburn," "Moby Dick," "Israel Potter," the "Piazza Tales," and the "Confidence Man," make up a catalogue which would prove, if it proved nothing more, our author's sincere devotion to his art, and would entitle him, therefore, to the interest and the respect of all who love American literature, and hope noble things for it.

Has that devotion been as wise as it has been fervent? is a question which, however, continually recurs to us, in perusing Mr. Melville's books, and we closed the "Confidence Man" with the conviction that it was time this question should be resolutely and clearly answered.

Everybody who read "Typee" thoughtfully (and, it was Mr. Melville's fault that so few people *could* read thoughtfully a book so full of fascination), was struck with a tendency to vague and whimsical speculation which constantly betrays itself in the turn of the hero's reflections, and in the character of his Yankee Sancho Panza, and seafaring man Friday—"Toby."

In the midst of the dreamiest, the most suggestively naïve

and unconscious passages of picturesque description, you stumble over quaint phrases of a vagrant philosophy, and find the most modern metaphysics mingled with the most primitive love-making, after a perfectly amazing fashion. It is as if that philosophic polygamist, John Buncle, gentleman, suddenly came upon you, while you were lazily happy under a palm-tree, in the company of Bernardin de St. Pierre and Daniel Defoe. This was annoying, certainly; but then we had only to remember that "Typee" was a first book, and that as no man suddenly becomes a thorough villain, so no man suddenly becomes a complete author.

An ardent and ingenious young writer sits down to his first book, as if it were to be his last also. There are a thousand thoughts busy in his brain—a thousand experiences fermenting in his heart. How does he know whether he shall ever have another opportunity of uttering them? So, fitly, or unfitly, germanely or extravagantly they come into speech, hints of them crop out everywhere, in unexpected places; in short, the general idiosyncrasy of a writer is, at least, quite as apt to be betrayed in his first book as his special intention is.

Mr. Melville was not only a young man, but a young American, and a young American educated according to the standard of our day and country. He had all the metaphysical tendencies which belong so eminently to the American mind—the love of antic and extravagant speculation, the fearlessness of intellectual consequences, and the passion for intellectual legislation, which distinguish the cleverest of our people. It was inevitable that he should have stamped himself pretty clearly on his book, and his book was all the more interesting that he had so stamped himself upon it. Still we waited anxiously for number two. It came, and with it came more than we had anticipated of the metaphysics of "Typee," and less than we had hoped of its poetry. Had not Mr. Melville been impelled to a good deal of sharp, sensible writing in "Omoo," by his wrath against the missionaries, it is clear, we think, that he would have plunged headlong into the vasty void of the obscure, the oracular, and the incomprehensible. But a little wholesome indignation is a capital stimulus to good writing, and the beneficial effects of it were never more clearly apparent than in this very book. We trembled for its successor, and we trembled with reason; for, when "Mardi" came, or rather when we came to "Mardi," our "voyage thither" affected us much as it would to be literally knocked into the middle of next week.

We frankly own here, and now, and once for all, that we have not, and never expect to have, the faintest notion of why we took a voyage to "Mardi," nor of what we found when we reached "Mardi," if we ever did reach it, nor of how we got away from "Mardi" again, if we ever did get away from that enchanted, mysterious place. We would just as soon undertake to give anybody a connected and coherent account of the *Mardi gras* of Paris, on coming out of the *Bal de l'Opéra* at three in the morning, as criticise, or describe, or analyze the "Mardi" of our friend Mr. Melville. Do we believe, then, that Mr. Melville meant nothing by taking us to "Mardi"—that he had no purpose at all in his mind, but was *carnivalizing* when he wrote the book? Not a bit of it; for, dull of perception, and still more dull of instinct must the critic be who does not recognize in every page of Mr. Melville's writings, however vague, and obscure, and fantastic, the breathing spirit of a man of genius, and of a passionate and earnest man of genius. It is precisely because we are always sure that Mr. Melville *does* mean something, and something intrinsically manly and noble, too, that we quarrel with him for hiding his light under such an impervious bushel.

Mr. Melville is not a *dilettante* in metaphysics. If he is fantastically philosophical in his language, it is because he wants to say something subtle and penetrating which he has discerned, or *thinks he has* discerned, and takes this to be the most effective way of saying it. And this is just the issue we have to make with him. We made it when we read "Mardi;" we have been obliged to make it, again and again, in reading his subsequent books. What, for instance, did Mr. Melville mean when he wrote "Moby Dick?" We have a right to know; for he carried us floundering on with him after his great white whale, through all manner of scenes, and all kinds of company—now perfectly exhausted with fatigue and deafened with many words whereof we understood no syllable, and then suddenly refreshed with a brisk sea breeze and a touch of nature kindling as the dawn. There was so much truth in the book that we knew the author must have meant to give us more, and we were excessively vexed with him for darkening his counsel by words which we could not but esteem to be words without knowledge. Is it not a hard case, O sympathizing reader? Here is a man of distinct and unquestionable genius; a man who means righteously and thinks sensibly; a man whose aims do honor to himself and to his country; a man who wishes to understand life himself, and to help other people to understand it; a man, too, who has proved not once only but fifty, yea, a hundred times, that he can write good English—good, strong, sweet, clear English— a man who has music in his soul, and can ring fair chimes upon the silver bells of style—and this man will persist in distorting the images of his mind, and in deodorizing the flowers of his fancy; a man born to create, who resolves to anatomize; a man born to see, who insists upon speculating.

The sum and substance of our fault-finding with Herman Melville is this. He has indulged himself in a trick of metaphysical and morbid meditations until he has almost perverted his fine mind from its healthy productive tendencies. A singularly truthful person—as all his sympathies show him to be—he has succeeded in vitiating both his thought and his style into an appearance of the wildest affectation and untruth. His life, we should judge, has been excessively introverted. Much as he has seen of the world, and keen as his appreciation is of all that is true and suggestive in external life, he has turned away habitually, of late years, at least, to look in upon his own imaginations, and to cultivate his speculative faculties in a strange, loose way. We do not know a more curious and instructive spectacle than some of his books afford, of the conflict between resolute nature and stubborn cultivation.

Nature says to Herman Melville, "You shall tell the world what you have seen and see, in a warm, quick, nervous style, and bring the realities of life and man before your readers in such a way that they shall know your mind without calling on you to speak it. You shall be as true as Teniers or Defoe, without the coarseness of the Fleming or the bluntness of the Englishman."

Obstinate cultivation rejoins: "No! you shall dissect and divide; you shall cauterize and confound; you shall amaze and electrify; you shall be as grotesquely terrible as Callot, as subtly profound as Balzac, as formidably satirical as Rabelais."

Sometimes, nature, for a while, carries her point, and then

what charming pages we have; what pictures, rather than pages, pregnant with truth and wise with beauty! Sometimes obstinate cultivation has it all her way, and then what a maze we get into; what a whirl of fantastic names—of unintelligible quotations—of alarming mysteries! Skeletons grin at us; waves wash over us; monsters glower at us, until, in our bewilderment and despair, we are ready to take the place of that Casabianca of the Pacific, Tashtego, who goes down in the story of "Moby Dick," nailing the red flag of Ahab to the mast of the sinking Pequod, and, with the flag, the wing of an unhappy falcon which swoops down at a fatal moment for itself upon the fluttering ensign. Take the novel of "Redburn," for instance, which, though one of the least known, is by no means one of the least clever of Mr. Melville's works. A more extraordinary mixture of sense and nonsense, of accuracy and extravagance, of exact portraiture, and of incredible caricature, than this novel presents, can hardly be found. Master Redburn, going to England, meets in that country (which one would say ought to be tolerably well known by this time to the world in general, and to writers of fiction in particular) with things untold before in song or story, book of travels or cyclopædia. He encounters gentlemen of decayed families who go about from door to door of respectable houses with their faces blacked, and banjos in their hands, singing "at the service" of the amiable inmates in their handsome drawing-rooms. He also sees, standing at the open window of a flashing carriage, and in a very interesting posture, an extremely elegant gentleman, with a small, glossy head, like a seal's, who *"poses with the sole of one boot vertically exposed so as to show the stamp on it—a coronet!"*

He also visits a wonderful place of entertainment, wherein good or bad wine and good or bad luck are dispensed by "a very handsome florid old man with snow-white hair and whiskers, and in a snow-white jacket, who *looked like an almond-tree in blossom.*" And he falls in with an individual, whose "aspect was damp and death-like; the blue hollows of his eyes being like vaults full of snakes." All this is sufficiently startling, unnatural, and lamentable; and, by the side of all this, we come suddenly upon the freshest and finest writing—upon stories of nautical adventure, told with a grace that Marryat never approached, and a fire that Cooper never surpassed!

As with the larger so is it with the smaller works of Mr. Melville. He balances the charm, and truth, and hazy golden atmosphere of "Las Encantadas" against the grotesque absurdity and incomprehensible verbiage of the "Lightning-Rod Man."

The two latest published books of our author differ considerably from their predecessors, in the degree in which they exhibit the characteristics of the classes of writing to which they respectively belong. "Israel Potter" is a comparatively reasonable narrative, embodying a story of the national war of independence, which may almost be considered a national legend. In the main, it is a coherent story, and is told with considerable clearness and force, but it lacks the animation that pervades those writings of Mr. Melville which, in other respects, it resembles. Two characters of a somewhat fantastic strain figure in it, Benjamin Franklin being represented as one of the prosiest possible old maxim-mongers, though the epoch of his life selected for the story is just that time at which he was living brilliantly at Paris, and cracking rather irreverent jokes with the Abbé Morellet; and Paul Jones comes and goes through the story—a veritable hero of melo-drama—sullen, scornful, unappeasable, and impracticable.

The "Confidence Man," on the contrary, belongs to the metaphysical and Rabelaistical class of Mr. Melville's works, and yet Mr. Melville, in this book, is more reasonable, and more respectful of probabilities, possibilities, and the weak perceptions of the ordinary mind than he usually is when he wraps his prophetic mantle about him. The "Confidence Man" is a thoroughly American story; and Mr. Melville evidently had some occult object in his mind, which he has not yet accomplished, when he began to paint the "Masquerades" of this remarkable personage.

The "Confidence Man" comes into the book, a mute, on board of a Mississippi steam-boat. He is "a man in cream-colors, whose cheek was fair, whose chin downy, and whose hair flaxen, and whose hat was of white fur with a long, fleecy nap." But for the fact that this singular being is presented to us as quite *dumb,* one might suppose that Mr. Melville meant to give us the portrait of a distinguished metropolitan editor [Horace Greeley], and, in this way, to suggest some clue to his purpose in the story. But this theory, of course, cannot be advanced for a moment, and the cream-colored man in the white hat goes off again into space at the end of this part (for the volume already published only begins the work) just as much masked as when he came.

In the interval, he does a great many very odd and rather reprehensible things. He comes and goes very mysteriously, and assumes new shapes, though he always betrays himself by a certain uniformity in the style of his thoughts and his machinations, which also communicates itself to the conduct and the conversation of the parties whom he meets. From the barber on the Mississippi boat to the Methodist minister, who believes in the sword of the Lord, there is not a character in the book who does not talk very much like all the others. Save for its greater reasonableness and moderation, the "Confidence Man" ought to be ranked with "Moby Dick" and "Mardi," as one of those books which everybody will buy, many persons read, and very few understand.

Ought Mr. Melville to write such books? Will he continue to write such books always? We do not hesitate to return an emphatic "No!" to both these questions. Mr. Melville has rare gifts; he has a sound heart, a warm and lively, though not now healthy, imagination, a vigorous intellect—somewhat given to crooked courses—and a brilliant reputation, which is also a gift, as enabling a man to work his best work to the best advantage. We expect much from him. To use the emphatic words of a Winnebago chief, who dissented from the missionary doctrine of the goodness of Providence, on the ground that the Winnebagoes invariably had more rain in their country than they wanted, while the Sacs and Foxes had more cattle than they could eat, we expect, from Mr. Melville, "more beef and less thunder." We desire him to give up metaphysics and take to nature and the study of mankind. We rejoice, therefore, to know that he is, at this moment, traveling in the Old World, where, we hope, he will enjoy himself heartily, look about him wisely, and come home ready to give us pictures of life and reality. It cannot be possible, that a man of Mr. Melville's genius is to go on forever producing books which shall deserve such praise as was bestowed upon "Mardi" by a bewildered French critic in the *Revue des Deux Mondes*—books which resemble "the dream of a badly-educated midshipman, drunk on hasheesh, and swinging asleep at the mast-head of a ship in a warm, tropical night!"

The thing is absurd; and Maga, who loves her step-son Melville, as if he were wholly her own, knows perfectly well that he is destined to do her and his country much honor and much good.

Honor and good, too, Maga expects from Mr. Melville's younger brother in letters, Mr. George William Curtis. For he, too, has an individuality of his own, and has won for himself a distinct place in our young literature.

If the five volumes, which bear his name, and lie before us now, cannot be taken as the measure of their author's capacity, they do, at least, indicate very fairly the qualities of his mind. A stronger contrast than they afford to the works of Mr. Melville it would be hard to find. Both writers are, evidently, men who wish to be thought and felt to be in earnest; but Mr. Melville takes as much pains to protest his earnestness as Mr. Curtis takes to conceal his. Mr. Melville is always as grave in his gayeties as Mr. Curtis is gay in his gravities. Mr. Melville has so much fancy and so little taste that he goes about accompanied by a grotesque troop of notions, whose preposterous attire more provokes the laugh than their numbers excite the respect of the world. Mr. Curtis has not so much fancy, but a great deal of fine instinctive grace, and the ideas which he introduces always do him credit by their style and accoutrements. Neither of these writers is natural enough, and enough at his ease to do himself full justice; for, while Mr. Melville throws himself off his balance by an over-eagerness to be prophetic and impressive, Mr. Curtis loses his through an over-anxiety to be moderate, judicious, and experienced.

The same kind of mischief which has been done to Mr. Melville, by his study of Rabelais, has been done to Mr. Curtis by his admiration of Thackeray. In the one case, as in the other, we cannot but commend the fanaticism whose effects we deplore and try to point out; for a good, hearty, unreasonable love of anything or anybody is an excellent thing for body and soul, and we shall never quarrel with it. But, in the one case as in the other, we wish to see the admirers shake themselves free of their admiration so far as to find out that it is leading them astray. If Mr. Melville is as little like the *curé* of Meudon in his character as in the circumstances of his life, Mr. Curtis resembles Thackeray neither in the constitution of his mind nor in the position from which he contemplates the world. . . .

Review of *The Confidence-Man*

ANONYMOUS

'The Confidence-Man' is a morality enacted by masqued play-ers. The credulous and the sceptical appear upon the stage in various quaint costumes, and discourse sententiously on the art of human life, as developed by those who believe and those who suspect. We leave the inference to be traced by Mr. Melville's readers,—some of whom, possibly, may wait for a promised se-quel to the book before deciding as to the lucidity or opaque-ness of the author's final meaning. There is a stage, with a set of elaborate scenery, but there is strictly no drama, the incidents being those of a masquerade, while the theatre is a steam-palace on the Mississippi. Here "the Confidence-Man" encounters his antagonists and disciples,—and their dialogues occupy the chief part of the volume. Mr. Melville is lavish in aphorism, epigram, and metaphor. When he is not didactic, he is luxuriously pic-turesque; and, although his style is one, from its peculiarities, difficult to manage, he has now obtained a mastery over it, and pours his colours over the narration with discretion as well as prodigality. All his interlocutors have studied the lore of old philosophy: they have all their wise sayings, of satire or specu-lation, to enrich the colloquy; so that, while the mighty river-boat, Fidèle, steams up the Mississippi, between low, vine-tan-gled banks, flat as tow-paths, a voyage of twelve hundred miles, "from apple to orange, from clime to clime," we grow so familiar with the passengers that they seem at last to form a little world of persons mutually interested, generally eccentric, but in no case dull. Mr. Melville has a strange fashion of inaugurating his moral miracle-play,—the synopsis of which, in the Table of Con-tents, is like a reflection of 'The Ancient Mariner,' interspersed with some touches vaguely derived from the dialecticians of the eighteenth century. One sentence, leading into the first chapter, immediately fixes the attention:—

"At sunrise on a first of April, there appeared, suddenly as Manco Capac at the lake Titicaca, a man in cream colours, at the water-side, in the city of St.-Louis."

London *Athenaeum*, No. 1537 (11 April 1857) 402–3.

This is a mute. The other personages are fantastically attired, or rather, by an adroit use of language, common things are suggested under uncommon aspects. The cosmopolitan himself is an oracle of confidence; and, finally, bargains with a barber, whose motto has been "No trust," to indemnify him against any loss that may ensue from the obliteration of that motto for a certain term, during which the barber shall not only shave mankind for ready money, but grant credit. The agreement is signed.—

" 'Very good,' said the barber, 'and now nothing remains but for me to receive the cash.' Though the mention of that word, or any of its singular numerous equivalents, in serious neighbourhood to a requisition upon one's purse, is attended with a more or less noteworthy effect upon the human countenance, producing in many an abrupt fall of it—in others a writhing and screwing up of the features to a point not undistressing to behold, in some, attended with a blank pallor and fatal consternation—yet no trace of any of these symptoms was visible upon the countenance of the cosmopolitan, notwithstanding nothing could be more sudden and unexpected than the barber's demand. . . .

'. . . Now what sort of a beginning is this? You, barber, for a given time engage to trust man, to put confidence in men, and, for your first step, make a demand implying no confidence in the very man you engage with. But fifty dollars is nothing, and I would let you have it cheerfully, only I unfortunately happen to have but little change with me just now.'—'But you have money in your trunk, though?'—'To be sure. But you see—in fact, barber, you must be consistent. No, I won't let you have the money now; I won't let you violate the inmost spirit of our contract, that way. So good-night, and I will see you again.' "

Such is the spirit of the book. These are the masqueraders among whom moves the cosmopolitan philanthropist, honeying their hearts with words of benignity and social faith.—

"Natives of all sorts, and foreigners; men of business and men of pleasure; parlour men and backwoodsmen; farm-hunters and fame-hunters; heiress-hunters, gold-hunters, buffalo-hunters, bee-hunters, happiness-hunters, truth-hunters, and still keener hunters after all these hunters. Fine ladies in slippers,

and moccasined squaws; Northern speculators and Eastern philosophers; English, Irish, German, Scotch, Danes; Santa Fé traders in striped blankets, and Broadway bucks in cravats of cloth
of gold; fine-looking Kentucky boatmen, and Japanese-looking
Mississippi cotton-planters; Quakers in full drab, and United
States soldiers in full regimentals; slaves, black, mulatto, quad-
roon; modish young Spanish Creoles, and old-fashioned French
Jews; Mormons and Papists; Dives and Lazarus; jesters and
mourners, teetotalers and convivialists, deacons and blacklegs;
hard-shell Baptists and clay-eaters; grinning negroes, and Sioux
chiefs solemn as high-priests."

A "limping, gimlet-eyed, sour-faced" discharged custom-
house officer,—a crippled Nigritian beggar,—a blue-eyed epis-
copalian,—a prime and palmy gentleman with gold sleeve-but-
tons,—a young Byronic student,—a plump and pleasant lady,—a
rich man,—a business man,—"a man with a travelling-cap,"—a
soldier of fortune,—a man with no memory, come under the
influence of the philanthropist's experimental doctrine, with
varying results, and much cordial philosophy is extracted from
their talk, fragrant with poetry or bitter with cynicism. The
"Confidence-Man" confides even in wine that has a truthful
tinge. "He who could mistrust poison in this wine would mistrust consumption in Hebe's cheek." And then is pronounced
the eulogy of the Press,—not that which rolls, and groans, and
rattles by night in printing-offices, but that which gushes with
bright juice on the Rhine, in Madeira and Mitylene, on the
Douro and the Moselle, golden or pale tinted, or red as roses in
the bud. Passing this, we select one example of Mr. Melville's
picture-making.—

"In the middle of the gentleman's cabin burned a solar lamp,
swung from the ceiling, and whose shade of ground glass was
all round fancifully variegated, in transparency, with the image
of a horned altar, from which flames rose, alternate with the
figure of a robed man, his head encircled by a halo. The light
of this lamp, after dazzlingly striking on marble, snow-white
and round—the slab of a centre-table beneath—on all sides went
rippling off with ever-diminishing distinctness, till, like circles
from a stone dropped in water, the rays died dimly away in
the furthest nook of the place."

Full of thought, conceit, and fancy, of affectation and originality, this book is not unexceptionably meritorious, but it is
invariably graphic, fresh, and entertaining.

———

Review of *The Confidence-Man*

ANONYMOUS

The precise design of Mr. Herman Melville in *The Confidence-
Man, his Masquerade,* is not very clear. Satire on many American smartnesses, and on the gullibility of mankind which en-
ables those smartnesses to succeed, is indeed an evident object
of the author. He stops short of any continuous pungent effect;
because his plan is not distinctly felt, and the framework is very
inartistical; also because the execution is upon the whole flat,
at least to an English reader, who does not appreciate what
appear to be local allusions.

A Mississippi steam-boat is the scene of the piece; and the
passengers are the actors, or rather the talkers. There is a misan-
thropist, looking like a dismissed official soured against the
government and humanity, whose pleasure it is to regard the
dark side of things and to infuse distrust into the compassionate
mind. There is the President and Transfer Agent of the "Black
Rapids Coal Company," who does a little business on board, by
dint of some secret accomplices and his own pleasant plausibility
and affected reluctance. A herb-doctor is a prominent person,
who gets rid of his medicine by immutable patience and his dex-
terity in playing upon the fears and hopes of the sick. The "Confidence-Man" is the character most continually before the reader.
He is collecting subscriptions for a "Widow and Orphan Asylum
recently founded among the Seminoles," and he succeeds greatly
in fleecing the passengers by his quiet impudence and his insinuating fluency; the persons who effectually resist being middle-
aged or elderly well-to-do gentlemen, who cut short his advances: "You—pish! why will the captain suffer these begging

London *Spectator*, Vol. 30 (11 April 1857) 398–99.

fellows to come on board?" There are various other persons who bear a part in the discourses: one or two tell stories; and the author himself sometimes directly appears in a chapter of disquisition.

Besides the defective plan and the general flatness of execution, there seems too great a success on the part of the rogues, from the great gullibility of the gulls. If implicit reliance could be placed on the fiction as a genuine sketch of American society, it might be said that poverty there as elsewhere goes to the wall, and that the freedom of the constitution does not extend to social intercourse unless where the arms and physical strength of some border man compel the fears of the genteel to grudgingly overcome their reluctance for the time. This reliance we cannot give. The spirit of the satire seems drawn from the European writers of the seventeenth and eighteenth centuries, with some of Mr. Melville's own Old World observations superadded. It sometimes becomes a question how much belongs to the New World, how much to the Old, and how much to exaggerated representation, impressing a received truth in the form of fiction. The power of wealth, connexion, and respectability, to overbear right, while poor and friendless innocence suffers, may be illustrated in the following story of a begging cripple, told to the herb-doctor; or it may instance the unscrupulous invention of vagrant impostors; but it can scarcely be taken as a true picture of justice towards the poor at New York. . . .

Review of *The Confidence-Man*

ANONYMOUS

We are not among those who have had faith in Herman Melville's South Pacific travels so much as in his strength of imagination. The "Confidence-Man" shows him in a new character —that of a satirist, and a very keen, somewhat bitter, observer. His hero, like Mr. Melville in his earlier works, asks confidence

Westminster Review, Vol. 12 (1 July 1857) 310–11.

of everybody under different masks of mendicancy, and is, on the whole, pretty successful. The scene is on board an American steamboat—that epitome of the American world—and a variety of characters are hustled on the stage to bring out the Confidence-Man's peculiarities: it is, in fact, a puppet-show; and, much as Punch is bothered by the Beadle, and calmly gets the better of all his enemies, his wife in the bargain, the Confidence-Man succeeds in baffling the one-legged man, whose suspicions and snappish incredulity constantly waylay him, and in counting a series of victims. Money is of course the great test of confidence, or credit in its place. Money and credit follow the Confidence-Man through all his transformations—misers find it impossible to resist him. It required close knowledge of the world, and of the Yankee world, to write such a book and make the satire acute and telling, and the scenes not too improbable for the faith given to fiction. Perhaps the moral is the gullibility of the great Republic, when taken on its own tack. At all events, it is a wide enough moral to have numerous applications, and sends minor shafts to right and left. Several capital anecdotes are told, and well told; but we are conscious of a certain hardness in the book, from the absence of humour, where so much humanity is shuffled into close neighbourhood. And with the absence of humour, too, there is an absence of kindliness. The view of human nature is severe and sombre—at least, that is the impression left on our mind. It wants relief, and is written too much in the spirit of Timon; who, indeed, saw life as it is, but first wasted his money, and then shut his heart, so that for him there was nothing save naked rock, without moss and flower. A moneyless man and a heartless man are not good exponents of our state. Mr. Melville has delineated with passable correctness, but he has forgotten to infuse the colours that exist in nature. The fault may lie in the uniqueness of the construction. Spread over a larger canvas, and taking in more of the innumerable sides of humanity, the picture might have been as accurate, the satire as sharp, and the author would not have laid himself open to the charge of harshness. Few Americans write so powerfully as Mr. Melville, or in better English, and we shall look forward with pleasure to his promised continuation of the masquerade. The first part is a remarkable work, and will add to his reputation.

Review of *Battle-Pieces*

ANONYMOUS

Mr. Melville's work possesses the negative virtues of originality in such degree that it not only reminds you of no poetry you have read, but of no life you have known. Is it possible—you ask yourself, after running over all these celebrative, inscriptive, and memorial verses—that there has really been a great war, with battles fought by men and bewailed by women? Or is it only that Mr. Melville's inner consciousness has been perturbed, and filled with the phantasms of enlistments, marches, fights in the air, parenthetic bulletin-boards, and tortured humanity shedding, not words and blood, but words alone?

Mr. Melville chooses you a simple and touching theme, like that of the young officer going from his bride to hunt Mosby in the forest, and being brought back to her with a guerrilla's bullet in his heart,—a theme warm with human interests of love, war, and grief, and picturesque with green-wood lights and shadows,—and straight enchants it into a mystery of thirty-eight stanzas, each of which diligently repeats the name of Mosby, and deepens the spell, until you are lost to every sense of time or place, and become as callous at the end as the poet must have been at the beginning to all feeling involved, doubting that

"The living and the dead are but as pictures."

Here lies the fault. Mr. Melville's skill is so great that we fear he has not often felt the things of which he writes, since with all his skill he fails to move us. In some respects we find his poems admirable. He treats events as realistically as one can to whom they seem to have presented themselves as dreams; but at last they remain vagaries, and are none the more substantial because they have a modern speech and motion. We believe ghosts are not a whit more tangible now that they submit to be photographed in the sack-coats and hoop-skirts of this life, than before they left off winding-sheets, and disappeared if you spoke to them.

With certain moods or abstractions of the common mind

Atlantic Monthly, Vol. 19 (February 1867) 252–53.

during the war, Mr. Melville's faculty is well fitted to deal: the unrest, the strangeness and solitude, to which the first sense of the great danger reduced all souls, are reflected in his verse, and whatever purely mystic aspect occurrences had seems to have been felt by this poet, so little capable of giving their positive likeness.

The sentiment and character of the book are perhaps as well shown in its first poem as in any other part of it. Mr. Melville calls the verses "The Portent (1859)"; but we imagine he sees the portent, as most portents are seen, after the event portended.

> "Hanging from the beam,
>   Slowly swaying (such the law),
> Gaunt the shadow on your green,
>   Shenandoah!
> The cut is on the crown
> (Lo, John Brown),
> And the stabs shall heal no more.
>
> "Hidden in the cap
>   Is the anguish none can draw;
> So your future veils its face,
>   Shenandoah!
> But the streaming beard is shown
> (Weird John Brown),
> The meteor of the war."

There is not much of John Brown in this, but, as we intimated, a good deal of Mr. Melville's method, and some fine touches of picturesque poetry. Indeed, the book is full of pictures of many kinds,—often good,—though all with an heroic quality of remoteness, separating our weak human feelings from them by trackless distances. Take this of the death of General Lyon's horse a few moments before he was himself struck at Springfield,—a bit as far off from us as any of Ossian's, but undeniably noble:—

> "There came a sound like the slitting of air
>   By a swift sharp sword—
> A rush of the sound; and the sleek chest broad
>   Of black Orion
> Heaved, and was fixed; the dead mane waved toward Lyon."

We have never seen anywhere so true and beautiful a picture as the following of that sublime and thrilling sight,—a great body of soldiers marching:—

> "The bladed guns are gleaming—
>   Drift in lengthened trim,
>   Files on files for hazy miles
>   Nebulously dim."

A tender and subtile music is felt in many of the verses, and the eccentric metres are gracefully managed. We received from the following lines a pleasure which may perhaps fail to reach the reader, taking them from their context in the description of a hunt for guerillas, in the ballad already mentioned:—

> "The morning-bugles lonely play,
>   Lonely the evening-bugle calls—
> Unanswered voices in the wild;
>   The settled hush of birds in nest
>   Becharms, and all the wood enthralls:
>   Memory's self is so beguiled
>   That Mosby seems a satyr's child."

He does so; and the other persons in Mr. Melville's poetry seem as widely removed as he from our actual life. If all the Rebels were as pleasingly impalpable as those the poet portrays, we could forgive them without a pang, and admit them to Congress without a test-oath of any kind.

JOHN SEELY HART [1810–77], a frequent contributor to religious and educational journals, was after 1872 professor of rhetoric and the English language at Princeton.

Melville

JOHN S. HART

Melville is the author of several exciting works based upon his adventures. The following are the principal: Typee, or Four Months in the Marquesas; Omoo; Mardi, and a Voyage Thither; Redburn, or the Confessions of a Gentleman's Son in the Merchant Service; White Jacket, or the World in a Man-of-War; the Piazzi [*sic*] Tales, a series of stories published in Putnam's Magazine; The Confidence Man. His two best works are, perhaps, Typee and Redburn. In the former, life among the savages is described in an almost idyllic style, too idyllic, it has been observed, to be wholly accurate. At least one may be permitted to doubt whether the savages of Typee were quite as interesting as Melville has represented them. The work itself and its successors attracted great attention at the time of their appearance, and although interest in them has since abated, they are still excellent in point of style. Melville is a writer of forcible and graceful English, although in some of his works he lapses into mysticism.

FRANCIS H. UNDERWOOD [1825–94], free-soiler, assistant manager of the *Atlantic Monthly* in its first two years, author of several books on literary history and biography, and magazine critic.

Melville

FRANCIS H. UNDERWOOD

Typee closes with the account of his escape from Nukuheva. A second work, Omoo, published in 1847, takes up the narrative at that point. These are among the most delightful books of

A *Manual of American Literature: A Text-Book for Schools and Colleges* (Philadelphia: Eldredge & Brother 1872) p. 486.

A *Hand-Book of English Literature: American Authors* (Boston: Lee and Shepard, 1872) p. 458.

travel in the language. The style is charmingly easy, the descriptions are novel and picturesque, and the incidents are, if not absolutely true, related with an air of verisimilitude that gives the reader perfect confidence. . . . In 1851 he published Moby Dick, the White Whale, an imaginative story, and not altogether probable. . . .

EDMUND CLARENCE STEDMAN [1833–1908]. The attribution is traditional and plausible, if only from the rarity of such attention to Melville and Stedman's known interest in him. Stedman was a major literary figure in his day—a critic, editor, poet, and influential anthologizer. His son Arthur Stedman discussed with Melville the reissue of his most popular works and brought out editions of *Typee, Omoo, White-Jacket,* and *Moby-Dick* after his death.

Review of *Clarel*

Attributed to EDMUND CLARENCE STEDMAN

After a long silence, Mr. Herman Melville speaks again to the world. No more a narrator of marvelous stories of tropical life and adventure, no more a weird and half-fascinating, half-provoking writer of romances, but now as a poet with a single work, in four parts, and about 17,000 lines in length. We knew already that Mr. Melville's genius has a distinctly poetical side; we remember still his stirring lines on Sheridan's Ride, commencing:

> Shoe the steed with silver,
> That bore him to the fray!

But the present venture is no less hazardous than ambitious. A narrative poem of such a length demands all the charms of verse, the strength and interest of plot, the picturesqueness of episode, and the beauty of sentimental or reflective digression which the author's art is capable of creating; and even then it may lack the subtle spell which chains the reader to its perusal. "Clarel," we must frankly confess, is something of a puzzle, both

New York *Tribune,* 16 June 1876.

in design and execution. A short excursion in Palestine—the four parts of the poem being entitled Jerusalem, the Wilderness, Mar Saba, and Bethlehem—gives a framework of landscape and incident to the characters, who are Clarel, a student, a doubter and dreamer; Nehemiah, an old Rhode Island religious enthusiast; Vine, a problematic character; Rolfe, "a messmate of the elements;" Derwent, an English clergyman; Glaucon, a Smyrniote Greek; and Mortmain, an eccentric Swede. After a love-passage between Clarel and Ruth, a young Jewish girl, in Jerusalem, the above characters make up a party for Jericho, the Jordan and the Dead Sea, returning by way of the Greek monastery of Mar Saba and Bethlehem. The excursion lasts but a few days: they return to Jerusalem by night, and find Ruth dead and about to be buried by torch-light. Passion Week follows, and with it the poem closes. Clarel with his grief, and the other characters with their several eccentricities, disappear suddenly from our view.

There is thus no plot in the work; but neither do the theological doubts, questions, and disputations indulged in by the characters, and those whom they meet, have any logical course or lead to any distinct conclusions. The reader soon becomes hopelessly bewildered, and fatigues himself vainly in the effort to give personality to speakers who constantly evade it, and connection to scenes which perversely hold themselves separate from each other. The verse, frequently flowing for a few lines with a smooth, agreeable current, seems to foam and chafe against unmanageable words like a brook in a stony glen: there are fragments of fresh, musical lyrics, suggestive both of Hafiz and of William Blake; there are passages so rough, distorted, and commonplace withal, that the reader impatiently shuts the book. It is, in this respect, a medley such as we have rarely perused,—a mixture of skill and awkwardness, thought and aimless fancy, plan shattered by whim and melody broken by discords. It is difficult to see how any one capable of writing such excellent brief passages should also write such astonishingly poor ones—or the reverse.

The descriptive portions of the poem are often bold, clear, and suggestive of the actual scenes. We might make a collection of admirable lines and couplets, which have the ring and sparkle of true poetry. On the other hand it would be equally easy to multiply passages like the following, the sense of which is only reached with difficulty, and then proves to be hardly worth the trouble of seeking:

> But one there was (and Clarel he)
> Who, in his aspect free from cloud,
> Here caught a gleam from source unspied,
> As cliff may take on mountain-side,
> When there one small brown cirque ye see,
> Lit up in mole, how mellowly,
> Day going down in somber shroud—
> October pall.
>   But tell the vein
> Of new emotion, inly held
> That so the long contention quelled—
> Languor and indecision, pain.
> Was it abrupt resolve? a strain
> Wiser than wisdom's self might teach?
> Yea, now his hand would boldly reach
> And pluck the nodding fruit to him,
> Fruit of the tree of life.

As a contrast, we take at random a few of the lyrical passages scattered through the work:

> Noble gods at the board,
>   Where lord unto lord
> Light pushes the care-killing wine:
>   Urbane in their pleasure,
>   Superb in their leisure—
>   Lax ease—
> Lax ease after labor divine!
>   *   *   *   *
> With a rose in thy mouth
>   Through the world lightly veer;
> Rose in the mouth
>   Makes a rose of the year!
>   *   *   *   *
> But through such strange illusions have they passed
>   Who in life's pilgrimage have baffled striven—
> Even death may prove unreal at the last,
>   And stoics be astounded into heaven.

The ordinary reader will find himself in the position of one who climbs over a loose mound of sliding stones and gravel, in the search for the crystals which here and there sparkle from the mass. Some may suspect a graver enigma hidden in the characters of the story, and study them with that patience which the author evidently presupposes; but all will agree that a little attention to the first principles of poetic art would have made their task much more agreeable. An author has the right, simply as an individual, to disregard those principles, and must therefore be equally ready to accept the consequences. There is a vein of earnestness in Mr. Melville's poem, singularly at variance with the carelessness of the execution; but this only increases the impression of confusion which it makes.

Review of *Clarel*

ANONYMOUS

The reader who undertakes to read a poem of 600 pages in length, thirty-five lines to the page, is more than apt to receive the reward given by Jupiter to the man whom he caused to seek a grain of wheat in a bushel of chaff—to wit, the chaff. Good lines there must be, but they and their effect will alike be lost in the overwhelming tide of mediocrity. There are very few themes capable of such expansion, and the theme being found, very, very few authors capable of conducting it successfully to the close. In the present instance, Mr. Melville has for subject the story of a short pilgrimage in the Holy Land, and as characters an old religious enthusiast of Yankee birth; a Swede; an English clergyman; a Greek; a Jewish girl, Ruth; a very nondescript genius, Vine; and another, Rolfe, who

> Was no scholastic partisan
> Or euphopist of Academe,
> But supplemented Plato's theme
> With daedal life in boats and tents,
> A messmate of the elements.

New York *World,* 26 June 1876.

Last comes the hero who gives the name to the poem, Clarel, a doubting, dreaming student. There is no particular reason why these characters should be assembled, but they are. Clarel falls in love with Ruth at Jerusalem, leaves her for a brief tour through the Holy Land, and returns to, as the French would say, assist at her funeral by torchlight, the book concluding with a description of Passion Week, and the characters vanish with about as much reason as they had for appearing at the first. There is thus no plot to sustain the interest of the reader, but there is a constant opportunity, fatal to such a facile writer as Mr. Melville, for digression, discussion, and, above all, description. Given these characters, and that scene, there is no earthly reason why the author should have turned the faucet and cut off his story at 21,000 lines instead of continuing to 221,000. Not being in his confidence we cannot of course say why he wrote the book, and what he intended it to mean, whether it has any cause or object. In the absence of this information, the reader is harassed by constant doubt whether the fact that he hasn't apprehended its motive and moral is due to his own obtuseness, or—distracting thought!—to the entire absence of either. The style is just as provoking. After a lot of jog-trot versifying—Mr. Melville rhymes "band" and "sustained," and "day" and "Epiphany" in the first ten lines—and just as he is prepared to abandon the book as a hopeless case, he stumbles on a passage of striking original thought, or possessing the true lyrical ring and straightway is lured over another thousand lines or so, the process being repeated till the book ends just where it began. There has been much action but nothing has been accomplished. There is some very break-neck reading, as for instance:

> "The chiffonier!" cried Rolfe: "e'en grim
> Milcom and Chemosh scowl at him,
> Here nosing underneath their lee
> Of pagod heights."

The philosophizing of the book is its least agreeable part, nor can the analyzations of character—or what appear to be intended therefor—receive much higher praise. Its best passages, as a rule, are the descriptive ones, which, notwithstanding frequent turgidness and affectation, are frequently bold, clear, and judicious. On the whole, however, it is hardly a book to be commended, for a work of art it is not in any sense or measure, and if it is an attempt to grapple with any particular problem of the universe, the indecision as to its object and processes is sufficient to appal or worry the average reader.

Review of *Clarel*

ANONYMOUS

The appearance of a poem in two volumes of three hundred pages each from a writer of Mr. Herman Melville's undoubted talent cannot fail to be a matter of interest to a wide circle of readers. The poem is upon the Holy Land, and is descriptive, narrative, and religious. It is in four parts, "Jerusalem," "The Wilderness," "Near [*sic*] Sabe," and "Bethlehem," and among these regions the scene of the work is laid. *Clarel* is not without signs of power such as we should have expected from Mr. Melville. Here and there we have delicate and vigorous pieces of description. But of the poem as a whole we do not think we can be far wrong when we say that it should have been written in prose. The author's genius is evidently not of the kind which must express itself in numbers. Nor has he that minor gift of facile verse which constitutes him one of the "mob of gentlemen who write with ease." The metre selected is the octosyllable, which Scott used in his narrative poems. But from the "fatal facility" which Byron said inhered in this verse Mr. Melville does not appear to have suffered. It is often very difficult work with the author. In describing the familiar fact that a horseman going down hill leans backward in order to preserve his centre of gravity, Mr. Melville writes:

> How fair
> And light he leaned with easeful air
> Backward in saddle, so to frame
> A counterpoise, as down he came.

New York *Times*, 10 July 1876.

The next three lines are better:

> Against the dolorous mountain side
> His Phrygian cap in scarlet pride,
> Burned like a cardinal flower in glen.

Indeed, there are many good pieces of description in the book, showing how sensible the author's mind is to the noble scenery of the East, to the poetic interest which attaches to man's handiwork in those ancient and remote regions, and to the misery of the contemporaneous society, so trifling and transitory do the living in that land of shadow and antiquity seem by the side of the dead. The following, addressed to Clarel as he enters this Gate of Zion by the lepers, is forcible:

> Behold, proud worm, (if such can be,)
> What yet may come, yea, even to thee.
> Who knoweth? Canst forecast the fate
> In infinite ages? Probe thy state:
> Sinless art thou? Then these sinned not,
> These, these are men; and thou art—what?

The following gives poetical expression to a well-known fact:

> Jerusalem, the mountain town
> Is based how far above the sea;
> But down, a lead-line's long reach down,
> A deep-sea lead, beneath the zone
> Of ocean's level, Heaven's decree
> Has sunk the pool whose deep submerged
> The doomed Pentapolis fire-scourged.
>   Long then the slope, though varied oft,
> From Zion to the seats abject;
> For rods and roods ye wind aloft
> By verges where the pulse is checked;
> And chief both height and steepness show
> Ere Achor's gorge the barrier rends
> And like a thunder-cloud impends
> Ominous over Jerico.

The thread of the story which *Clarel* contains the reader will find some difficulty in deciphering. If Mr. Melville had condescended to follow the example of Milton, he might have

eased the reader's task by placing before his poem an "argument." Clarel is a young American student of theology, who
goes to Palestine. By a Christian saint of the country he is taken
to the house of a convert to Judaism from New-England. This
is Nathan, the mother [*sic*] of Agar and the father of the heroine
Ruth. Nathan had met and loved, in a sea-port town of his own
country, Agar, a Jewess. Her he married, and she made him a
convert to her own religion. He left his scant acres, became
a tradesman, and grew rich. When, however, there arose a sect
which announced that the time had arrived when Judah should
be reinstated in her ancient glory, Nathan, with a zeal which
belongs to proselytes, determined to leave his Western home
and with his family take up his abode in Palestine. Agar and
their daughter Ruth, though not sharing Nathan's belief, accompanied him:

> Happy was Agar ere the seas
> She crossed for Zion. Pride she took—
> Pride, if in small felicities—
> Pride in her little court, a nook
> Where morning glories starred the door:
> So sweet without, so snug within.
> At sunny matin meal serene
> Her damask cloth she'd note. It bore
> In Hebrew text, about the hem
> 'Mid broidered cipher and device,
> *"If I forget thee, O, Jerusalem!"*
> And swam before her humid eyes
> In rainbowed distance Paradise.
> Faith, ravished, followed Fancy's path
> In more of bliss than Nature hath.

But Agar found Palestine a country rather to dream of than
to live in. Ruth had grown to girlhood when Clarel finds his
way to Palestine. The women receive him gladly as one from
the home to which they long to return. There are some pretty
descriptions of Ruth, the heroine. The story, we are sorry to
say, ends badly. Clarel and Ruth are plighted lovers. Nathan,
the father, has been slain by robbers. Jewish custom forbids
the entrance to the house after a death of all but Jews. So
Clarel, despairing of meeting Ruth, starts for a short journey

with a company of friends and sees Ruth no more. If Mr. Melville has any special tenets of religion to advance he has chosen a vehicle somewhat at variance with intelligibility, and the reader will have some trouble in making them out. In the "epilogue" the poet thus speaks of faith and science:

> Yes, ape and angel, strife and old debate—
> The harps of heaven and dreary gongs of hell;
> Science the feud can only aggravate—
> No umpire she betwixt the chimes and knell:
> The running battle of the star and clod
> Shall run forever—if there be no God.

Such merit as Mr. Melville's poem has is in its descriptions and in the Oriental atmosphere which he has given his work. There is no nonsense about the book; it is written in an honest and sincere style, but verse is certainly not the author's forte.

Review of *Clarel*

ANONYMOUS

These volumes are thoroughly described in their title. An American traveller in the Holy Land, full of Western thought, formed by modern civilisation, wanders among Eastern shrines where dawned a faith which seems now dying, now possessed of a strange vitality: at one time changeless, at another capable of adapting itself to every age and time. The traveller falls in with companions in his journey and makes new friends, nor is a more tender element wholly wanting. The scenes of the pilgrimage, the varying thoughts and emotions called up by them, are carefully described, and the result is a book of very great interest, and poetry of no mean order. The form is subordinate to the matter, and a rugged inattention to niceties of rhyme and metre here and there seems rather deliberate than careless. In this, in the musical verse where the writer chooses to be musical,

London *Academy*, Vol. 10 (19 August 1876) 185.

in the subtle blending of old and new thought, in the unexpected turns of argument, and in the hidden connexion between
things outwardly separate, Mr. Melville reminds us of A. H.
Clough. He probably represents one phase of American thought
as truly as Clough did one side of the Oxford of his day. The
following lines on the Holy Sepulchre are striking:—

> "In Crete they claimed the tomb of Jove,
> In glen o'er which his eagles soar,
> But through a peopled town ye rove
> To Christ's low tomb, where, nigh the door,
> Settles the dove. So much the more
> The contrast stamps the human God
> Who dwelt among us, made abode
> With us, and was of woman born;
> Partook our bread and thought no scorn
> To share the humblest, homeliest hearth,
> Shared all of man except the sin and mirth."
>
> Vol. i., p. 16.

We must make room for one more quotation, which is typical
of the tone and spirit as well as the poetry of the whole:—

> "He espied
> Upon the mountain humbly kneeling
> Those shepherds twain, while morning tide
> Rolled o'er the hills with golden healing.
> It was a rock they kneeled upon,
> Convenient for their rite avowed—
> Kneeled and their turbaned foreheads bowed—
> Bowed over till they kissed the stone:
> Each shaggy sur-coat heedful spread
> For rug such as in mosque is laid.
> About the ledge's favoured hem
> Mild fed their sheep enringing them,
> While facing as by second sight
> Toward Mecca they direct the rite.
> 'Look; and their backs on Bethlehem turned,'
> Cried Rolfe. The priest then, who discerned
> The drift, replied 'Yes, for they pray
> To Allah.' Well, and what of that?

Christ listens standing in heaven's gate,
Benignant listens, nor doth stay
Upon a syllable in creed,
Vowels and consonants indeed."

–Vol. ii., p. 477.

We advise our readers to study this interesting poem, which deserves more attention than we fear it is likely to gain in an age which craves for smooth, short, lyric song, and is impatient for the most part of what is philosophic or didactic.

Academic Neglect and Prophecies of Renown: 1884-1912

W. CLARK RUSSELL [1844–1911], journalist, and the major late nineteenth-century English sea novelist.

From "Sea Stories"

W. CLARK RUSSELL

Cooper pleases and has pleased, and is to this day read and admired by thousands; but speaking from a sailor's point of view, I really have no words to express the delight with which I quit his novels for the narratives of his countrymen, Dana and Herman Melville.

Whoever has read the writings of Melville must I think feel disposed to consider "Moby Dick" as his finest work. It is indeed all about the sea, whilst "Typee" and "Omoo," are chiefly famous for their lovely descriptions of the South Sea Islands, and of the wild and curious inhabitants of those coral strands; but though the action of the story is altogether on shipboard, the narrative is not in the least degree nautical in the sense that Cooper's and Marryat's novels are. The thread that strings a wonderful set of fancies and incidents together, is that of a whaler, whose master, Captain Ahab, having lost his leg by the teeth of a monstrous white whale, to which the name of Moby Dick has been given, vows to sail in pursuit of his enemy. The narrator embarks in the ship that is called the *Pequod,* which he describes as having an "old-fashioned, claw-footed look about her."

"She was apparelled like any barbaric Ethiopic Emperor, his neck heavy with pendants of polished ivory. She was a thing of trophies. A cannibal of a craft, tricking herself forth in the chased bones of her enemies. All round her unpanelled, open bulwarks were garnished like one continuous jaw, with the long sharp teeth of the sperm-whale, inserted there for pins to fasten her old hempen thews and tendons to. Those thews ran not through base blocks of land wood, but deftly travelled over sheaves of ivory. Scorning a turnstile wheel at her reverend helm she sported there a tiller; and that tiller was in one mass,

The London *Contemporary Review,* Vol. 46 (September 1884) 356–59.

curiously carved from the long narrow jaw of her hereditary foe. The helmsman, who steered by that tiller in a tempest, felt like the Tartar when he holds back his fiery steed by clutching its jaw. A noble craft, but somehow a most melancholy! All noble things are touched with that."

Melville takes this vessel, fills her full of strange men, and starts her on her insane quest, that he may have the ocean under and around him to muse upon, as though he were in a spacious burial-ground, with the alternations of sunlight and moonlight and deep starless darkness to set his thoughts to. "Moby Dick" is not a sea-story—one could not read it as such—it is a medley of noble impassioned thoughts born of the deep, pervaded by a grotesque human interest, owing to the contrast it suggests between the rough realities of the cabin and the forecastle, and the phantasms of men conversing in rich poetry, and strangely moving and acting in that dim weather-worn Nantucket whaler. There is a chapter where the sailors are represented as gathered together on the forecastle; and what is made to pass among them, and the sayings which are put into their mouths, might truly be thought to have come down to us from some giant mind of the Shaksperean era. As we read, we do not need to be told that seamen don't talk as those men do; probabilities are not thought of in this story. It is like a drawing by William Blake, if you please; or, better yet, it is of the "Ancient Mariner" pattern, madly fantastic in places, full of extraordinary thoughts, yet gloriously coherent—the work of a hand which, if the desire for such a thing had ever been, would have given a sailor's distinctness to the portrait of the solemn and strange Miltonic fancy of a ship built in the eclipse and rigged with curses dark. In "Typee," and "Omoo," and "Redburn," he takes other ground, and writes—always with the finest fancy—in a straight-headed way. I am concerned with him only as a seafarer. In "Redburn" he tells a sailor's yarn, and the dream-like figures of the crew of the *Pequod* make place for Liverpool and Yankee seamen, who chew tobacco and use bad language. His account of the sufferings of the emigrants in this book leaves a deep impression upon the mind. His accuracy is unimpeachable here, for the horrors he relates were as well known thirty and forty years ago as those of the middle passages were in times earlier still. In "Omoo," again, he gives us a good deal of the sea, and presumably relates his own experiences on board a whaler. He seems proud of his calling, for in "Moby Dick" he says:—

"And as for me, if by any possibility there be any as yet undiscovered prime thing in me; if I shall ever deserve any real repute in that small but high-hushed world which I might not be unreasonably ambitious of; if hereafter I shall do anything that, upon the whole, a man might rather have done than left undone; if at my death my executors, or more properly my creditors, find any precious MSS. in my desk, then here I prospectively ascribe all the honour and the glory to whaling; for a whale-ship was my Yale College and my Harvard."

He returns to the whalemen in "Omoo," and in his barque, the *Little Jule,* charms the nautical reader with the faithfulness of his portraiture, and the humour and the poetry he puts into it. There is some remarkable character-drawing in this book: notably John Jermin, the mate of the *Little Jule,* and Doctor Long Ghost, the nickname given by the sailors to a man who shipped as a physician, and was rated as a gentleman and lived in the cabin, until both the captain and he falling drunk, he drove home his views on politics by knocking the skipper down, after which he went to live forward. He is as quaint, striking, and original a personage as may be found in English fiction, and we find him in the dingy and leaky forecastle of the *Little Jule,* where he is surrounded by coarse and worn whalemen in Scotch caps and ragged clothes quoting Virgil, talking of Hobbes, "besides repeating poetry by the canto, especially 'Hudibras.'" Yet his portrait does not match that of John Jermin, the mate, whom, spite of his love of rum and homely method of reasoning with a man by means of a handspike, one gets to heartily like and to follow about with laughter as, intoxicated, he chases the sun all over the deck at noon with an old quadrant at his eye, or tumbles into the forecastle after a seaman who has enraged him by contemptuous remarks. Both Melville and Dana, who deal with the Merchant Service, show us in their books how trifling has been the change in the inner life of the sea during the forty or fifty years since they wrote about it. . . .

It is well indeed when men who have suffered the experiences and preserved the knowledge of sailors write books about the sea, that they should include all harsh facts which may help to teach the world what the mariner's life is. Dana and Melville have written thus, and whatever they say is stamped with genius and truth. The ocean is the theatre of more interests than boys would care to follow. We laugh with Marryat; we read Cooper for his "plots;" we find much that is dashing and flattering to our patriotism in the "Tom Bowlings," and "Will Watches," and "Tough Yarns," and "Topsail Sheet-blocks;" in the sprawling and fighting and drinking school of sea yarns; but when we turn to Dana and Melville, we find that the real life of the sea is not to be found between yellow covers adorned with catching cuts; that all the romance does not lie in cocked-hats and epaulets, but that by far the largest proportion of the sentiment, the pathos of the deep, the bitterness and suffering of the sailor's life, must be sought in the gloomy forecastle of the humble coaster, in the deckhouses of the deep-laden cargo-steamer, in the crew's dwelling-place on board the big ship trading to Australia and India and China. It is because only two or three writers have kept their eye steadfastly on this walk of the marine calling, and it is because all the rest who have written about the sea have represented the sailor as a jolly, drinking, dancing, sky-larking fellow, that the shore-going public have come to get the wildest, absurdest notion of Jack's real character and professional life. For one who reads Dana and Melville, thousands read Marryat and Michael Scott, and Chamier, and Cupples, and Neale.

ROBERT WILLIAMS BUCHANAN [1841–1901], English poet, remembered for his attack on the Pre-Raphaelites, "The Fleshly School of Poetry." Tantalizingly little is known of the English "cultists" who read and wrote about Melville in the 1880's and 1890's, but Buchanan's interest may have been inspired by his friend Charles Reade (d. 1884), whose copy of *Moby-Dick* was extensively annotated in a way to suggest to Michael Sadlier that he had thought of issuing an abridged edition of it.

Melville

ROBERT BUCHANAN

Meantime my sun-like music-maker,
    Shines solitary and apart;
Meantime the brave sword-carrying Quaker
    Broods in the peace of his great heart,—
While Melville,* sea-compelling man,
Before whose wand Leviathan
Rose hoary white upon the Deep,
With awful sounds that stirred its sleep,
Melville, whose magic drew Typee,
Radiant as Venus, from the sea,
Sits all forgotten or ignored,
While haberdashers are adored!
He, ignorant of the drapers' trade,
    Indifferent to the art of dress,
Pictured the glorious South-sea maid
    Almost in mother nakedness—
Without a hat, or boot, or stocking,
A want of dress to most so shocking,
With just one chemisette to dress her
She *lives,*—and still shall live, God bless her!
Long as the sea rolls deep and blue,
    While heaven repeats the thunder of it,
Long as the White Whale ploughs it through,
The shape my sea-magician drew
    Shall still endure, or I'm no prophet!

---

* Hermann Melville, author of *Typee, The White Whale,* &c. I sought everywhere for this Triton, who is still living somewhere in New York. No one seemed to know anything of the one great imaginative writer fit to stand shoulder to shoulder with Whitman on that continent.

From "Socrates in Camden, with a Look Round," The London *Academy,* No. 693 (15 August 1885) 102–3.

HENRY STEPHENS SALT [1851–1939], English classicist and biographer of
—among others—Thoreau and James Thomson ("B.V.").

Herman Melville

H. S. SALT

'Instead of a landsman's grey-goose quill, he seems to have
plucked a quill from a skimming curlew, or to have snatched it,
a fearful joy, from a hovering albatross, if not from the wings
of the wind itself.'

This extract, from the pages of a bygone review, is a sam-
ple of the outburst of interest and admiration which greeted
the appearance of Herman Melville's earlier volumes more than
forty years ago. Such books as *Typee*, *Omoo*, and *Mardi* challenged attention by the originality of their style, their suggestive
piquancy of tone, the strangeness of the experiences of which
they purported to be the record, and not least by the very gro-
tesqueness of the titles themselves. Who and what was the
narrator of these mysterious adventures among the islands of
the Pacific? Was he, as his stories implied, a common seaman
serving before the mast—now on a whaler, now on an American
frigate, and devoting the interim of his voyages to the publication of his diary; or was he rather, as might be surmised from
the cultured tone of his writings and the fictitious aspect of
some of his 'narratives,' a man of liberal education and imaginative temperament, who promulgated these romantic accounts
of perils in the South Seas from some comfortable quarters in
London or New York? The critics, intent on such questions as
these, were fairly puzzled as to Herman Melville's identity;
even his name was declared by some to be a *nom de plume*.
'Separately,' said one wiseacre, 'the names are not uncommon;
we can urge no valid reason against their juncture; yet, in this
instance, they fall suspiciously on our ear.'

Herman Melville, once the cause of this lively commotion
in the dovecots of criticism, but now so far forgotten by a later
and ungrateful generation as to be too often confused with Herman Merivale on the one side, or Whyte Melville on the other,

The Scottish Art Review, Vol. 2 (June–December 1889) 186–90.

was born at New York, August 1st, 1819. . . . At the present time he is still living, an old man of seventy years.

✓ His books may be roughly divided into two classes, according to the predominance of the practical or the fantastic element. *Typee*, the 'narrative of a four months' residence in the Marquesas Islands,' appeared in 1846, and takes precedence of all his other writings, in merit no less than in date. Few indeed are the books of adventure that can vie with this charming little volume in freshness, humour, and literary grace, above all in the extraordinary interest which the story, simple as it is, inspires in the mind of the reader, from the first page to the last. The rhythmical drifting of the whaler 'Dolly' before the equable trade-winds of the Pacific; the arrival in the dream-like harbour of Nukahiva; the escape of the two malcontents Tom and Toby; their wanderings on the mountains, and descent into the dreaded valley of the redoubtable Typees; their hospitable reception by the natives; the departure of Toby and long retention of 'Tommo'; the wild beauty of the valley, with its flashing streams and rich groves of bread-fruit trees and cocoa-nuts; the mild, placid, healthful life of the inhabitants, varied by an occasional indulgence in a cannibal banquet,—all this is depicted with the firmness of outline indicative of a true narrative, yet invested (such is the literary skill of the narrator) with the filmy mystery of a fairy tale. . . .

Omoo (*i.e.*, in Polynesian dialect, 'a rover') was published a year later than *Typee*, to which it supplies the sequel. It is altogether a more desultory and discursive book than its predecessor; but there is much vigour in the narrator's description of his voyage from Typee to Tahiti on board the 'Little Jule,' and his subsequent adventures in the Society Islands. Some remarks in which he commented severely on the errors committed by Christian missionaries in their treatment of the native Polynesians gave great offence to the critics, who attempted to discount the effect by impeaching the character of the sailor-novelist, especially on the subject of his relations with the charming Fayaway. 'We shall not pollute our pages,' wrote one grandiloquent reviewer, 'by transferring to them the scenes in which this wretched profligate appears self-portrayed as the chief actor.' But, as a matter of fact, these scenes are drawn with the most admirable tenderness of feeling and delicacy of touch, and contain nothing whatever of which their author had cause to be ashamed.

Redburn (1849) and *White Jacket* (1850) complete the category of Melville's distinctly autobiographical writings. The former has already been mentioned as giving an account of his first voyage; the latter embodies the experiences which he gained during his year's service on the American man-of-war with which he returned from a Pacific harbour to Boston, after the events narrated in *Omoo*. This vessel, which he calls the 'Never-sink,' is said to have been in reality the 'United States,' which in 1812 captured the English frigate 'Macedonian.' *White Jacket* is a careful study of all the doings on board a man-of-war, its sum and substance being a strong protest, on humane grounds, against the overbearing tyranny of the naval officers and the depravity of the crew. 'So long as a man-of-war exists,' he says, 'it must ever remain a picture of much that is tyrannical and repelling in human nature.' The serious tone of the book is, however, relieved and diversified by some brilliant touches of humorous description, among which may be mentioned the account of the white jacket (whence the title), an extempore surtout manufactured for himself by the narrator, in default of the ordinary seaman's costume, out of a white duck frock, stuffed for the sake of warmth with old socks and trouser-legs. A coating of paint to make it waterproof was the crowning desideratum; but owing to the scarcity of the commodity in question this was denied him. 'Said old Brush, the captain of the paint-room, "Look ye, White Jacket," said he, "ye can't have any paint." ' The ill-fated garment accordingly acted as a sort of sponge, a 'universal absorber,' so that White Jacket's heartless shipmates would dry themselves at his expense by standing up against him in damp weather. 'I dripped,' he says, 'like a turkey a-roasting; and long after the rainstorms were over, and the sun showed his face, I still stalked a Scotch mist, and when it was fair weather with others, alas! it was foul weather with me.' He is at length rid of his encumbrance by nothing less than a fall from the masthead, in which he entirely loses his white jacket, and nearly loses his life.

Melville's later works must be considered as phantasies rather than a relation of sober facts. He was affected, like so many of his countrymen, by the transcendental tendency of the age, and the result in his case was a strange blending of the practical and the metaphysical, his stories of what purported to be plain matter-of-fact life being gradually absorbed and swallowed up in the wildest mystical speculations. This process was already discernible in *Mardi,* published as early as 1849, the first volume of which is worthy to rank with the very finest achievements of its author, while the rest had far better have remained altogether unwritten. The story of *Mardi* is apparently an imaginary variation of that told in *Typee,* for here too the narrator deserts from a whaling-vessel in the Pacific, and makes his way in the boat 'Chamois,' together with old Jarl, a fellow-mariner, to an island of ideal felicity, where he is entertained by a chieftain, Media, who bears considerable resemblance to the royal Mehevi of *Typee.* The 'watery world' of the Pacific, with its blazing tropical sun by day and magical phosphores-cence by night, as seen from the solitary whale-boat, is described in Melville's most graphic and suggestive manner, the chapter on sharks, in particular, being a masterpiece of fact melting into phantasy. The Pacific, he tells us, is 'populous as China. Trust me, there are more sharks in the sea than mortals on land;' and he proceeds to expatiate on the various species of the sea-mon-ster—the brown shark, 'a grasping, rapacious varlet, that in spite of the hard knocks received from it often snapped viciously at our steering-oar'; the dandy blue shark, 'a dainty spark,' like a Bond Street beau, that 'lounged by with a careless fin and an indolent tail'; the tiger shark, 'a round, portly gourmand, with distended mouth and collapsed conscience'; and the ghastly white shark, a 'ghost of a fish,' for ever gliding solitary just below the surface. But the great charm of the book centres round Yillah, the mysterious white maiden—a sort of spiritualised Fayaway—whom the hero rescues from being sacrificed to the pagan deities, and takes with him to the island of Mardi, only to lose her there through some mystic supernatural agency. At this point an extraordinary change comes over the whole tone of *Mardi,* the remainder of which is devoted to the search for Yillah, who is apparently typical of ideal love, and the rejection of the allurements of Hautia, the goddess of earthly passion—all of which, with much more, is narrated with an excess of fantastic conception and gorgeous word-painting that is positively be-wildering. A writer in the *Revue des deux Mondes* has de-scribed *Mardi* as 'the dream of a badly-educated midshipman, drunk on hasheesh, and swinging asleep at the masthead of a ship in a warm tropical night.' As applied to the latter portion of the book, this criticism is scarcely exaggerated; never did a story which began with such promise end in such disappointment.

Moby Dick; or, The White Whale (1851) is perhaps more successful as a whole than *Mardi*, since its very extravagances, great as they are, work in more harmoniously with the outline of the plot. Ishmael, the narrator, having embarked on board a whaling-vessel with a savage harpooner named Queequeg, whose character is admirably drawn, gradually discovers that they are committed to an extraordinary voyage of vengeance. It seems that, in a former expedition, Captain Ahab, their com-mander, a mysterious personage, who 'looked like a man cut away from the stake when the fire has overrunningly wasted all the limbs without consuming them,' had lost one of his legs, which had been 'reaped away' by Moby Dick, a famous white sperm-whale of unequalled strength and malignity. Frenzied by his loss, he was now devoting the rest of his life to the single object of destroying Moby Dick, who 'swam before him as the monomaniac incarnation of all those malicious agencies which some deep men feel eating in them.' The book is a curious com-pound of real information about whales in general and fantas-tic references to this sperm-whale in particular, that 'portentous and mysterious monster,' which is studied (as the bird is studied by Michelet) in a metaphysical and ideal aspect—'a mass of tremendous life, all obedient to one volition, as the smallest insect.' Wild as the story is, there is a certain dramatic vigour in the 'quenchless feud' between Ahab and Moby Dick which at once arrests the reader's attention, and this interest is well maintained to the close, the final hunting-scene being a perfect nightmare of protracted sensational description.

Moby Dick was published when Melville was still a young man of thirty-three. Before he was forty he produced several other volumes, none of which were calculated to add in any de-gree to his fame, one of them, entitled *Pierre; or, The Ambi-guities*, being perhaps the *ne plus ultra* in the way of meta-physical absurdity.

'Physic of metaphysic begs defence,
And metaphysic calls for aid on sense.'

It may seem strange that so vigorous a genius, from which stronger and stronger work might reasonably have been expected, should have reached its limit at so early a date; but it must be remembered that the six really notable books of which I have made mention were produced within a period of less than six years. Whether the transcendental obscurities in which he latterly ran riot were the cause or the consequence of the failure of his artistic powers is a point which it would be difficult to determine with precision. His contemporary critics were inclined, not unnaturally, to regard his mysticism as a kind of *malice prepense,* and inveighed mournfully against the perversity of 'a man born to create, who resolves to anatomise, a man born to see, who insists upon speculating,'[1] and warned him, after the publication of *Pierre,* that his fame was on the edge of a precipice, and that if he were wise he would thenceforth cease to affect the style of Sir Thomas Browne, and study that of Addison. Yet how successfully he could at times reproduce the quaint conceits of the earlier writer may be seen from the following passage of *Mardi:*—

'And truly, since death is the last enemy of all, valiant souls will taunt him while they may. Yet, rather, should the wise regard him as the inflexible friend, who, even against our own wills, from life's evils triumphantly relieves us.

'And there is but little difference in the manner of dying. To die, is all. And death has been gallantly encountered by those who have never beheld blood that was red, only its light azure seen through the veins. And to yield the ghost proudly, and march out of your fortress with all the honours of war, is not a thing of sinew and bone. . . . 'Tis no great valour to perish sword in hand and bravado on lip cased all in panoply complete. For even the alligator dies in his mail, and the swordfish never surrenders. To expire, mild-eyed, in one's bed, transcends the death of Epaminondas.'

The chief characteristic of Herman Melville's writings is this attempted union of the practical with the ideal. Commencing with a basis of solid fact, he loves to build up a fantastic

[1] *Putnam's Magazine,* 1857.

structure, which is finally lost in the cloudland of metaphysical speculation. He is at his best, as in *Typee,* when the mystic element is kept in check, and made subservient to the clear development of the story; or when, as in certain passages of *Mardi* and *Moby Dick,* the two qualities are for the time harmoniously blended. His strong attraction to the sea and to ships, which has already been alluded to as dating from his earliest boyhood, was closely connected with this ideality of temperament; for the sea, he tells us, was to him 'the image of the ungraspable phantom of life,' while a ship was 'no piece of mechanism merely, but a creature of thoughts and fancies, instinct with life, standing at whose vibrating helm you feel her beating pulse.' 'I have loved ships,' he adds, 'as I have loved men.'

The tone of Melville's books is altogether frank and healthy, though of direct ethical teaching there is little or no trace, except on the subject of humanity, on which he expresses himself with strong and genuine feeling. He speaks with detestation of modern warfare, and devotes more than one chapter of *White Jacket* to an exposure of the inhuman system of flogging, then prevalent in the navy, asking at the close if he be not justified 'in immeasurably denouncing this thing.' In *Typee* and *Omoo* he again and again protests against the shameful ill-usage of the harmless Pacific islanders by their 'civilised' invaders. 'How often,' he says, 'is the term *savages* incorrectly applied! None really deserving of it were ever yet discovered by voyagers or by travellers. They have discovered heathens and barbarians, whom by horrible cruelties they have exasperated into savages. It may be asserted without fear of contradiction, that in all the cases of outrages committed by Polynesians Europeans have at some time or other been the aggressors.'

That Melville, in spite of his early transcendental tendencies and final lapse into the 'illimitable inane,' possessed strong powers of observation, a solid grasp of facts, and a keen sense of humour, will not be denied by any one who is acquainted with his writings. Among the best of his humorous passages may be instanced the admirable scene in *Redburn* where the young Peter Simple of the story, who imagines that a sailor's life will be one of dignified comfort, has his first interview with the wily Captain Riga; or the difficulties experienced by the narrator of *Mardi* in correctly playing the part of 'the White Tagi,' a long-expected demi-god for whom he is mistaken by the delighted islanders; or, again, the amusing account in *Moby Dick* of the terrors of sharing a bed at a crowded hostelry with Queequeg, the barbarian harpooner. As a portrayer of character Melville is almost always successful. His sea-captains, from the effeminate 'Miss Guy' to the indomitable Ahab, and his seamen one and all, from Toby to old Jarl, are lifelike pictures; nothing could be better than the brief, pointed sketch of Doctor Long Ghost, the odd, cadaverous, mischief-loving physician, who figures so largely in the pages of *Omoo;* while his characters of the natives of Polynesia are probably more faithful, as they are certainly more vivid, than those drawn by any other writer. His literary power, as evidenced in *Typee* and his other early volumes, is also unmistakable, his descriptions being at one time rapid, concentrated, and vigorous, according to the nature of his subject, at another time dreamy, suggestive, and picturesque. The fall from the mast-head in *White Jacket* is a swift and subtle piece of writing of which George Meredith might be proud; the death of the white whale in *Moby Dick* rises to a sort of epic grandeur and intensity. Here is a charming passage of the contrary kind, taken from an early chapter of *Typee:*—

'The sky presented a clear expanse of the most delicate blue, except along the skirts of the horizon, where you might see a thin drapery of pale clouds which never varied their form or colour. The long, measured, dirge-like swell of the Pacific came rolling along with its surface broken by little tiny waves, sparkling in the sunshine. Every now and then a shoal of flying fish, scared from the water under the bows, would leap into the air, and fall the next moment like a shower of silver into the sea. Then you would see the superb albicore, with his glittering sides, sailing aloft, and, often describing an arc in his descent, disappear on the surface of the water. Far off, the lofty jet of the whale might be seen, and nearer at hand the prowling shark, that villainous foot-pad of the seas, would come skulking along, and at a wary distance regard us with his evil eye. At times some shapeless monster of the deep, floating on the surface, would, as we approached, sink slowly into the blue waters, and fade away from the sight. But the most impressive feature of the scene was the almost unbroken silence that reigned over sky and water. Scarcely a sound could be heard but the occasional breathing of the grampus and the rippling at the cutwater.'

When one reads such passages as this (and it is but one taken almost at random out of many others of equal excellence), it is hard to account for the indifference of the present generation to Herman Melville's writings.[1] In an age which has witnessed a marked revival of books of travel and adventure, and which, in its greed for narrative or fiction of this kind is often fain to content itself with works of a very inferior quality, it is a cause for regret that the author of *Typee* and *Mardi* should have fallen to a great extent out of notice, and should be familiar only to a small circle of admirers, instead of enjoying the wide reputation to which his undoubted genius entitles him.

A Mention of Melville

ANONYMOUS

The death of Herman Melville, the author of 'Typee' and other works, recalls to one's memory the quantity of good literature which was published by John Murray in his Home and Colonial Library. Many of the volumes in that series are still worthy of reproduction, and it seems singular that Albemarle Street does not see its way to re-issue a considerable number of these books at popular prices.

[1] When Mr. Robert Buchanan was on a visit to America, he heard that Herman Melville was dwelling 'somewhere in New York, having resolved, on account of the public neglect of his works, never to write another line.'—*Universal Review*, May 1889.

London *Bookman*, Vol. 1 (November 1891) 50.

JULIAN HAWTHORNE [1846–1934], journalist and novelist, was the only son of Nathaniel Hawthorne. He became a bewildered and resentful witness of the Melville revival.

LEONARD LEMMON [b. 1860] was superintendent of schools at Sherman, Texas. In 1903 he was coeditor with Mimmie Halley Smith of *Our Country's Readers.*

An Early Sea-Novelist

JULIAN HAWTHORNE AND LEONARD LEMMON

Forty years ago, few American authors had so wide a reputation as Melville, whose books of sea-adventure, part fact and part fancy, were read and praised in England quite as much and as warmly as in this country. Not to have read "Typee" and "Omoo" was not to have made the acquaintance of the most entertaining and novel current literature: and those who take them up to-day find their charm and interest almost unimpaired. The leading sea-novelist of the present day has acknowledged Melville as his master; and there is no doubt that he possessed not only exhaustive technical knowledge of his chosen field, but that his talent for exploiting it amounted to genius. The main substance of his books is plainly founded on fact; but the facts are so judiciously selected as to produce the effect of art, while the flavoring of fiction is so artfully introduced as to seem like fact. All the stories are told in the first person, and there is a fascination and mystery in the narrator's personality that much enhances the interest of the tale. But Melville's imagination has a tendency to wildness and metaphysical extravagance; and when he trusted to it alone, he becomes difficult and sometimes repulsive. There seems, also, to be a background of gloom in his nature, making itself felt even in the midst of his sunshine: and now and then his speculations and rhapsodies have a tinge almost of insanity. "Typee" and "Omoo" are stories of adventure in the Pacific archipelago, as is also "Mardi," but the latter merges into a quasi-symbolic analysis of human life, perplexing to the general reader, though the splendor and poetic beauty

American Literature: A Text-Book for the Use of Schools and Colleges (Boston: D. C. Heath, 1892), 208–9.

of the descriptions win his admiration. "Redburn" is the narrative of a voyage to Liverpool before the mast, in an American clipper, and is a model of simplicity and impressiveness: "White Jacket" describes life on an American man-of-war, and overflows with humor, character, adventure and absorbing pictures of a kind of existence which has now ceased forever to exist. "Moby Dick, or The Whale" takes up the whole subject of whaling, as practised in the '30's and '40's, and is, if anything, more interesting and valuable than "White Jacket"; the scenes are grouped about a wildly romantic and original plot, concerned with the chase round the world of an enormous white whale—Moby Dick—by a sea-captain who has previously lost a limb in a conflict with the monster, and has sworn revenge. This is the most powerful of Melville's books; it was also the last of any literary importance. "Pierre, or The Ambiguities" is a repulsive, insane and impossible romance, in which the sea has no part, and one or two later books need not be mentioned. But Melville's position in literature is secure and solitary: he surpasses Cooper, when Cooper writes of the sea; and no subsequent writer has even challenged a comparison with him on that element.

From A Claim for American Literature

W. CLARK RUSSELL

Herman Melville, as I gather from an admirable account of this fine author by Mr. Arthur Stedman, a son of the well-known poet, went to sea in 1841. He shipped before the mast on board a whaler and cruised continuously for eighteen months in the Pacific. He saw much ocean life, and his experiences were wild and many. I will not compare him with Dana: his imagination was soaring and splendid, yet there are such passages of pathos and beauty in Dana's book as persuade me that he might have matched Melville's most startling and astonishing inventions,

North American Review, Vol. 154 (February 1892) 138–49.

had taste prompted him or leisure invited. There is nothing in Melville to equal in simple, unaffected beauty Dana's description of an old sailor lying over a jibboom on a fine night and looking up at the stirless canvas white as sifted snow with moonlight. Full of rich poetry, too, is Dana's description of the still night broken by the breathing of shadowy shapes of whales. Melville is essentially American: Dana writes as a straight-headed Englishman would; he is clear, convincing, utterly unaffected. A subtle odor of the sea freshens and sweetens his sentences. An educated sailor would swear to Dana's vocation by virtue of his style only—a style as plain and sturdy as Defoe's. In truth, I know of no American writer whose style is so good. Yet are Melville's pictures of the forecastle life, his representation of what goes on under the deck of that part of the ship which is thumped by the handspike of the boatswain when he echoes in thunder the order of "All hands!" marvellously and delightfully true. I will not speak of his faithful and often beautiful and often exquisite sketches of the life and scenery of the South Sea Islands, nor of his magnificent picture of Liverpool, and the descriptions of London and of English scenery in "Redburn," and the wonderful opening chapters of "Moby Dick." I link him with Dana; I place the two side by side as men of genius, but sailors first of all, and I claim, in their name, that to American literature the world owes the first, the best, and the enduring revelation of the secrets of one great side of the ocean life.

"When I go to sea," Melville says in "Moby Dick," "I go as a simple sailor, right before the mast, plumb down into the forecastle, aloft there to the masthead." His "Redburn" supplemented Dana's book. It is a further upheaval of secrets sheer through the forescuttle into the eye of the landsman. No such book as that was to be found in literature in the English language. Plenty there was, and always was, about the navy, royal and republic. One might have thought that Melville, having read Dana's famous work, had said to himself: "I, too, have suffered and seen and know; I will help to brighten the glittering beam this fine fellow* has darted into the ocean parlors; which has even now made all English readers understand that

* Mr. Melville, I know, greatly admired the genius of Dana. His praise of "Two Years Before the Mast" half fills a letter I possess.

we merchant seamen form a great world of human beings of whom nobody that takes pen in hand appears to know anything at all, who are carefully neglected by British naval writers because, from the elevation of a man-o'-war's decks, even the biggest merchantman looks to sit low, humanly speaking very low indeed, and who by the inexpert are hideously muddled under that vague term of 'Jack,' confounded with the blue-jacket, and elbowed in with the 'longshoreman."

Melville wrote out of his heart and out of wide and perhaps bitter experience; he enlarged our knowledge of the life of the deep by adding many descriptions to those which Dana had already given. His "South Seaman" is typical. Dana sighted her, but Melville lived in her. His books are now but little read. When he died the other day,—to my sorrow! for our correspondence had bred in me a deeper feeling than kindness and esteem, —men who could give you the names of fifty living American poets and perhaps a hundred living American novelists owned that they had never heard of Herman Melville; which simply means that to all intents and purposes the American sailor is a dead man, and the American merchant service to all intents and purposes a dead industry. Yet a famous man he was in those far days when every sea was bright with the American flag, when the cotton-white canvas shone starlike on the horizon, when the nasal laugh of the jolly Yankee tar in China found its echo in Peru. Famous he was; now he is neglected; yet his name and works will not die. He is a great figure in shadow; but the shadow is not that of oblivion. . . .

Two American sailors, men of letters and of genius, seizing the pen for a handspike, prized open the sealed lid under which the merchant-seaman lay caverned. The light of heaven fell down the open hatch, and the story of what had been happening for centuries in the British service, for years in the American, was read. Did any good come of it? I should have to ask your patience for a much longer paper than this to answer *that* question. But as a literary feat! in an age, too, when men thought most things known. Americans! honor your Dana and your Melville. Greater geniuses your literature has produced, but none who have done work so memorable in the history of their native letters.

From the Review of the Stedman Edition of *Moby-Dick*

ANONYMOUS

In this story Melville is as fantastically poetical as Coleridge in the "Ancient Mariner," and yet, while we swim spellbound over the golden rhythms of Coleridge feeling at every stroke their beautiful improbability, everything in "Moby-Dick" might have happened. The woe-struck captain, his eerie monomania, the half-devils of the crew, the relentless pursuit of the ever-elusive vindictive white whale, the storms and calms that succeed each other like the ups and downs of a mighty hexameter, all the weird scenery of the pursuit in moonlight and in daylight, all are so wonderfully fresh in their treatment that they supersede all doubt and impress one as absolutely true to the life. Even the recondite information about whales and sea-fisheries sprinkled plentifully over the pages does not interfere seriously with the intended effect; they are the paraphernalia of the journey. The author's extraordinary vocabulary, its wonderful coinages and vivid turnings and twistings of worn-out words, are comparable only to Chapman's translations of Homer. The language fairly shrieks under the intensity of his treatment, and the reader is under an excitement which is hardly controllable. The only wonder is that Melville is so little known and so poorly appreciated.

The New York *Critic*, Vol. 22 (15 April 1893) 232.

JOHN ST. LOE STRACHEY [1860–1927], English journalist, political writer, and editor of the *Spectator* from 1898 until 1925.

Herman Melville

J. ST. LOE STRACHEY

Though Melville has not the literary power of Mr. Stevenson, the description in *Typee* of the life he led among a cannibal tribe in the Marquesas islands has a charm beyond the charm of *The Wrecker*, the *Island Nights*, or those studies of the Marquesas which Mr. Stevenson contributed to the earlier numbers of *Black and White*. *Typee* is the "document" *par excellence* of savage life, and a document written by one who knew how to write as well as to look. We have said that Mr. Melville does not write as well as Mr. Stevenson, but this does not mean that he is not a literary artist. Mr. Melville is no mean master of prose, and had his judgment been equal to his feeling for form, he might have ranked high in English literature on the ground of style alone. Unfortunately, he was apt to let the last great master of style he had been reading run away with him. For example, in *Moby Dick*—one of the best and most thrilling sea-stories ever written—Mr. Melville has "hitched to his car" the fantastic Pegasus of Sir Thomas Browne. With every circumstance of subject favourable, it would be madness to imitate the author of *Urne Burial*. When his style is made the vehicle for describing the hunting of sperm-whales in the Pacific, the result cannot but be disastrous. Yet so great an artist is Mr. Melville and so strong are the fascinations of his story, that we defy any reader of sense to close this epic of whaling without the exclamation,—"With all its faults I would not have it other than it is." Discovering a right line in obliquity and by an act of supreme genius forcing his steed to run a pace for which he was not bred, Mr. Melville contrives, in spite of Sir Thomas Browne, to write a book which is not only enchanting as a romance, but a genuine piece of literature. No one who has read the chapter on "Nantucket" and its seafarers, and has learned how at night-fall the Nantucketer, like "the landless gull that at sunset folds her wings and is rocked to sleep between billows," "furls his sails and lays him to his rest, while under his very pillow rush herds of walruses and whales," will have the heart to cavil at Melville's style. In *White Jacket*—a marvellous description of life on a man-of-war—we see yet another deflection given to Mr. Melville's style, and with still worse results. He had apparently been reading Carlyle before he wrote it; and Carlylisms, mixed with the dregs of the *Religio Medici,* every now and then crop up to annoy the reader. In spite, however, of this heavy burden, *White Jacket* is excellent reading, and full of the glory of the sea and the spirit of the Viking. And here we may mention a very pleasant thing about Mr. Melville's books. They show throughout a strong feeling of brotherhood with the English. The sea has made him feel the oneness of the English kin, and he speaks of Nelson and the old Admirals like a lover or a child. Though Mr. Melville wrote at a time when English insolence and pig-headedness, and Yankee bumptiousness, made a good deal of ill-blood between the two peoples, he at heart feels that, on the sea at least, it is the English kin against the world. . . .

[Here Strachey quotes two now-famous passages: from "The Ship," the paragraph beginning "Now, Bildad, like Peleg, and indeed many other Nantucketers, was a Quaker," and from "Nantucket" the paragraph beginning "And thus have these naked Nantucketers." Then he adds: "If there is not high imagination and true literature in this, we know not where to find it."]

ARCHIBALD MACMECHAN [1862–1933], an author of critical essays and an anthologizer of Canadian literature. In 1889, the year he wrote Melville that he was "anxious to set the merits of your books before the public," he had just been granted a Ph.D. from Johns Hopkins and had been made Munro professor of English at Dalhousie University.

"The Best Sea Story Ever Written"

ARCHIBALD MAC MECHAN

Anyone who undertakes to reverse some judgment in history or criticism, or to set the public right regarding some neglected man or work, becomes at once an object of suspicion. Nine times out of ten he is called a literary snob for his pains, or a

Queen's Quarterly, Vol. 7 (October 1899) 120–30.

prig who presumes to teach his betters, or a "phrase-monger," or a "young Osric," or something equally soul-subduing. Besides, the burden of proof lies heavy upon him. He preaches to a sleeping congregation. The good public has returned its verdict upon the case, and is slow to review the evidence in favour of the accused, or, having done so, to confess itself in the wrong. Still, difficult as the work of rehabilitation always is, there are cheering instances of its complete success; notably, the rescue of the Elizabethan dramatists by Lamb and Hazlitt and Leigh Hunt. Nor in such a matter is the will always free. As Heine says, ideas take possession of us and force us into the arena, there to fight for them. There is also the possibility of triumph to steel the raw recruit against all dangers. Though the world at large may not care, the judicious few may be glad of new light, and may feel satisfaction in seeing even tardy justice meted out to real merit. In my poor opinion much less than justice has been done to an American writer, whose achievement is so considerable that it is hard to account for the neglect into which he has fallen.

This writer is Herman Melville, who died in New York in the autumn of 1891, aged eighty-three. That his death excited little attention is in consonance with the popular apathy towards him and his work. The civil war marks a dividing line in his literary production as well as in his life. His best work belongs to the *ante-bellum* days, and is cut off in taste and sympathy from the distinctive literary fashions of the present time. To find how complete neglect is, one has only to put question to the most cultivated and patriotic Americans north or south, east or west, even professed specialists in the nativist literature, and it will be long before the Melville enthusiast meets either sympathy or understanding. The present writer made his first acquaintance with *Moby Dick* in the dim, dusty Mechanics' Institute Library (opened once a week by the old doctor) of an obscure Canadian village, nearly twenty years ago; and since that time he has seen only one copy of the book exposed for sale, and met only one person (and that not an American) who had read it. Though Kingsley has a good word for Melville, the only place where real appreciation of him is to be found of recent years is in one of Mr. Clark Russell's dedications. There occurs the phrase which gives this paper its title. Whoever takes the trouble to read this unique and original book will concede that Mr. Russell knows whereof he affirms.

Melville is a man of one book, and this fact accounts possibly for much of his unpopularity. The marked inferiority of his work after the war, as well as changes in literary fashion, would drag the rest down with it. Nor are his earliest works, embodying personal experience like *Redburn* and *White Jacket,* quite worthy of the pen which wrote *Moby Dick. Omoo* and *Typee* are little more than sketches, legitimately idealized, of his own adventures in the Marquesas. They are notable works in that they are the first to reveal to civilized people the charm of life in the islands of the Pacific, the charm which is so potent in *Vailima Letters* and *The Beach of Falesà.* Again, the boundless archipelagos of Oceanica furnish the scenes of *Mardi,* his curious political satire. This contains a prophecy of the war, and a fine example of obsolete oratory in the speech of the great chief Alanno from Hio-Hio. The prologue in a whale-ship and the voyage in an open boat are, perhaps, the most interesting parts. None of his books are without distinct and peculiar excellences, but nearly all have some fatal fault. Melville's seems a case of arrested literary development. The power and promise of power in his best work are almost unbounded; but he either did not care to follow them up or he had worked out all his rifts of ore. The last years of his life he spent as a recluse. . . .

After his marriage, he lived at Pittsfield for thirteen years, in close intimacy with Hawthorne, to whom he dedicated his chief work. My copy shows that it was written as early as 1851, but the title page is dated exactly twenty years later. It shows as its three chief elements this Scottish thoughtfulness, the love of literature and the love of adventure.

When Mr. Clark Russell singles out *Moby Dick* for such high praise as he bestows upon it, we think at once of other sea-stories,—his own, Marryat's, Smollett's perhaps, and such books as Dana's *Two Years before the Mast.* But the last is a plain record of fact; in Smollett's tales, sea-life is only part of one great round of adventure; in Mr. Russell's mercantile marine, there is generally the romantic interest of the way of a man with a maid; and in Marryat's the rise of a naval officer through various ranks plus a love-story or plenty of fun, fighting and prize-money. From all these advantages Melville not only cuts himself off, but seems to heap all sorts of obstacles in his self appointed path. Great are the prejudices to be overcome; but he triumphs over all. Whalers are commonly regarded as a sort of sea-scavengers. He convinces you that their business is poetic; and that they are finest fellows afloat. He dispenses with a love-story altogether; there is hardly a flutter of a petticoat from chapter first to last. The book is not a record of fact; but of fact idealized, which supplies the frame for a terrible duel to the death between a mad whaling-captain and a miraculous white sperm whale. It is not a love-story but a story of undying hate.

In no other tale is one so completely detached from the land, even from the very suggestion of land. Though Nantucket and New Bedford must be mentioned, only their nautical aspects are touched on; they are but the steps of the saddle-block from which the mariner vaults upon the back of his sea-horse. The strange ship "Pequod" is the theatre of all the strange adventures. For ever off soundings, she shows but as a central speck in a wide circle of blue or stormy sea; and yet a speck crammed full of human passions, the world itself in little. Comparison brings out only more strongly the unique character of the book. Whaling is the most peculiar business done by man upon the deep waters. A war-ship is but a mobile fort or battery; a merchant-man is but a floating shop or warehouse: fishing is devoid of any but the ordinary perils of navigation; but sperm-whaling, according to Melville, is the most exciting and dangerous kind of big game hunting. One part of the author's triumph consists in having made the complicated operations of this strange pursuit perfectly familiar to the reader; and that not in any dull, pedantic fashion, but touched with the imagination, the humor, the fancy, the reflection of a poet. His intimate knowledge of his subject and his intense interest in it make the whaler's life in all its details not only comprehensible but fascinating. . . .

For a tale of such length, *Moby Dick* is undoubtedly well constructed. Possibly the "Town-Ho's Story," interesting as it is, somewhat checks the progress of the plot; but by the time the reader reaches this point, he is infected with the leisurely, trade-wind, whaling atmosphere, and has no desire to proceed faster than at the "Pequod's" own cruising rate. Possibly the book might be shortened by excision, but when one looks over the chapters it is hard to decide which to sacrifice. The interest begins with the quaint words of the opening sentence: "Call me Ishmael"; and never slackens for at least a hundred pages. Ishmael's reasons for going to sea, his sudden friendship with Queequeg, the Fijian harpooner, Father Mapple's sermon on Jonah, in the seamen's bethel, Queequeg's rescue of the country bumpkin on the way to Nantucket, Queequeg's Ramadan; the description of the ship "Pequod" and her two owners, Elijah's warning, getting under way and dropping the pilot, make up an introduction of great variety and picturesqueness. The second part deals with all the particulars of the various operations in whaling from manning the mast-heads and lowering the boats to trying out the blubber and cleaning up the ship, when all the oil is barrelled. In this part Ahab, who has been invisible in the retirement of his cabin, comes on deck and in various scenes different sides of his vehement, iron-willed, yet pathetic nature, are made intelligible. Here also is much learning to be found, and here, if anywhere, the story dawdles. The last part deals with the fatal three days' chase, the death of Ahab, and the escape of the White Whale.

One striking peculiarity of the book is its Americanism—a word which needs definition. The theme and style are peculiar to this country. Nowhere but in America could such a theme have been treated in such a style. Whaling is peculiarly an American industry; and of all whale-men, the Nantucketers were the keenest, the most daring, and the most successful. Now, though there are still whalers to be found in the New Bedford slips, and interesting as it is to clamber about them and hear the unconscious confirmation of all Melville's details from the lips of some old harpooner or boat-header, the industry is almost extinct. The discovery of petroleum did for it. Perhaps Melville went to sea for no other purpose than to construct the monument of whaling in this unique book. Not in his subject alone, but in his style is Melville distinctly American. It is large in idea, expansive; it has an Elizabethan force and freshness and swing, and is, perhaps, more rich in figures than any style but Emerson's. It has the picturesqueness of the new world, and, above all, a free-flowing humour, which is the distinct *cachet* of American literature. No one would contend that it is a perfect style; some mannerisms become tedious, like the constant moral turn, and the curiously coined adverbs placed before the verb. Occasionally there is more than a hint of bombast, as indeed might be expected; but, upon the whole, it is an extraordinary style, rich, clear, vivid, original. It shows reading and is full of thought and allusion; but its chief charm is its freedom from all scholastic rules and conventions. Melville is a Walt Whitman of prose.

Like Browning he has a dialect of his own. The poet of *The Ring and the Book* translates the different emotions and thoughts and possible words of pope, jurist, murderer, victim, into one level uniform Browningese; reduces them to a common denominator, in a way of speaking, and Melville give us not the actual words of American whalemen, but what they would say under the imagined conditions, translated into one consistent, though various Melvillesque manner of speech. The life he deals with belongs already to the legendary past, and he has us completely at his mercy. He is completely successful in creating his "atmosphere." Granted the conditions, the men and their words, emotions and actions, are all consistent. One powerful scene takes place on the quarter-deck of the "Pequod" one evening, when, all hands mustered aft, the Captain Ahab tells of the White Whale, and offers a doubloon to the first man who "raises" him. . . .

Then follows the wild ceremony of drinking round the capstan-head from the harpoon-sockets to confirm Ahab's curse. "Death to Moby Dick. God hunt us all, if we do not hunt Moby Dick to the death!" The intermezzo of the various sailors on the forecastle which follows until the squall strikes the ship is one of the most suggestive passages in all the literature of the sea. Under the influence of Ahab's can, the men are dancing on the forecastle. The old Manx sailor says:

"I wonder whether those jolly lads bethink them of what they are dancing over. I'll dance over your grave, I will—that's the bitterest threat of your night-women, that beat head-winds round corners. O, Christ! to think of the green navies and the green-skulled crews."

Where every page, almost every paragraph, has its quaint or telling phrase, or thought, or suggested picture, it is hard to make a selection; and even the choicest morsels give you no idea of the richness of the feast. Melville's humour has been mentioned; it is a constant quantity. Perhaps the statement of his determination after the adventure of the first lowering is as good an example as any:

"Here, then, from three impartial witnesses, I had a deliberate statement of the case. Considering, therefore, that squalls and capsizings in the water, and consequent bivouacks in the deep, were matters of common occurrence in this kind of life; considering that at the superlatively critical moment of going on to the whale I must resign my life into the hands of him who steered the boat—oftentimes a fellow who at that very moment is in his impetuousness upon the point of scuttling the craft with his own frantic stampings; considering that the particular disaster to our own particular boat was chiefly to be imputed to Starbuck's driving on to his whale, almost in the teeth of a squall, and considering that Starbuck, notwithstanding, was famous for his great heedfulness in the fishery; considering that I belonged to this uncommonly prudent Starbuck's boat; and finally considering in what a devil's chase I was implicated, touching the White Whale: taking all things together, I say, I thought I might as well go below and make a rough draft of my will.

'Queequeg,' said I, 'come along and you shall be my lawyer, executor and legatee.'"

The humour has the usual tinge of Northern melancholy, and sometimes a touch of Rabelais. The exhortations of Stubb to his boat's crew, on different occasions, or such chapters as "Queen Mab," "The Cassock," "Leg and Arm," "Stubb's Supper," are good examples of his peculiar style.

But, after all, his chief excellence is bringing to the landsman the very salt of the sea breeze, while to one who has long known the ocean, he is as one praising to the lover the chiefest beauties of the Beloved. The magic of the ship and the mystery of the sea are put into words that form pictures for the dullest eyes. The chapter, "The Spirit Spout," contains these two aquarelles of the moonlit sea and the speeding ship side by side:

"It was while gliding through these latter waters that one serene and moonlight night, when all the waves rolled by like scrolls of silver; and by their soft, suffusing seethings all things made what seemed a silvery silence, not a solitude; on such a silent night a silvery jet was seen far in advance of the white bubbles at the bow. Lit up by the moon it looked celestial; seemed some plumed and glittering god uprising from the sea. . . .

Walking the deck, with quick, side lunging strides, Ahab commanded the t'gallant sails and royals to be set, and every stunsail spread. The best man in the ship must take the helm. Then, with every mast-head manned, the piled-up craft rolled down before the wind. The strange, upheaving, lifting tendency of the taffrail breeze filling the hollows of so many sails made the buoyant, hovering deck to feel like air beneath the feet."

In the chapter called "The Needle," ship and sea and sky are blended in one unforgettable whole:

"Next morning the not-yet-subsided sea rolled in long, slow billows of mighty bulk, and striving in the "Pequod's" gurgling track, pushed her on like giants' palms outspread. The strong, unstaggering breeze abounded so, that sky and air seemed vast outbellying sails; the whole world boomed before the wind. Muffled in the full morning light, the invisible sun was only known by the spread intensity of his place; where his bayonet rays moved on in stacks. Emblazonings, as of crowned Babylonian kings and queens, reigned over everything. The sea was a crucible of molten gold, that bubblingly leaps with light and heat."

It would be hard to find five consecutive sentences anywhere containing such pictures and such vivid, pregnant, bold imagery: but this book is made up of such things.

The hero of the book is, after all, not Captain Ahab, but his triumphant antagonist, the mystic white monster of the sea, and it is only fitting that he should come for a moment at least into the saga. A complete scientific memoir of the Sperm Whale as known to man might be quarried from this book, for Melville has described the creature from his birth to his death, and even burial in the oil casks and the ocean. He has described him living, dead and anatomized. At least one such description is in place here. The appearance of the whale on the second day of the fatal chase is by "breaching," and nothing can be clearer than Melville's account of it:

"The triumphant halloo of thirty buckskin lungs was heard, as—much nearer to the ship than the place of the imaginary jet, less than a mile ahead—Moby Dick bodily burst into view! For not by any calm and indolent spoutings; not by the peaceable gush of that mystic fountain in his head, did the White Whale now reveal his vicinity; but by the far more wondrous phenomenon of breaching. Rising with his utmost velocity from the furthest depths, the Sperm Whale thus booms his entire bulk into the pure element of air, and piling up a mountain of dazzling foam, shows his place to the distance of seven miles and more. In those moments the torn, enraged waves he shakes off seem his mane; in some cases this breaching is his act of defiance.

'There she breaches! there she breaches!' was the cry, as in his immeasurable bravadoes the White Whale tossed himself salmon-like to heaven. So suddenly seen in the blue plain of the sea, and relieved against the still bluer margin of the sky, the spray that he raised for the moment intolerably glittered and glared like a glacier; and stood there gradually fading and fading away from its first sparkling intensity to the dim mistiness of an advancing shower in a vale."

This book is at once the epic and the encyclopaedia of whaling. It is a monument to the honour of an extinct race of daring seamen; but it is a monument overgrown with the lichen of neglect. Those who will care to scrape away the moss may be few, but they will have their reward. To the class of gentleman-adventurer, to those who love both books and free life under the wide and open sky, it must always appeal. Melville takes rank with Borrow, and Jefferies, and Thoreau, and Sir Richard Burton; and his place in this brotherhood of notables is not the lowest. Those who feel the salt in their blood that draws them time and again out of the city to the wharves and the ships, almost without their knowledge or their will; those who feel the irresistible lure of the spring, away from the cramped and noisy town, up the long road to the peaceful companionship of the awaking earth and the untainted sky; all those—and they are many—will find in Melville's great book an ever fresh and constant charm.

BARRETT WENDELL [1855–1921], biographer of Cotton Mather, professor of English at Harvard, and a prominent literary historian.

Melville

BARRETT WENDELL

. . . There are certain names which we might have mentioned; Mrs. Kirkland, for example. . . . Hermann Melville, with his books about the South Seas, which Robert Louis Stevenson is said to have declared the best ever written, and with his novels of maritime adventure, began a career of literary promise, which never came to fruition. Certain writers, too, who reached maturity later had already made themselves known,—Bayard Taylor, for example, and George William Curtis. . . .

––––––––

JULIAN W. ABERNETHY [1853–1923], American scholar, remembered as an early Thoreau collector and cofounder (with his brother Frank D. Abernethy) of the Abernethy Library of Middlebury College, his alma mater.

The Lesser Novelists

JULIAN W. ABERNETHY

From the scores of novelists who have won an undisputed success, it is difficult to select with any hope of justice the few who

A Literary History of America (New York: Charles Scribner's Sons, 1900), Chap. VI, "The Knickerbocker School," p. 229.

American Literature (New York: Maynard Merrill, & Co., 1902), pp. 456–57. The comment appears in Chapter 10, "Present Schools and Tendencies," after extended treatment of Howells, James, Crawford, Frank Richard Stockton, Edward Everett Hale, Celia Thaxter, Elizabeth Stuart Phelps, Julia C. R. Dorr, Sarah Orne Jewett, Rose Terry Cooke, Harriet Prescott Spofford, Margaret Deland, Mary Eleanor Wilkins.

can be named in a subordinate paragraph. The humor and pathos of New England life are strongly depicted by John Townsend Trowbridge (1827–   ), in "Neighbor Jackwood," "Coupon Bonds," and many other stories, and in his quaint poems of the soil, like the "Vagabonds." The breezy out-of-door novel "John Brent" will keep the name of Theodore Winthrop (1828–1861) green, and perhaps commend his other stories. With Winthrop perished, in the Civil War, the brilliant Irish-American Fitz-James O'Brien (1828–1861), whose "Diamond Lens" and other short tales do not suffer in comparison with the tales of Poe. Another forgotten New York novelist is Herman Melville (1819–1891), whose "Typee" and "Omoo," containing his adventures while a captive among the cannibals of the South Sea Islands, were once the sensation of two continents. Two powerful and artistic novels by Arthur Sherburn Hardy (1847–   ), "But Yet a Woman" and "Passe Rose," raised high hopes that may yet be fulfilled. The many novels of Julian Hawthorne (1846–   ), some of them remarkable for creative force, like "Archibald Malmaison," show the inheritance of a literary gift from his distinguished father from which achievements of permanent worth might reasonably be expected. Hjalmar Hjörth Boyesen (1848–1895), an adopted Norwegian, gathered the memories of his native land into the stories "Gunnar," "A Norseman's Pilgrimage," and "Ilka on the Hilltop," which were written with a free, spontaneous love and romantic fancy that disappear in his later novels, when he had become converted to the realism of Howells and Tolstoi. Frances Hodgson Burnett (1849–   ) will be affectionately remembered by "That Lass o' Lowrie's" and "Little Lord Fauntleroy," notwithstanding her later descent to the methods of the naturalistic school of fiction and the sensational stage in her "Lady of Quality."

JOHN PAYNE [1842–1916], English poet, translator—notably of Villon—
and friend of Swinburne and William Michael Rossetti. Payne's biographer,
Thomas Wright, makes this offhand comment on the contents of *Vigil and
Vision:* "Old friends such as Herman Melville, Mallarmé, Auguste Villiers
de l'Isle Adam, De Banville, E. J. W. Gibbs, John Trivett Nettleship and
others are feelingly commemorated."—*The Life of John Payne* (London:
T. Fisher Unwin Ltd., 1919), p. 134.

Herman Melville

JOHN PAYNE

None of the sea that fables but must yield
To Melville; whether with Whitejacket fain
We are to share, or Redburn, joy and pain;
Whether through Mardi's palaces, palm-ceiled,
We stray or wander in Omoo afield
Or dream with Ishmael cradled at the main,
High in the crow's-nest o'er the rocking plain,
Few such enchantments o'er the soul can wield.
But, over all the tale of Typee vale,
O'er all his idylls of the life afloat,
"The Whale" I prize, wherein, of all that wrote
Of Ocean, none e'er voiced for us as he
The cachalot's mad rush, the splintered boat,
The terrors and the splendours of the sea.

Vigil and Vision, New Sonnets (London: The Villon Society, 1903), p. 62.

WILLIAM EDWARD SIMONDS [1860–1947], American educator, scholar, and literary historian.

Fiction in the North

WILLIAM EDWARD SIMONDS

Rev. William Ware (1797–1852), a Massachusetts clergyman, was the author of three sober narratives dealing with the persecution of the Christians at Rome. To some extent *Zenobia* (1837), *Aurelian* (1838), and *Julian* (1841) still maintain their place among popular religious romances. Rev. Sylvester Judd (1813–1853) is more dimly remembered as the author of a transcendental romance, *Margaret* (1845), which was admired by Lowell for its description of humble rural life. The fiction of adventure is represented at its best in the novels of Herman Melville (1819–1891), a native of New York city. His own experiences on land and sea supplied the material of his most successful books, *Typee* (1846), *Omoo* (1847), and *Moby Dick, or the White Whale* (1851). Melville was, moreover, master of a brilliant style which gave his writings a distinction still retained. The tales of Catherine M. Sedgwick (1789–1867) employed an historical background; of these *Hope Leslie, or Early Times in Massachusetts* (1827), and *The Linwoods, or Sixty Years Since in America* (1835), were especially admired. Lydia Maria Child (1802–1880), whose philanthropic spirit brought her prominently into the antislavery agitation, began her modest literary career with the publication of two historical novels: *Hobomok* (1824), which depicted life in the colony at Salem, and *The Rebels* (1825), the scene of which is laid in Boston just previous to the Revolution.

A Student's History of American Literature (Boston: Houghton Mifflin Company, 1909), p. 304.

WILLIAM PETERFIELD TRENT [1862–1939], professor of English at Columbia, prolific editor of standard writers, student of Defoe and Simms, an early specialist in American literature, and one of the editors of the *Cambridge History of American Literature*.

JOHN ERSKINE [1879–1951], professor of English at Columbia, poet, novelist, literary critic, and also a joint editor of the *Cambridge History of American Literature*. Among his widely read novels were *The Private Life of Helen of Troy* and *Adam and Eve*.

Melville

W. P. TRENT AND JOHN ERSKINE

Of his other stories [besides *Typee*], the best are *Omoo: a Narrative of Adventures in the South Seas*, 1847, and *Moby Dick, or the White Whale*, 1851. This last is his masterpiece. Not even Cooper could surpass the grandeur of its sea-pictures, and some of its adventurous episodes have an uncanny quality found nowhere else. Melville could not repeat this success, nor again approach it. He died in New York, September 28, 1891.

The work of Simms, for extent and contemporary importance, is far more worthy of attention than all of Melville's writing, with the one exception of *Moby Dick;* and the character of Simms was most engaging. But his novels are now hardly known by name, whereas the praise of Stevenson and other craftsmen near at hand has given Melville's best work a new lease of life. Yet above them both Cooper still keeps his secure place, not much injured by unsympathetic criticism, nor even by some condescending praise.

Great American Writers (New York: Henry Holt and Company, 1912), pp. 56–57.

The Melville Revival:
1917-32

CARL VAN DOREN [1885–1950], a leading American historian, critic, and man-of-letters. Author of *The Roving Critic, American Literature: An Introduction,* and an editor of the *Cambridge History of American Literature,* his role in bringing about the Melville revival has never been quite adequately acknowledged.

Contemporaries of Cooper

CARL VAN DOREN

It was, however, while on this perilous border that [Melville] produced the best of his, and one of the best of American, romances; it is the peculiar mingling of speculation and experience which lends *Moby Dick* (1851) its special power.

The time was propitious for such a book. The golden age of the whalers was drawing to a close, though no decline had yet set in, and the native imagination had been stirred by tales of deeds done on remote oceans by the most heroic Yankees of the age in the arduous calling in which New England, and especially the hard little island of Nantucket, led and taught the world. A small literature of whaling had grown up, chiefly the records of actual voyages or novels like those of Cooper in which whaling was an incident of the nautical life. But the whalers still lacked any such romantic record as the frontier had. Melville brought to the task a sound knowledge of actual whaling, much curious learning in the literature of the subject, and, above all, an imagination which worked with great power upon the facts of his own experience. Moby Dick, the strange, fierce white whale that Captain Ahab pursues with such relentless fury, was already a legend among the whalers, who knew him as "Mocha Dick."[1] It remained for Melville to lend some kind of poetic or moral significance to a struggle ordinarily conducted for no cause but profit. As he handles the story, Ahab, who has lost a leg in the jaws of the whale, is driven by a wild desire for revenge which has maddened him and which makes him identify

[1] See Reynolds, J. N., *Mocha Dick, Knickerbocker Magazine,* May, 1839.

Cambridge History of American Literature, Vol. I (New York, 1917) 322-23. (Copyright 1917 Cambridge University Press; renewed 1945 The Macmillan Company.)

Moby Dick with the very spirit of evil and hatred. Ahab, not Melville, is to blame if the story seems an allegory, which Melville plainly declared it was not[1]; but it contains, nevertheless, the semblance of a conflict between the ancient and scatheless forces of nature and the ineluctable enmity of man. This is the theme, but description can hardly report the extraordinary mixture in *Moby Dick* of vivid adventure, minute detail, cloudy symbolism, thrilling pictures of the sea in every mood, sly mirth and cosmic ironies, real and incredible characters, wit, speculation, humour, colour. The style is mannered but often felicitous; though the book is long, the end, after every faculty of suspense has been aroused, is swift and final. Too irregular, too bizarre, perhaps, ever to win the widest suffrage, the immense originality of *Moby Dick* must warrant the claim of its admirers that it belongs with the greatest sea romances in the whole literature of the world.

[1] *Moby Dick*, Chap. XLV.

FRANK JEWETT MATHER, JR. [1868–1953], distinguished American art critic and art historian, and the most comprehensive and sympathetic critic of Melville during the revival.* He was professor of art and archeology at Princeton University and author of *Estimates in Art* and *Modern Painting*.

* The following quotation from Mather's review of Lewis Mumford's biography in the *Saturday Review of Literature*, Vol. 5 (27 April 1929) 945, is a fascinating afternote to Mather's centennial essay:

"Almost twenty-five years ago I sought Herman Melville's daughter, Elizabeth, who was living in the old Florence amid her father's books and pictures. She talked of him with constraint, but was interested in my quest, giving me the two privately printed pamphlets of poems, which completed my first editions, and letting me read casually from that japanned tin cakebox which contained Melville's letters and unpublished manuscripts. Thus I took a few notes from the diaries of travels, sampled "Billy Budd," and the last poems. Miss Melville generously promised me the use of all the papers except Melville's letters to his wife. In high hopes I wrote to the American publishers whose list is heaviest with our classics, and proposed a modest biography in one volume. The answer was friendly but decisive: Herman Melville was a hopelessly bad risk, and one that no prudent publisher could undertake even to the extent of a few hundred dollars.

"Some five or six years later, Mr. Raymond Weaver happily rediscovered the most precious of cake boxes, and with the wisdom of youth addressed a

Herman Melville

FRANK JEWETT MATHER, JR.

My introduction to Herman Melville is due to Edwin Lucas White, the author of "El Supremo" and of much verse equally notable, if too little known. Amid the rigors of philology, to which we were then both bound, we kept certain private delectations of a literary sort. One afternoon he took me to his study and instead of the expected sonorous passage from Victor Hugo's "Légende des Siècles" he read me the following words out of a stout, shabby, cloth-bound book named "Moby Dick, or The Whale":

> To a landsman, no whale, nor any sign of a herring, would have been visible at that moment; nothing but a troubled bit of greenish white water, and thin scattered puffs of vapor hovering over it, and suffusingly blowing off to leeward, like the confused scud from white rolling billows. The air around suddenly tingled and vibrated, as it were, like the air over intensely heated plates of iron. Beneath this atmospheric waving and curling, and partially beneath a thin layer of water also, the whales were swimming.

(Then began the chase)

> It was a sight full of wonder and awe! The vast swells of the omnipotent sea; the surging, hollow roar they made, as they rolled along the eight gunwales, like gigantic bowls in a boundless bowling green; the brief suspended agony of the boat, as it would tip for an instant on the knife-like edge of the sharper waves that almost seemed threatening to cut it in two; the sudden profound dip into the watery glens and hollows; the keen spurrings and goadings to gain the top of the opposite hill; the headlong, sled-like slide down

---

publisher who had no long list of historic American worthies and was willing to bet on an unsure thing. . . .

"This too long reminiscence is not written to claim an empty priority, but to show how completely a Melvillian and Melville himself were outsiders twenty-five years ago."

Review, Vol. I (August 1919) 276–78, 298–301.

its other side—all these, with the cries of the headsmen and harpooners, and the shuddering gasps of the oarsman, with the wondrous sight of the ivory Pequod bearing down upon her boats with outstretched sails, like a wild hen after her screaming brood—all this was thrilling. Not the raw recruit marching from the bosom of his wife into the fever heat of his first battle; not the dead man's ghost encountering the first unknown phantom in the other world—neither of these can feel stranger and stronger emotions than that man does, who for the first time finds himself pulling into the charmed, churned circle of the hunted sperm whale.

The tang of this was unforgettable. That reading made a Melvilleite out of me. I bought everything Melville published —it took me ten years to do it, and my collection was only completed with the two privately printed pamphlets of poems, through the gracious gift of Melville's daughter. I read my collection up and down with increasing delight. Gradually I learned that to love Melville was to join a very small circle. It was like eating hasheesh. Robert Louis Stevenson and Charles Warren Stoddard had given him brave praise. John La Farge told me of meeting in the South Seas two American beachcombers lured towards the Marquesas by the spell of "Typee." La Farge made the charming drawing of Fayaway standing in the bow of a canoe and serving as mast and sail. It was for the ill-fated reprint of "Typee" and "Omoo" edited by the late Arthur Stedman, and I saw another charming Fayaway in clay in the studio of the sculptress, Miss Elizabeth Cornwall. I owe to my enthusiasm for Melville acquaintance with extraordinary persons on both sides the seas; for no ordinary person loves Melville. So on the centenary of his birth it is a double debt of gratitude which I repay most inadequately in giving some account of one of the greatest and most strangely neglected of American writers. . . .

Melville, in prose, for he was also no mean poet, had three styles, like an old master. The swift lucidity, picturesqueness, and sympathy of "Typee" and "Omoo" have alone captured posterity. Melville lives by his *juvenalia*. "Redburn" and "White Jacket" are straightforward manly narratives, less colorful than their predecessors. They have not stood the competition with

Dana's quite similar "Two Years Before the Mast." They are not quite as solid as that classic, but their chief fault was merely in being later. Then Melville developed a reflective, mystical, and very personal style, probably influenced by Carlyle, which the public has from the first eschewed. It asserts itself first in the strange allegory, "Mardi, and a Voyage Thither," 1849, it pervaded "Pierre, or the Ambiguities," 1852, and other later books. "Moby Dick" shows an extraordinary blend of the first and the last style—the pictorial and the orphic; is Melville's most characteristic and, I think, his greatest book. Still, for the average reader Melville is merely the author of "Typee" and "Omoo." Chronology and the popular will, if it can be at all invoked in Melville's case, alike bid us slur his single historical novel, "Israel Potter," 1855, and his middlewestern character sketches in "The Confidence Man," 1857, and even the excellent "Piazza Tales," 1856, in favor of the Marquesan idyl and the picaresque account of Tahiti.

As Herman Melville staggered down the cliffs and cascades above the happy valley of Typee, a famished cripple fearing the redoubtable cannibals, the first human beings he saw were:

> A boy and girl, slender and graceful, and completely naked, with the exception of a slight girdle of bark, from which depended at opposite points two of the russet leaves of the bread-fruit. An arm of the boy, half screened from sight by her wild tresses, was thrown about the neck of the girl, while with the other he held one of her hands in his; and thus they stood together, their heads inclined forward, catching the faint noise we made in our progress, and with one foot in advance, as if half inclined to fly from our presence.

The direct, assured, unaffected style of this holds through the entire book.

Melville was adopted by the king, Mehevi, nursed back to health by the loveliest of mistresses, Fayaway, and most devoted of aged retainers, Kory Kory. For four months he saw the life of the gentlest of barbarians in every aspect. He chatted with the bachelors at the *Ti* (men's club); he saw the wild dancing at the feast of calabashes, shared in the rites of the puppet god Moa Artua, entered the funeral fastnesses where the effigies

of former heroes eternally paddled canoes adorned by the skulls
of their foes. He heard the clamor of a cannibal feast, and lifted
the cover of a tub where lay a fresh human skeleton. He heard
the superb warrior Marnoo incite the folk to resistance against
the invading French. He mused by pools, splashing with laughing bronze nymphs. Every evening these anointed him for the
healing of his wounds and better sleep. He saw, without fixed
religion or other law than a wholly capricious *tabu*, an entire
population living in brotherhood and peace. He saw honesty
without courts or prisons. He measured this idyllic life against
civilization and wrote:

> The term "Savage" is, I conceive, often misapplied, and
> indeed when I consider the vices, cruelties, and enormities
> of every kind that spring up in the tainted atmosphere of
> a feverish civilization, I am inclined to think that so far as
> the relative wickedness of the parties is concerned, four or
> five Marquesan Islanders sent to the United States as mis-
> sionaries, might be quite as useful as an equal number of
> Americans dispatched to the Islands in a similar capacity.

But it is, after all, less opinion than pictures which counts
in "Typee," and the pictures are so vivid because there is no
condescension in the observer's attitude. Melville was one of
the earliest literary travelers to see in barbarians anything but
queer folk. He intuitively understood them, caught their point
of view, respected and often admired it. Thus "Typee" in a
peculiar sense is written from the inside. The ready tolerance
that Melville had learned in the forecastle had not blunted the
gentleman in him, but had prepared him to be the ideal spectator of a beautiful life that has forever passed. As having distinctly saved a vanishing charm for posterity, "Typee" is perhaps
Melville's most important book.

Quite unlike the well-compacted proportions of the Marquesan idyl, is the straggling, picaresque vivacity of "Omoo."
From the unspoiled loveliness of Typee, Melville passed to the
tainted life of the Tahitian beaches. His companion was one
of those amazing derelicts which the sea best affords, Dr. Long
Ghost, reduced to the forecastle, but having at some time or
other "spent money, drunk Burgundy, and associated with gentlemen." They jumped ship, were imprisoned and put in the

stocks; wandered in rags from village to village; saw strange British despots who ruled by virtue of rifle and powder-horn; and even reached the presence of Queen Pomaree. The casual, care-free flavor of the book can not be suggested in quotations. Its manly vigor, as certain British reviewers duly pointed out, recalls the masterpieces of George Borrow. Among underworld romances it is strange that it has not taken the high place which on its merits it deserves. The style, as in the case of "Typee," had doubtless profited through Melville's habit of telling these yarns to friends. There is a clarity which tends to fade in the later and more consciously literary works. I don't know that any American writer has had a better eye than Melville. He is not merely a capital story-teller, but a most trenchant picture maker. In a few just strokes, without pretentiousness or faltering, he achieves his sketch. I choose, not from the famous books but from "Redburn," a picture whose original I have often seen— calm and the sea-approaches to New York:

> The ship lay gently swelling in the soft, subdued ocean swell; while all around were faint white spots; and nearer to, broad milky patches, betokening the vicinity of scores of ships, all bound to one common port, and tranced in one common calm. Here the long devious wakes from Europe, Africa, India, and Peru converged to a line, which braided them all in one.
>
> Full before us quivered and danced, in the noonday heat and mid-air, the green heights of New Jersey; and by an optical delusion, the blue sea seemed to flow under them.

In its combination of precise and delicate observation, curious felicity of phrase, and implications of mystery and immensity, with just a tinge of conceitfulness, this passage is purest Melville. In one sense "Typee," the adventure and the book, made Melville. At twenty-seven, from being an oddity of the forecastle, he jumped into fame. From "Typee" and his antecedent experience at sea came the subject of every book of his that has lived. In another sense "Typee" undid Melville. Its success barred other roads. Surviving himself by nearly forty years, Melville tried restlessly in one direction and another to work out a sort of philosophic romance in which he relatively failed. The sojourn under King Mehevi's palm trees had made a skeptic of Melville, yet a skeptic with philosophical yearnings and profoundly religious intuitions. It had destroyed also all political and social theories and gone far to efface conventional maxims of morality.

These may seem only long words for the forecastle mood, which "bolts down all events, all creeds, and beliefs, and persuasions, all hard things visible and invisible; as an ostrich of potent digestion gobbles down bullets and gunflints." It is a mood, however, endurable only for one who thinks little, and Melville thought tremendously. To doubt everything, yet to retain certain saving intuitions became his avowed programme. This work of critical destruction and reintegration was that of Melville's times—the Victorian mood. But few of Melville's contemporaries had gone so far in disillusion, few had razed prejudice so thoroughly, few had lived so much. What might have been a triumphant process of reconstruction—for Melville had the intelligence and apparently the force—lapsed through invalidism and misfortune into occasional strenuous gropings not without their nobility and pathos. Herman Melville was gradually eaten up by his desire to understand the eternal mysteries, and his activities were not of a sort to clarify his quest. His fate superficially was that of the Ohio honey hunter, described in "Moby Dick," who "seeking honey in the crotch of a hollow tree, found such exceeding store of it, that leaning too far over, it sucked him in, so that he died embalmed. How many think ye, have likewise fallen into Plato's honey head, and sweetly perished there?"

The human interest of Melville's later and forgotten work is so great that I can not follow my predecessors and betters in criticism who have agreed to ignore it as unreadable. We may best approach Herman Melville's cavernous phase from the vantage point of the great transitional romance "Moby Dick."

II

In 1849, about two years before "Moby Dick," appeared that strangest of allegories, "Mardi, and a Voyage Thither." The two works are companion pieces: "Mardi" is a survey of the universe in the guise of an imaginary voyage of discovery, "Moby Dick" is a real voyage skilfully used to illustrate the cosmos; "Mardi" is a celestial adventure, "Moby Dick" an infernal. "Mardi" is highly general—the quest of a mysterious damsel, Zillah, a sort of Beatrice, a type of divine wisdom; "Moby Dick" is specific, the insanely vengeful pursuit of the dreaded white whale. The people of "Mardi" are all abstractions, those of "Moby Dick" among the most vivid known to fiction. "Mardi" was far the most ambitious effort of Melville's, and it failed. Personally I like to read in it; for its idealism tinged with a sane Rabelaisianism, for its wit and rare pictorial quality, for the strange songs of Yoomy, which, undetachable, are both quaintly effective in their context, and often foreshadow oddly our modern free verse. It is often plethoric and over-written, it drops out of the Polynesian form in which it is conceived, and becomes too overt preaching and satire. It justifies the Bacchic philosopher Babbalanja's aphorism—"Genius is full of trash"; but it is also full of wisdom and fine thinking. It represents an intellectual effort that would supply a small library, and I suppose it is fated to remain unread. Perhaps its trouble is its inconclusiveness. Again Babbalanja is enlightening:

> Ah! my lord, think not that in aught I've said this night, I would assert any wisdom of my own. I but fight against the armed and crested lies of Mardi, that like a host, assail me. I am stuck full of darts; but tearing them from out me, gasping, I discharge them whence they came.

The very seriousness of "Mardi" tells against it. One feels something, a breaking heart under the literary horseplay. Thus it can not hold its own either with such neatly fashioned ideal republics as Edward Bellamy's "Looking Backward," nor with the Horatian elegance of Samuel Butler's "Erewhon," nor of course with the grim impassivity of "Gulliver's Travels." The occasional delver in "Mardi," however, will pluck out of it all sorts of surprises from foreshadowings of the superman to an anticipation of Samuel Butler's vitalism.

"Moby Dick" has the tremendous advantage of its concreteness. Captain Ahab's mad quest of the white whale imposes itself as real, and progressively enlists and appalls the imagination. Out of the mere stray episodes and minor characters of "Moby Dick" a literary reputation might be made. The retired Nantucket captains, Bildad and Peleg, might have stepped out of Smollett. Father Mapple's sermon on the Book of Jonah is in itself a masterpiece, and I know few sea tales which can hold their own with the blood feud of Mate Radney and sailor Steelkilt. The style still has the freshness and delicate power of "Typee," but is subtler. Take the very modern quality of a passage which a Loti might envy:

> It was while gliding through these latter waters that one serene and moonlight night, when all the waves rolled by like scrolls of silver; and by their soft, suffusing seethings, made what seemed a silvery silence, not a solitude; on such a silent night a silvery jet was seen far in advance of the white bubbles at the bow. Lit up by the moon, it looked celestial; seemed some plumed and glittering god uprising from the sea.

There is also a harsher note befitting the theme. The tang of it is in the passage with which this essay opened. The tragic and almost incredible motive of the quest of the demon whale gains credibility from the solid basis of fact, as mad captain Ahab himself is based, so to speak, on his ivory leg. The insane adventure itself grows real through the actuality of its participants: Was there ever such a trio as the savage harpooners? Their very names, Feddallah, Tashetego, Queequeg, are a guarantee of good faith. A reader instinctively hurrahs at the deeds of such mates as Starbuck and Stubbs while with them he cowers under the fateful eye of Captain Ahab. Throughout the book are shudders, sympathies, and laughs.

But "Moby Dick" is more than what it undisputedly is, the greatest whaling novel. It is an extraordinary work in morals and general comment. In the discursive tradition of Fielding and the anatomist of melancholy, Melville finds a suggestion or a symbol in each event and fearlessly pursues the line of association. As he and Queequeg plait a mat on the same warp, the differing woofs and resulting surfaces become a symbol for man's free will asserting itself against the background of fate. Such reflections are in a grave, slow-moving style in which Burton has counted for much and Carlyle for something. It is the interplay of fact and application that makes the unique character of the book. As for the Christian fathers the visible world was merely a similitude or foreshadowing of the eternal world, so for Melville the voyage of the Pequod betokens our moral life in the largest sense. An example may best show the qualities and defects of the method. "Ishmael" (Herman Melville) is at the wheel at night gazing at the witches' kitchen of "trying out" the blubber. The glare sends him into a momentary doze and a strange thing happens:

> Starting from a brief standing sleep, I was horribly conscious of something fatally wrong. The jaw-bone tiller smote my side, which leaned against it; in my ears was the low hum of sails just beginning to shake in the wind. I thought my eyes were open: I was half conscious of putting my fingers to my lids and mechanically stretching them still farther apart. But, spite of all this, I could see no compass before me to steer by; though it seemed but a minute since I had been watching the card, by the steady binnacle lamp illuminating it. Nothing seemed before me but a jet gloom, now and then made ghastly by flashes of redness. Uppermost was the impression, that whatever swift, rushing thing I stood on was not so much bound to any haven ahead as rushing from all havens astern. A stark, bewildered feeling, as of death, came over me. Convulsively my hand grasped the tiller, but with the crazy conceit that the tiller was, somehow, in some enchanted way, inverted. My God! what is the matter with me, thought I. Lo! in my brief sleep I had turned myself about, and was fronting the ship's stern with my back to her prow and the compass . . .
>
> Look not too long in the face of the fire, O man! Never dream with thy hand on the tiller! Turn not thy back to the compass; accept the first hint of the hitching tiller, believe not the artificial fire when its redness makes all things look ghastly. Tomorrow, in the natural sun, the skies will be bright; those who glared like devils in the forking flames will show in far other, at least gentler relief; the glorious, golden, glad sun, the only true lamp—all others but liars.

Upon the reader's slant towards this sort of parable will very much depend his estimate of "Moby Dick." Are we dealing with trimmings or essentials?—that is the critical question. Cut out the preachments, and you will have a great novel, some readers say. Yes, but not a great Melville novel. The preachments are the essence. The effect of the book rests on the blend

of fact, fancy, and profound reflection, upon a brilliant inter-
mingling of sheer artistry and moralizing at large. It is Kipling
before the latter crossed with Sir Thomas Browne, it comprises
all the powers and tastes of Herman Melville, is his greatest
and most necessary work. So while no one is obliged to like
"Moby Dick"—there are those who would hold against Dante
his moralizing and against Rabelais his broad humor—let such
as do love this rich and towering fabrique adore it whole-
heartedly—from stem to stern, athwart ships and from maintruck
to keelson.

In a sense "Moby Dick" exhausted Melville's vein. At
thirty-two he had put into a single volume all that he had been
in action, all that he was to be in thought. The rest is aftermath, yet it, too, is considerable. The year after "Moby Dick,"
1852, appeared "Pierre, or the Ambiguities." Legend assigns
the author's swift obscuration to the dispraise "Pierre" aroused.
It is too simple an explanation, as we shall see. The book is
repellent and overwrought, yet powerful. The theme is the
endeavor of a long-parted brother and sister, a mere lad and
lass, to cut loose and lead their own lives, as nominal husband
and wife. The ambiguity of their situation leads to misery, madness, and ruin. Convention triumphs over a boy's genius and
chivalry, as over a girl's unmeasured tenderness. The struggle
is painful, without winning much sympathy. The moral that
one must somewhat bend to things as they are is almost commonplace. The demonstration is powerful, but without much sequence; reflection and satire burgeon over the mishaps of the
luckless brother and sister, as if the red, red rose and the briar
should finally conceal the twin tombs of the ballad lovers. Yet
as a literary curiosity "Pierre" is worth reading, and it is at least
a curious coincidence that it completely anticipates in wire-
drawn fashion what was soon to be the leading motive of "The
Ordeal of Richard Feverel." The parallel is commended to
would-be doctors of philosophy.

In 1863 Herman Melville sold "Arrowhead" to his brother
Allan and soon went to New York and obscurity. A disastrous
driving accident in 1864 and the resultant shock for months
sapped the nerve of the former whaleman, and when he emerged
it was to a new and smaller life. Family cares now pressed
upon him, and in 1865 he took a position as customs' appraiser,
humble duties which he exercised at the old Gansevoort Mar-

ket for upwards of twenty years. He lived, a cheerful and courteous recluse, satisfied with his books and his home. Literary New York forgot him and social New York never knew him. Shortly before his death the magnanimous poet-critic, Edmund Clarence Stedman, managed a complimentary dinner for him, and with difficulty got him to attend it. It was about the only public recognition he ever received. I had the pleasure of seeing the home in which he died, an apartment in the now vanished "Florence," at 18th Street and Fourth Avenue. It was the mellowest home I have ever seen in Manhattan. There was a fine portrait of the Gansevoort grandsire, by Sully after Stuart; Washington Alston would have highly approved the prints after Claude and Salvator, and Charles Lamb would have reveled in the lustrous brown folios of the old English worthies. The simple old furniture was worthy of the rest. I liked to think that Herman Melville's last anchorage was in so sweet a port.

Perhaps Melville had written himself out, lasted just as long as his incomparable sea material, and no longer. For a smaller man the explanation would be adequate, as it is the simplest. I rather think poor health and brooding must chiefly account for the collapse. Among the numerous aphorisms in "Pierre" we read, "When a man is really in a profound mood, then all merely verbal or written profundities are unspeakably repulsive, and seem downright childish to him." And again, "Yoke the body to the soul, and put both to the plough, and the one or the other must assuredly drop in the furrow." "Pierre" is one long parable of living too intensely morbidly, and individually. It probably reflects a personal struggle of the author for a mental equipoise which he attained at the cost of surrender of old activities and ambitions. Meanwhile he had greatly isolated himself. By telling the truth about the Polynesian missionaries he had sorely ruffled the devout, and had increased the offense by skeptical asides in his novels. From the New England writers, most of whom too clearly revealed "the striped origin of their German and Neo-Platonical origins," he stood off. He came to a New York in the literary doldrums. Solitude easily became a habit which stuck.

For recreation he still occasionally turned to verse, but nothing except "Battle Pieces," 1866, was even intended for the public. Of the war poems only "Sheridan at Cedar Creek" is remembered—

> Shoe the steed with silver
> That bare him to the fray

is deservedly in the anthologies. There are single lines and stanzas in the volume that are thrilling. The poems to the Swamp Angel, the great gun that reduced Charleston, is fine, as a stanza proves, in sustained irony and symbol:

> There is a coal-black Angel
>   With a thick Afric lip
> And he dwells (like the hunted and harried)
>   In a swamp where the green frogs dip
> But his face is against a City
>   Which is over a bay of the sea,
> And he breathes with a breath that is blastment,
>   And dooms by a far decree.

There are again striking anticipations of the terse and sententious method that Kipling was to make famous. Kipling himself might have thought this prophetic stave to the Monitor's victory:

> Hail to victory without the gaud
>   Of glory; zeal that needs no fans
> Of banners; plain mechanic power
> Plied cogently in War now placed—
>   Where War belongs
> Among the trades and artisans.

Melville had rather the soul of a poet than great poetical capacity, or facility, but there is power and probity in his feelings that atone for halting verse and occasional makeshift rhyme. He is too original a figure in American poetry ever to be quite forgotten.

After "Battle Pieces" the rest with Melville if not silence is whisper. He sunk resignedly into his habits. In a literary way he was not idle. I have seen in manuscript an historical novel, half a dozen short stories, a volume of lyrics and some long narrative poems, but have had no opportunity to read this unpublished material. For a time Melville had the genial and accomplished Richard Henry Stoddard as an associate in the customs office. Towards the end he was in correspondence with the English writer of sea novels, W. Clark Russell. But in general Melville's situation was that which he treats in the privately printed poem, "John Marr," printed in 1888—a disillusioned

mariner living by great memories and by family affection, drawing ever more aloof from the surrounding world.

In his early fifties Melville made the Mediterranean trip,
leaving certain memories of it in his two privately printed volumes of verse and more comprehensively in the reflective poem,
"Clarel, a Pilgrimage in the Holy Land." Of those who have
actually perused the four books and two volumes of "Clarel"
I am presumably the only survivor. Yet there are in "Clarel"
vividness, humor, irony, and mind-stuff sufficient to stock the
entire imagist school; only the blend was never quite right and
the fashion of the poem has passed. Melville brings a group of
flippant and serious skeptics, theologians, men of action, poets,
and traders into Palestine and notes their reaction to the legend,
scenery, and shrines of the Holy Land. There are charming
lyrics, sharp and well-seen descriptions. The problem of faith
and doubt is turned over in every sense, the bearing of both on
public and private morals is constantly adumbrated often with
prophetic intuition.

> Arts are tools;
> But tools, they say are to the strong;
> Is Satan weak? weak is the Wrong?
> No blessed augury overrules;
> Your arts advance in faith's decay;
> You are but drilling the new Hun
> Whose growl even now can some dismay;
> Vindictive in his heart of hearts,
> He schools him in your mines and marts—
> A skilled destroyer.

This should show the vigor of the thinking in "Clarel," and pre-
pare the way for its eminently Victorian conclusion. Melville
admits all the doubts, but *quand même* lets the individual hold
his modicum of faith in humanity and a God, and his hope in
immortality.

> If Luther's day expand to Darwin's year,
> Shall that exclude the hope—foreclose the fear?
>
>   *   *   *   *
>
> Yea, ape and angel, strife and old debate,
> The harps of heaven and dreary gongs of hell;
> Science the feud can only aggravate—

No umpire she betwixt the chimes and knell;
The running battle of the star and clod
Shall run forever—if there be no God.

✿   ✿   ✿   ✿

Then keep thy heart, though yet but ill resigned—
Clarel, thy heart, the issues there but mind;
That like the crocus budding through the snow—
That like a swimmer rising from the deep—
That like a burning secret which doth go
Even from the bosom that would hoard and keep;
Emerge thou mayst from the last whelming sea
And prove that death but routs life into victory.

With its patent *longueurs* and lapses "Clarel" is about all America has to show for the poetical stirring of the deeper theological waters which marked the age of Matthew Arnold, Clough, Tennyson, and Browning. And we need not be ashamed of our representation.

In the deepening twilight of his later years Melville printed for private circulation two little pamphlets of verse, "John Marr and Other Sailors," 1888, and "Timoleon," 1891. Here and there are flashes of the old genius which the Melvilleite will cherish, many fine lines and no quite fine poems. The little brochures were fittingly dedicated to W. Clark Russell and to Elihu Vedder, artists who respectively accord with the objective and the mystical side of Melville's vein.

I have left myself little scope for discussing the problem of Melville's decline. He seemed written out at thirty-two, when most authors are just beginning to strike their gait. Yet it should not be forgotten that not even the most neglected works of his are negligible for a reader who values rich idiosyncrasy. "Pierre" is perhaps the only positively ill-done book, and it is stuffed with memorable aphorisms. Amid the somewhat dreary wastes of "The Confidence Man" are numerous tidbits of irony and wit. "Israel Potter" contains the best account of a seafight in American fiction. But it is undeniable that after "Moby Dick" Melville never conceived a good book—"White Jacket" was a hangover; his inventive processes became uncertain and fluctuating, the moralist in him eclipsed the man of letters. The extraordinary artistry, the ineffable magic of words so frequent in his beginnings becomes intermittent and rare. The new sententiousness and oracular eloquence never quite fulfill themselves. What he lacked was possibly only health and nerve, but perhaps even more, companionship of a friendly, critical, and understanding sort. In London, where he must have been hounded out of his corner, I can imagine Melville carrying the reflective vein to literary completion. As sensitive a friend as the poet Stoddard has written: "Whether any of Melville's readers understood the drift of Melville's mind, or whether he understood it himself, has often puzzled me." Yet there seems no mystery in the ambition to make great fulness of life contribute to fuller understanding of life's deeper enigmas. Robert Browning would readily have seen what Melville was driving at.

If Melville relatively failed in the synthesis he sought, he left the evidence of its possibility in "Moby Dick." In sheer capacity to feel most American writers look pale beside him. Out of his loins grows the recent "strong school." They have nothing in common with him but his emphasis. At his best he commanded a witchery of words beyond any American save only Edgar Allan Poe. He combined in an extraordinary degree impressionistic delicacy and precision with emotional and mental vigor, and withal robust humor; he was both drastic and refined, straightforward and deeply mystical, precious, and delightfully homely. He felt keenly the task of harmonizing so many opposites, and perhaps has left the sufficient key both to his ambitions and disappointments in one of the poems of "Timoleon." With it we take leave of the most personally alluring of American men of letters:

ART

In placid hours well-pleased we dream
Of many a brave unbodied scheme.
But form to lend, pulsed life create,
What unlike things must meet and mate;
A flame to melt—a wind to freeze;
Sad patience—joyous energies;
Humility—yet pride and scorn;
Instinct and study;—love and hate:
Audacity—reverence. These must mate,
And fuse with Jacob's mystic heart,
To wrestle with the angel—art.

From Herman Melville (1819-1891):
A Centenary Tribute

F. C. OWLETT

Melville's humour is of a subtler and more intimate quality than Lavengro's. It permeates his work—is, indeed, the vital essence of it—charging it through and through, and playing on it from without as it were, lambent always save in those great moments when it breaks and surges in riot. His style is spontaneous, buoyant, rich—with the richness of seventeenth century prose (Mr. Strachey has pointed out the literary kinship of Melville with Sir Thomas Browne). His best descriptive passages reach the highest level of impassioned prose, and even in those books where he falls farthest from literary grace, he never loses his sense of the force and the colour of words. It may even be contended that the badness of his worst work is due to an over-development of this same sense, which, in its relation to our author's other excellent qualities, exhibited at times the dangerous tendencies of an Aaron's rod. Let it be conceded that Borrow on occasion achieves greater effects, in spite of—shall we say because of?—his terser statement of fact, and the simplicity and angularity that are the marks of his style. The throes of composition were very real with Borrow; his books were produced only after sore travail. He (who never confessed anything) might have confessed with Milton that he wrote prose as it were with his left hand (which is not to say that the Lavengro ever wrote, or was capable of writing, *poetry*). . . .

London *Bookman*, Vol. 56 (August 1919) 164–67.

The member of the staff referred to is H. M. Tomlinson [1873–1958], who was literary editor of *The Nation and Athenaeum* from 1917 until 1923. An English writer, his novels include *The Sea and the Jungle* and *Gallions Reach*.

A Testimonial for *Moby-Dick*

ANONYMOUS

It is clear that the wind of the spirit, when it once begins to blow through the English literary mind, possesses a surprising power of penetration. A few weeks ago it was pleased to aim a simultaneous blast at the direction of a book known to some generations of men as "Moby Dick." A member of the staff of THE NATION was thereupon moved in the ancient Hebrew fashion to buy it and to read it. He then expressed himself on the subject, incoherently indeed, but with signs of emotion as intense and as pleasingly uncouth as Man Friday betrayed at the sight of his long-lost father. While struggling with his article, and wondering what the deuce it could mean, I received a letter from a famous literary man, marked on the outside "Urgent," and on the inner scroll of the MS. itself "A Rhapsody." It was about "Moby Dick." Having observed a third article on the same subject, of an equally febrile kind, I began to read "Moby Dick" myself. Having done so I hereby declare, being of sane intellect, that since letters began there never was such a book, and that the mind of man is not constructed so as to produce such another; that I put its author with Rabelais, Swift, Shakespeare, and other minor and disputable worthies; and that I advise any adventurer of the soul to go at once into the morose and prolonged retreat necessary for its deglutition. And having said this, I decline to say another word on the subject now and for evermore.

A WAYFARER

London *Nation*, Vol. 28 (22 January 1921) 572. (Reprinted by permission of the *New Statesman*, London.)

RAYMOND M. WEAVER [1888–1948], Melville's first biographer, was professor of English at Columbia.

Moby-Dick

RAYMOND M. WEAVER

Born in hell-fire, and baptised in an unspeakable name, *Moby-Dick* is, with *The Scarlet Letter,* among the few very notable literary achievements of American literature. There has been published no criticism of Melville more beautiful or more profound than the essay of E. L. Grant Watson on *Moby-Dick* (*London Mercury,* December, 1920). It is Mr. Watson's contention in this essay, that the *Pequod,* with her monomaniac captain and all her crew, is representative of Melville's own genius, and in the particular sense that each character is deliberately symbolic of a complete and separate element. Because of the prodigal richness of material in *Moby-Dick,* the breadth and vitality and solid substance of the setting of the allegory, the high quality of *Moby-Dick* as a psychological synthesis has very generally been lost sight of. Like Bunyan, or Swift, Melville has enforced his moral by giving an independent and ideal verisimilitude to its innocent and unconscious exponents. The self-sustaining vitality of Melville's symbols has been magnificently vouched for by Mr. Masefield in his vision of the final resurrection. And the superb irony—whether unconscious or intended—of *Moby-Dick's* "towing the ship our Lord was in, with all the sweet apostles aboard of her," would surely have delighted Melville. *Pilgrim's Progress* is undoubtedly a tract; but, as Brownell observes, if it had been only a tract, it would never have achieved universal canonisation. Both *Pilgrim's Progress* and *Moby-Dick* are works of art in themselves, each leaning lightly—though of course to all the more purpose—on its moral. Most persons probably read *Gulliver* for the story, and miss the satire. In the same way, a casual reader of *Moby-Dick* may skip the more transcendental passages and classify it as a book of adventure. It is indeed a book of adventure, but upon the highest plane of spiritual daring. Ahab is, of course, the atheistical captain of the tormented soul; and his crew, so Melville says, is "chiefly made of mongrel renegades, and cast-aways and cannibals." And Ahab is "morally enfeebled, also, by the incompetence of mere unaided virtue or rightmindedness in

Herman Melville: Mariner and Mystic (New York: George H. Doran Company, 1921) pp. 331–33. (By permission of Cooper Square Publishers, Inc.)

Starbuck, the invulnerable jollitry of indifference or recklessness of Stubb, and the pervading mediocrity of Flash." But Ahab is Captain; and his madness is of such a quality that the white whale and all that is there symbolised, needs must render its consummation, or its extinction. On the waste of the Pacific, ship after ship passes the *Pequod,* some well laden, others bearing awful tidings: yet all are sane. The *Pequod* alone, against contrary winds, sails on into that amazing calm, that extraordinary mildness, in which she is destroyed by *Moby-Dick.* "There is a wisdom that is woe, and there is a woe that is madness." And in *Moby-Dick,* the woe and the wisdom are mingled in the history of a soul's adventure.

Though *Moby-Dick* is not only an allegory, but an allegory designed to teach woeful wisdom, nowhere in literature, perhaps, can one find such uncompromising despair so genially and painlessly administered. Indeed, the despair of *Moby-Dick* is as popularly missed as is the vitriolic bitterness of *Gulliver.* There is an abundance of humour in *Moby-Dick,* of course: and there is mirth in much of the laughter. In *Moby-Dick,* it would appear, Melville has made pessimism a gay science. "Learn to laugh, my young friends," Nietzsche counsels, "if you are at all determined to remain pessimists." If there are tears, he smiles gallantly as he brushes them aside. "There are certain queer times and occasions in this strange mixed affair we call life," Melville says, "when a man takes this whole universe for a vast practical joke, though the wit thereof he but dimly discovers, and more than suspects that the joke is at nobody's expense but his own. There is nothing like the perils of whaling to breed this free and easy sort of genial, desperado philosophy; and with it I regard this whole voyage of the *Pequod,* and the great white whale its object." And for the most part, he does. But he declares, withal, that "the truest of all men was the Man of Sorrows, and the truest of all books is Solomon's, and Ecclesiastes is the fine hammered steel of woe. All is vanity. ALL." *Moby-Dick* was built upon a foundation of this wisdom, and this woe; and so keenly did Melville feel the poignancy of this woe, so isolated was he in his surrender to this wisdom, that this wisdom and this woe, which he had learned from Solomon and from Christ, he felt to be of that quality which in our cowardice we call madness.

From the Review of Raymond Weaver's
Herman Melville: Mariner and Mystic

J. ST. LOE STRACHEY

Before I leave the subject of Melville I should like to point out that the latest biographer of the great American does not seem to realize how strong the feeling about Melville has always been in England. I well remember some thirty years ago writing a review in the *Spectator* on a new edition of Melville's works which had just appeared. A reference thereto shows that a Melville boom was then proceeding. But this is not all. I remember that when my article appeared a lady of letters who could remember the 'fifties remarked to me that she was glad to see people were reading Melville again, and added: "I can't tell you how enthusiastic we all were, young and old, at the end of the 'forties and beginning of the 'fifties, over *Typee*, *Omoo*, and *Moby-Dick*. There was quite a furore over Melville in those days. All the young people worshipped him."

––––––––––

LINCOLN COLCORD [1883–1947], novelist, poet, and journalist and an associate editor of *The Nation*, 1919–20.

Notes on "Moby Dick"

LINCOLN COLCORD

I

Fresh from a second reading of Melville's "Moby Dick," I am surprised by the heterodoxy of certain strong impressions. It is a book which leads to violent convictions. I first read it as a boy, on shipboard, somewhere about the world; I was enthralled

The London *Spectator*, Vol. 128 (6 May 1922) 560.

Freeman, Vol. V (August 1922) 559–62, 585–87.

by the story, but beyond a keen sensation of pleasure I retained no definite recollection of it. Thus, upon a second reading, the book had for me all the delight of a new discovery. Again I was enthralled, this time by more than the story; by all the infernal power and movement of the piece, by that intangible quality which, through suggestion and stimulation, gives off the very essence of genius. I do not mean atmosphere—Conrad creates atmosphere—but something above atmosphere, the aura of sublime and tragic greatness; not light but illumination, the glance of a brooding and unappeasable god.

The art of "Moby Dick" as a masterpiece of fiction lies in the element of purposeful suspense which flows through the tale from beginning to end in a constantly swelling current; and in the accumulating grandeur and terror evoked by the whale-*motif*. This achievement which, like every such feat of genius, defies either description or criticism, is what makes the book superlatively great. Melville performs the most difficult task of literary creation—that of encompassing and fixing the vague form of a tremendous visionary conception.

The high-water mark of inspiration in the book is reached in the dramatic dialogue between Ahab and the carpenter over the making of the wooden leg. This scene is preceded by the finest piece of descriptive characterization in the volume, written in Melville's own style (not aped after Sir Thomas Browne): the sketch of the old ship-carpenter. Starting abruptly from the heights of this description, the dialogue soars straight to the realm of pure literary art. It is the equal of Shakespeare's best dialogue. One longs to hear it given by a couple of capable actors: the scene, the confusion of the "Pequod's" deck by night on the whaling-grounds; the lurid flame of the smithy in the background, in the foreground the old bewhiskered carpenter planing away at Ahab's ivory leg; before the footlights an audience familiar with the book, or, lacking this, any intelligent audience, the want of special knowledge being supplied by a plain prologue. The scene exactly as it stands is magnificently dramatic.

This, however, is a burst of inspiration. The ablest piece of sustained writing in "Moby Dick" unquestionably is the extraordinary chapter on "The Whiteness of the Whale." Here we have a *tour de force* without excuse in the narrative, a mere joyous rush of exhilaration and power, a throwing out of the arms with a laugh and a flash of the eye. "The Whiteness of the Whale," I said to myself, as I came to this chapter; "what the devil have we now?" I feared that Melville would exceed his licence, that he might be going to strain the case a little. For it seemed an inconsequential heading for a chapter; and when I ran over the leaves, noting how long the effort was, my heart misgave me. But before a page is finished, the reader catches the idea and perceives the masterliness of the attack. Through-out the chapter, as one watches the author play with his theme, letting it rise and fall naturally (nothing is ever still that comes from Melville's hand—even his calms shimmer and shake with an intensity of heat); as one follows this magically dexterous exercise, all of which, apart from its intrinsic beauty, contributes in some ineffable manner to the charm and mystery of the tale; one is aware of the thrill which comes but seldom in a lifetime of reading.

As a piece of sheer writing, this chapter on the whiteness of the whale is a remarkable achievement. Its creator could do anything with words. I wonder that it has not been more com-monly utilized in the higher teaching of English; I know of no effort in the language which affords a better study of what can be accomplished by the magic of literary power.

II

"Moby Dick" stands as one of the great nautical books of the world's literature. What I have to say of it on this score, therefore, may to Melville's public, which is almost exclusively a shore-public, appear to be malicious heresy. But I am con-cerned only with establishing what seems to me an interesting verity; I want to find the real Melville, because he is so well worth finding; I would not be engaged in criticism had I not first become engaged in love and admiration.

I am surprised, when all is said and done, to find how little of real nautical substance there is in "Moby Dick." It would not be overstating the case to say that the book lacks the final touch of nautical verisimilitude. In criticizing the book from this viewpoint, one must, of course, make due allowance for the refining and rarifying influence of the imaginative pitch to which the whole work is cast; an influence which naturally tends to

destroy a share of nautical realism, as, indeed, it tends to destroy all realism. Yet, when this allowance is made, there remains in "Moby Dick" a certain void, difficult of estimate or
description, where the shadows, at least, of nautical reality
should stand.

This void, of course, appears only to the sailor who reads
the book; no one else would notice it. It is not that the book
lacks the framework of nautical reality; it would be idle for me
to attempt to deny what plainly exists. "Moby Dick," indeed,
is in the generic sense of the term a nautical piece; it is a tale
of ships, sailing, and the sea. We have a view of the "Pequod,"
of certain seafaring scenes and operations; we have a picture of
the business of whaling, the handling of boats, the cutting in of
the great fish alongside the ship, the final labours on deck and
in the hold; we have a general background of nautical affairs, so
that the scenes inevitably stand out against a tracery of sails,
clouds, horizon and sea; and all this is correctly written, from
the nautical standpoint, save in a few insignificant particulars.
Melville's treatment of the whaling-industry, in fact, is classic.
No one else has done such work, and no one ever will do it
again; it alone serves to rescue from oblivion one of the most
extraordinary episodes of human enterprise.

But this fidelity to the business of whaling is not precisely
what I mean by nautical verisimilitude. How, then, shall I define the lack of this verisimilitude which I find in "Moby Dick"?
Shall I put it that there is not quite enough of sure detail, in
any instance where a nautical scene or evolution is described,
to convince the sailor-reader that the man who wrote the words
understood with full instinctive knowledge what he was writing
about? A sailor, a seaman in the real sense of the word, would
involuntarily have followed so closely the scene or evolution in
hand, that he could not have fallen short of the final touch of
realism; he would himself have been a part of the picture, he
would quite unconsciously have written from that point of view,
and the added colour and particularity, in the case of "Moby
Dick," far from detracting from the strength and purpose of
the work, would on the contrary have considerably augmented
them.

Melville, quite unconsciously, did not write the book that
way. To his eye, indeed, it plainly was not so much a nautical

work as it was a study in the boundless realm of human psychology. Yet, having taken the sea for his background, he could not have failed, had he been a sailor, to fill the void I mention. From this one gets a measure of Melville's spiritual relation to seafaring.

Most mysteries submit to a simple explanation; they are no mysteries at all. In the present case, a closer view of seafaring alone is needed. All Melville's seafaring experience lay before the mast. He gives no indication that he was in the least degree interested in this experience as a romantic profession; he speaks of obeying orders, admitting that those who commanded his activities on the sea had a right to require him to do anything under the sun; but I have never seen a passage in which he celebrated the task of learning to be a good seaman—except as a piece of extraneous description—or one showing the slightest interest in the sea professionally. He was decidedly not looking towards the quarter-deck. When afloat, he seems simply to have been mooning around the vessel, indulging his fancy to the full, chiefly observing human nature; realistically intent on the ship's company, but merely romanticizing over the ship herself; in short, not making any advance towards becoming himself a sailor, towards the acquisition of those instinctive reactions which make man and ship dual parts of the same entity.

I would not be thought so absurd as to blame Melville for not becoming a true sailor; I am merely trying to run the fact to earth. He was divinely inefficient as a seaman; he never learned the lore of a ship, beyond attaining the necessary familiarity with her external parts, with the execution of simple commands, and with the broader features of her control and operation. His nautical psychology was that of the forecastle, the psychology of obeying orders. For months on end, at sea, he felt no curiosity to know where the ship was or whither she was going; he never understood exactly why she was made to perform certain evolutions; he helped to execute the order, and watched the result with a mild and romantic perplexity. The psychology of the quarter-deck, the psychology of handling a vessel, was foreign to him.

This is why his nautical atmosphere is made up of relatively unimportant details and insignificant evolutions, such as a green man before the mast would have compassed; while infinitely more important details and more significant evolutions, and the grasp of the whole ship as a reality, all of which would have been in the direct line of the narrative, and would only have intensified the effect he was striving to produce, were passed over in silence because they were beyond his ken. He might have made the ship, as well as the whale, contribute to the mysterious grandeur of the book's main theme; in no single instance does he attempt to do so. The "Pequod," to all intents and purposes, is a toy ship; when, indeed, she is not a ship nautically fictitious, a land-lubber's ship, a ship doing the impossible.

If Captain Ahab says "Brace the yards!" once, he says it a hundred times; whereas there are dozens of commands that he might have shouted with stronger effect, both realistic and literary; whereas, furthermore, the order to "brace the yards" means nothing in particular, without a qualifying direction, and never would be given in this incomplete form on a ship's deck. This is a minor instance; but the sum of these nautical ineptitudes throughout the book is fairly staggering.

To cite a major instance, the account of the typhoon off the coast of Japan is a sad failure; it might have been written by one of your Parisian arm-chair romanticists, with a knowledge of the sea derived from a bathing-beach experience. The ship is an imaginary piece of mechanism; no coherent sense of the storm itself is created; no realization of the behaviour of a vessel in a typhoon runs behind the pen. Ahab's battered quadrant, thrown to the deck and trampled on the day before, is allowed to come through the storm reposing as it fell, so that his eye may be caught by it there when the weather has cleared. In fact, both as a piece of writing and as an essential of the tale, the scene wholly fails to justify itself. It serves no apparent purpose; it seems to have been lugged in by the ears.

How a man with an experience of some years on the sea, a man who could write the superlative chapter on the whiteness of the whale, should fail so completely to present an adequate or even an understanding picture of a ship beset by a heavy circular storm—here is a mystery not so easy of solution. It would seem to be plainly evident that Melville had never passed through a typhoon, and never, probably, had been on the Japan whaling-grounds. But he must have seen plenty of storms at sea. With all his passionate descriptive power, however, he is strangely handicapped when he comes to imagine a scene beyond the range of his experience; his literary equipment did not readily lend itself to the translation of an imaginative picture in terms of reality.

Certainly Melville had in his blood none of the "feeling of the sea," that subtle reaction which is the secret animating spring of the real sailor. Romantic appreciation he had, and imaginative sentiment; but these must never be confounded with seamanship. Yet, in defence of his nautical laxity in the latter half of "Moby Dick," it should be recognized that, by the time he had reached these chapters, he must have been exhausted with the intensity of the emotional effort; and that, after juggling with forms for two-thirds of the volume, he had now definitely forsaken all attempts at realism. Ahab alone would have worn out an ordinary man in short order.

III

I do not remember having seen in print a discussion of the extraordinary technical development of "Moby Dick." In terms of the craft of writing, the book is a surpassing feat of legerdemain. Briefly, "Moby Dick" is the only piece of fiction I know of, which at one and the same time is written in the first and the third persons. It opens straightforwardly as first-person narration. "Call me Ishmael"—"I thought I would sail about a little"—"I stuffed a shirt or two into my carpet bag, tucked it under my arm, and started for Cape Horn and the Pacific." So it runs throughout the opening scenes in New Bedford and Nantucket; the characters are real persons, seen through Ishmael's eyes; they speak real speech; the scenes are delineated with subjective realism. Melville is telling a story. His (or Ishmael's) meeting with Queequeg, and their first night together in the big feather bed at the Spouter Inn, are intensely human and alive. Even Bildad and Peleg are creations of realism. The first note of fancifulness is introduced with the Ancient Mariner who accosts Ishmael and Queequeg on the pier in Nantucket. The book, however, still holds to the technical channel of first person narration; and it is through Ishmael's eyes that one sees the "Pequod" sail from Nantucket.

Then, without warning, the narrative in Chapter twenty-nine jumps from the first to the third person; begins to relate conversations which could not possibly have been overheard by Ishmael and to describe scenes which his eye could not possibly have seen; follows Ahab into his cabin and Starbuck into the recesses of his mind, and launches boldly on that sea of mystical soliloquy and fanciful unreality across which it sweeps for the remainder of the tale. As it progresses, Ishmael sinks farther and farther from sight, and the all-seeing eye of the third person comes more and more into play.

Yet, even at this stage, the technical form of first-person narration is not entirely abandoned; is kept along, as it were, like an attenuated wraith. As the "Pequod" sights ship after ship, the narrative momentarily reappears, only to be discarded once more at the first opportunity; so that, of the main body of the book, it may truly be said that it is written in both the first and the third persons. For instance, chapter ninety-one, "The 'Pequod' Meets the 'Rosebud'": "It was a week or two after the last whaling-scene recounted, and when we [not they] were slowly sailing over a sleepy, vapoury, midday sea. . . ." This is a recurrence to first person narration in the midst of pages of third-person soliloquy. But turning to Chapter CXXVIII, "The 'Pequod' Meets the 'Rachel'": "Next day, a large ship, the 'Rachel,' was descried, bearing directly down upon the 'Pequod,' all her spars thickly clustering with men"—this might be either first or third person; the context shows it to be the latter. Ishmael has been definitely forsaken, and hereafter remains in abeyance until the end of the book; when, suddenly, he re-emerges in the epilogue.

The quarrel between the persons, however, does not by any means comprise the whole technical irregularity of "Moby Dick." There is the introduction of the form of dramatic dialogue; an innovation singularly successful, and remarkably in keeping both with the mood of the moment when it is introduced and with the general tone of mystical formlessness pervading the whole work. There is the adroit suspending of the narrative by those absorbing chapters of plain exposition, descriptive of whales and whaling; the gradual revealing of the secrets of the whale, while the final nameless secret is withheld, while fancy and terror feed and grow on suspense. There is the totally ideal development of the characterization, as Ahab and Starbuck and Stubbs and all the rest indulge themselves in the most high-flown and recondite reflections and soliloquies. Finally, there is the bizarre method of chaptering—each chapter a little sketch, each incident having its own chapter; some of the chapters only half a page in length, others a page or two; a hundred and thirty-five chapters in all, together with forewords on etymology and extracts, and an epilogue. In short, "Moby Dick" as a technical exercise is utterly fantastic and original. Melville has departed from every known form of composition; or rather, he has jumbled many forms into a new relation, choosing among them as fancy dictated.

It is safe to say that no literary craftsman of the present day would so much as dream of attempting the experiment which "Moby Dick" discloses on its technical side. Such an attempt would be answered by both critics and public with the ostracism which modern Western culture reserves for irregularity. Here we have a striking commentary on the rigidity of our present literary technique; a technique which rules style and matter, and dominates the literary field, as never before. We speak of ourselves as individualists, freely developing new forms; we like to regard the period of 1840 as a time of stilted and circumscribed literary expression. Yet the truth of the matter seems to be quite otherwise. We are slaves to the success of a literary convention, while the writers of 1840 were relatively free. I am not aware that "Moby Dick" was received at the time of its publication with any degree of surprise at its technical form, whatever surprise or opposition may have been called forth by its content. Neither am I aware that Melville himself felt that he was doing an extraordinary thing in adopting a unique but natural technical form for the expression of an original creative effort. His letters to Hawthorne during the composition of "Moby Dick" betray no self-consciousness on this score. In fact, he seems to have retained a perfectly free relation with his technical medium.

IV

The exhaustion in the latter part of "Moby Dick," of which I have already spoken, seems to me to become startlingly apparent at the crisis of the book, which is reached in the last chapter. Cavilous as the criticism may sound from the viewpoint of a broader appreciation, I sincerely feel that Melville failed to reap in his crisis all that he had sown throughout the body of the tale. The chase of the white whale is splendid; in the daily fight between Ahab and this sinister embodiment of evil Melville is at his best, everything goes magnificently up to the very last; but the final attack of Moby Dick on the ship, and the sinking of the "Pequod" with all her company, are inadequate to the point of anti-climax.

There should have been a more generous descriptive effort at this pass; Melville could picture a scene superbly, and he should have spared no pains to do it here. He seems instead to have adopted an affectation of simplicity. He will rest on his oars now, let the momentum of the book carry it forward, allow the various lines of suspense and horror to culminate of their own accord; in fine, he will sketch the winding up of the piece, leaving the actual descriptive effort to the reader's imagination.

But in this he made a critical error; while it is a fine thing to utilize the reader's imagination, it is disastrous to tax it too far. The last pages of "Moby Dick" do not give us the ending for which we have been prepared; which, with the keenest anticipation, we have been awaiting. Having created such intense suspense, Melville was under the imperative obligation to provide for its satisfaction a flash of equally intense realism. The imagination, having too readily devoured the feast that he has set forth, and finding its hunger only increased thereby, is suddenly let down and disappointed. In this unhappy, defrauded state, it fastens upon the first thing at hand, which is the catastrophe itself; recognizing at once the fantastic nature of that complete oblivion which so causelessly descends on the "Pequod" and her company. For, as a matter of sober fact, a ship of her size would not, in sinking, have drawn down into her vortex an agile cat, much less a crew of whalers, used to being pitched out of boats in the open sea, and surrounded with quantities of dunnage for them to ride when the decks had gone from under.

Turning to the last chapter of "Moby Dick," one may note that it contains but a brief paragraph describing the whale's frantic attack on the vessel. No horror is created, no suspense, no feverish excitement. It is another of art's vanished opportunities. There should have been a close-packed page or two of tumultuous visualization; then, with the gigantic whale dashing head-on toward the devoted "Pequod," a pause in the narrative, to let suspense rankle, while a few paragraphs were occupied with a dissertation on the sinking of vessels—not the sinking of vessels by whales, which matter has already been examined, but the sinking of vessels; about how difficult, how unusual, it would be for a ship to carry her whole company beneath the waves; about Starbuck's knowledge of this fact; about their frantic preparations for escape—then, loosing every ounce of reserve literary power, a description of the crash, the catastrophe, the peculiar and malignant combination of circumstances, easily to be imagined, which, in spite of common experience, did actually destroy this whole ship's company. The whale should have dashed among the debris and floating men, after the ship had gone down, to complete the work of destruction. The scene should have been cast in the form of first-person narration, and Ishmael should have been near enough to see it all. (He was adrift, it will be remembered, and did not go down with the vessel; but the return to the first person is reserved for the epilogue, while the crisis of the story is told in an especially vague form of the third person.) We should have been given a final view of the white whale, triumphantly leaving the scene and resuming the interrupted course of his destiny. In short, there are dozens of strokes of realism neglected in this chapter which plainly demand to be driven home.

Melville chose to end the book on a note of transcendentalism; he himself does not seem to have visualized the scene at all. The influence of Hawthorne, one suspects, was largely responsible for this grave error. Hawthorne was living just over the hill in the Berkshires that summer. The intense and lonely Melville had fallen under his fascination; he thought that he had at last found a friend. He was captivated, also, by that vague imaginative method of thought and style out of which Hawthorne wove his tales; and, quite naturally, his own work reflected this influence. For Melville was that man of genius known as the passionate hunter; he was the taster of all sensations, the searcher of all experience, the sampler of every form and style. And, as so often happens with such people, it was his tragic fate never entirely to find himself. The secret quarry of life constantly eluded him.

The influence of Hawthorne is painfully evident throughout the last two-thirds of "Moby Dick"; painfully evident, because it is so incongruous with Melville's natural manner which is that of narrative realism; he must be there in person—he makes the scene alive with amazing vitality where he stands. In the same sense, his natural power of characterization is in the descriptive or analytical field; I am not aware that he has ever put into the mouth of a single character a realistic speech. Wherever, in "Moby Dick," he gets his best effects, he gets them through the exercise of his natural manner. Certain scenes stand out vividly. Certain pages of analytical characterization are instinct with truth and greatness. The natural impulse keeps bursting through. But the bulk of the characterization is cast in a method artificial to him; he constantly tries to raise the pitch of the tale, to inflate the value of the words. Too much of the descriptive matter likewise is forced through unnatural channels, losing the air of mastery in its adaptation to the less vigorous form of the third person.

Thus the book, in its composition, represents a struggle between realism and mysticism, between a natural and an artificial manner. It begins naturally, it ends artificially. This in a measure explains the strange confusion of the technique, the extravagant use of the two separate persons. Only the most extraordinary creative power could have struck art and achievement from such an alien blend.

What, then, of the allegory?—for we are told that "Moby Dick" is a masterpiece of this form of composition. I must confess that I did not follow the allegory closely, and did not find that it was forced on my attention; and now that I look back on the book, I fail exactly to see wherein it lies. What, for instance, does Ahab represent, and what the white whale? I am not certain that Melville meant the story to be an allegory. In fact, does he not somewhere fiercely disclaim the imputation? But it is the fate of all work done in the manner of transcendentalism to land sooner or later in the rarified atmosphere of allegory, whether it means anything or not, whether or not the allegory seems to point anywhere in particular. Transcendentalism is the stuff of allegory. Melville hated allegory, and would have hated transcendentalism, had he not just then happened to come under the influence of a transcendentalist. This put him in a bad fix, and made him, whether he willed it or not, write a book which looked like allegory. Do we need a better explanation of his turning so fiercely against the imputation?

Not because of its allegorical significance, and not, indeed, because of its mysticism, considered as a thing apart, does this book of the chase of the white whale live among the immortal works of literature; but rather because of its irrepressible triumph of realism over mysticism, because of the inspired and gripping story that builds itself up out of a passionate flow of words. For my part, I like Ahab as Ahab, not as a symbol of something or other; and Ahab lives as Ahab, marvellously enough, in spite of the wild unreality of his constant meditations and ebullitions. Yes, and because of it; the overshadowing demoniac terror of the story lends reality to unreality, charm and substance to mystical formlessness. This is the mark of genius in the creator. Yet even genius may carry things too far; Ahab manages to live as Ahab, but Starbuck—well Starbuck struts and swells a little, betrayed by an overdose of transcendentalism.

v

If I have seemed to wish that "Moby Dick" had been written in the form of unalloyed narrative realism, that Melville had left off altogether his dalliance with transcendentalism, I would correct the impression now. As a piece of pure realism, the book obviously would not have been the inspired achievement that it is in its present form. The creative struggle that Melville was undergoing at the time of its composition was the intensifying medium through which the work rose to superlative heights. The chapters flow easily, as though he did not realize their duality of form and temper, but felt them to be parts of a unified, continuous product; but the grievous battle taking place within him caused him to produce what actually are gigantic fragments, struck from mountains of fire and anguish, which slowly and ponderously arrange themselves into the delineation of a majestic idea.

"Moby Dick" is not the allegory of Ahab's struggle with destiny; it is rather the story of Melville's struggle with art and life. Without this struggle, there would have been no agonizing greatness; only another "Typee," a splendid tale, a perfect example of literary realism. But, given the struggle, there had to be from page to page this singular conflict in style and form and matter, the confused, reflected gleams of a hidden conflagration; so that to wish the conflict away would be to wish away the book's divinity.

ARNOLD BENNETT [1867–1931], the English novelist, made his reputation as a master in fiction with *The Old Wives' Tale* and the *Clayhanger* series.

Pierre

ARNOLD BENNETT

My second important large work [the first was Dreiser's *An American Tragedy*] read this year is Herman Melville's *Pierre*, which ought to be issued separately—at present it can only be had in the standard edition of Melville's works in heaven knows how many volumes. Melville was once famous as the author of those rather second-class (at any rate as bowdlerized for print) South Sea romances, *Typee* and *Omoo*. Then, much later, he became known as the author of *Moby Dick*—a great novel. He may still later become famous as the author of *Pierre*.

Pierre is transcendental, even mystical, in spirit. The basic idea of its plot is entitled to be called unpleasant. It contains superb writing, and also grotesque writing, which its author mistakenly thought to be superb. It is full of lyrical beauty which the veriest sentimentalist could not possibly confuse with ugliness. It is conceived in an heroical, epical vein, and executed (faultily) in the grand manner. It has marked originality. In it the author essays feats which the most advanced novelists of to-day imagine to be quite new.

Melville was an exalted genius. *Pierre*, though long, is shorter than *An American Tragedy;* but it is even more difficult to read. I recommend it exclusively to the adventurous and the fearless. These, if the book does not defeat them, will rise up, after recovering from their exhaustion, and thank me. I intend to pursue my researches into Herman Melville.

The Savor of Life: Essays in Gusto (Garden City: Doubleday, Doran & Company, Inc., 1928), pp. 305–7. (Reprinted by permission of the publisher, Mrs. Cheston Bennett, and Cassell & Co. Ltd.)

LEWIS MUMFORD [1895–   ] is an influential American critic of literature and the arts whose books include *Sticks and Stones, The Brown Decades,* and *The Culture of Cities.*

Moby-Dick

LEWIS MUMFORD

It is absurd and ineffectual to give a summary of Moby-Dick, or to quote, dismembered, some of its great passages. Like the paintings in the Ajanta caves, the beauty of Moby-Dick can be known only to those who will make a pilgrimage to it, and stay within its dark confines until what is darkness has become light, and one can make out, with the help of an occasional torch, its grand design, its complicated arabesque, the minute significance of its parts. No feeble pencil sketch can convey a notion of Moby-Dick's extravagant beauty; but at the same time, without a hint of its design and its manner of execution, all subsequent commentary must seem flatulent and disproportionate. For three-quarters of a century Moby-Dick has suffered at the hands of the superficial critic: it has been condemned because to one man it seemed confused, to another it was not a novel, to a third the characters were not "real," and to a fourth it was merely a weird, mystical, impossible tale of dubious veracity, an example of Bedlam literature, while to a fifth, it was just a straightforward account of the whaling industry, marred by a crazy captain and an adventitious plot. The final answer to all these criticisms lies, of course, in the book itself: but the foregoing outline will perhaps aid us a little in defining the qualities and limits of Melville's vast epic.

Before we can take the measure of Moby-Dick we must, however, throw aside our ordinary measuring-sticks: one does not measure Saturn with the aid of an opera-glass and a dressmaker's tape. The conventional critic has dismissed Moby-Dick because it is "not a novel," or if it is a novel, its story is marred by all sorts of extraneous material, history, natural history, philosophy, mythological excursions, what not. This sort of criticism

Herman Melville (New York: Harcourt, Brace and Company, Inc., 1929), pp. 176–81, 193–95. Copyright 1957 by Lewis Mumford. By permission of the publishers and of Martin Secker & Warburg Ltd.)

would belittle Moby-Dick by showing that it does not respect canons of a much pettier nature than the work itself, or because its colossal bulk cannot be caught in the herring-net of the commonplace story or romance. Even Mr. John Freeman, one of the most sympathetic interpreters of Melville, falls into this error; for while acknowledging the great qualities of Moby-Dick, he refers to its "digressions and delays" as if they were in fact digressions and delays; that is, as if the "action" in the common novelist's development of plot carried the thread of the story.

The matter is very easily put to rights if we simply abandon these false categories altogether. Moby-Dick stands by itself as complete as the Divine Comedy or the Odyssey stands by itself. Benedetto Croce has correctly taught us that every work of art is indeed in this same position: that it is uniquely what it is, and cannot be understood except in terms of its own purpose. If, for purely practical reasons, we ignore this in dealing with the ruck of novels and stories, because their inner purpose is so insignificant, we must respect it strictly when we confront a work that does not conspicuously conform to the established canons; for, needless to say, an imaginative work of the first rank will disclose itself through its differences and its departures, by what it originates, rather than by what it is derived from or akin to. Had Melville seriously sought in Moby-Dick to rival the work of Trollope or Reade or Dickens, had he simply desired to amuse and edify the great bourgeois public that consumed its three-decker novels as it consumed its ten-course public dinners, and wanted no delay in the service, no hitch in the round of food, drink, toasts, speeches, and above all, no unaccustomed victuals on such occasions, then Moby-Dick would have been a mistake and failure. But one cannot count as a failure what was never an attempt. Moby-Dick does not belong to this comfortable bourgeois world, any more than horse-hair shirts or long fasts; it neither aids digestion nor increases the sense of warm drowsy good nature that leads finally to bed: and that is all there is to it.

The same criticism that disposes of the notion that Moby-Dick is a bad novel, by admitting freely that it is not a novel at all, equally disposes of its lack of verisimilitude. Although Melville was at first challenged on his facts, such as the ramming of the Pequod by Moby-Dick, events were just as kind to his reputation here as they were in the case of Typee: for while Moby-Dick was on the press, news came of the sinking of the whaler Ann Alexander by the ferocious attack of a whale. No one of authority has attempted to quarrel with Melville's descriptions of the life and habits of whalemen and the whale: the testimony of every observer is that Melville left very little for any one else to say about the subject. This does not, however, dispose of the charge; for those who are wisely captious of Melville here will confine themselves to saying that no such crew ever existed, no such words ever passed human mouth, and no such thoughts could enter the mind of a Nantucketer, as entered Ahab's.

Again, one is tempted to grant the objection; for it makes no difference in the value of Moby-Dick as a work of art. In the realistic convention, Moby-Dick would be a bad book: it happens that the story is projected on more than one plane, and a good part of it belongs to another, and equally valid, convention. Melville himself was aware of the difference, and early in the book he calls upon the Spirit of Equality, which has spread its royal mantle of humanity over all his kind, to defend him against all mortal critics "if, then, to the meanest mariners, and renegades, and castaways, I shall hereafter ascribe high qualities, though dark; weave round them tragic graces; if even the most mournful, perchance the most abased among them all shall at times lift himself to the exalted mounts; if I shall touch that workman's arm with some ethereal light; if I shall spread the rainbow over his disastrous set of sun." Now, the convention in which Melville cast this part of Moby-Dick was foreign to the nineteenth century; obscure people, like Beddoes, alone essayed it: to create these idealized figures called for such reserves of power that only minor poets, for the most part, unconscious of their weaknesses, attempted the task.

The objections to Melville's use of this convention would be fair enough if, like the minor poets, he failed; but, through his success, one sees that the limitations of naturalism are no closer to reality than the limitations of poetic tragedy; and, on the contrary, Melville's valiant use of this convention enabled him to present a much fuller picture of reality than the purely external suggestions of current realism would have permitted him to show. What we call realism is a method of approaching reality: an external picture of a Cowperwood or a Gantry may have as little human truth in it as a purely fanciful description of an elf: and the artist who can draw upon more than one convention is, at all events, free from the curious illusion, so common in the nineteenth century, alike in philosophy, with its pragmatism in science, with its dogmatic materialism, and in imaginative writing, with its realism, that this convention is not limited, and so far arbitrary, but the very stuff and vitals of existence. The question to settle is not: Did an Ahab ever sail from Nantucket? The question is: Do Ahab and Stubb and Starbuck and Tashtego live within the sphere where we find them? The answer is that they are tremendously alive; for they are aspects of the spirit of man. At each utterance, one feels more keenly their imaginative embodiment; so that by the time Ahab breaks into his loftiest Titanisms, one accepts his language, as one accepts his pride: they belong to the fibre and essence of the man. Ahab is a reality in relation to Moby-Dick; and when Melville projects him, he ceases to be incredible, because he is alive.

We need not concern ourselves particularly with those who look upon Moby-Dick solely as a sort of World's Almanac or Gazetteer of the Whaling Industry, unhappily marred by the highly seasoned enticements of the narrative. This criticism is, indeed, but the other side of the sort of objection I have disposed of; and it tells more about the limitations of the reader than it does about the quality of Moby-Dick. For the fact is that this book is a challenge and affront to all the habits of mind that typically prevailed in the nineteenth century, and still remain, almost unabated, among us: it comes out of a different world, and presupposes, for its acceptance, a more integrated life and consciousness than we have known or experienced, for the most part, these last three centuries. Moby-Dick is not Victorian; it is not Elizabethan; it is, rather, prophetic of another quality of life which Melville had experienced and had a fuller vision of in his own time—a quality that may again come into the world, when we seek to pass beyond the harassed specialisms which still hold and preoccupy so many of us. To fathom this quality of Melville's experience and imagination, we must look a little deeper into his myth and his manner of projecting it. What is its meaning? And first, in what manner is that meaning conveyed to us? . . .

Moby-Dick, then, is one of the first great mythologies to be created in the modern world, created, that is, out of the stuff of that world, its science, its exploration, its terrestrial daring, its concentration upon power and dominion over nature, and not out of ancient symbols, Prometheus, Endymion, Orestes, or mediaeval folk-legends, like Dr. Faustus. Moby-Dick lives imaginatively in the newly broken soil of our own life: its symbols, unlike Blake's original but mysterious figures, are direct and explicit: if the story is bedded in facts, the facts themselves are not lost in the further interpretation. Moby-Dick thus brings together the two dissevered halves of the modern world and the modern self—its positive, practical, scientific, externalized self, bent on conquest and knowledge, and its imaginative, ideal half, bent on the transposition of conflict into art, and power into humanity. This resolution is achieved in Moby-Dick itself: it is as if a Shakespeare and a Bacon, or, to use a more local metaphor, as if an Eakins and a Ryder, had collaborated on a single work of art, with a heightening of their several powers. The best handbook on whaling is also—I say this scrupulously—the best tragic epic of modern times and one of the fine poetic works of all time.

That is an achievement; and it is also a promise. Whitman went as far in his best poems, particularly in the Song of Myself; and, with quite another method, Tolstoy went as far in War and Peace, Dostoyevsky in the Brothers Karamazov; Hardy, less perfectly, approximated it perhaps in The Dynasts; but no one went further. It is one of the great peaks of the modern vision of life. "May God keep us," wrote Blake, "from single vision and Newton's sleep." We now perhaps see a little more clearly what Blake's enigmatic words mean. In Moby-Dick Melville achieved the deep integrity of that double vision which sees with both eyes—the scientific eye of actuality, and the illumined eye of imagination and dream.

I have dwelt for a little on some of the meanings of Moby-Dick; but this does not exhaust the matter. Each man will read into Moby-Dick the drama of his own experience and that of his contemporaries: Mr. D. H. Lawrence sees in the conflict a battle between the blood-consciousness of the white race and its own abstract intellect, which attempts to hunt and slay it: Mr. Percy Boynton sees in the whale all property and vested privilege, laming the spirit of man: Mr. Van Wyck Brooks has found in the white whale an image like that of Grendel in Beowulf, expressing the Northern consciousness of the hard fight against the elements; while for the disciple of Jung, the white whale is the symbol of the Unconscious, which torments man, and yet is the source of all his proudest efforts.

Each age, one may predict, will find its own symbols in Moby-Dick. Over that ocean the clouds will pass and change, and the ocean itself will mirror back those changes from its own depths. All these conscious interpretations, however, though they serve the book by approaching its deeper purpose, do not, cannot, quite penetrate the core of its reality. Moby-Dick has a meaning which cannot be derived or dissociated from the work itself. Like every great work of art, it summons up thoughts and feelings profounder than those to which it gives overt expression. It introduces one, sometimes by simple, bald means, to the depths of one's own experience. The book is not an answer, but a clue that must be carried further and worked out. The Sermon on the Mount has this quality. It does not answer all the difficult problems of morality, but it suggests a new point of view in facing them: it leads one who is sufficiently moved to follow through all the recesses of conduct which can be influenced by mildness, understanding, and love, but not otherwise. So with Moby-Dick: the book itself is greater than the fable it embodies, it foreshadows more than it actually reflects: as a work of art, Moby-Dick is part of a new integration of thought, a widening of the fringe of consciousness, a deepening of insight, through which the modern vision of life will finally be embodied.

The shadow cast by Moby-Dick throws into obscurity not merely the sand-hills, but likewise some of the mountains, of the last three centuries. Noting the extent of that shadow, one begins to suspect how high the mountain itself is, and how great its bulk, how durable its rock.

CESARE PAVESE [1908–50], Italian poet and novelist, became the foremost translator and interpreter of American literature in Italy. Among his principal books are *Dialogues with Leucò* and *House on the Hill*.

The Literary Whaler

CESARE PAVESE

The importance today of Herman Melville, the nineteenth-century writer who is only now returning to fame, can be condensed in a contrast; we, the descendants of the nineteenth century, have in our bones that taste for adventure, for the primitive, and for real life which is the aftermath of culture, freeing us from complications, providing a balm to the plague sores of decadence, to the diseases of civilization. The names of our heroes are still Rimbaud, Gauguin and Stevenson, while Herman Melville instead lived first through real adventures, through the primitive state. He was first a barbarian and then, later, he entered the world of culture and thought, bringing with him the sanity and balance he had acquired in the life he had been leading. It is clear that for some time we have been feeling a growing need for a return to barbarity. This can be seen from the increasing popularity of travel, of sport, of films and of jazz, from the interest in Negroes and from a hundred other signs which it seems banal to recall and which we label as anti-literary. All this is doubtless very fine. But it is the manner which offends. It seems to me that, in this anti-literary frenzy, there is a tendency towards a primitivism bordering on imbecility. Imbecility, or rather, weakness: it is cowardly to take refuge from the complications of life in an over-simplified paradise which, after all, is only another of the many refinements of civilization. I was wrong before: our hero is not Rimbaud, or Gauguin or Stevenson, it is the wreck of a man. Melville's ideal, on the other hand, is Ishmael, a sailor who can row half a day behind a whale with his illiterate companions, and then retire to a masthead to meditate on Plato.

It is not for nothing that Melville is a North American. We have much to learn in this connection from these newcomers

Sewanee Review (summer 1960), pp. 407–18. First published (in Italian) in*La Cultura*, January–March 1932.

in the field of culture, who have been held responsible by its defenders, not without justice, though without blame, for the return of our ideals to barbarism. The Americans for their part discovered how to re-invigorate culture, sieving it through primitive and actual experience, not like us, by substituting one term for another, but by enriching, modifying and strengthening literature through what is called life.

That a thought has no meaning unless it is thought by the whole man is an American concept, and this is the ideal toward which the whole of the literature of the United States, from Thoreau to Sherwood Anderson, either consciously or unconsciously aims. It created powerful individuals, passing a good many years in a barbarous state, living and absorbing, and then dedicating themselves to culture, and presenting the reality which they had known in thoughts and images that had something of the harmony we associate with the Greeks. This is a far cry from the artificial paradises situated at the ends of the earth in which our own fastidious neo-barbarians make their return to nature.

Herman Melville began life sickly and with a sense of isolation. He was scribbling when he was about nineteen. Then, suddenly, the sea: four years of wandering and companionship, whaling, the Marquesas, a woman, Tahiti, Japan, sperm whales, some reading, many dreams, Callao, Cape Horn; and in October, 1844, there turned up in Boston a complete man, sunburnt, experienced in human vices and human values. Melville was to say later, surrounded as he was by difficulties, melancholy, and sickness, that a fully developed gentleman is always robust and healthy. For these practical men are by no means as easy-going and superficial as might be expected. Almost all the North American writers who have brought this ideal of balance and serenity to literature worked in the midst of serious difficulties, of need and sickness. (Whitman is a typical example, paralyzed for almost twenty years, permanently on the rocks.) For this, too, contributed to their experience of reality, concentrating their thought, making them more intensely aware. The health of these men lay not only in their bodies but also in the vitality and purity of their spirits which outlasted physical well-being.

Nor was Melville, in the long literary career which began on the day he turned up in Boston, the prolific, fluent and rather superficial writer that we might expect of one who has travelled so much and among such exotic scenes. A number of his books were destined to be failures, despite his heroic struggles, even when, as is the case with *Mardi,* they are magnificent attempts, while others, like *Moby Dick* were rewritten and agonized over until they undermined his health. In this Melville was the brother of the many *barbarous* Americans who were indeed among the least easily satisfied and most refined craftsmen of the century.

Melville was a true Greek. Reading European evasions of literature makes you feel more literary than ever; you feel tiny, cerebral, effeminate; reading Melville, who was not ashamed to begin *Moby Dick,* his poem of barbarous life, with eight pages of quotations and to go on by discussing, quoting again, and being the man of letters, you expand your lungs, you enlarge your brain, you feel more alive and more of a man. And though *Moby Dick,* like Greek tragedy, may be dark and gloomy, yet the serenity and clarity of the chorus (Ishmael) is so great that you leave the theatre each time with a sense of increased vitality.

Herman Melville is therefore above all a man of letters and a thinker who began life as a whaler, a Robinson Crusoe, and a wanderer. A good example of his way of being primitive is to be seen in the fragments of *The Lusiad,* that hymn in praise of seafaring which the well-known and respected old sea-wolf, Jack Chase, used to quote to the most worthy of his comrades in moments of repose. It is the barbarian, the man who discovered the south seas in literature who writes:

> Ay, Camoens was a sailor once! Then, there's Falconer, whose "Shipwreck" will never founder, though he himself, poor fellow, was lost at sea in the *Aurora* frigate. Old Noah was the first sailor. And St. Paul, too, knew how to box the compass, my lad! mind you that chapter in Acts? I couldn't spin the yarn better myself. Were you ever in Malta? They called it Melita in the Apostle's day . . . There's Shelley, he was quite a sailor. Shelley—poor lad! . . . he was drowned in the Mediterranean, you know, near Leghorn . . . Trelawny was by at the burning; and he was an ocean-rover, too! Ay, and Byron helped put a piece of keel on the fire . . . And was not Byron a sailor? an amateur forecastle man . . . I say, White Jacket, d'ye mind me? there

never was a very great man yet who spent all his life inland . . . I'll swear Shakespeare was once a captain of the
forecastle. Do you mind the first scene in *The Tempest,*
White Jacket? . . . A snuff of the sea, my boy, is inspiration
. . . for, d'ye see, there's no gammon about the ocean; it
knocks the false keel right off a pretender's bows; it tells
him just what he is, and makes him feel it, too.

It is necessary to have a clear idea of what Melville's culture, the culture which plays so large a part in his works, consists
of. It would be a mistake to believe that this man had an
eighteenth-century training. For him, as for the whole literary
world of the United States between the years of 1830–1850
(Poe, Emerson, Hawthorne, Alcott, etc.) the eighteenth century, although very well known, had been left behind, at least
in its most typically eighteenth-century aspects. Benjamin Franklin no longer interested anyone except the patriots. The tastes
of this "golden age" are close to the tastes of the English poets
Coleridge, Keats, and Shelley; the great century for them is
the seventeenth century which includes a good half of the six-
teenth century as well. Yet, while Keats or Shelley were looking to the early seventeenth century mainly for a lyrical and
stylistic tradition, the North Americans, and Melville above all,
found deeper roots, not only in the memories of the historical
crises from which their colony originated, but in the need they
felt to recall the proud thirst for spiritual liberty, for the unknown and for the distant land which gave life and traditions
to this colony.

These New Englanders were great Bible readers (and, it
should be remembered, the authorized version dates from 1611).
In *Moby Dick* the Bible is to be felt at every step, not only in
the sound of the names of Ahab, Ishmael, Rachel, Jeroboam,
Bildad, Elijah and the rest, but in the constant presence of a
spirit of Puritan awe and severity, turning what might have been
a scientific tale of terror in the Poe tradition into a dark moral
tragedy, where the catastrophe is brought about not by human
or natural forces but by a monster known as the leviathan.

The curious fact is that Melville retained an unprejudiced
rationalistic attitude towards the Bible. In *Moby Dick* there is
a highly amusing chapter on "Jonah historically regarded." And
this is where the seventeenth century really comes in.

At the same time the lively tone of the new scientific and philosophic terminology which was in the process of formation, mixing together solemn Latinisms with nervous, almost vernacular, expressions of the new sensibility, is often re-echoed in the pages of the Puritan whaler. If I could be certain that he had read him, I should say that Melville took more from Giordano Bruno than from anyone. But these are thorny questions. In any case the writers with which he can most justifiably be connected are Rabelais and the Elizabethans, in whom the same love of catalogues, of verbal profusion and of *vivez joyeux* are present. At times Melville even reaches the point of introducing burlesque quotations. And the Elizabethans gave him the dazzling style, those thick-piled images, that love of contrasts which is however, in the end a mark of over facility of imagination. But the current at which Melville drank most deeply, which lies at the roots of all seventeenth-century thought, was Platonizing rationalism, especially the rationalism of the English essayists. Naturally, as with the Bible, he read Plato, and, I imagine, the Neoplatonists and the mystics, from beginning to end. But the historical guise in which these tendencies appeared to him was undoubtedly that of the English seventeenth century. Thomas Browne was not only his teacher of style, but his spiritual father, and the sentence of *Religio Medici* ". . . that this visible World is but a Picture of the invisible, wherein, as in a Pourtraict, things are not truely, but in equivocal shapes . . ." is not only to be found again in the epigraph to Coleridge's *Ballad of the Ancient Mariner*—another essential clue to the understanding of *Moby Dick*—but it returns once more in the latter work on the lips of Captain Ahab, who (mad though he was) belonged to the same philosophical school as the author. Now Thomas Browne, besides being a sort of mystic magician, is also a subtle rationalist, and puts forward certain arguments for the Christian religion that have led rigid doctrinaires to take him for a heretic or an atheist.

Such was Melville's attitude. In his early books about Polynesia—*Typee* (1846) and *Omoo* (1847)—and in *White Jacket* (1850), he is still a strong young man who loves the wind and the sun and the beautiful native girls and adventures with happy endings: he is, we might say, still unaware. But if you open *Mardi* (1848) and finally *Moby Dick* (1851) you find the wider experience of a man tortured by insoluble doubts, driving him, in *Mardi,* into curious allegorical confusions, and in *Moby Dick,* into a few exasperated declamations; but, above all, to a lucid and subtle investigation, to a scientific examination, meditation and continuous quotation, in order to solve the mystery.

Melville is no quack who makes use of a halo of mystery every time he wants to produce an effect and does not know what to say. He is one of the doubting Thomases who are to be found precisely in the seventeenth century. As the Apostles would not believe in the Resurrection, Melville in *Moby Dick* does not want to believe in the breathless phantom, one of the supernatural effects hinted at; he does not want to believe that Fedallah, the head of Ahab's Malays, has such an odor of brimstone about him; he does not want to believe in omens, and even tries to explain away the shoals which follow Ahab's boat by the fact that sharks prefer the flesh of Malays to any other. The mystery which remains in *Moby Dick:* the demonism of the universe, the conscious power which underlies natural destructive forces, the invisible world of which the visible is but a picture, this is a real mystery (given Melville's peculiar turn of thought) and a critic allowing rein to his imagination might say that the fate of Captain Ahab awaits whoever tries to solve this mystery.

The same fate awaited Melville when, in 1852, he attempted in *Pierre* with increased confidence the psychological analysis of the diseases of the world, which in 1848 he had attempted in a more muted form in *Mardi:* the contradictions of morals and the rigid barrier against which all inquirers are in the end brought up short. Given Melville's eyes, his culture, his training and experience, this "half of the world" had inevitably to remain a mystery. Such it remains in *Moby Dick* and it is for this that *Moby Dick* is a great work. All Melville's other books —excluding those he wrote in his youth which are not concerned with this problem, and some of his minor works, the stories of *The Encantadas* (1854) and *Benito Cereno* (1855)—fail more or less for this reason. In them the rational element might be said to kill the transcendental. A notable example, among others, is *The Confidence Man* (1857), a kind of human attempt to get to the bottom of humanity, for polemical and pessimistic ends, but which instead turns into long drawn out, confused and heavy satire.

And in *Mardi*—the symbolic tale of Taji's wanderings in search of a vague ideal, through a Polynesia transformed into a sad key map in which every name corresponds to a State or institution of the western world—the balance between the rational and transcendental elements essential to Melville's mature art is lost in the allegorical and philosophical vivisection of the "enigmas." And in spite of its setting in the South seas (the setting of *Typee* and *Omoo*), in spite of innumerable happy touches of satire, parody and philosophic dialogue, in spite of the elegance and precision of certain symbols, the book as a whole is a failure. But, as I said, there is the excuse that the growing pains of *Mardi* opened the way to *Moby Dick*.

There is no such excuse instead for *Pierre or The Ambiguities,* an attempt to prove psychologically that society and the universe are badly conceived, that even moral perfection cannot lead to good, that an act of abnegation (Pierre's marriage with his natural sister, to provide her with a home) becomes in the channels of society—and of life—a monstrosity, in the more than fraternal love of the two. It is the evil of the White Whale that Melville is trying to come to grips with in all these analyses, leaving no place for the supernatural and the mysterious. This results inevitably in lack of balance: the style becomes convulsive, the inspiration epileptic and fragmentary, the sense of proportion is lost and the few pages still cut to his old measure are bogged down in a swamp of big words, of false notes and supersubtleties, boring, but above all naïve. The book really looks as though it had been written by Ahab.

As with all great works, you never get to the end of *Moby Dick;* you discover new points of view, new meanings and new values.

I have already mentioned what seems to me to be the deepest meaning of the story, but in spite of this, how much the reader has still to learn from its austere legendary tone, from that style which, above and beyond its wealth of fantasy, is pregnant with strict moral thought. Or from the tense and solemn pace, accompanied at times by a mischievous smile, with which the chapters of realistic description, information, and discussion, proceed. But above all it is the constant sense of the enormous, of the superhuman, toward which the whole book converges, in a miracle of construction by which little by little the gay and puritanical atmosphere of the beginning and the learned atmosphere of the long explanations of the central passages are finally blended in a spirit of conscious and daring action which is almost mythical, as the name and fame of the White Whale, which only appears toward the end of the book, grow until they seem gigantic and occupy all places, all actions, and all thoughts.

There remain Melville's minor works, the first short works which were more strictly autobiographical: *Typee*, the primitive and idyllic life among the cannibals of the Marquesas; *Omoo*, wanderings among south sea islands, among colonials and natives; *White Jacket*, Melville's experience of service life on board a man-of-war, a deluge of figures, or sketches, a school for learning how to live, and what humanity is. And these, even for those who have not read them, can be seen to be barbarous books which the whaler, no longer a puritan but a pagan, might be expected to have written.

I have already quoted a passage from *White Jacket* which gives the measure of Melville's barbarism even in these books, but it can always be objected that *White Jacket* was written in 1850, after *Mardi*, that is to say, and that undeniably the Polynesia of his early books has a much naïver tone than the settings of the three novels discussed: *Mardi, Moby Dick* and *Pierre*. This, I might add, is particularly obvious in *Mardi;* though Yillah (the ideal woman the hero follows through the islands) is not only the Fayaway of *Typee*—innocence and primitive grace in flesh and blood—but is also a metaphysical symbol of these and other accompanying virtues; yet in the story with which the book opens the idyll with Yillah in the paradise of Mardi, and some later landscapes which shine among the allegories, still have the quiet unsophisticated tone of the best pages of *Typee* and *Omoo*. Now it is just this contrast between the two parts of *Mardi* which marks the difference between the Melville of the minor works and the Melville of *Moby Dick* and *Pierre*. The intrusion of new ideological concerns, in the guise of allegory, of baroque psychology or of mystery, was to be the ruin but also the glory of the future Melville. His minor works ignore the mystery of the universe, the so-called problem of the White Whale. In this way they avoid the dramatic failure of *Pierre*, but they are also cut off from the miracle of a *Moby Dick*.

Here lies the difference. But the spiritual relationship with the rest of his work is still to be found in the tone, which even in its simplicity is knowledgeably self-conscious, and for this the more dignified. The fascination of the three books, to return to the first direct impression they make, lies without doubt in the unbroken flow of their narrative, in the sparkle of wit, of carica-ture and of the joy of life, against a background of immense serenity, like the shimmer of the ocean they describe. But if we come to think of it, what is *Typee* but a continual comparison, made by a man with a completely western education, between certain trends and certain aberrations of his civilization and the living testimony of a civilization simpler, yet essentially more curious, not lacking, that is, in pure exhibitionism? And what are *Omoo* and *White Jacket* but a lively comedy, where judge Dante smiles in the best of health and spirits at his comrades, but underneath is different from them and on the islands of the archipelago holds learned communion with the doctor; or on the man-of-war, with Jack Chase (the Jack of Camoens): judg-ing, that is to say, everyone else, including the bigwigs, consul, captain, and Commodore, with the calm certainty of the man who has *studied?*

But I don't want to give the impression that Melville was a tremendous pedant, bent on instilling, under the guise of ad-venture, a modicum of dusty book learning. Simply it gives one pleasure to note how Melville, when writing, recalls and quotes the books he has read, measuring them, without humility, at their just value, and all the time with a half smile under his beard. In him this humorous tone of a man of learning at large on the ocean is, I might say, the epidermic layer of a system of thought which is extraordinarily deep and comprehensive. A paragraph of *Moby Dick* where, when the head of a sperm whale is fastened to the side of the *Pequod*, another of a Right whale is fixed in the course of the hunt to the other side, concludes with the following words:

> As before, the *Pequod* steeply leaned over towards the sperm-whale's head, now, by the counterpoise of both heads, she regained her even keel; though sorely strained, you may well believe. So, when on one side you hoist in Locke's head, you go over that way; but now, on the other

side, hoist in Kant's and you come back again; but in very poor plight. Thus, some minds for ever keep trimming boat. Oh, ye foolish! throw all these thunder-heads overboard, and then you will float light and right.

Finally Melville left collections of verses, written in his old age, or when he was growing old, poems with rhymes and rhythms. But what use could Melville, after writing *Moby Dick* and *The Encantadas* in prose, have for verse?

There is something in this which connects him with Walt Whitman. Melville had more in common with the sage of Camden than his rebellion against the small reality of his own time, his Anglo-Dutch parentage and his year of birth (and almost of death: 1819–91, –92). They are linked by slow disintegration in old age, in weariness and solitude, accompanied by the rather melancholy sight of literature which has become a habit, by the "garrulity" of these last years, which so desperately tries to repeat a note of the oceanic symphonies of their prime.

Walt Whitman was the more fortunate, for after the obstinate optimism of his creative years, he discovered in pain and delusion a fresh if shallow vein of poetry, of "celestial death," and of crepuscular resignation. Sad instead was the fate of Herman Melville, who had already expressed pain, the unknown beyond and nothingness in his great legend of the sea, and who now found himself at the end, worn out and empty, with nothing but an echo in his heart:

> . . . Summer and winter, and pleasure and pain
> And everything everywhere in God's reign,
> They end, and anon begin again:
> Wane and wax, wax and wane:
> Over and over and over again . . .
> . . . Since light and shade are equal set
> And all revolves, nor more ye know;
> Ah, why should tears the pale cheek fret
> For aught that waneth here below.
> Let go, let go!

Academic Recognition:
1938-67

WILLARD THORP [1899–   ] is Holmes professor of belles-lettres at Princeton University. Among his books are *A Southern Reader,* and *American Writing in the Twentieth Century.*   He is a coauthor of *The Literary History of the United States.*

The Trilogy: *Mardi, Moby-Dick, Pierre*

WILLARD THORP

With a slightly malicious smile Melville announced in the preface to *Mardi:* "Having published two narratives of voyages in the Pacific, which, in many quarters, were received with incredulity, the thought occurred to me of indeed writing a romance of Polynesian adventure, and publishing it as such; to see whether the fiction might not, possibly, be received for a verity: in some degree the reverse of my previous experience." But it was not simply a romance he had undertaken. "This thought was the germ of others, which have resulted in *Mardi,*" the preface continues. It was for the sake of uttering those "other thoughts" that *Mardi* was really written. It is the first of the three books, *Moby-Dick* and *Pierre* being the other two, where a theme arising from Melville's spiritual quest is merged with the ostensible story.

His ambition to be more than a spinner of yarns was formed, and the time had come to tell his readers, under the necessary guise of romance and allegory, what conclusions he had struggled toward in the realms of social and religious thought. The fictional device was simple but well-adapted to his ends. With a companion he would desert his ship, the *Arcturion,* and take to the open ocean. After a series of adventures not too improbable to be believed in, including the rescue, from a native priest, of Yillah, a mysterious and beautiful girl who supposed she had once lived in Oroolia, the Polynesian paradise, he would land on Odo and be received there as the demigod Taji, as Captain Cook had been received by the Hawaiians as Lono the war-god. To this point Melville introduced nothing which was not credible. He carefully makes Taji doubt the supernatural parts of

Herman Melville: Representative Selections (New York: American Book Co., 1938), pp. lxv–lxxxiv.

Yillah's story and seek a natural explanation of her history. After his setting forth on a tour of the islands of Mardi (the world) with King Media, marvelous scenes soon appear, but the accounts of the first three kingdoms visited contain only traces of satire. A reader might have traveled thus far with a growing belief that Melville was forcing him to take for fiction what might indeed be fact.[103]

Melville makes Taji and his companions visit a group of island-states whose names suggest they are modern countries in disguise. Their voyage allows him to give vent to his fermenting ideas on kingship, democracy, social revolution, the new plutocracy in England and America, imperialism, slavery, and nationalist war. In none of these nations do the travelers find a perfect commonwealth. The realms which are controlled by the church (Maramma) are no better, and in them, in addition, the ecclesiastical sins prevail. Pilgrims who are humble of heart, poor, and truth-seeking, are not wanted there.

In Serenia, at length, a Utopia is discovered where the ethics of Alma (Christ) form the constitution of the people.

---

[103] Actually Melville's fabulous islands do owe much to his memory of definite places in the South Seas, Hawaii in particular, and to his reading of the voyagers. No one seems to have noticed that the description of surfboard-riding in the chapter entitled "Rare Sport at Ohonoo" recalls what Melville had seen at Waikiki beach on Oahu and that the valley where the visitors feasted (Monlova) is really Manoa. There are many other passages which circumstantially refer to Hawaiian geography and history. Chapter XCII—"The God Keevi and the Precipice of Mondo"—describes, for instance, the cliff of the Pali over which, in 1795, the conquering invader Kamehameha drove scores of the defenders to their death on the rocks below. Melville seems also to have made some use of the Hawaiian folk-tales.

Melville's recourse to the voyage literature in writing *Mardi* is discussed in David Jaffé's "Some Sources of Melville's *Mardi*," *American Literature*, IX, 56–69. To indicate the way he transformed his originals, an example from Ellis's *Polynesian Researches* may be cited. In "The Tale of a Traveler" (I, 98) Samoa tells the marvelous story of how he once, in performing a trepanning operation on a wounded friend, replaced a portion of the injured brain with part of a pig's brain. Ellis reports the operation on hearsay: "It is also related, although I confess I can scarcely believe it, that on some occasions, when the brain has been injured as well as the bone, they have opened the skull, taken out the injured portion of the brain, and, having a pig ready, have killed it, taken out the pig's brains, put them in the man's head, and covered them up. They persist in stating that this has been done; but add, that the persons always became furious with madness, and died" (ed. of 1829, II, 277). Melville, with a characteristic twist, makes the patient survive for a time in a perverse-minded, piggish state.

Without priests, kings, or statutes to govern them, they dwell in peace under the Master.

> The Master's great command is Love; and here do all things wise, and all things good, unite. Love is all in all. The more we love, the more we know; and so reversed. Oro [God] we love; this isle; and our wide arms embrace all Mardi like its reef. How can we err, thus feeling? We hear loved Alma's pleading, prompting voice, in every breeze, in every leaf; we see his earnest eye in every star and flower.[104]

Babbalanja, the philosopher, greatly moved by a mystic vision, elects to stay among the Serenians, and tries to persuade Taji to stay with him. But the phantom of the blue firmament eyes and Golconda locks of Yillah, whose disappearance impelled him first to set out, lures Taji toward his doom of an endless quest.

How are we to interpret Taji's pursuit of the mysterious Yillah and the equally mysterious pursuit of Taji by the dark lady, Hautia? Beneath the symbolism of this myth Melville concealed the dualistic enigma which had begun to wrack his spirit. The theme here first announced is augmented in *Moby-Dick, Pierre,* and *Billy Budd*.

Melville, in the days since his homecoming, had wrestled with the chronic problems of philosophy. In *Mardi,* as he had done with his friends in conversation, he threshed over the old arguments for the proof of consciousness, the debate between necessity and free will, the problem of a sinful world and a righteous God, the question of the moral responsibility of the natural man. To us who in the course of a systematic education encounter these dilemmas first in the textbooks and are cognizant of all the traditional answers, these iterative passages in *Mardi* seem a little sophomoric. To Melville the ideas were new and the rehearsal of them helped to purge away the remnants of the Calvinistic orthodoxy of his upbringing.

What troubled him ceaselessly was to know whether a master key to all these teasing questions could ever be found. An urge, deep in his nature, compelled him to "grind away at the nut of the universe" though it crack his jaws. The Penulti-

---

[104] *Works,* IV, 370.

mate will not satisfy him; he must have the Ultimate. That he might be dragged asunder in the effort to reconcile heaven and earth and find the Absolute, he knew, as well as did his creature Babbalanja. In the conversion of Taji's companions to the way of life of the Serenians, Melville represents the inclination he often felt to content himself with the natural "theology in the grass and the flower," and to follow the promptings of the heart, supplemented by Christ's gospel. "Yet, alas! too often do I swing from these moorings." [105]

When Babbalanja is granted a vision of the Mardian Paradise he dares to ask there the question, "Why create the germs that sin and suffer, but to perish?"

> "That," breathed my guide, "is the last mystery which underlieth all the rest. Archangel may not fathom it; that makes of Oro the everlasting mystery he is; that to divulge, were to make equal to himself in knowledge all the souls that are; that mystery Oro guards; and none but him may know." [106]

This evasion contents Babbalanja. Taji it did not content. He would solve the mystery or pull down heaven. Leaving his companions behind he seizes the helm, eternity in his eye, and steers for the outer ocean.[107]

As with most great books into which the writer has poured his whole thought and energy, the reader can make of *Moby-*

---

[105] *Works*, IV, 126.

[106] *Ibid.*, 376.

[107] Melville's critics have identified Yillah and Hautia and their supplementary symbols in various ways. They are in fundamental agreement, however, since the general meaning is sufficiently clear. Plainly Yillah stands for the ultimate revelation. If she connotes happiness, as Homans contends ("The Dark Angel," *New England Quarterly*, V, 708), then the identification must mean happiness of a heavenly sort, something like the heavenly beauty of Spenser and the intellectual beauty of Shelley. As for Hautia, the dark charmer who entices Taji to her Circean island with the intimation that there he will find Yillah, the best I can suggest is that to Melville she represents whatever soul-deadening worldly lures impede the search for truth (she offers him "beauty, health, wealth, long life, and the last lost hope of man"). The symbol is given a theological cast from the suggestion of the theme of the fall of man and original sin which Melville introduces into the story of Hautia's ancestry (*Works*, IV, 385–386). We might be led to interpret Yillah's captivity in Hautia's bower as a simple allegory of truth's temporary subservience to evil, did we not know, from Melville's subsequent development of the Yillah-Hautia dualism, that he had in mind the ambiguity of the moral universe and the inextricability of good and evil.

Dick pretty much what he pleases. He can read it as the most thrilling of sea stories which at the same time far outranks the sober works of Beale and Cheever in presenting a definitive account of the short-lived whaling industry that brought fabulous wealth to New England in the 1840's. To some it epitomizes the romantic generation's "pursuit of death." For others it records the experience, which Melville was not the only man of the century to endure, of the clash of a transcendental optimism with the new realistic perception of the natural world, which would culminate in the end of the century in the "capricious sub-rational fatalism" of such men as Hardy and Housman. It is also Melville's *Anatomy of Melancholy*, large enough in scope to allow him to include within its covers the strange miscellaneous lore, that he, like the seventeenth-century "Democritus" whom he loved, gathered in from the remotest sources. These various elements he fused together into an artistic performance whose skill his admirers, though they prized the book for other excellencies, have been late in recognizing. Even Van Wyck Brooks had to look a second time before he observed the "careful disorderliness" of his method and the accelerations of the rhythm when the voyage begins which portend the fate that will overwhelm the mad Ahab and his crew.[108]

What we are more particularly concerned with here is the place of *Moby-Dick* in Melville's quest for the Ultimate. When *Mardi* ended, Taji held the prow toward the open sea and the realm of shades that harbors Yillah. The action of *Moby-Dick* begins when Ahab, whose "quenchless feud," Melville declares, "seemed mine,"[109] tells the crew that they have signed on to chase the White Whale "round perdition's flames," till he "spouts black blood and rolls fin out." The new voyage is the continuation of the first, with this great difference, that the object of the quest has been transformed. Taji still hoped to recover the lost happiness of the days when Yillah was his in Odo; Ahab seeks revenge against an inscrutable and apparently capricious foe.

What is this White Whale which swam before the lunatic captain as the "monomaniac incarnation of all those malicious agencies which some deep men feel eating in them, till they are

[108] *Emerson and Others,* 196.
[109] *Works,* VII, 222.

left living on with half a heart and half a lung"? [110] The exegetes are ready with many answers. Is he, as D. H. Lawrence said, "the deepest blood-being of the white race" which is hunted by the "maniacal fanaticism of our white mental consciousness"? This is close, for Starbuck cried out to Ahab in the third day's chase, "Moby-Dick seeks thee not. It is thou, thou, that madly seekest him!" [111] Is Lewis Mumford right in seeing in him "the brute energies of existence, blind, fatal, overpowering"? [112] This shoots somewhat wide of the mark, for what chiefly torments Ahab is to know whether he is fighting against energies from the void of death which man has himself animated, or against "some unknown but still reasoning thing." [113] Whichever guess may be the true one, what Ahab chiefly hates is the inscrutableness of his enemy who impales him first on one and then the other of these desperate answers.

The frightfulness of the whale is incarnate in his whiteness, the "colorless, all-color of atheism," of the universal charnel-house inhabited by nothingness. To pursue him is to pursue death. If we try to solve the incantation of his whiteness, we must to the grave to learn it. Sometimes Ahab, in this mood, thinks "there's naught beyond" the mask, behind which his foe fights, but blankness. [114] But this mood is not frequent. To whalers who encountered Moby-Dick in times past his seeming infernal aforethought of ferocity was "not wholly regarded as having been inflicted by an unintelligent agent." [115] Their inclination to believe in his demoniac purpose became at length in Ahab an obsession of certainty. The beast, whether agent of a devil-god or the god himself, showed purposeful malice beneath his outrageous strength. All the suspected malice of the universe, all the "subtle demonisms of life and thought" crazy Ahab saw at last practically assailable in Moby-Dick. [116]

[110] *Ibid.*, 229.
[111] *Works*, VIII, 361.
[112] *Herman Melville*, 184.
[113] *Works*, VII, 204.
[114] *Loc. cit.*
[115] *Works*, VII, 228.
[116] *Ibid.*, 229. In concentrating here on the symbolism of the White Whale, I do not infer that Moby-Dick is to be taken only as a symbol. The book has been read by most—with no harm done—as the story of a mad sea-captain's pursuit of a vengeful creature whom the rest of the whaling masters shun. The

Before his mind was overthrown by this fatal obsession Ahab was sensitive to other elements than the demonism of the world. We are allowed glimpses, as in the words of Ophelia about the Hamlet of other days, of an Ahab who responds to the clear, strong, and steadfast mildness of the trade winds. The "long-drawn virgin vales; the mild blue hillsides" of the ocean have yet their temporary effect upon him.[117] He can still weep and, in conversation with Starbuck, remember Nantucket and home and child. In his calmer moments, such as prevail in this colloquy with Starbuck in "The Symphony," he looks back longingly to the world of reason and love which he has put behind him.[118] But these moods are few and are annihilated by the remorseless commands of the emperor who rules him. He feels himself the Fates' lieutenant acting under orders. His act is immutably decreed and was rehearsed a billion years before the ocean rolled.[119] He and the crew are turned round and round like the ship's windlass, and Fate is the handspike.

So Ahab wills to believe. His creator knows this is delusion. Once when the ship, aglow with the flame and smoke of the try-works, drove on through the night, Ishmael-Melville dozed at the helm. The tiller smote his side, and he awoke in fright, having turned himself about in his sleep. Grateful to have escaped the fatal contingency of being brought by the lee, he

---

whole force of the book is, of course, directed by Melville to the end of creating in the reader an impression of the monster's terrible actuality. The details of the preparation for the voyage, the operation of the ship, the digressions on the natural history of the whale, the encounters with other ships, and the final mighty three-day struggle with Moby-Dick, serve, chapter by chapter, to convince the reader that he is real, a part of nature like the other whales which have been killed, their blubber tried out and stowed in the hold. It is by means of the energy in this external story that its allegorical significance is, in Ahab's word, "shoved" near us.

In this connection attention should be called to Melville's statement to Mrs. Hawthorne, in a letter of Jan. 8, 1852: "I had some vague idea while writing it [*Moby-Dick*], that the whole book was susceptible of an allegorical construction, and also that parts of it were—but the specialty of many of the particular subordinate allegories were first revealed to me after reading Mr. Hawthorne's letter, which, without citing any particular examples, yet intimated the part-and-parcel allegoricalness of the whole." (See Bibliography: "An Unpublished Letter from Herman Melville to Mrs. Hawthorne.")

[117] *Works*, VIII, 264.

[118] *Ibid.*, 329.

[119] *Ibid.*, 352.

meditates: "Look not too long in the face of the fire, O man! Never dream with thy hand on the helm! Turn not thy back to the compass; accept the first hint of the hitching tiller; believe not the artificial fire, when its redness makes all things look ghastly." [120] Such wisdom Ahab trampled on. He had gazed too long on the unholy fires. He willed his mind to follow the cursed fiends who beckoned him down among them. In the chapter called "The Chart" Melville represents him as starting from his hammock at night, forced by intolerable dreams. His explanation of Ahab's anguish is explicit, and we should not pass it by. The Ahab who rushed from his sleep was not, he says, the crazy Ahab who pursued the whale. It was the innocent living soul of him that for a moment, in sleep, dissociated itself from and escaped the characterizing mind, which at other times employed it for its outer vehicle or agent.

"But as the mind does not exist unless leagued with the soul, therefore it must have been that, in Ahab's case, yielding up all his thoughts and fancies to his one supreme purpose; that purpose, by its own sheer inveteracy of will, forced itself against gods and devils into a kind of self-assumed, independent being of its own. Nay, could grimly live and burn, while the common vitality to which it was conjoined, fled horror-stricken from the unbidden and unfathered birth. Therefore, the tormented spirit that glared out of bodily eyes, when what seemed Ahab rushed from his room, was for the time but a vacated thing, a formless somnambulistic being, a ray of living light, to be sure, but without an object to colour, and therefore a blankness in itself. God help thee, old man, thy thoughts have created a creature in thee; and he whose intense thinking thus makes him a Prometheus; a vulture feeds upon that heart forever; that vulture the very creature he creates." [121]

This significant passage makes plain the symbolic meaning of the mysterious Fedallah, the Parsee whom Ahab smuggles aboard the ship and who led his chase against the whale. Though they never spoke while they kept watch together, a potent spell joined them, "as if in the Parsee Ahab saw his forethrown

---

[120] *Ibid.*, 181.
[121] *Works*, VII, 252–253.

shadow, in Ahab the Parsee his abandoned substance." [122] Which is to say, that Ahab brought his own fate on board with him. This vulture that feeds upon his heart he himself created.[123]

How is *Moby-Dick* to be read as the allegory of Melville's spiritual state in 1851? To what point has he come in his quest for the Ultimate? He invites us to inquire in the passage which admits his sympathy with Ahab's feud.[124] The wall of the mystery had been shoved menacingly near. He was like a prisoner whose only escape was by thrusting through. The ultimate answer, if it could be reached, would be complex, he now realized, and its quest perhaps dangerous to the sanity. He might have to impute the evil omnipresent in the universe to its ruler. But was this evil the work of principal or of agent? He began to suspect even that the intricate subject of all his speculations might dissolve in nothing, that there was, as he wrote to Hawthorne, no secret, "like the Freemason's mighty secret, so terrible to all children," which turns out, at last, "to consist in a triangle, a mallet, and an apron,—nothing more." In this same illuminating letter he notes that as soon as man begins to objectify the invisible world, to talk of *Me*, a *God*, a *Nature*, he prepares the noose that will hang him, like Ahab who sought to fight the intangible malignities only when he found in the White Whale their tangible incarnation.

Although Ahab was mad, as Melville knew him to be, and though he tried revenge, which is no solution to man's predicament, we must not suppose that Melville, even though defiant, would now choose to follow Ahab into the gulf, as Taji had turned his prow towards the racing tide. It is not merely for the purpose of saving the narrator that Ishmael-Melville survives

---

[122] *Works*, VIII, 320.

[123] This point has been overlooked or minimized by critics of *Moby-Dick*. It would seem to be of the utmost importance. There are other passages in the book which show even more plainly Melville's feeling at this time that within the lines of necessity which control man's world there is room for the play of free will. In the chapter called "The Mat-Maker," for example, Ishmael weaves a sword-mat, using his own hand for a shuttle, while Queequeg ever and anon with his oaken sword carelessly drives home every yarn. To Ishmael this suggests "the straight warp of necessity"; free will, "still free to ply her shuttle between given threads"; and chance, which has the "last featuring blow at events."

[124] The chapter entitled "Moby-Dick."

the White Whale's assault. However much he sympathized with Ahab's Promethean determination to stare down the inscrutableness of the universe, Melville hurled, not himself, but Ahab, his creature, at the injurious gods. Like the mountain eagle, though he had swooped into the blackest gorge, that gorge lay within the lofty mountains.[126] He had written a wicked book for which Ahab was made to suffer vicariously, and he felt as spotless as the lamb.

Melville's contemporaries dismissed *Pierre* as not only a dead failure but as a work so "repulsive, unnatural and indecent"[127] that it might endanger one's mental health to read it. With his admirers of more recent times, enthusiasts over the neglected *Moby-Dick*, it did not fare much better. Only in the past half dozen years has it been studied objectively with the intent of elucidating its mysteries and determining what Melville thought he had accomplished.

Pierre is still a difficult book. To us of this generation who read with ease Meredith and James and Woolf, and think we fathom the expressionism of Joyce's *Ulysses* and Lawrence's *The Rainbow*, Melville's methods are not utterly confusing, as they were to an earlier generation. Our difficulty is not to understand the drift and significance of the story but to know how much of what we think we see was placed there by Melville, and how much we read into the text because we have lived through the Freudian era.[128] So startling is Melville's prescience about such subjects as adolescent psychology and the unconscious[129]

---

[126] This position is summed up in the passage from which this figure comes (*Works*, VIII, 182): "There is a wisdom that is woe; but there is a woe that is madness." In other words, the perception of the dualism in the universe brings woe, but man is not fated to allow that woe to pass into madness.

[127] *American Whig Review*.

[128] In this connection one may object to some of the terminology in E. L. Grant Watson's "Melville's *Pierre*" (*New England Quarterly*, April, 1930). He is inclined to treat the novel as if it were the work of a contemporary whose symbolism shows him to be thoroughly familiar with the concepts of the Freudian school. In *Pierre* the story takes place in the realm where moral values are paramount, in society that is, and chiefly within the family. But the theme which the story embodies is metaphysical as well as moral and the symbols which Melville invents to add depth to it belong therefore to both orders of thought. When they seem to be startlingly erotic as well, the presumption is that they are often so only by the accident that Melville's plot necessarily involves various sex relationships.

[129] For passages showing Melville's interest in the psychology of childhood and adolescence, see particularly *Works*, IX, 96, 111–114, 123–127, 164, 301.

and so modern is his literary use of dreams and myths that one has constantly to remind oneself of the date of the novel.

As a barrier to our enjoyment of *Pierre,* and sometimes to comprehension, we cannot overlook the insecurity of its style. In *Moby-Dick* potentially dissonant passages of realism, rhapsody, instruction, humor, and tragedy are modulated to the universally heroic tone of the book. These various elements have one trait in common. In *Pierre* this is not the case. Time and again it is impossible without weighing and comparing to apprehend the intended tone of a particular passage. Two examples will sufficiently demonstrate this. The over-sweet Arcadian opening of the book, disclosing Pierre the Innocent in the center of his earthly paradise, is probably intended as satire and is artistically satisfying when read as such.[130] But it is so near to the style of the "thee-and-thou" school of sentimental fiction contemporary with it that one cannot be quite sure. For a second example consider Plinlimmon's pamphlet on "Chronometricals and Horologicals," advocating a "virtuous expediency" in moral actions, which opens Pierre's eyes though it does not affect his will. So unemphatic is Melville's attitude toward the pamphlet that some critics have been convinced that he sided with Plinlimmon, though if such were the case, the novel would contain insoluble contradictions.

In spite of these difficulties *Pierre* is a fascinating book. It possesses the vigor and promise of greater things to come which any primitive displays. André Gide has said that more interesting than the finished novel itself would be the journal of a great novelist like Stendhal or Dostoevsky showing the progress of the fight to achieve it. In *Pierre* we see Melville struggling, as M. Gide says of his central figure in *Les Faux Monnayeurs,* "entre ce que lui offre le réalité et ce que, lui, prétend en faire." The substance of the book is Melville's struggle to fathom the mystery of Pierre, who in turn is struggling to understand his author-hero Vivia, who is struggling to write a novel about his own "pursuit of the highest health of virtue and truth."

Modern ideas of the unconscious are suggested in pages 97–98, 150–151, 396–397, 407.

[130] Braswell believes that the aberrances of style throughout the book are deliberate on Melville's part and reveal his satiric purpose ("The Satirical Temper of Melville's *Pierre," American Literature,* VII, 432–435).

Melville knew that he would have to disrupt the confines of the conventional novel which laboriously spins veils of mystery, "only to complacently clear them up at last." His readers need not expect him to unravel his mysteries, because in human life there are no proper endings, but only "imperfect, unanticipated, and disappointing sequels," which "hurry to abrupt intermergings with the eternal tides of time and fate."[131] He was about to descend into the heart of man by a spiral stair without an end, "where that endlessness is only concealed by the spiralness of the stair, and the blackness of the shaft." In two earlier books he had presented the tormenting dualism which is masked behind the inscrutableness of the universe, as it is embodied in the political and economic realm (*Mardi*) and as it may be discovered in the world of nature (*Moby-Dick*). He wished to work it out anew in the plane of metaphysical values. His search for the Ultimate here brought him, as it did Browning, into conflict with the dominant belief of the nineteenth century fostered by the scientist, that reality is to be found in the natural world.

Melville wished to show in *Pierre* that there are some men, "Enthusiasts to Duty," who will obey the highest behest of their souls, though they lose their worldly felicity and bring upon themselves a "not-to-be-thought-of-woe." They stake all on the good faith of God. The world casts them out and mocks them. Heaven gives no sign, either of having ordained their fall or of being concerned for it. They are befooled by Truth, Virtue, and Fate. This theme would be projected through the story, deliberately Hamletian in outline, of Pierre Glendinning, gently born and reared in innocence and piety. He reveres the memory of his father as the personification of a goodness which is almost divine. He adores his haughty, worldly mother and worships Lucy Tartan, to whom he is engaged, as if she were almost more than mortal. Suddenly there invades this heaven on earth a mysterious dark-haired girl (Isabel) who, he is convinced, is an unacknowledged daughter of his father. He faces a dilemma. Heaven-decreed Duty compels him to receive Isabel, yet to receive her as his sister will shame his father's memory and cast down his mother's pride. He cuts the knot by the fantastic device of a pseudo-marriage to her. Lucy nearly dies of the

[131] *Works*, IX, 199.

shock and his mother, after disinheriting Pierre, is killed by grief and anger. In the city whither the couple have gone, Pierre struggles to write a novel, which is a failure. Lucy follows him to the city, pursued by Glen Stanly, Pierre's cousin and former friend, who wishes to save her. Pierre is goaded into killing him. Lucy dies of shock. Pierre and Isabel end the tragedy with poison.

What Pierre learns in the boundless expansion of his life, how society judges the folly of men like him, what the philosophers have to tell the Pierres of the world about the disparity between heavenly and terrestrial morality, what Melville had concluded about the issue, were all to find a place within the plot of this *Hamlet raisonné*.

A few ludicrously melodramatic scenes in *Pierre* have induced critics to overlook the fact that Melville invented an external plot which could be excellently manipulated to embody his theme and was capable of appropriate symbolic elaboration. There is scarcely a situation in the story which is not sound psychological realism except the pseudo-marriage between Pierre and his half-sister Isabel. The exception is a large one, but Melville could not avoid the episode. The incest motive was symbolically indispensable to the development of the idea of the ambiguity and the terrestrial taint of heavenly truth. Yet Pierre, since he represents in the beginning absolute innocence (though he is soon made alarmingly aware of the inversions of Truth) could not be made a deliberate partner in a physically incestuous relationship, however much this might have enhanced the probability of the external plot. The solution of the pseudo-marriage Melville recognized as a weak link and he devotes most of Book X—"The Unprecedented Final Resolution of Pierre"— to an analysis of the motives which induced his hero to take this way out. In the course of it he uncovers two psychological facts which nearly convince the reader. Isabel's mysterious nature had already begun to work an ambiguous charm upon Pierre so that the performance of his heaven-appointed duty was not single-motived; nor was the act, for another reason, entirely unprepared for. The artificial and ambiguous brother-sister relationship which Pierre and his mother had established between themselves was the preparative to this "nominal conversion of a sister into a wife."

The characters in *Pierre,* their actions, even objects which they touch, like Isabel's guitar and Pierre's Terror Stone, have symbolic value. The whole novel is a "continued allegory or dark conceit." Pierre is the Demigod whose parentage is half heavenly and half earthly. Because half his nature is divine he has a natural and insatiable appetite for God and seeks to regain his paternal birthright "even by fierce escalade." Pierre's father symbolizes the Deity; his haughty mother, the World. His betrothed Lucy, his Good Angel, who seeks to recapture him in the end, is heavenliness, as Pierre, while still the innocent and the enthusiast, apprehended it. The mysterious Isabel, whose unjust fate and irresistible charm attract Pierre into the pseudo-marriage, symbolizes Melville's maturing intuition of the nature of ultimate truth. She is heaven-born—Pierre's father is her father—but her mother was earthborn, and so Isabel's birth was tainted. His love for her grows imperceptibly warm and earthly, and is finally revealed as such to Lucy.[132] In the allegory, abstract truth, to follow which a righteous man has sacrificed his world, proves at last to be ambiguous, casting two shadows, Virtue and Vice. The tragic course of Pierre—the Demigod who seeks to recover his lost heaven—proves the indisputableness of Melville's maxim: "In those Hyperborean regions, to which enthusiastic Truth, and Earnestness, and Independence, will invariably lead a mind fitted by nature for profound and fearless thought, all objects are seen in a dubious, uncertain, and refracting light. Viewed through that rarefied atmosphere the most immemorially admitted maxims of men begin to slide and fluctuate, and finally become wholly inverted; the very heavens themselves being not innocent of producing this confounding effect, since it is mostly in the heavens themselves that these wonderful mirages are exhibited."[133]

In *Moby-Dick* Melville stood outside the tragedy; though sympathizing with Ahab's feud, he believed the captain's thirst for revenge was not fated and that he might have avoided the woe that is madness. Melville is not Ahab. What is the circumstance in *Pierre?* Does Melville identify himself with his hero; are we permitted to suppose Pierre's tragedy is his also? Actually, Melville, even more directly than in *Moby-Dick,* cau-

132 *Works,* IX, 465.
133 *Ibid.,* 231.

tions us against assuming that hero and author are one: "But the thoughts we here indite as Pierre's are to be very carefully discriminated from those we indite concerning him." [134]

Commenting on the dangerous state to which "enthusiastic Truth" has brought Pierre, he goes so far as to declare that the "example of many minds forever lost, like undiscoverable Arctic explorers, amid those treacherous regions, warns us entirely away from them; and we learn that it is not for man to follow the trail of truth too far, since by so doing he entirely loses the directing compass of his mind; for arrived at the Pole, to whose barrenness only it points, there, the needle indifferently respects all points of the horizon alike." [135]

These words do not prove, of course, that when Melville was at work on *Pierre* he had abandoned his speculations on the nature of ultimate truth. Though he would stop short of Ahab's madness and Pierre's self-destruction, he had still much to say, explicitly and by implication, on the quest initiated in *Mardi*.

There can be no doubt, in the first place, of Melville's disgust with the prudent materialism with which the world, represented by Mrs. Glendinning, her white-handed pastor, and Pierre's cousin Glen, views Pierre's agony, which these people would be quite incapable of comprehending. The desire to satirize their hypocrisy persisted with Melville until the writing of *The Confidence Man*. But there is another way of viewing the problem which obsesses Pierre, that offered by the transcendentalist philosopher Plotinus Plinlimmon, in his lecture on "Chronometricals and Horologicals." His comfortable doctrine proclaims a "virtuous expediency" as the best way for the heaven-conscious mortal to live on earth. When he goes to heaven it will be quite time enough to live by heaven's chronometrical time.

By introducing Plinlimmon and his pamphlet, which promised a later (unaccomplished) reconciliation of God's truth to man's truth, Melville intended a satire on all shallow and amiable transcendental "reconcilers" of the "Optimist" or "Compensation" school.[136] Their waving away of the problem he found quite as distasteful as the worldly hypocrisy of the Rev. Mr. Falsgrave.

---

[134] *Ibid.*, 233.
[135] *Ibid.*, 231.
[136] *Works*, IX, 385.

To know at what position Melville had now positively arrived in his quest for the Ultimate, we must study a passage in
Book XIV of *Pierre* where he sets down candidly his own conclusions. He testifies there to the conviction of divine origin
which the beauty of the Sermon on the Mount carries to the
heart of an earnest or enthusiastic youth. When he first looks
about him in the world he cannot believe that the professed
Christian can live so totally at variance with it. Unless his faith
fades, or he fails to see the lying world around him or unless "he
can find the talismanic secret, to reconcile this world with his
own soul, then there is no peace for him, no slightest truce for
him in this life." [137] The talismanic secret has never been found,
nor does Melville suppose it will be found. Philosophers pretend
to have it—"Plato, and Spinoza, and Goethe,[138] and many more
belong to this guild of self-imposters, with a preposterous rabble
of Muggletonian Scots and Yankees, whose vile brogue still the
more bestreaks the stripedness of their Greek or German Neo-
platonical originals." They lie when they assert they have received an answer from the "Voice of our God." How can a man
"get a Voice out of Silence"? [139]

Here in 1852 ended, for the moment, Melville's quest for
the Ultimate. His mood had changed from the reckless high
adventure of Taji, not content with Serenia, to partial sympathy
with the vengeful Ahab who longed to strike through the mask
of whiteness and so lay bare the malice or the blankness which
lay beyond, to the desponding and skeptical mood of *Pierre*.
There seems to be no answer, least of all a transcendental one,
yet for Melville there could be no truce in the war to wrest one
from the silent heavens.

If Melville could have continued to objectify his quest in
books like *Mardi, Moby-Dick,* and *Pierre,* he might have saved

---

[137] *Ibid.,* 290.

[138] The inclusion of Goethe here is illuminated by Melville's remark in a letter
to Hawthorne (see p. 393, below): "In reading some of Goethe's sayings, so
worshipped by his votaries, I came across this, 'Live in the all.' That is to say,
your separate identity is but a wretched one,—good; but get out of yourself,
spread and expand yourself, and bring to yourself the tinglings of life that are
felt in the flowers and the woods, that are felt in the planets Saturn and Venus,
and the Fixed Stars. What nonsense! Here is a fellow with a raging toothache,
'My dear boy,' Goethe says to him, 'you are sorely afflicted with that tooth;
but you must *live in the all,* and then you will be happy!'"

[139] *Loc. cit.*

himself from the emotional collapse which darkened the next ten years of his life. But the story of his truceless war was told on all possible planes. Chaos was come again, but there was no further possibility of subliming it into another *Moby-Dick,* for the "fullness" was gone. He abandoned himself in private conversation to continued wandering over the deserts of speculation.

In the end Melville called the truce. On April 19, 1891— five months before he died—he put the last words to "Billy Budd, Foretopman," a story which Mr. Watson has named his "testament of acceptance." In this tale of an innocent and beautiful young sailor accused of mutiny by a master-at-arms in whom breeds "a depravity according to nature," Melville achieves unsurpassable tragedy. His own passionate rage at the inscrutableness of the universe is spent. He acquiesces in the magnanimous Captain Vere's sentence of death on Billy, for Captain Vere, like Melville, had learned that here below we have no concern with the "mystery of iniquity." "We fight at command," but for the "law and the rigor of it, we are not responsible." This is the blight man was born for, and when we weep for the undoing of such men as Billy Budd it is for ourselves we mourn.

LEON HOWARD [1903–   ] is professor of English at the University of California at Los Angeles. His books include *The Connecticut Wits, Victorian Knight-Errant: A Study of the Early Literary Career of James Russell Lowell,* and an edition of Jonathan Edwards' *The Mind* (*The Mind: A Reconstructed Text*). Besides his standard biography of Melville, he wrote the University of Minnesota pamphlet on Melville.

Melville's Struggle with the Angel

LEON HOWARD

The common denominator of most—if not all—critical discussions of Herman Melville is their dependence upon the logical fallacy of "distribution." Since all successful writers are "artists" within the collective meaning of the word, a conscious artistry

Modern Language Quarterly, Vol. 1 (June 1940) 195–206.

in Melville's work is usually taken for granted. The fallacy in this logical assumption arises, however, when the term "artist" is extended to include notions of craftsmanship drawn from the dispositions of the critics rather than the findings of a comprehensive scholarship. When the concept of art is derived from the crossword puzzle, critical interpretation sinks into the complete absurdity of presenting Captain Ahab's artificial leg as evidence of Melville's belief that "the Will is limited by Fate." [1] But when a more plausible extension defines the artist as an expert narrative craftsman, the interpretation of his books becomes less obviously unsound: still based upon bad logic, it nevertheless presents both the author and his work in a way that leaves them recognizable though unreal.

For example: The best general discussion of Melville in print insists that "with *Mardi*, *Moby-Dick*, and *Pierre* . . . . he deliberately set himself against the main currents of fiction-writing of his time"; it refers to "architectural skill" as a permanent characteristic of his art and admires his lesser works as illustrations of "how thoroughly he had mastered the technique of his craft." [2] Yet Melville himself, at the end of his life, made a poetic comparison of his artistic struggle with the wrestling of Jacob in terms that by no means suggest any attainment of professional skill. [3] Through a combination of circumstances, on one occasion, he did prevail over "the angel—Art"; but the circumstances seem to have been unusual, and his success was in the mastery of particular materials rather than the technique of his craft. My purpose here is to illustrate the limitations of his technical skill by giving a brief survey of (1) the major technical devices he gradually cultivated in his early books, (2) the new artistic influences that produced *Moby-Dick*, and (3) the inef-

[1] W. S. Gleim, "A Theory of Moby Dick," *New England Quarterly*, II (July, 1929), 411. Cf. the same author's *The Meaning of Moby Dick* (New York, 1938).

[2] Willard Thorp, *Herman Melville* (New York 1938), pp. xliv, li, lii. Although Mr. Thorp's statement serves as an excellent point of departure for the argument in this paper, his treatment of Melville is by far the sanest general discussion in print. His editorial work, also, has been so admirable that most of the minor documents pertinent to a study of Melville's art may be found—in their best available text—among his selections.

[3] "Art," originally published in *Timoleon* (1891) and reprinted by Thorp, *op. cit.*, p. 365, with interesting notes (pp. 427–428) on MS variations showing Melville's efforts toward the exact representation of his artistic difficulties.

fectiveness of these influences in developing a permanent, dependable craftsmanship.

II

Melville's first five books clearly reveal how he developed, by trial and error, one major literary device which he eventually used with considerable skill. This was the rather elementary device of suspense as it might be achieved by raising melodramatic questions that had to be answered before the book was finished. It appeared first in *Typee,* where the author deviated from an actual record of experiences[4] by extending the period of his captivity, introducing an idyllic narrative into the simple adventure story, and unifying the two by adding an element of suspense. While the narrator was wandering with Kory-Kory and Fayaway, the chief men of Typee were eating another stranger. How would Melville escape a similar fate? The question apparently was more exciting to contemporary readers than it is to us, and it seems to have been deliberately introduced in order to make the idyll something of an adventure and so give a crude unity to the whole.[5] Yet the device was of no very great importance in *Typee,* and Melville abandoned it entirely in *Omoo* for the rambling, picaresque method. *Mardi* began in the narrative manner of its predecessor; but as the excitement of his rapid intellectual development overwhelmed Melville's desire to tell a story,[6] he returned to the device of suspense in an effort to sustain narrative interest through a hundred and fifty chapters of social criticism and philosophical speculation which he substituted for the adventure story he had planned. Would the hero find the mysterious blonde? Would he be seduced by the sensuous brunette? Or would he be done to death by three vengeful specters for a crime innocently committed? Melville

[4] See Robert S. Forsythe, "Herman Melville in the Marquesas," *Philological Quarterly,* XV (January, 1936), 1–5; Charles R. Anderson, *Melville in the South Seas* (New York, 1939), pp. 179–195.

[5] Contemporary advertisements and allusions, as well as Melville's own petulance at his reputation as the "man who lived among the cannibals" (see letter to Hawthorne [1851], Thorp, *op. cit.,* p. 392), bear witness to the effect of South Sea cannibalism upon the imaginations of early readers of *Typee.*

[6] For evidence concerning the close relationship between *Mardi* and the intellectual stimuli affecting Melville during the period of its composition see Luther S. Mansfield, *Herman Melville: Author and New Yorker, 1844–1851* (unpublished doctoral dissertation; the University of Chicago, 1936).

obviously spent a good deal more time and thought on the visions of Yillah, the messengers of Hautia, and the spectral pursuers than he had upon the reminders of cannibalism in *Typee;* and, though these devices did not accomplish their artistic purpose, they did establish suspense as a permanent element in his crafts-manship. The anticipation of some malign result from the in-fluence of Jackson was a major constituent in the narrative technique of *Redburn,* and in *White Jacket* Melville revealed conclusively his increasing emphasis upon suspense as a literary device. In his first book he had used suspense for the purpose of binding a certain amount of fiction to the framework of his true narrative. In his fifth, he introduced most of the fiction for the purpose of creating suspense. Almost all of the invention in *White Jacket* is connected with two questions: What would the author do when threatened with a flogging? How would the white jacket almost cost him his life? And the questions them-selves are entirely artificial, for Melville is known neither to have been brought to the gratings nor to have worn a white jacket.[7]

The second literary device cultivated by Melville during the early stages of his career was one later revealed in theory by the "Agatha letter" to Hawthorne[8] and illustrated in practice by his transformation of a chapter from Captain Delano's *Voy-ages* into the story *Benito Cereno.*[9] This was the device of allu-siveness, or the use of the incident and phraseology for the purpose of giving intellectual significance to the story and of achieving imaginative coherence. In the later books it was used, in part, to support the structural device of suspense; and, by its constant reminders and anticipations of events, it reveals an un-usual degree of mental awareness on the part of the author and demands an equal alertness from the reader.[10] Yet Melville was

---

[7] See Anderson, *op. cit.,* pp. 409–418.

[8] S. E. Morison, "Melville's 'Agatha' Letter to Hawthorne," *New England Quar-terly,* II (April, 1929), 296–307.

[9] H. H. Scudder, "Melville's *Benito Cereno* and Captain Delano's Voyages," *PMLA,* XLIII (June, 1928), 502–532.

[10] The importance of this quality of allusiveness can hardly be exaggerated in any discussion of Melville's more ambitious works. The cross currents of allu-sion in *Moby-Dick,* for instance, reveal a turbulent mental energy which dashes at words and incidents from two or three or even more points of reference. To illustrate: When Melville refers to Ahab occasionally as *king* Ahab the title may allude to the captain's biblical prototype, his characteristic arrogance, his absolute power over the ship and its crew, his occupation of the conventionally

extraordinarily slow in developing it, and his characteristic alertness is missing from his earliest books. In *Typee,* for example, he was capable of referring to "the lofty jet of the whale" as a lethargic influence upon a ship's crew and of attributing the "alleged savagery" of the South Sea Islanders to European influences—completely unaware, it would seem, that he had just traced the lethargy to a persistent failure to sight whales and had just been writing about the traditional barbarity of the natives toward their nearest neighbors.[11] In *Mardi,* however, the

---

royal role of tragic hero—or to all of these at once. Melville's visible cultivation of an increasing allusiveness shows that it was a conscious literary device; but I believe that it was a supporting device rather than a primary one. In the language of the "Agatha" letter, he used it in developing the "significances" with which his material happened to be "instinct," although, of course, he grew more and more inclined to select material that lent itself to such treatment. This opinion is based on two sorts of evidence that supplement the revelations of the "Agatha" letter: The first of these is my failure to find, in any of Melville's major works, anything more than an occasional, momentary example of the influence of allusiveness upon his narrative invention such as is to be found, for instance, in James Branch Cabell's *Figures of Earth,* the entire plot of which grows out of this literary device. The second is Melville's wasteful use of the device when it can serve no possible purpose, as when he revises the description of the black fish given in one of the sources for the chapter on "cetology" from "the angles of the lips are curved upwards, giving the physiognomy of the animal an innocent, smiling expression" to "the inner angles of his lips are curved upward, he carries an everlasting Mephistophelean grin on his face" (Frederick Dobell Bennett, *Narrative of a Whaling Voyage Round the World from the year 1833 to 1836* [London, 1840], II, 233; *Moby-Dick* ["Standard edition," London, 1922], I, 174). Even Mr. John Freeman, who identifies the whale with Lucifer, and Mr. Raymond Weaver, who identifies it with "demonism at the cankered heart of nature," would have difficulty making this change signify more than mental exuberance; and Miss Viola White, who identifies the whale with "the Old Testament Jehovah," and Mr. Carl Van Doren, who found Ahab representing Lucifer, would have even more trouble.

But this aspect of Melville's art is too complex for full discussion in a footnote, although it needs a considerable amount of attention. It might best be approached formally, I believe, through a study of his humor. Informally, an attentive reading of *Mardi* or *Moby-Dick* and either *Figures of Earth* or Elinor Wylie's *The Venetian Glass Nephew* should reveal the great difference between the use of allusiveness as an exuberant supporting device and its use as a primary element in meticulous craftsmanship.

[11] *Typee* (London, 1922), p. 10, and chapter iv, in which a discussion of the "hereditary warfare" waged between the Happars and Typees "from time immemorial" is interrupted by a digression attributing "the cruel and bloodthirsty disposition of some of the islanders" to the influence of examples of European aggression. In the next sentence Melville refers to traditional "predatory excursions" of natives "to cut off any imprudent straggler" from the body of his tribe or to "make a descent upon the inmates of some sequestered habitation" (p. 34).

device of allusiveness was luxuriantly cultivated. To a considerable extent it grew out of the indirection necessary to the
presentation of social criticism in the guise of "romance" after
the manner of Rabelais and Swift. In part it was the result of
Melville's curious fondness for the sentimental flower language
of Victorian elegance.[12] But its most skillful cultivation was in
the method of characterization newly developed in that book,
for in *Mardi,* for the first time, Melville created a group of
fictitious characters who were identifiable by their underlying,
individual points of view rather than by any peculiar mannerisms. Although Babbalanja, the philosopher, was a "humor"
character, his portrayal required much more thought and subtlety than was needed for the caperings of Doctor Long Ghost
in *Omoo;* and this subtlety is revealed in the extraordinary allusiveness of the conversations in which he engaged. Babbalanja
can hardly be described as a caricature, but his creator never
forgot that a philosopher should speak "most philosophically." [13]
When Melville shackled his exuberance by a return to a basic
pattern of autobiography in *Redburn* and *White Jacket,* he sacrificed much of the allusiveness that he had felt free to cultivate
in pure fiction; hence, these books, though they have more intellectual depth and imaginative coherence than the first two,
seem superficial in comparison with *Mardi.* Melville himself was
more critical of them than they deserved.[14] His creative energies
had been stimulated by the disguise of fiction; he was impatient
with the restraint of actuality; and by the time he began *Moby-
Dick* he was anxious to speak again in a role other than his own.
     Melodramatic suspense and allusiveness were the two major

---

[12] In a forthcoming article on "The Flower Symbolism of *Mardi*" Mr. Merrell R.
Davis will supply material for a precise, though hardly profound, interpretation
of the "quest" in this novel.

[13] My guess is that the creation of Babbalanja opened Melville's eyes to the
possibilities of dramatic self-expression in the novel. Though the author certainly stood aside from his creation, the philosopher expressed himself freely on
many subjects that interested his creator; and the allusive subtlety of Babbalanja's
discourse, as his attitudes are changed by the impact of his experiences, seems
reasonably good evidence that Melville was identifying himself, dramatically
and imaginatively, with his fictitious character.

[14] See his expression of surprise at the favorable reception given his "beggarly
'Redburn' " (letter to Duyckinck [December 14, 1849], Thorp, *op. cit.,* p. 376)
and compare the tone of his comments on *Mardi,* which, though disparaging,
indicate that he considered the book anything but "beggarly."

artistic devices that Melville developed during the early part of his literary career. He may possibly have cultivated one other: the intensification of action by representing the ship as a micro-cosm.[15] But there is a more than reasonable doubt whether this was a conscious artistic device or merely an effect incidental to his general allusiveness. His failure to make successful use of it, some years later, in *The Confidence Man* suggests that it was not the well-tested trick of his trade that it might otherwise appear to be. In any case it seems reasonably clear that by 1850 Melville still had a great deal to learn about the craft of fiction and that he did not have at his command a skilled artistry that would enable him deliberately to set himself against the main currents of fiction-writing of his time.

III

As a matter of fact, *Moby-Dick*, more completely than any of Melville's novels, may be described in terms of new influences

---

[15] Thorp (*op. cit.*, p. xlviii) believes that Melville began in *Omoo* to explore "the ship-microcosm which [was] to constitute a large element of the formal structure of *White-Jacket* and *Moby-Dick*." It seems to me, however, that Melville's method of composition was just opposite to that implied in this comment. Instead of designing a "ship-microcosm" and selecting his material to fit the plan, he started with material that came to hand and, by stylistic allusiveness and an alertness to all possible "significances" (cf. the "Agatha" letter, *loc. cit.*, and note 10 above), made it as suggestive as possible, thus achieving the effect of a microcosm largely through the accident of his material. In other words, Melville's method of composition seems to have been one of constant leaping and then looking rather than the reverse process of the skilled craftsman. Babbalanja's comments on Lombardo's methods of composition, in the 180th chapter of *Mardi*, suggest as much, and they are so extraordinarily like Melville's own comments on himself (see the letters to Duyckinck and Hawthorne printed by Thorp, pp. 376–377, 383–384, 390, 391, 394) that the suggestion becomes important. Furthermore, a comparison of the chronology of the composition of *Mardi* with the chronology of some of the events reflected in it shows that Melville could not have written the book, as it stands, had he not adopted Lombardo's method: i.e., "He did not build himself in with plans; he wrote right on; and so doing got deeper and deeper into himself; and like a resolute traveller, plunging through baffling woods, at last was rewarded for his toils." Melville's account of another imaginary author, in chapter xxv of *Pierre*, is similar; and, in general, he seems to have had little conception of any method of composition that required careful looking before he leaped.

In this connection it should be noticed that the researches of Albert Mordell ("Melville and 'White-Jacket,'" *Saturday Review of Literature*, VII [July 4, 1931], 946) and the supplementary investigation of Anderson (*op. cit.*, pp. 361 ff.) show that Melville probably did not contribute a single invented character to the ship-microcosm in *White-Jacket*.

upon the author's craftsmanship. The technical details of whaling had been carefully reserved for special treatment,[16] and soon after Melville's return from England, in February, 1850, he seems to have gone to work on the book. By August of that year Evert Duyckinck was able to write that his friend had "a new book mostly done—a romantic, fanciful & literal & most enjoyable presentment of the Whale Fishery." [17] What was in this original version we do not know. A literal account of the whaling industry, the fanciful but not unprecedented destruction of the vessel, the romantic element of suspense that anticipated it, and a most enjoyable style—all these may have been in the "presentment," for all these Melville had at his command by the middle of 1850. But he had not yet demonstrated any mastery of the tragic characterization, dramatic intensity, and purposeful narration revealed in the finished novel; and it is reasonable to believe that the year of agonized struggle so clearly reflected in his letters represented an effort to achieve these qualities. Also, it seems reasonable to accept as evidence of literary influence his fervid appreciation, during this period, of exactly these qualities as he found them in Shakespeare and Nathaniel Hawthorne.

Actually Melville dated his admiration for Shakespeare from February, 1849, when he heard Fanny Kemble read the part of Lady Macbeth and was inspired to re-read the plays.[18] By 1850, however, he was exhibiting a tendency to despise the "popular," visible evidences of Shakespeare's art and to admire him primarily as a literary artist, especially as revealed in what Melville called the "dark characters of Hamlet, Timon, Lear, and

[16] Cf. the preface to *Omoo*.

[17] Luther S. Mansfield, "Glimpses of Herman Melville's Life in Pittsfield, 1850–1851," *American Literature*, IX (March, 1937), 32 n. In a letter written to Hawthorne, presumably in June, 1851, Melville indicated that though part of the book was "driving through the press" it was still unfinished (Thorp, *op. cit.*, pp. 390, 391). Duyckinck was able to speak of it, in the following August, as completed (Mansfield, *op. cit.*, p. 39); and it was published in London in October, probably being printed from proof sheets for the New York edition of November. Since all the available correspondence recording Melville's labors on the book is from the year *following* August, 1850, I considered the statement that it was "mostly done" by that time sufficiently arresting to justify a query. Mr. Mansfield, however, assures me that it is accurate.

[18] Letter to Duyckinck, Thorp, *op. cit.*, pp. 370–371. Melville's statement that he had "until a few days ago, never made close acquaintance with the divine William" is more indicative of his new enthusiasm than of anything else, for he had been quoting Shakespeare with some frequency and aptness in his books.

Iago."[19] The tragic dramatist who created Hamlet and Lear apparently appealed most strongly to the man engaged in writing *Moby-Dick;* and his annotation of the plays has recently been presented as further evidence of the close imaginative connection between the tragedies and the novel.[20]

The dramatic character and the Elizabethan qualities of *Moby-Dick* are well known, and Melville's enthusiasm for Shakespeare during the period of its composition is clearly established. But it has not been pointed out that Melville learned—or thought he learned—from Shakespeare a specific creative method that filled a large vacancy in his artistic bag of tricks. For Melville looked at Shakespeare through the medium of Samuel Taylor Coleridge, and, in doing so, he discovered an artistry that appealed strongly to the author of *Mardi* and that solved some of the problems which had hitherto prevented progress from the creative point reached in that book. Instead of fictitious "humor" characters, Melville was enabled by these influences to create a life-like tragic hero and so to summon up a dramatic intensity he had never before achieved.

Investigations into Melville's reading have not been made with sufficient exactitude to make the evidence complete, but it is known that Melville's closest intellectual associate at the time he discovered Shakespeare was Evert Duyckinck and that Duyckinck was a particular admirer of Coleridge. It may be that when Melville wrote his friend a letter of enthusiastic comment on "the divine William," Duyckinck directed his attention to Coleridge's interpretations of Shakespeare's art in his *Literary Remains.*[21] In any case, *Moby-Dick* itself indicated that Cole-

[19] See the comments in "Hawthorne and His Mosses," Thorp, *op. cit.,* pp. 333–334. All further citations of this essay will be by page number to this reprint from the *Literary World,* August 17 and 24, 1850.

[20] Charles Olson, "Lear and Moby-Dick," *Twice a Year,* I (1938), 165–189. See also R. G. Hughes, "Melville and Shakespeare," *Shakespeare Association Bulletin,* VII (July, 1932), 103–112.

[21] Mansfield says that Lamb was "perhaps the supreme literary god of the Duyckinck household" with Browne, Rabelais, Coleridge, and Richter only "slightly less exalted" (*Herman Melville, Author and New Yorker,* p. 180); and he refers to the enthusiasm for Lamb and Coleridge reflected in the *Literary World,* which Melville regularly read (*ibid.,* p. 182). Melville displayed a general familiarity with "Coleridgean" philosophy in his journal for October 12, 1849 (see selections printed in Raymond Weaver, *Herman Melville: Mariner and Mystic* [New York, 1921], p. 285) and with Coleridge's poems in *Moby-Dick* and elsewhere; but mention of the *Literary Remains* does not appear in

ridge's lecture on *Hamlet* came into Melville's mind whenever he stopped to comment on Captain Ahab as an artistic creation. Remembering the dictum that "one of Shakespeare's modes of creating characters is to conceive any one intellectual or moral faculty in *morbid* excess, and then to place himself . . . . thus *mutilated* or *diseased,* under given circumstances," [22] Melville prepared for the introduction of his own hero as "a mighty pagent creature, formed for noble tragedies," by explaining that it would not "at all detract from him, dramatically regarded, if either by birth or other circumstances, he have what seems a half-wilful *over-ruling morbidness* at the bottom of his nature." "For all men tragically great," he added, "are made so through a certain *morbidness*"; and he insisted, in the same passage, that "all mortal greatness is but *disease*." [23] Later, in a rather elaborate discussion of Ahab's disease, Melville used an ambiguous phrase that again echoed Coleridge and apparently referred both to the captain's physical and mental disability: "deliriously transferring" his broodings to the white whale, in his "frantic morbidness," Ahab "pitted himself, *all mutilated,* against it." [24] Melville's reference to the "royal mantle" over all humanity in defense of his attempt to ascribe "high qualities, though dark," and weave "tragic graces" around "meanest mariners" [25] and his effort, as a "tragic dramatist," to justify his selection of a hero who lacked "all outward majestical trappings" [26] is further evidence that he consciously thought of his protagonist as a tragic hero of the sort found in *Hamlet* and *King Lear.*

The Coleridgean version of Shakespeare's creative methods,

---

the incomplete record of his readings, and his acquaintance with the volume can be asserted only on the grounds of probability and on the evidence of parallels between the lecture on *Hamlet* and the language of *Moby-Dick.* His reading of *Wilhelm Meister,* which he borrowed from Duyckinck in 1850 (probably just before leaving for Pittsfield, according to Mansfield), may have directed his attention to the psychological criticism of *Hamlet,* although, of course, he could not have found in Goethe the suggestions of creative method discussed below.

[22] "Hamlet" in Coleridge's *Complete Works* (New York, 1884), IV, 145. The italics in this and all the quotations given below are my own.

[23] *Moby-Dick,* I, 92.

[24] *Ibid.,* I, 229.

[25] *Ibid.,* I, 144.

[26] *Ibid.,* I, 183.

however, did not solve all the new technical problems overcome during the production of *Moby-Dick*. Melville had never written a book without a "message," and he persistently criticized the Elizabethans for their shortcomings in what he called "the great Art of Telling the Truth." [27] He referred to "the muzzle which all men wore on their souls in the Elizabethan day" and declared that even "Shakespeare was not a frank man to the uttermost." [28] Melville had to turn to contemporary novelists for the art of frankness and also for methods of more purposeful narration than the drama demanded or he himself had achieved by his own experiments.

There is some evidence—not yet fully explored—that he had read and been affected by Disraeli, Bulwer-Lytton, and Dickens; [29] but the narrative methods which Melville adopted as most suitable to his requirements were those of Hawthorne. He had read some of Hawthorne's tales before 1850 and had not been greatly impressed. [30] He opened the *Mosses from an Old Manse* in the summer of that year, however, under different circumstances: he had practically exhausted the autobiographical pattern of personal experience, and the problem of narrative invention had become acute. Hawthorne's four-year-old book immediately aroused a profound admiration. Here was an American novelist who "approached" the Elizabethan dramatist. "Not a great deal more," he exclaimed, "and Nathaniel were verily

[27] See, for example, "Hawthorne and His Mosses," p. 334.

[28] Letter to Duyckinck (March 3, 1849), Thorp, *op. cit.*, p. 372.

[29] Mr. Norman Pearson has pointed out to me some interesting parallels between Melville's work and Disraeli's; the phrase in Melville's annotation of Shakespeare which so puzzles Olson (*op. cit.*, pp. 175–176) may have been borrowed from Bulwer's *The Last Days of Pompeii*; and Mansfield (*op. cit., passim*) has given evidence of an interest, on Melville's part, in comic illustrators of Dickens and other novelists which seems to me indicative of a possible influence of both the illustrations and their text. Mansfield in calling attention to "Melville's Comic Articles on Zachary Taylor," (*American Literature*, IX [January, 1938], 411–418), has provided, I believe, a concrete example of the influence of caricature upon Melville's methods of characterization, and I suspect that a further study of this subject would show that Melville usually drew his portraits with the bold strokes of the artists in whom he was most interested —or, perhaps more accurately, in the manner of the novelists whom they were illustrating. Cf., in this connection, Thorp, *op. cit.*, p. lxiii, n. 99.

[30] At least I think this is the implication of his comments in the letter to Duyckinck (February 12, 1851), Thorp, *op. cit.*, p. 385, when considered in relation to "Hawthorne and His Mosses," pp. 340, 345.

William!" [31] The stories of Hawthorne, Melville found, possessed their full complement of the mysterious, tragic "blackness" which he so admired as a literary characteristic in Shakespeare[32]; and his enthusiasm led him to express a momentary preference for "the still, rich utterance of a great intellect in repose" over the dramatist's "noise and show." [33] Hawthorne also, in Melville's opinion, was the more consistent master "of the great Art of Telling the Truth," for he directly and regularly revealed depths of truth that Shakespeare revealed only "covertly and by snatches." [34] The long, appreciative essay which he dashed off before he had even finished reading the book shows all the enthusiasm of a struggling young author who had discovered the man who could teach him his art. "Already," he announced in a sort of postscript to the essay, "I feel that this Hawthorne has dropped germinous seeds into my soul." [35] And, cultivated by a quick intimacy, the seeds developed into the narrative technique of *Moby-Dick*—although by the time he finished the book Melville had come to qualify his first admiration by a feeling that Hawthorne might be improved by a little less intellectual repose and more robust vigor.[36]

This emphasis upon new influences on Melville's craftsmanship does not imply that the author of *Moby-Dick* neglected any of the literary devices cultivated in his earlier books. They are all there. But the distinctive qualities of *Moby-Dick* may be described almost entirely in terms applicable to Hawthorne or actually applied by Coleridge to Shakespeare. The plot is that of the "quest" story, unified by its complete dependence upon the character of the protagonist. It is the sort of plot found in the stories of Hawthorne rather than the casual quest plot found in *Mardi*. The plot is further unified by a parabolic significance which, again, is more like the stories of Hawthorne than anything hitherto achieved by Melville; and, to make the

[31] "Hawthorne and His Mosses," pp. 335, 336.

[32] *Ibid.*, pp. 333, 343.

[33] *Ibid.*, p. 335.

[34] Cf. *ibid.*, p. 334 and the implications of pp. 331–333, 341–343.

[35] *Ibid.*, p. 341.

[36] See the letter to Duyckinck (February 12, 1851), Thorp, *op. cit.*, p. 386. The dedication of *Moby-Dick*, however, displays the continued admiration which is also expressed in the letter.

similarity even closer, Melville seems to have been attempting to illustrate the same "profound" and "appalling" moral found in "Earth's Holocaust"—a story which he particularly admired in the *Mosses from an Old Manse*.[37] Yet for all the signs of Hawthorne's influence, there is none of his intellectual repose in *Moby-Dick*. Ahab is a Shakespearean tragic hero, created according to the Coleridgean formula. He is certainly not Melville, but he is certainly vivified by Melville's sympathetic emotions as though the author fancied himself "thus mutilated or diseased" under the "given circumstances." Furthermore Ahab's disease has many symptoms of that diagnosed by Coleridge: surely he may be described as a man with a "craving after the indefinite," who "looks upon external things as hieroglyphics," and whose mind, with its "everlasting broodings," is "unseated from its healthy relation" and "constantly occupied with the world within, and abstracted from the world without—giving substance to shadows, and throwing a mist over all commonplace actualities."[38] The difference between Melville's Ahab and Coleridge's Hamlet is not so much in the disease as in the basic character "thus mutilated" and in the "given circumstances" in which he is placed. To put the matter briefly: The literary art which makes *Moby-Dick* different from Melville's earlier works was an art learned from Shakespeare under the tutelage of Coleridge and adjusted to Melville's own peculiar temperament and to the requirements of the novel according to the example set by Hawthorne.

IV

In his painful struggle with "the angel—Art" from August, 1850, to August, 1851, Melville learned more about the technical requirements of a successful novel than he had learned during the preceding five years of his literary career. And there can be no doubt that on this occasion he thought himself blessed with

[37] "Hawthorne and His Mosses," p. 332. The moral concerns the "all-engendering heart of man" as the source of "vanities and empty theories"; but this point (and a similar one, below, concerning *Pierre*) will have to be taken on whatever faith still survives in the reader. The all-engendering hearts of the Melville exegetes have surrounded these books with so many vanities and empty theories that an adequate commentary on their "meaning" will require a second—and perhaps even a third—full essay.

[38] See Coleridge, *op. cit.*, p. 146.

victory. Hawthorne at least understood what he had been trying to do, and as a result Melville felt "a sense of unspeakable security"[39] that had not come to him after any other book. Inevitably he tried to repeat the achievement.

And with his habitual economy in the use of artistic methods he tried not only a repetition but almost a duplication of the achievement. Pierre was merely a younger man, in different circumstances, whom Melville infected with the same disease that governed Ahab. The same descriptive terms that were transferred from Coleridge's Hamlet to the hero of *Moby-Dick* may be used with equal validity in describing Pierre. The plot was again—though somewhat less obviously—that of a quest, unified by its dependence upon the character of the protagonist. The same parabolic significance reappears with possibly the same "appalling" moral. The chief differences between the two books grow out of the complete differences in the "given circumstances" in which the characters were placed. Melville, in *Pierre*, tried to create another novel by the rather simple process of nipping a successful character in the bud rather than by blasting him in full bloom.

Naïve though the plan was, however, it might have been reasonably successful had it not been for a peculiar limitation of Melville's genius and a peculiar requirement of the literary art developed in *Moby-Dick*. One of the restrictions upon Melville's imagination seems to have been that he could not "place himself" in a mutilated, diseased, or any other condition in "given circumstances" that were completely disassociated from his actual experience. Accordingly he placed Pierre in circumstances closely related to those of his own boyhood and let his "appalling" fable develop in the commonplace environment of Victorian New York. Hawthorne, with his air of intellectual repose, might have managed such a situation; but an Elizabethan tragic hero in the familiar haunts of the Duyckincks was as out of place as Lucifer among the Buchmanites. For the art of fiction which Melville had cultivated required a more expansive, a more vigorous, and potentially a more dramatic atmosphere in order to be convincing than was supplied by Melville's life in the neighborhood of Albany and New York. Violent rebellion in

---

[39] See the letter to Hawthorne (1851), Thorp, *op. cit.*, p. 394.

a polite environment is never an artistic success, and neither was *Pierre*.

The empirical quality of Melville's constructive imagination, together with the exhaustion of his own experiences, forced him to abandon the literary technique developed during his one successful struggle with the art of the novel. He attempted Hawthorne's more restrained manner in a number of short stories, tried dramatic tale-telling without a parable in *Israel Potter*, and made an effort towards a parable without a dramatic hero in *The Confidence Man*—but with no real success in any instance. When he found a story ready to hand that needed only the element of suspense and the development of its incidental "significances," as in *Benito Cereno*, he could accomplish remarkable results. But his later artistic struggles produced no new skill that would enable him to continue his career. Perhaps (to elaborate his own comparison) his one completely successful wrestling bout left him too disabled for any further exercise of his whole energies in a struggle with the art of fiction during the long period between *The Confidence Man* and *Billy Budd*.

At any rate, when at the age of thirty-seven he closed his early career as a writer of fiction, he did so when his artistic craftsmanship was little more than that of an extraordinarily talented amateur—effective only when external influences and personal experiences were united in a fortunate, but largely fortuitous, combination.

MERTON M. SEALTS, JR. [1915–   ], professor of English at the University of Wisconsin, is the author of *Melville's Reading* and *Melville as Lecturer*. With Harrison Hayford he is coeditor of the definitive edition of *Billy Budd, Sailor*, and he is one of the editors of the *Journals and Miscellaneous Notebooks of Ralph Waldo Emerson*.

Herman Melville's "I and My Chimney"

MERTON M. SEALTS, JR.

The five years between the publication of *Moby-Dick* and his advent to the Holy Land were the most crucial in Melville's long life. . . ."[1] So Raymond Weaver has written of the obscure period in Herman Melville's career between 1851 and 1856 which included the writing of *Pierre* (1852), a number of short stories and sketches for periodicals (1853–1856), and *The Confidence-Man* (1857). At this time Melville was living at Arrowhead, his farm-house near Pittsfield, Massachusetts, which provided the setting for some of his less familiar prose. Such is the case with "I and My Chimney," a short sketch in a humorous vein probably written near the end of 1855,[2] in which "Melville makes the old chimney at Arrowhead the chief character in a sketch of his domestic life at Pittsfield. . . ."[3] But the story, as will be shown, is more than a mere descriptive sketch: it is Melville's subtle comment on a major spiritual crisis of his life. The clue to certain elements in *Pierre* is also afforded by an understanding of Melville's procedure in writing "I and My Chimney."

A brief account of the plot of the story should be useful in further discussion. The action turns on the affection of its narrator for his beloved old chimney, which he describes in detail,

[1] In the Introduction to his edition of Melville's *Journal up the Straits, October 11, 1856–May 5, 1857* (New York, 1935), p. xii.

To Herman Melville's granddaughter, Mrs. Eleanor Melville Metcalf, and to the Committee on Higher Degrees in the History of American Civilization, Harvard University, I am indebted for permission to quote from manuscript material as indicated below. This material, hitherto unpublished, is now in the Melville Collection of the Harvard University Library. Mr. William Braswell of Purdue University has also allowed me to quote from his unpublished dissertation, *Herman Melville and Christianity*. For these and other favors connected with the preparation of this article, I am grateful.

[2] [Published anonymously in *Putnam's Monthly Magazine*, VII (March 1856), 269–283; from a reference in George W. Curtis' editorial correspondence with John A. Dix it is now known that the manuscript was in the editors' hands prior to September 7, 1855. Jay Leyda, *The Melville Log* (New York, 1951), II, 504, suggests that Melville may have submitted it as early as mid-July of that year.—MMS, 1966.]

[3] Raymond Weaver, *Herman Melville, Mariner and Mystic* (New York, 1921), p. 308.

American Literature, Vol. 13 (May 1941) 142–51.

and his lengthy dispute with his wife over her proposals to alter it and later to remove it entirely from the house. Over the protests of her husband, the wife employs an architect and stonemason, Scribe by name, to make a thorough examination of the chimney. Scribe startles the family by suggesting the possible existence of a secret closet within the structure, and the wife and daughters immediately conjure up visions of treasure hidden away by the late builder of the house—the narrator's mysterious kinsman, Captain Julian Dacres. But the husband, to put a stop to such foolishness and to gain a little peace for himself, eventually bribes the not unwilling Scribe to accept fifty dollars in return for a certificate attesting to the entire soundness of the chimney. Fortified with this evidence, which he hangs prominently above the fireplace, the narrator refuses to countenance the slightest alteration to the chimney, but as the story closes he is still facing minor assaults of the opposition and "standing guard over my mossy old chimney; for it is resolved between me and my chimney, that I and my chimney will never surrender." [4]

This rather slight plot has attracted less attention to the story than has its setting, drawn as it is from Melville's surroundings at Arrowhead. Weaver, noting this factual background, states that the farmhouse itself was built in 1780 by a Captain David Bush, but he does not call attention to Bush's transformation by Melville into the narrator's kinsman, Captain Dacres. This is but one example of Melville's free handling of details in the story, which Weaver does not discuss,[5] nor have Melville's other full-length biographers added appreciably to Weaver's treatment of the story. John Freeman remarks only that it is "an example of Melville writing like Hawthorne," [6] and Lewis Mumford says merely that it is more an essay "in character" than a tale.[7] Yet Mumford himself sees "a glimpse of Melville's own drift of mind" in other prose of this period,[8] and more recent

---

[4] "I and My Chimney," in *Billy Budd and Other Prose Pieces* (Vol. XIII in the Standard Edition of Melville's works, 16 vols., London, Constable and Co., 1922–24), p. 311. All succeeding references to Melville's works are to volumes of the Constable edition.

[5] Weaver, *Herman Melville, Mariner and Mystic*, pp. 308 ff.

[6] John Freeman, *Herman Melville* (London, 1926), p. 52.

[7] Lewis Mumford, *Herman Melville* (New York, 1929), p. 236.

[8] *Ibid.*, p. 238.

investigation has found Melville's penchant for symbolism revealed even in one of his most matter-of-fact sketches.[9] With this in mind, the extent of Melville's departures from literal truth in "I and My Chimney" should be carefully considered.

First, as pointed out above, Melville makes the builder of the house a kinsman of the narrator, naming him "Dacres." Secondly, he places in the story a household of four persons: the husband and wife with their two daughters, Anna and Julia. Melville's own daughters were younger than these two characters: Elizabeth was born in 1853 and Frances in 1855, both before the probable time of composition of the story. In addition, the family at Arrowhead included two older sons, Melville's own sisters, and his mother. The presence of Melville's mother is significant because of a notation made by Melville's wife concerning the spouse of the story: "All this about his wife, applied to his mother—who was very vigorous and energetic about the farm, etc." If Mrs. Melville is correct, this represents still another departure from literal truth. The nagging spouse, far from an attractive figure, is scarcely typical of Melville's own wife, whereas according to family tradition his mother was persistently critical. More than one writer toys with the idea that the domineering Mary Glendinning in *Pierre* is based on the character of Maria Gansevoort Melville, and the wife of "I and My Chimney" may be cut from the same pattern. But Mrs. Melville's notation goes still further: "The proposed removal of the chimney," she continues, "is purely mythical."[10] Not only the

[9] E. H. Eby, "Herman Melville's 'Tartarus of Maids,'" *Modern Language Quarterly*, I, 95–100 (March, 1940). Eby holds that here "Melville's main intention is to represent through the medium of the story the biological burdens imposed on women because they bear the children. This is conveyed by symbolism remarkably consistent and detailed" (p. 97).

[10] Weaver prints this notation with the text of the story in the Constable edition, p. 287. He is inaccurate in his accompanying statement that it is taken from the *manuscript* of the story, which has apparently not survived. Mrs. Melville made her notation on a printed copy of the story which, with clippings of other periodical pieces by her husband, she collected in a binder. [This volume, formerly in the possession of her granddaughter, the late Mrs. Henry K. Metcalf, is now in the Harvard College Library. What Mrs. Melville termed the "purely mythical" proposal to remove the chimney may have been suggested by alterations made at the nearby Broadhall in 1851 after Melville's friends the J. R. Morewoods bought the property from his uncle Thomas. As Mrs. Morewood explained in a letter of November 7, 1851, to George L. Duyckinck (Duyckinck

characters, then, but also the motivation of the plot itself shows Melville's inventive touch—and Melville never invents without purpose. In *Mardi, Moby-Dick,* and *Pierre,* Melville's myth-making is intentionally allegorical and symbolic. If the removal of the chimney is "purely mythical," has Melville more to communicate than the mere spinning of a yarn? And why should he write of a chimney?

In *Pierre,* published four years before, Melville had described "the gray and grand old tower" of the Church of the Apostles, "emblem to Pierre of an unshakable fortitude, which, deep-rooted in the heart of the earth, defied all the howls of the air." [11] The chimney in the present story is a similar emblem of fortitude, "for it is resolved between me and my chimney, that I and my chimney will never surrender." Again in *Pierre* Melville writes: "Deep, deep, and still deep and deeper must we go, if we would find out the heart of a man; descending into which is as descending a spiral stair in a shaft, without any end, and where that endlessness is only concealed by the spiralness of the stair, and the blackness of the shaft." [12] So Melville in his writing, like the poet Lombardo in *Mardi,* "got deeper and deeper into himself." [13] It is with the same purpose that in the present story he traces the shaft of the chimney: "Very often I go down into my cellar, and attentively survey that vast square of masonry. I stand long, and ponder over, and wonder at it. It has a druidical look, away down in the umbrageous cellar there, whose numerous vaulted passages, and far glens of gloom, resemble the dark, damp depths of primeval woods." [14] As it would be vain to search for the bottom of the endless shaft described in *Pierre,* so the narrator of "I and My Chimney" digs in vain about the foundation of the chimney. The vast area of this lower part of the structure is emphasized: ". . . large as it

---

Collection, New York Public Library), "a chimney had to come down" in order to allow enlargement of the dining room. J. E. A. Smith, *The History of Pitts-field, 1800–1876* (Springfield, Mass., 1876), p. 7, referring to the alterations at that time, mentions "removal of the broad chimney and the old-fashioned balustrade which surrounded the roof."—MMS, 1966.]

[11] *Pierre,* p. 378.
[12] *Ibid.,* p. 402.
[13] *Mardi,* II, 326.
[14] "I and My Chimney," p. 283.

appears above the roof," says Scribe, the architect, "I would not have inferred the magnitude of this foundation, sir." [15]

The significance of all this may be summarized briefly: the shaft is the image of "the heart of a man"; the chimney is an emblem of fortitude; what lies at its bottom is hidden in darkness. Like a pyramid in its shape, the chimney is thus discovered to have its greatest area shrouded in mystery. This consistent likening to the pyramids is important: "The architect of the chimney must have had the pyramid of Cheops before him; for after that famous structure it seems modelled. . . ." [16] Had the wife's projected tunnel been thrust into the chimney "some Belzoni or other might have succeeded in future ages in penetrating through the masonry, and actually emerging into the dining-room. . . ." [17] Belzoni was an Egyptologist. And again: "We seemed in the pyramids; and I, with one hand holding my lamp over head, and with the other pointing out, in the obscurity, the hoar mass of the chimney, seemed some Arab guide, showing the cobwebbed mausoleum of the great god Apis." [18] A commentary on this passage is afforded by an often-quoted sentence in *Pierre:* "By vast pains we mine into the pyramid; by horrible gropings we come to the central room; with joy we espy the sarcophagus; but we lift the lid—and no body is there—appallingly vacant as vast is the soul of a man!" [19] What Melville is saying in the story is that in pondering over and wondering at his "chimney" he is introspectively surveying his own soul—and that introspection is an endless, empty-handed search.

Melville's identification of the chimney with himself is made certain by the amusing connotations of other passages in the story. Built around the structure were "the most rambling conceivable" rooms which (like the organs of the body), "as it were,

---

[15] *Ibid.,* p. 295.

[16] *Ibid.,* p. 280.

[17] *Ibid.,* p. 292.

[18] *Ibid.,* p. 295. Apis was "supposed to be the image of the soul of Osiris. . . . He was also regarded as the reincarnation (or the son) of Ptah—except by Greek writers . . ." (*Encyclopaedia Britannica,* 14th ed., II, 99).

[19] *Pierre,* p. 397. Note the significance of other references to the pyramids: in a letter to Hawthorne written in 1851 as printed by Julian Hawthorne, *Nathaniel Hawthorne and His Wife* (2 vols., Boston, 1885), I, 405 ff.; a passage in "Bartleby the Scrivener," *Piazza Tales,* p. 64; the profound effect on Melville of the pyramids themselves, described in his *Journal up the Straits,* pp. 56–59.

dovetailed into each other. They were of all shapes; not one mathematically square room among them all. . . ."[20] Almost every room "was in itself an entry, or passageway to other rooms . . . —never was there so labyrinthine an abode. Guests will tarry with me several weeks, and every now and then, be anew astonished at some unforeseen apartment."[21] This jocular anatomizing depicts perfectly the enigma Herman Melville presented to his acquaintances, who were anew astonished every now and then by what he said and did. Carrying on the anatomical figure, Melville's narrator exclaims at his wife's proposal *"in toto* to abolish the chimney":

> What! . . . abolish the chimney? To take out the backbone of anything, wife, is a hazardous affair. Spines out of backs, and chimneys out of houses, are not to be taken like frosted lead-pipes from the ground. Besides, . . . the chimney is the one grand permanence of this abode. If undisturbed by innovators, then in future ages, when all the house shall have crumbled from it, this chimney will still survive—a Bunker Hill monument. No, no, wife, I can't abolish my backbone.[22]

"Backbone," the colloquial term for fortitude, together with the reference to the enduring Bunker Hill monument (like the church tower in *Pierre*), further amplifies the connotation of the chimney. No wonder that to Scribe "this house would appear to have been built simply for the accommodation of your chimney";[23] that "I and my chimney could not be parted";[24] that "it is never out of my house, and never out of my mind";[25] that "I

---

[20] "I and My Chimney," p. 306. For still another physiological connotation, cf. pp. 286 ff.: the "mysterious closet." This passage should be read in the light of Eby's article, cited above, and with reference to the chronology of Melville's family life in 1855. Those familiar with E. L. Grant Watson's article, "Melville's *Pierre*," *New England Quarterly*, III, 195–234 (April, 1930), should also compare the description of Pierre's chambers (*Pierre*, pp. 413 ff.), noting reference to "the dining room" there as in the present story (p. 292).

[21] *Ibid.*, pp. 292 ff.

[22] *Ibid.*, p. 294. Cf. the dedication of *Israel Potter* (dated June 17, 1854) to the Bunker Hill monument.

[23] *Ibid.*, p. 295.

[24] *Ibid.*, p. 298.

[25] *Ibid.*, p. 297.

look upon this chimney less as a pile of masonry than as a personage." [26] All this is entirely true, for the "chimney" is the heart and soul of Herman Melville.

II

The identification of the chimney with Melville's own personality would constitute nothing more than a piece of subtle ingenuity on the part of both author and reader were it not for the larger implication of "I and My Chimney." This centers in the "purely mythical" proposal to remove the chimney and the subsequent examination made of it by Scribe. Scribe's report of his findings reads in part as follows:

> It is my solemn duty to warn you, sir, that there is architectural cause to conjecture that somewhere concealed in your chimney is a reserved space, hermetically closed, in short, a secret chamber, or rather closet. How long it has been there, it is for me impossible to say. What it contains is hid, with itself, in darkness. But probably a secret closet would not have been contrived except for some extraordinary object, whether for the concealment of treasure, or what other purpose, may be left to those better acquainted with the history of the house to guess. [27]

The wife and daughters, on receipt of this report, immediately conclude that the mysterious kinsman who built the house must have hidden something away—another excuse for probing the chimney:

> Although they had never before dreamed of such a revelation as Mr. Scribe's; yet upon the first suggestion they instinctively saw the extreme likelihood of it. In corroboration, they cited first my kinsman, and second, my chimney; alleging that the profound mystery involving the former, and the equally profound masonry involving the latter, though both acknowledged facts, were alike preposterous on any other supposition than the secret closet. [28]

From this point on, the secret closet becomes the central topic of argument: over its possible existence the family quarrel

[26] *Ibid.*, p. 284.
[27] *Ibid.*, p. 300.
[28] *Ibid.*, p. 302.

bitterly. The wife argues that "when you think of that old kinsman of yours, you *know* there must be a secret closet in this chimney." [29] The husband, unable to silence his wife by out-talking her, finally resorts to the bribing of Scribe to certify, as "a competent surveyor," that having examined the chimney he "found no reason to believe *any unsoundness; in short, any—any secret closet* in it." [30] This studied phrasing makes the secret closet signify unsoundness, so that the reason for probing the chimney becomes to ferret out its weakness. The likelihood of such "unsoundness," it will be recalled, was corroborated by "first my kinsman, and second, my chimney."

In the story the specific kinship of the highly mysterious Captain Dacres is never disclosed. But in *Pierre* the immediate relatives of the hero are all marked at one time or other by mental unsoundness. Isabel, whom Pierre takes for his half sister, had been kept in a madhouse; [31] Pierre's father had died in delirium, [32] and Pierre's mother also had died insane. [33] "Nor did this remarkable double-doom of [Pierre's] parents wholly fail to impress his mind with presentiments concerning his own fate—his own hereditary liability to madness." [34] And behind this fear in Pierre lay Melville's knowledge of what had befallen one of his own parents. His mother was still living when *Pierre* was written, but in 1832 his father had died under the cloud of mental derangement. His condition on his deathbed is briefly described in a letter to Lemuel Shaw, Herman Melville's future father-in-law, from Thomas Melville (Herman Melville's uncle): "I found him *very sick*—induced by a variety of causes—under great mental excitement—at times fierce, even *maniacal.*—in short, my dear sir, Hope, is no longer permitted of his recovery, in the opinion of the attending Physicians. . . ." [35]

---

[29] *Ibid.*, p. 304. The ensuing dispute over the ash-hole is a strange passage, dealing with the wife, the cat, and St. Dunstan's devil. Cf. Isabel's mention of the cat in *Pierre*, "softly scratching for some hidden thing among the litter of the abandoned fire-places" (p. 163).

[30] *Ibid.*, p. 308. Italics mine.

[31] *Pierre*, pp. 168 ff.

[32] *Ibid.*, pp. 96 ff.

[33] *Ibid.*, p. 398.

[34] *Ibid.*, p 400.

[35] From an unpublished letter dated Albany, January 15, 1832, now in the Melville Collection of the Harvard University Library, printed with permission of Mrs. Eleanor Melville Metcalf and authorities of Harvard University. Peter

The pattern of "I and My Chimney" now begins to emerge, becoming more clear as the plot of the story unfolds. Following the bribing of Scribe, the narrator cites the certificate attesting to the chimney's soundness in an effort to put an end to the argument:

> Wife, . . . why speak more of that secret closet, when there before you hangs contrary testimony of a master mason, elected by yourself to decide. Besides, even if there were a secret closet, secret it should remain, and secret it shall. Yes, wife, here, for once, I must say my say. *Infinite sad mischief has resulted from the profane bursting open of secret recesses.* Though standing in the *heart* of this house, though hitherto we have all nestled about it, unsuspicious of aught hidden within, this chimney may or may not have a secret closet. *But if it have, it is my kinsman's. To break into that wall would be to break into his breast.*[36]

The tone of this passage contrasts with the general light tone of the earlier part of the story, as even a casual reading will show. The sudden seriousness here, in speaking of the "profane" meddling with any secrets of the kinsman, is more in keeping with the reverent mood of Pierre in approaching the image of his "sacred father"[37] enshrined in his mind,[38] or in retiring to the "locked, round-windowed closet . . ., *sacred*" to his privacies, where the ambiguous chair-portrait of his father is hung.[39] Though the beloved image is later so tragically shattered, the memory of his father "for right cause or wrong" remains ever *sacred and inviolate*" to Pierre.[40] That such a mood was also Herman Melville's is strikingly indicated by the name given the kinsman in "I and My Chimney," "Dacres" being simply an anagram for *sacred!* This is startling confirmation that both

---

Gansevoort had touched upon the matter five days earlier in a letter to Thomas Melville, now in the Gansevoort-Lansing Collection of the New York Public Library (Willard Thorp, *Herman Melville: Representative Selections*, New York, 1938, p. xii and n.).

[36] "I and My Chimney," p. 309. Italics mine.

[37] *Pierre*, p. 89.

[38] *Ibid.*, p. 93.

[39] *Ibid.*, p. 98. Italics mine.

[40] *Ibid.*, p. 267. Italics mine.

Dacres and Pierre's father are based on memories of the unfortunate Allan Melville.

Besides explaining the first of the two reasons given for the possible unsoundness of the chimney, this analysis is important in an understanding of Melville's intentions in *Pierre*. Many of the details of Pierre's situation, from his surroundings at Saddle Meadows to the torture of his failing eyesight, are unquestionably drawn from Melville's own life. Some critics, cautioned by Melville's distinct warning that "the thoughts we here indite as Pierre's are to be very carefully discriminated from those we indite concerning him,"[41] object to any interpretation of *Pierre* as its author's spiritual autobiography. But from this new evidence it is obvious that a fundamental element in Pierre's situation is taken straight from his creator's experience. When Pierre "dropped his angle into the well of his childhood, to find what fish might be there,"[42] he brought forth dark memories of the unhappy death of his father. And Isabel, supposedly his father's illegitimate daughter, is mysteriously connected with the father's fate just as the chimney in Melville's short story is related to the mysterious kinsman. There is general agreement among recent critics that Isabel, again like the chimney, symbolizes the depths of Melville's mind.[43] As it was impossible to reach the bottom of the endless shaft of the soul, the ultimate foundation of the chimney, so Pierre "renounced all thought of ever having Isabel's dark lantern illuminated to him. Her light was lidded, and the lid was locked." Such is the dark mystery surrounding the girl; though, Melville continues, by interrogating relatives "on his father's side" Pierre "might possibly rake forth some few small grains of *dubious and most unsatisfying things,* which, *were he that way strongly bent,* would only serve the more hopelessly *to cripple him in his practical resolves.* He determined

[41] *Ibid.,* p. 233.
[42] *Ibid.,* p. 396.
[43] Note the similarity in terms employed by Lewis Mumford, *Herman Melville,* pp. 220 ff.; E. L. Grant Watson, "Melville's *Pierre," New England Quarterly,* III, 201 (April, 1930); George C. Homans, "The Dark Angel: The Tragedy of Herman Melville," *New England Quarterly,* V, 723 (Oct., 1932); William Braswell, "The Satirical Temper of Melville's *Pierre," American Literature,* VII, 431 n. (Jan., 1936); Willard Thorp, *Herman Melville: Representative Selections,* p. lxxx.

to pry not at all into this *sacred* problem."[44] So in "I and My Chimney" Melville warns against the profane disturbance of secrets relating to his sacred kinsman.

I interpret this passage as the expression of Melville's own fear that, "were he that way strongly bent," he would experience the same fate as his father's by continued delving into the depths of his mind. His dilemma was something like that of Pierre over the symbolic Isabel: to acknowledge her publicly is impossible without hurting his mother; to vindicate openly her relationship to him means tarnishing his father's honorable memory. Melville's advice to his hero is to "quit Isabel" and to "beg humble pardon of thy mother," but Pierre is unable to free himself so easily from his problem. In the confusion of his soul at these "absurdities" he "would fain have disowned the very *memory* and the *mind* which produced to him such an immense *scandal upon his common sanity.*"[45] This sounds suspiciously like the two reasons offered for the existence of the symbolic secret closet, in "I and My Chimney." At the time of *Pierre* Melville had nevertheless continued his introspection just as Pierre in the novel gave himself over to Isabel. No wonder that he later concluded in "I and My Chimney" that he had been "a little out of my mind, I now think," in trying to lay bare the very *foundation* of the structure which his kinsman had established.[46]

That Melville's family shared his uneasiness is suggested by Mrs. Melville's private account of this portion of her husband's career, from the writing of *Moby-Dick* "under unfavorable circumstances" in 1850 and 1851 until the period now under discussion.[47] "We all felt anxious about the strain on his health in spring of 1853," writes Mrs. Melville: she is confirmed by authentic tradition. At the time of the publication of *Pierre*, Melville, says William Braswell, "had worked himself into so frightful a nervous condition that his family had physicians examine him for insanity. The physicians pronounced him sane and assumed responsibility for his actions; but authoritative tradition sur-

---

[44] *Pierre*, p. 199. Italics mine.
[45] *Ibid.*, p. 239. Italics mine.
[46] "I and My Chimney," p. 283.
[47] Weaver prints a lengthy quotation from Mrs. Melville's pocket diary in his Introduction to Melville's *Journal up the Straits*, pp. xv ff. [The diary itself is now in the Berkshire Athenaeum at Pittsfield.—MMS, 1966.]

vives that tells a pathetic story of his life during this period." In a note Braswell adds: "I base this statement upon personal talks with Mrs. Eleanor Melville Metcalf [Melville's granddaughter] and with Professor Raymond Weaver." [48]

Mrs. Metcalf, with whom I have also discussed the entire situation, agrees with me that "I and My Chimney" is an allegorical version of the circumstances leading to this examination. Melville's own serious mental condition was the primary cause, made doubly distressing to his family by the tragic memory of his father's death, which Melville himself had recalled in *Pierre*. Hence the relation of the chimney itself and the "kinsman" of the story to the possible unsoundness of the structure. It is conceivable that Melville's analysis of his own condition in writing *Pierre* played a part in the decision of the family to have his mind examined. According to tradition the subtler meanings of his work were a mystery even to his closest relatives,[49] but the pointed allusion to Pierre's father probably did not escape the notice of those familiar with the facts of Allan Melville's death— particularly Maria Gansevoort Melville and Lemuel Shaw. It is significant that Melville's mother is said to be the original of the character in "I and My Chimney" who instigates the examination, who is actively hostile to the narrator's "philosophical

[48] William Braswell, *Herman Melville and Christianity* (unpublished University of Chicago dissertation, 1934), p. 166 and n., quoted with permission of the author. [See William Braswell, *Melville's Religious Thought* (Durham, 1943), p. 106.—MMS, 1966.] Cf. also Weaver's discussion in his Introduction to Melville's *Journal up the Straits*, pp. xii–xxiv.

[49] Concerning *Mardi* Mrs. Melville had written her mother: "I suppose by this time you are deep in the 'fogs' of 'Mardi'—if the mist ever does clear away, I should like to know what it reveals to you . . ." (from an unpublished letter dated New York, April 30, 1849, now in the Melville Collection of the Harvard University Library, printed with permission of Mrs. Eleanor Melville Metcalf and authorities of Harvard University). Melville himself told Mrs. Hawthorne that she was "the only *woman*" who liked *Moby-Dick*, but that with her spiritualizing nature" she could "see more things than other people" (from a letter dated New York, Jan. 8, 1852, printed in part in "An Unpublished Letter from Herman Melville to Mrs. Hawthorne in Explanation of 'Moby-Dick.' " *American Art Association–Anderson Galleries Catalogue of Sale*, No. 3911, p. 9 [New York, 1931]). [In the Berkshire Athenaeum, as a bequest of the late Miss Agnes Morewood, granddaughter of Melville's brother Allan, is a copy of *Putnam's* for March, 1856, inscribed "Allan Melville. Arrowhead—/ Pittsfield / Mass. / (I and my chimney)"; there are question marks in the margins of the sketch on pages 269, 272, 277 (two), 280, and 283 and a check mark in the margin of page 280.—MMS, 1966.]

jabber," [50] and who even after Scribe's report continues to tap the wall of the chimney after the manner of a physician examining a man for life insurance.[51]

The possible identification of one other character in the story is worth considering—that of Scribe, the examiner. Again referring to Mrs. Melville's journal we find that Melville's physical health remained poor for several years after the writing of *Pierre*. "In Feb 1855 he had his first attack of severe rhumatism [*sic*] in his back—so that he was helpless—and in the following June an attack of sciatica. Our neighbor in Pittsfield Dr. O. W. Holmes attended & prescribed for him." [52] The relation between Holmes and Melville was more than that of doctor and patient. Holmes's "The Last Leaf" was written about Melville's own grandfather, Major Thomas Melville, and interesting records survive of vigorous conversations between the two younger men when both were in residence at Pittsfield.[53] Reviewing these points, we find that the literary doctor was on familiar terms with Melville and had served him in a professional capacity twice during the very year in which "I and My Chimney" was probably written. It has been shown that as the architect found no unsoundness in the chimney, that is, in Melville's mind; so doctors had "pronounced him sane and assumed responsibility for his actions." Is it possible that Holmes had been one of the doctors, and that Melville meant to indicate the fact in the story by giving the examiner there the name of "Scribe," or *writer*? In view of Melville's general procedure in composing the story, this identification is at least not implausible.

The significance of "I and My Chimney" may now be summarized briefly. It is Melville's account of the examination of his mind made a few years before the story was written, at the instigation of his family. This meaning is conveyed in disguised form by the plot itself, with the aid of symbolism parallel to that of *Pierre* though the terms are dissimilar. The examination

---

[50] Cf. "I and My Chimney," pp. 309 ff.

[51] *Ibid.*, p. 308.

[52] Introduction to *Journal up the Straits*, p. xvi. Note the reference to sciatica in "I and My Chimney," pp. 287 ff.; this may be of some value in confirming the suggested date of the story.

[53] See a letter of Evert A. Duyckinck to his wife dated Pittsfield, August 6, 1850, printed by Luther S. Mansfield, "Glimpses of Herman Melville's Life in Pittsfield, 1850–1851," *American Literature*, IX, 29–31 (March, 1937); M. B. Field, *Memories of Many Men and of Some Women* (New York, 1874), p. 202.

was made because of anxiety over Melville's nervous condition, represented by the speculation concerning the chimney, and with the knowledge of the tragic circumstances surrounding the death of his father, represented by the mystery concerning the late kinsman of the story. This fear of possible hereditary insanity was alluded to by Melville himself in *Pierre*. The characterization of "I and My Chimney" points to Melville's mother as the person responsible for the consultation of physicians, one of whom may have been Dr. Oliver Wendell Holmes. The examination revealed that Melville's nervous condition was not a manifestation of insanity, and the subsequent course of his life confirmed the judgment of his examiners.

Of the evidence afforded by records of Melville's career after this time, Forsythe observes that "no one who has any knowledge of Melville in his later years" needs such testimony. "For thinking people, the question . . . of Melville's sanity has long since been completely settled."[54] With these words there can be only thorough agreement. In the present study Herman Melville himself has been allowed to explain how the question was first raised: it cannot be too strongly emphasized that any suspicions based on his own nervousness and associated with memories of his father had been entirely groundless. This is not to minimize the seriousness of his condition in 1852–1853, though in a day when a better understanding of nervous disorders prevails than in Melville's own lifetime there is no reason for describing his difficulties in sensational terms. Had modern mental therapeutic knowledge been available to Melville himself, he and his family would doubtless have been spared much of the distress they were forced to endure. More important than misguided amateur psychologizing at this late date, however, is an appreciation of the unexpected extent to which, through employment of symbols, Melville committed his deepest spiritual problems to subtle analysis in print. There is further evidence for this practice in other work of the period of "I and My Chimney," as I plan to discuss in a future publication, but for the present it is sufficient to take leave of him still "standing guard over my mossy old chimney; for it is resolved between me and my chimney, that I and my chimney will never surrender."

[54] Robert S. Forsythe, reviewing Weaver's edition of *Journal up the Straits*, *American Literature*, VIII, 85 (March, 1936).

F. O. MATTHIESSEN [1902–50], critic and professor of English at Harvard. His books include biographies of Sarah Orne Jewett and Theodore Dreiser, *The Achievement of T. S. Eliot,* an edition (with Kenneth B. Murdock) of *The Notebooks of Henry James,* and *The James Family.* His most significant achievement was *American Renaissance.*

"A Bold and Nervous Lofty Language"

F. O. MATTHIESSEN

At the time of Melville's death, Richard Henry Stoddard, one of his few professed defenders, felt obliged to state that 'his vocabulary was large, fluent, eloquent, but it was excessive, inaccurate, and unliterary.' Some just application can be found for all the first five adjectives, for the fourth and fifth especially in *Pierre;* but the reaction of the modern reader to the last is that the Melville of *Mardi,* and, on occasion, even of *Moby-Dick,* could all too easily fall into the 'literary.' Stoddard's conventional standards betray themselves in his further remark that Melville's early books made him 'famous among his countrymen, who, less literary in their tastes and demands than at present, were easily captivated by stories of maritime life.' Actually Melville had felt himself constrained by just such genteel demands. In *White Jacket,* for instance, he said that his aim was to be a chronicler of the navy exactly as it was, of what might become obsolete, 'withholding nothing, inventing nothing.' Yet he found that he quickly reached the limits that were permitted him. When he wanted to present the scene of a flogging, the captain's abusive epithet had to be left blank, with the note, 'The phrase here used I have never seen either written or printed and should not like to be the first person to introduce it to the public.' His own modesty joined again with the taboos of his age when he came to probe the daily life of the men, for he skirted the subject with remote allusions to the *Oedipus* and to Shelley's *Cenci,* and with the remark that 'the sins for which the cities of the plain were overthrown still linger in some of these wooden-walled Gomorrahs of the deep.'

American Renaissance (New York: Oxford University Press, 1941), pp. 421–31. (Copyright 1941 by Oxford University Press, Inc.)

More fundamental than these evasions is the fact that Melville never felt impelled to the kind of discipline that was soon to actuate Flaubert in his desire to sacrifice everything to finding the word that would evoke the very look and gesture. Melville had a good ear for speech rhythms: in his review of Ross Browne's *Etchings of a Whaling Cruise,* his own memories of a mate's lingo, 'Pull, pull, you lubberly *hay makers!,*' foreshadowed his creation of Stubb and Flask. But even in *Moby-Dick* he was very intermittent in what would now be a main concern for many writers: to base the talk of their common men as closely as possible on American idioms. His deepest interest was other, as he had already phrased it in *White Jacket:* to 'dive into the souls' of men, even if that meant 'to bring up the mud from the bottom.' In *Mardi* he had attempted this by the device of Babbalanja's demon, but he had not yet developed a controlled heightening of diction that could make the reader accept the lack of verisimilitude. In *White Jacket* he fell between two goals. He was a master there neither of realism, nor of an intensified reality. The general level of honest but stiff writing, which had tended also to characterize his early travel books, can be briefly instanced by this description of a dying sailor: 'I could not help thinking, as I gazed, whether this man's fate had not been accelerated by his confinement in this heated furnace below; and whether many a sick man round me might not soon improve, if but permitted to swing his hammock in the airy vacancies of the half-deck above, open to the port-holes, but reserved for the promenade of the officers.' The defects need hardly be labored. The style is workmanlike enough, but its want of vividness comes from conventional rather than idiomatic phrasing ('if but permitted'), and from a diction still influenced ('accelerated by his confinement') by merely formal standards of correctness.

Melville suggests how he found the lead to the freedom of speech he needed, in a note on one of his war poems, 'Lee in the Capitol.' In trying to present, not what the General had actually said when summoned before the congressional Reconstruction Committee in 1866, but what might be imagined to have been his deepest feelings on that occasion, and in aiming to invest his words with heroic dignity, Melville was aware that he had taken 'a poetical liberty.' 'If for such freedom warrant be necessary, the speeches in ancient histories, not to speak of those in Shakespeare's historic plays, may not unfitly perhaps be cited.'

His liberation in *Moby-Dick* through the agency of Shakespeare was almost an unconscious reflex. Unlike Emerson he discussed at no point the origins and nature of language. The great philologian Jacob Grimm had, as Renan was to perceive, arrived at mythology through his investigation of speech.[1] Words and fables became finally inseparable for him, and he sought their common source in the most primitive and most profound instincts of the race, in its manner of feeling and imagining. It may be said of Melville that he intuitively grasped this connection. In his effort to endow the whaling industry with a mythology befitting a fundamental activity of man in his struggle to subdue nature, he came into possession of the primitive energies latent in words. He had already begun to realize in the dream-passages of *Mardi* that meaning had more than just a level of sense, that the arrangement of words in patterns of sound and rhythm enabled them to create feelings and tones that could not be included in a logical or scientific statement. But he did not find a valuable clue to how to express the hidden life of men, which had become his compelling absorption, until he encountered the unexampled vitality of Shakespeare's language.

We have already observed that other forces beside Shakespeare conditioned his liberation. Thomas Browne had taught him that musical properties of prose could help increase its symbolical richness. Carlyle's rhetoric may have drugged him into obscurities, but it had also the value of helping him rediscover what the Elizabethan dramatists had known, that rhetoric did not necessarily involve a mere barren formalism, but that it could be so constructed as to carry a full freight of emotion. But his possession by Shakespeare went far beyond all other influences, and, if Melville had been a man of less vigor, would have served to reduce him to the ranks of the dozens of stagey nineteenth-century imitators of the dramatist's stylistic mannerisms. What we actually find is something very different: a man of thirty awakening to his own full strength through the challenge of the most abundant imagination in history. Since Melville meditated more creatively on Shakespeare's meaning than any other Ameri-

[1] See Renan's preface to the translation of Grimm, *De l'Origine du Langage* (1859).

can has done, it is absorbing to try to follow what the plays meant
to him, from the superficial evidence of verbal echoes down
through the profound transformation of all his previous styles.

Shakespeare's phrasing had so hypnotized him that often
he seems to have reproduced it involuntarily, even when there
was no point to the allusion, as was the case with the 'tiger's
heart.'[2] On other occasions he enjoyed a burlesque effect: in
omitting from his account such dubious specimens as the Quog
Whale or the Pudding-headed Whale, he says that he 'can hardly
help suspecting them for mere sounds, full of leviathanism, but
signifying nothing.' He came closer to the feeling of the original
passage when he found an equivalent for the gravedigger in the
ship's carpenter, at work on a new whale-bone leg for Ahab,
who had broken his former one by jumping into his boat. Melville had marked Hamlet's answer to the King's demand for
Polonius: 'But, indeed, if you find him not within this month,
you shall nose him as you go up the stairs into the lobby.' Now
he transferred that to the situation where the carpenter, sneez-
ing over his job, since 'bone is rather dusty, sir,' is told by Ahab:
'Take the hint, then; and when thou art dead, never bury thyself
under living people's noses.'

You could trace such kaleidoscopic variations of Shakespeare's patterns throughout this book, since, once you become
aware of them, you find fragments of his language on almost
every page. Even Ishmael's opening remark about having 'no
money in my purse' probably re-echoes *Othello*. 'The Spirit
Spout,' that scene when a whale was sighted eerily by moonlight, and which, incidentally, was one of the episodes wherein
Mrs. Hawthorne read an allegorical significance that Melville
said he did not intend, seems to owe something of its enchanted atmosphere to the last act of *The Merchant of Venice*,
if you can judge from the effect that is built up to by the phrase,
'on such a silent night a silvery jet was seen.' The end of *Othello*
is more integral to the account of Moby-Dick's former assault
upon Ahab; but, as an instance of how Melville's imagination
instinctively reshaped its impressions to suit his own needs, it
is to be noted that

[2] In view of the enormous impression that *King Lear* made upon him, it is possible that even his chapter title 'Knights and Squires' was suggested by Goneril's
'Here do you keep a hundred knights and squires.'

> Where a malignant and a turban'd Turk
> Beat a Venetian and traduced the state,

is altered to: 'No turbaned Turk, no hired Venetian or Malay, could have smote him with more seeming malice.' On such levels, where the borrowed material has entered into the formation of Melville's own thought, the verbal reminiscences begin to be significant. What he implied by calling the crew 'an Anacharsis Cloots deputation' is made sharper by the addition that they are going 'to lay the world's grievances at the bar from which not very many of them ever come back.' The hidden allusion to Hamlet's 'bourn' from which 'no traveller returns,' serves to increase our awed uncertainty over what lies before them.

The most important effect of Shakespeare's use of language was to give Melville a range of vocabulary for expressing passion far beyond any that he had previously possessed. The voices of many characters help to intensify Ahab's. For instance, as he talks to the blacksmith about forging his harpoon, he finds the old man "too calmly, sanely woeful . . . I am impatient of all misery . . . that is not mad.' This seems to have drawn upon the mood of Laertes' violent entrance, 'That drop of blood that's calm proclaims me bastard'; or since it has been remarked that 'Ahab has that that's bloody on his mind,' it probably links more closely to Hamlet's 'My thoughts be bloody, or be nothing worth.' The successive clauses, with their insistent repetitions, 'Thou shouldst go mad, blacksmith; say, why dost thou not go mad?' have built upon the cadences of Lear. Finally, as Ahab takes up the blacksmith's statement that he can smooth all dents, and sweeping his hand across his own scarred brow, demands, 'Canst thou smoothe this seam?,' Melville has mingled something of Lady Macbeth's anguish with her husband's demand to the physician, 'Canst thou not minister to a mind diseased?'

In view of Shakespeare's power over him, it is not surprising that in 'The Quarter Deck,' in the first long declaration from Ahab to the crew, Melville broke at times into what is virtually blank verse, and can be printed as such:

> But look ye, Starbuck, what is said in heat,
> That thing unsays itself. There are men
> From whom warm words are small indignity.
> I meant not to incense thee. Let it go.

> Look! see yonder Turkish cheeks of spotted tawn—
> Living, breathing pictures painted by the sun.
> The pagan leopards—the unrecking and
> Unworshipping things, that live, and seek and give
> No reasons for the torrid life they feel!

That division into lines has been made without alteration of a
syllable, and though there are some clumsy sequences, there is
no denying the essential pattern. Nor is this a solitary case.
Ahab's first soliloquy begins:

> I leave a white and turbid wake;
> Pale waters, paler cheeks, where'er I sail.
> The envious billows sidelong swell to whelm
> My track; let them; but first I pass.

Starbuck's meditation opens the next chapter:

> My soul is more than matched; she's overmanned;
> And by a madman! Insufferable sting . . .

The danger of such unconsciously compelled verse is always
evident. As it wavers and breaks down again into ejaculatory
prose, it seems never to have belonged to the speaker, to have
been at best a ventriloquist's trick. The weakness is similar in
those speeches of Ahab's that show obvious allusions to a series
of Shakespearean characters. The sum of the parts does not
make a greater whole; each one distracts attention to itself and
interferes with the singleness of Ahab's development.

Emerson had thought about this problem. Writing in his
journal in 1838 about the experience of having re-read *Lear* and
Hamlet on successive days, he did not feel obliged to assume
his platform manner, and to call for the emergence of a super
philosopher-poet. He was lost in wonder at 'the perfect mastery'
of the architectural structure of these wholes. Yet they faced
him as always with the question of the derivative literature of
his own country, since he knew that, despite all his admiration,
he could not construct 'anything comparable' even to one scene.
'Set me to producing a match for it, and I should instantly depart
into mouthing rhetoric.'

That Melville so departed on many occasions may hardly
be gainsaid. Yet *Moby-Dick* did not become another *Prince of
Parthia*. This first tragedy by an American, composed in 1759

by Thomas Godfrey, a young Philadelphian, foreshadowed the romantic conventions that still were prevailing on the stage in Melville's day. It set its scene in a country of whose life its author knew nothing, at the beginning of the Christian era. It passed over contemporary themes, with which, as an officer in the militia shortly to undertake the expedition to Fort Duquesne, Godfrey was to become better acquainted. But even if he had written his tragedy after he had gone as a tobacco factor to North Carolina—where he was to die of a sunstroke at twenty-seven—it is improbable that he would have brought his poetry nearer home. For it resumed the debate between love and honor where Dryden had left off, and made its lines a pastiche of familiar quotations from Shakespeare, and of some less familiar from Beaumont and Fletcher. By the time of Boker the manner had been more subtly assimilated, but the main problem still remained unsolved. Emerson came near to suggesting its resolution in his journal of 1843:

> Do not write modern antiques like Landor's *Pericles* or Goethe's *Iphigenia* . . . or Scott's *Lay of the Last Minstrel*. They are paste jewels. You may well take an ancient subject where the form is incidental merely, like Shakespeare's plays, and the treatment and dialogue is simple, and most modern. But do not make much of the costume. For such things have no verity; no man will live or die by them. The way to write is to throw your body at the mark when your arrows are spent, like Cupid in Anacreon. Shakespeare's speeches in *Lear* are in the very dialect of 1843.

No matter whether Shakespeare's language seems to us anything but 'simple,' Melville's feeling that such words spoke to him directly of life as he knew it called forth from him an almost physical response. The first result might be that he started to write high-flown speeches entirely under the dramatist's spell. But they did not remain mere posturing, since he was able 'to throw his body at the mark.' The weight of his experience backed up what he wanted to do with words. He knew what he was about in the way he prepared the reader for the improbability of Ahab's diction. He stated that there were instances, among the 'fighting Quakers' of Nantucket, of men who, 'named with Scripture names—a singularly common fashion on the island,' had in childhood naturally imbibed 'the stately dramatic thee and thou of the Quaker idiom.' Such men were substantially schooled in the 'daring and boundless adventure' of whaling; they were led, 'by the stillness and seclusion of many long night-watches in the remotest waters,' to think 'untraditionally and independently.' Moreover—and here is a telling factor that operated on Melville as well as on Ahab—they received 'all nature's sweet or savage impressions fresh from her own virgin voluntary and confiding breast,' and had come, 'thereby chiefly, but with some help from accidental advantages, to learn a bold and nervous lofty language.'

In Melville's case the accident of reading Shakespeare had been a catalytic agent, indispensable in releasing his work from limited reporting to the expression of profound natural forces. Lear's Fool had taught him what Starbuck was to remark about poor Pip, that even the exalted words of a lunatic could penetrate to the heavenly mysteries. But Melville came into full possession of his own idiom, not when he was half following Shakespeare, but when he had grasped the truth of the passage in *The Winter's Tale* that 'The art itself is nature,'[3] when, writing out of his own primary energy, he could end his description of his hero in language that suggests Shakespeare's, but is not an imitation of it: 'But Ahab, my captain, still moves before me in all his Nantucket grimness and shagginess; and in this episode touching emperors and kings, I must not conceal that I have only to do with a poor old whale-hunter like him; and, therefore, all outward majestical trappings and housings are denied me. Oh, Ahab! what shall be grand in thee, it must needs be plucked at from the skies, and dived for in the deep, and featured in the unbodied air!' The final phrase seems particularly Shakespearean in its imaginative richness, but its two key words appear only once each in the plays, 'featured' in *Much Ado* ('How wise, how noble, young, how rarely featured'), 'unbodied' in *Troilus and Cressida* ('And that unbodied figure of the thought That gave't surmised shape'), and to neither of these usages is Melville indebted for his fresh combination. The close concatenation of 'dived' and 'plucked' is probably dependent upon their presence in Hotspur's

[3] See above, p. 386.

> By heaven methinks it were an easy leap,
> To pluck bright honour from the pale-fac'd moon,
> Or dive into the bottom of the deep,
> Where fathom-line could never touch the ground,
> And pluck up drowned honour by the locks.

But Melville has adapted these verbs of action so entirely to his own usage that they have become his possession as well as Shakespeare's.

In driving through to his conception of a tragic hero who should be dependent upon neither rank nor costume, Melville showed his grasp of the kind of art 'that nature makes,' and fulfilled Emerson's organic principle. His practice of tragedy, though it gained force from Shakespeare, had real freedom; it did not base itself upon Shakespeare, but upon man and nature as Melville knew them. Therefore, he was able to handle, in his greatest scenes, a kind of diction that depended upon no source, and that could, as Lawrence noted, convey something 'almost superhuman or inhuman, bigger than life.' This quality could be illustrated at length from the language of 'The Grand Armada' or 'The Try-Works' or the final chase, or from Ishmael's declaration of what the white whale signified for him. One briefer example of how Melville had learned under Shakespeare's tutelage to master, at times, a dramatic speech that does not encroach upon verse, but draws upon a magnificent variety and flow of language, is Ahab's defiance of fire:

> Oh! thou clear spirit of clear fire, whom on these seas I as Persian once did worship, till in the sacramental act so burned by thee, that to this hour I bear the scar; I now know thee, thou clear spirit, and I now know that thy right worship is defiance. To neither love nor reverence will thou be kind; and e'en for hate thou canst but kill; and all are killed. No fearless fool now fronts thee. I own thy speechless, placeless power; but to the last gasp of my earthquake life will dispute its unconditional, unintegral mastery in me. In the midst of the personified impersonal, a personality stands here. Though but a point at best; whenceso'er I came; whereso'er I go; yet while I earthly live, the queenly personality lives in me, and feels her royal rights. But war is pain, and hate is woe. Come in thy lowest form of love,

and I will kneel and kiss thee; but at thy highest, come as
mere supernal power; and though thou launchest navies of
full-freighted worlds, there's that in here that still remains
indifferent. Oh, thou clear spirit, of thy fire thou madest me,
and like a true child of fire, I breathe it back to thee.

The full meaning of that speech can be apprehended only
in its context in the tumultuous suddenness of the storm, and in
relation to Ahab's diabolic bond with the fire-worshipping Parsee. Even in that context it is by no means clear exactly how
much Melville meant to imply in making Ahab regard the fire
as his father, and presently go on to say: 'But thou art my fiery
father; my sweet mother, I know not. Oh, cruel! what hast thou
done with her? There lies my puzzle.' Immersed in primitive
forces in *Moby-Dick*, Melville soon learned that—as he made
Ishmael remark concerning 'the gliding great demon of the seas
of life'—there were 'subterranean' levels deeper than his understanding could explain or fathom. But whatever the latent radia-
tions of intuition in this passage, they emanate from a core of
articulated thought. Here, if Emerson's prejudice against the
novel had only allowed him to see it, was the proof that the
dialect of mid-nineteenth-century America could rise to dramatic heights. That does not mean that any American ever
spoke like this, any more than Elizabethans talked like Lear;
but it does mean that the progressions of Melville's prose are
now based on a sense of speech rhythm, and not on anybody
else's verse. The elaborate diction should not mislead us into
thinking that the words have been chosen recklessly, or merely
because they sounded well. For they are combined in a vital
rhetoric, and thereby build up a defense of one of the chief doc-
trines of the age, the splendor of the single personality. The
matching of the forces is tremendous: the 'placeless,' 'supernal
power,' a symbol of the inscrutable mystery which Ahab so
hates, is set over against his own integrity, which will admit
the intrusion of nothing 'unintegral,' and which glories both in
its 'queenly' magnificence and in the terrible violence of its
'earthquake life.' The resources of the isolated man, his courage
and his staggering indifference to anything outside himself, have
seldom been exalted so high.

The verbal resources demonstrate that Melville has now
mastered Shakespeare's mature secret of how to make language

itself dramatic. He has learned to depend more and more upon verbs of action, which lend their dynamic pressure to both movement and meaning. A highly effective tension is set up by the contrast between 'thou launchest navies of full-freighted worlds' and 'there's that in here that still remains indifferent.' The compulsion to strike the breast exerted by that last clause suggests how thoroughly the drama has come to inhere in the words. Melville has also gained something of the Shakespearean energy of verbal compounds ('full-freighted'); and something, too, of the quickened sense of life that comes from making one part of speech act as another—for example, 'earthquake' as an adjective, or the coining of 'placeless,' an adjective from a noun.

But Melville's new ripeness of power should not be thought of solely in relation to his drama. It is just as apparent in his narrative, as can be suggested very briefly by one of his many Biblical allusions, which for once he makes not for solemnity but to heighten humor. He is just finishing his chapter on 'The Tail': 'Dissect him how I may, then, I but go skin deep; I know him not, and never will. But if I know not even the tail of this whale, how understand his head? much more, how comprehend his face, when face he has none? Thou shalt see my back parts, my tail, he seems to say, but my face shall not be seen. But I cannot completely make out his back parts; and hint what he will about his face, I say again he has no face.'

The effect of that burlesque is to magnify rather than to lessen his theme, not to blaspheme Jehovah, but to add majesty to the whale. Melville's inner sureness was now such that it freed his language from the constrictions that had limited *White Jacket*. He had regained and reinforced the gusto of *Typee* on a level of greater complexity. Whether or not he consciously intended to symbolize sex in the elemental energies of fire or of the white whale, when he wanted to deal with the subject directly he did not resort to guarded hints, but handled very simply the Whitmanesque comradeship between Ishmael and Queequeg. In 'The Cassock' he could also write a chapter about the heroic phallus of the whale.

NATHALIA WRIGHT [1913–   ] is professor of English at the University of Tennessee. She has written *Horatio Greenough: The First American Sculptor* and *American Novelists in Italy* and is one of the editors of a new edition of Washington Irving.

Imagery

NATHALIA WRIGHT

All Melville's writing from the realistic *Typee* onward is highly imagistic, and all his images have an interrelationship which constantly enhances their individual effect. His penchant for calling the names of remote lands and forgotten cities is scarcely separable from his fondness for the sea, nor his fondness for the sea from his sensibility to movement and to light and shadow. His preference for massive objects in nature is akin to his liking for kings and for gods. Akin to both is his use of hyperbole, and his exaggerations themselves lead eventually to his paradoxes.

Nor do Melville's Biblical images form a group distinct from all the rest. True, this is the aspect of his writing in which the influence of the Bible is most immediately apparent. But so largely a matter of general enrichment is it that there is hardly a topic, a sensibility, or a form manifest throughout his imagery which is not exemplified by Scriptural allusion. Even upon his titanic characters and his grand themes the effect is less extensive, though it may appear to be more significant. Yet as the imagery of any author reflects more clearly than the most direct exposition his principal interest, Melville's above all else reveals the extent and the depth of this influence upon him.

I

Considered as to content, his Biblical figures represent a convergence of the two subjects most prominent in all Melville's imagery: the antique and the marvelous. They seem to have dominated his imagination, as light attracted Bacon and as nature preoccupied Shakespeare. Probably his interest in the former was fostered by the archeological discoveries of the early nineteenth century, especially since the most notable were in

Melville's Use of the Bible (Durham, N.C.: Duke University Press, 1949), pp. 20–45.

Egypt, Babylonia, and Assyria, the ancient regions to which he most often alluded. The names of Belzoni and Champollion occur in his figures of speech, and Robinson's explorations in Palestine were among those familiar to him.

At any rate, Melville handled these two subjects in his imagery very much as a historian or an archeologist. That is, he spoke not of the generally old or wonderful but of actual men, countries, battles, books, and marvels of the past. Among these proper names Scriptural ones are prominent, and in their selection may be seen the preferences, unconfined to his Biblical material, which constitute the individuality of Melville's images. Of Biblical places, he preferred mountains and cities, especially ruined cities; of persons, kings and spiritually gifted or supernatural beings; of events, those of violence and those of vision or revelation.

Actually, except in *Clarel*, most of the place names on Melville's pages have little geographical significance. The words *Ararat, Tarsus, Bethlehem, Gaza, Gath, Uz, Sinai* are as likely to call to mind a character as a place. And so Melville meant them to do, when Redburn criticizes his Liverpool guidebook for not pushing back to "the man of Uz," and when Fayaway is said to prefer "the garb of Eden."[1] With the names of still other places the association is one of condition rather than topography. Tophet and Gehenna mean hell; Cities of the Plain mean doomed societies. "Let us freely enter this Golgotha,"[2] is White Jacket's way of introducing the subject of flogging through the fleet. Sacred and secular geography are allegorized together when Melville exclaims: "Out of some past Egypt, we have come to this new Canaan; and from this new Canaan, we press on to some Circassia."[3] Shinar, too, is emblematic, as the building of the bell tower is compared with the erection of the tower of Babel: "No wonder that, after so long and deep submersion, the jubilant expectation of the race should, as with Noah's sons, soar into Shinar aspiration."[4]

Generally more prominent in Melville's images than such places are persons, and most conspicuous of all are kings, whom

[1] *Redburn*, p. 190; *Typee*, p. 116.
[2] *White Jacket*, p. 465.
[3] *Pierre*, p. 44.
[4] *The Piazza Tales*, p. 253.

he preferred above all men in or out of the Bible. In *Moby-Dick*
alone the captain of the *Pequod* is compared to King Ahab and
King Belshazzar; the harpooner Daggoo to King Ahasuerus,
whom apparently Melville never identified with Xerxes; the fin-
back whale, making a shadow on the water, to King Ahaz's sun-
dial, for on "that Ahaz-dial the shadow often goes back."[5] The
cone of another whale is likened to Queen Maachah's idol:

> Such an idol as that found in the secret groves of Queen
> Maachah in Judea; and for worshipping which, King Asa,
> her son, did depose her, and destroyed the idol, and burnt
> it for an abomination at the brook Kedron [*sic*], as darkly
> set forth in the fifteenth chapter of the first book of Kings.[6]

Night cries heard by the *Pequod's* watch sound like the ghosts
of King Herod's victims. Moby-Dick, maddened by the sight
of the splintered boats, resembles King Antiochus's elephants
when grapes and mulberries were cast before them. A passing
whaler is named for King Jeroboam, and the masts of the *Pequod*
itself stand up like "the spines of the three old kings of Co-
logne,"[7] as fable designates the magi.

Indeed, for all his democracy, Melville's world has an aristocratic cast. When invoking the spirit of equality his aim was
not to degrade but to ennoble, to exalt the common multitudes,
and to infuse the veins of all creatures with one royal blood.
In so doing he more than once cited the Old Testament's gen-
ealogy of the race, as he did in Taji's exclamation:

> King Noah, God bless him! fathered us all. Then hold up
> your heads, oh ye Helots, blood potential flows through your
> veins. All of us have monarchs and sages for kinsmen; nay,
> angels and archangels for cousins; since in antediluvian
> days, the sons of God did verily wed with our mothers, the
> irresistible daughters of Eve.[8]

So it is with Melville's supernatural world, which he peopled also with individuals of rank. Rolfe, observing Margoth
gather geological specimens, declares that Milcom and Chemosh

[5] *Moby-Dick*, I, 171.
[6] *Ibid.*, II, 175.
[7] *Ibid.*, I, 86.
[8] *Mardi*, I, 13–14.

are scowling at him. As Clarel dreams of Ruth, who has shed a light in his room like that of the angel who released Peter from prison, he is as frightened as Eliphaz was at the spirit which passed before his face. The Arab troopers encountered by the pilgrims have the appearance at one time of the Witch of Endor, at another of the Carmel prophets. The palm tree is now addressed as a seraph, now as the Paraclete.

In addition to these Biblical types there were also a few individuals whom, judging by his repeated allusions to them, Melville preferred. They reappear in his pages in this order: Jesus, Jonah, Adam and Eve, Abraham, Solomon, Noah, Moses, Lazarus and Dives, Job, Samson, David and Goliath, Paul. Familiar as they are, they none the less exemplify his love of the erudite and the esoteric, since it is often one of the less familiar events of their lives which is commemorated. Thus, Noah is repeatedly introduced imbibing wine (Judah is in "'The true wine-zone of Noah'"),[9] Paul buffeted by the wind Euroclydon, David hiding in the Adullam cave (the sun is a hermit, "hutted in an Adullum cave"[10]), Abraham entertaining angels. Jesus, on the other hand, is most often pictured in some aspect of his passion.

Of course, Melville was not always original, and on occasion he treated individuals as the types which they popularly represent: Anak and Og as giants, Cain and Abel as participants in the first crime, the Hittites, Jebusites, and Philistines as enemies. In Job, says Clarel, "'Hamlets all conglobe,'"[11] and to Nathan's ancestors the Indians were Hittites. Jarl looks on Yillah as an Ammonite siren who might lead Taji astray. A robin or a canary arriving among the aquatic birds of Galápagos would be falling into the hands of the Philistines. The Elizabethans are Anaks among men. More than one South Sea island queen is called a Jezebel.

Most of all, however, Melville's imagery was enriched by the events of the Bible. Their tone varies considerably, from God's walking in Eden in the evening to the confusion of the Last Judgment. Yet, as Melville paused oftenest before the grand aspects of nature and the most dramatic moments of his-

---

[9] *Clarel*, II, 264.
[10] *The Piazza Tales*, p. 6.
[11] *Clarel*, II, 109.

tory, nearly all these events are of a spectacular nature. Many of them are miracles. Walking among the cripples at the Liverpool dock, Redburn mused:

> . . . I could not but offer up a prayer, that some angel might descend, and turn the waters of the docks into an elixir, that would heal all their woes, and make them, man and woman, healthy and whole as their ancestors, Adam and Eve, in the garden.[12]

In the course of compiling a list of the distinguished whale hunters of the past, Ishmael ingeniously proves first that the dragon which St. George vanquished was in all probability a sea and not a land creature, and finally that it was none other than leviathan himself:

> In fact, placed before the strict and piercing truth, this whole story will fare like that fish, flesh, and fowl idol of the Philistines, Dagon by name; who being planted before the ark of Israel, his horse's head and both the palms of his hands fell off from him, and only the stump or fishy part of him remained.[13]

The Biblical incidents to which Melville repeatedly referred, however, fall into two groups: events of violence and destruction, and events of vision and revelation. Prominent among the retold stories of violence is the destruction of Sodom and Gomorrah, which he cited in describing such dissimilar objects and occurrences as the dismal Liverpool houses, those ships manned by what White Jacket considers evil crews, the sinking of the *Bon Homme Richard,* the ash box outside the Negro church in New Bedford, the sounds of the sharks tapping against the *Pequod,* and, in *The Confidence-Man,* all wicked thoughts. Other violent narratives recurring on his pages are those of Lot's wife, the Final Judgment, Jael's murder of Sisera, David's conquest of Goliath, Cain's murder of Abel, the drowning of the Egyptians in the Red Sea, Herod's slaughter of the innocents, the Crucifixion, the swallowing up of Korah by the earth. Avows Ishmael:

---

[12] *Redburn,* p. 242.
[13] *Moby-Dick,* II, 103. See also *Poems,* pp. 62, 403, for other allusions to Dagon.

Preternatural terrors rested upon the Hebrews, when under the feet of Korah and his company the live ground opened and swallowed them up forever; yet not a modern sun ever sets, but in precisely the same manner the live sea swallows up ships and crews.[14]

The Biblical visions or revelations which Melville mentioned most often form almost as long a list as his favorite stories of violence. Among them are the dreams of Daniel and John, the Ascension, the Pentecost, the adoration of the seraphim, the appearances of angels and archangels. The waterspouts on the sea remind Taji of Jacob's ladder, descended and ascended by angels; and the deaf-mute in *The Confidence-Man,* because he is sleeping beneath the ladder leading to the next deck, suggests to his fellow-passengers that he is " 'Jacob dreaming at Luz.' " [15] In the poem "Art" Jacob's other angel visitant is introduced to propound an aesthetic theory in which hatred and love

must mate
And fuse with Jacob's mystic heart,
To wrestle with the angel—Art.[16]

The sphere of the marvelous and the supernatural which Melville thus entered was not of course compassed by these Biblical events any more than his ancient world was peopled only by Hebrews. As his sacred verges on his secular history, so these stories blend with others as spectacular in his imagery: accounts of unusual natural phenomena, such as St. Elmo's fire and the phosphorescent ocean; excerpts from Greek, Egyptian, Norse, and Hindu mythology; excursions into the realm of memories, dreams, and the processes of thought. The series is infinite, its progression revealing each of his sources at more than one point.

II

More than content, however, composes the anatomy of imagery, and more than Melville's mental interests determined the individuality of his pictures of the sea, history, and the Bible.

[14] *Moby-Dick,* I, 348.
[15] *The Confidence-Man,* p. 6.
[16] *Poems,* p. 270.

His sensibility also fashioned them. It was a sensibility first of all to movement, next to mass and line, finally to light.

Though all these qualities are of a visual nature, Melville's other senses were by no means undeveloped, as the abundant sensuousness of *Mardi* in particular testifies. He could smell the burning of Gomorrah and the pit; hear the trumpet in the Valley of Jehoshaphat, "the minstrels, who sang in the Milky Way"[17] at Jesus's birth, the "sounding brass" and "tinkling cymbal"; taste Belshazzar's feast; feel the heat of the fiery furnace. They are impressions whose quality is often extreme. His ear caught sounds audible only in the midst of a vast calm, as when he heard in *Billy Budd* the bony creak of the sea fowls' pinions. The scent of ambergris and the stench of the dead whale from which it comes afford a memorable contrast. Extremes of heat and cold, fire and ice, are his thermal stimuli. Hence part of the attraction which the story of Lazarus and Dives had for him was the contrast it represented between the coolness of Abraham's bosom and the infernal fires. The islands of Galápagos are personified:

> Like split Syrian gourds left withering in the sun, they are cracked by an everlasting drought beneath a torrid sky. "Have mercy upon me," the wailing spirit of the Encantadas seems to cry, "and send Lazarus that he may dip the tip of his finger in water and cool my tongue, for I am tormented in this flame."[18]

But in general Melville's feeling for movement is keenest of all his sensibilities. The motion of waves, ships, clouds, fish, and aquatic birds often provided him with descriptive figures for entirely unaquatic scenes, while outside this sphere his figure of the loom captures the same restless spirit. The subject matter of a preponderance of the Biblical events he recalled involves violent movement: battles, burnings, murders, flood, captivity, shipwreck, earthquake. White Jacket cites one such catastrophe as he complains of the tides, his figure, characteristically, appealing to opposite tactile senses at the same time:

> During the pleasant night-watches, the promenading officers, mounted on their high-heeled boots, pass dry-shod,

[17] *Mardi*, I, 14.
[18] *The Piazza Tales*, p. 182.

like the Israelites, over the decks; but by daybreak the roaring tide sets back, and the poor sailors are almost overwhelmed in it, like the Egyptians in the Red Sea.[19]

On a calm day, Ishmael observes, the sea "heaved with long, strong, lingering swells, as Samson's chest in his sleep."[20]

So keenly did he perceive this movement of life that to Melville its absence signified spiritual death. It is the unceasing and inconclusive motion of the sea rather than the sea itself which constitutes his symbol for truth. So in *Mardi, Moby-Dick,* and *Clarel* the quiet water and the still air are oppressive, and the calm which pervades the scene is often a "dead calm." White Jacket distinguishes between the future and the past: "Those who are solely governed by the Past stand like Lot's wife, crystallised in the act of looking backward, and forever incapable of looking before."[21] Ahab, in the midst of a stillness which arouses melancholy speculations in him, cries: "'Would now St. Paul would come along that way, and to my breezelessness bring his breeze!'"[22]

Next to movement Melville was most sensitive to mass and to line. He spoke oftener of architecture and sculpture than of other art forms, of hills more than plains. *Pierre* is dedicated to Greylock Mountain, and *Israel Potter* to the Bunker Hill monument. Many of the Biblical places he named are themselves celebrated for some kind of form: the Beautiful Gate, the gates of Gaza, the stones at Gilgal, the ladder at Luz, the Tower of Babel; neither Solomon's Temple nor the two-pillared temple of the Philistines was forgotten. The mountains of Scripture add their bulk to his pages: ". . . Romara flooded all Mardi, till scarce an Ararat was left. . . ."[23] His imagination saw giants even where there were none: the head of the slain whale is pictured hanging "to the *Pequod's* waist like the giant Holofernes's from the girdle of Judith."[24]

Often inseparable from this mass, in Melville's eyes, was

[19] *White Jacket*, p. 109.
[20] *Moby-Dick*, II, 326.
[21] *White Jacket*, p. 188.
[22] *Moby-Dick*, II, 38.
[23] *Mardi*, II, 239.
[24] *Moby-Dick*, II, 37. Nothing in the Bible indicates that Holofernes was a man of unusual size.

line. All varieties of hieroglyphics, inscriptions, writing, tattooing, charts, labyrinths, and mazes interested him; among them were the twisted streets of Constantinople, the skeleton of the whale, the parts of the idol Dagon and the Beast of the Apocalypse, the handwriting on Belshazzar's wall, the mysterious lots called Urim and Thummim, the mark of Cain. The tattooing on the person of Lem Hardy combines sacred and profane lines: upon his chest was "a sort of Urim and Thummim engraven,"[25] and his forehead bore the figure of a blue shark, a mark which was

> Far worse than Cain's—*his* was, perhaps, a wrinkle, or a freckle, which some of our modern cosmetics might have effaced; but the blue shark was a mark indelible, which all the waters of Abana and Pharpar, rivers of Damascus, could never wash out.[26]

A passage in *Mardi* characterizes Daniel not only as a prophet but a reader of inscriptions, as Taji and Jarl discover a barge of biscuit aboard the *Parki:*

> Our castle the bread-barge was of the common sort; an oblong oaken box, much battered and bruised, and like the Elgin Marbles, all over inscriptions and carving:—foul anchors, skewered hearts, almanacs, burton-blocks, love verses, links of cable, kings of clubs; and divers mystic diagrams in chalk, drawn by old Finnish mariners, in casting horoscopes and prophecies. Your old tars are all Daniels.[27]

To light Melville seems to have been more sensitive than to color, and it is another testimony of his susceptibility to sensory extremes that he passed continually from brilliance into shadow and out again. Biblical Hebrew itself has few color words, and when he turned to the Bible for a description of this contrast he often found one ready made. The *Pequod* plunges, in the phrase of Jude, through "blackness of darkness" after Moby-Dick, who is as white as the robes worn by the twenty-four elders in Revelation. The volcanic mountain Narborough sends up smoke by day and flame by night, in imitation of the

[25] *Omoo*, p. 38.
[26] *Ibid.*, pp. 32–33.
[27] *Mardi*, I, 73.

pillars of cloud and fire which led the Israelites through the wilderness. On the island of Juam the sun shines on one side of the mountain wall of the glen Willamilla, leaving the other side in darkness, while Taji fancies: "Thus cut in twain by masses of day and night, it seemed as if some Last Judgment had been enacted in the glen." [28]

Like the Hebrew poets, too, whose imagery of the sky he often marked in his Bible, Melville derived much of the light in his pages from allusions to the sun and the stars. In *Mardi*, where they lend support to Taji's fiction that he is a demigod from the sun, they are most noticeable, but other novels have their own astronomy. Exclaims White Jacket: "Quick! take the wings of the morning, or the sails of a ship, and fly to the uttermost parts of the earth." [29] The dawn in "Billy Budd" is compared to Elijah: "Like the prophet in the chariot disappearing in heaven and dropping his mantle to Elisha, the withdrawing night transferred its pale robe to the peeping day." [30]

As many of these figures suggest, the absence of light symbolized death to Melville, as did the absence of movement. This, too, is a conventional figure, which he sometimes gave doctrinal character by references to the "outer darkness," black Tophet, and the eternal night of the damned. "'Blindness seems a consciousness of death,'" [31] observes Pani, the blind guide of Maramma, whose particular blindness recalls Jesus's epithet for the scribes and Pharisees: "Ye blind guides."

The absence of color, however, signified quite a different thing to Melville from the absence of light. If the meaning of the white objects he mentioned varies from book to book, and within a single book sometimes becomes too uncertain to have consistent symbolic value, [32] there is about them all a suggestion of the infinite. The blond Yillah is inscrutable; the white whale is uncapturable; the pockets, crevices, and voluminous folds of the white jacket are inexhaustible; the first, blond incarnation

---

[28] *Ibid.*, I, 253.

[29] *White Jacket*, p. 4.

[30] *Billy Budd and Other Prose Pieces*, p. 101.

[31] *Mardi*, II, 21.

[32] F. O. Matthiessen has pointed out how the symbolic values of black and white change, from the simplicity of *Typee*, *Mardi*, and *Redburn*, through the difficult imagery of *Moby-Dick* and *Pierre*, to the Agatha story, "Benito Cereno," and *Billy Budd* (*American Renaissance* [New York, 1941], pp. 502 ff.).

of the Confidence-Man—the deaf-mute—is uncommunicative; the fate of the fair, white-clad Billy Budd is inexplicable. Most of the Biblical white objects he cited actually touch the subject of immortality: Ezekiel's valley of dry bones (from which Benito Cereno's vessel seems launched), the leper Naaman, the apparel of the twenty-four elders, the fleece of the Lamb, the pale horse of Death.

That death itself was, in fact, less disturbing an idea to Melville than infinity is often suggested in his imagery. When, for example, the artist in the prose section of "Rip Van Winkle" encounters the lean moralist and his white horse he is reminded of the Evangelist's vision of Death on the pale horse. "A cadaver!" he exclaims, applying the epithet both to the horseman and to the near-by white church, and inevitably calling to mind the Scriptural phrase, "whited sepulchres." In contrast, however, he introduces an image not simply of life but of a distinctly human life, for he thinks of the temples of Greece, their marble mellowing with age and "taking on another and more genial tone endearing it to that polytheistic antiquity, the sense whereof is felt or latent in every one of us." [33] Far more awesome than the specter of death is the whole monotheistic tradition—unfixed by place, shadowed by a sense of imminent physical dissolution, looking to a disembodied life of the spirit.

Within the realm of life and humanity, however, certain colors do brighten Melville's pages, especially in *Mardi* and *The Confidence-Man*. Most of them are primary colors of brilliant hue, emanating, like his whiteness, from objects of symbolic value themselves. Brightest of all and most recurrent is red, especially the red of fire. "Fiery" is one of his commonest adjectives, and in *Moby-Dick* even a squall at sea is called a prairie fire. His allusions to the pit, the burning bush, the fiery furnace, the pentecostal tongues, the pillar of fire—all augment this effect. And all, because they represent excruciating trials of the spirit, have the peculiarity common among Melville's figurative fires: they burn without consuming. Ahab, whose fire worship has a Zoroastrian character, "looked like a man cut away from the stake, when the fire has overrunningly wasted all the limbs without consuming them. . . ." [34] The *Pequod* itself burns with

[33] *Poems*, p. 328.
[34] *Moby-Dick*, I, 152.

corposants which do not destroy it, and which Ishmael compares to a Biblical scene in which fire actually has no part: ". . .
seldom have I heard a common oath when God's burning finger
has been laid on the ship; when His 'Mene, Mene, Tekel Up-
harsin' has been woven into the shrouds and the cordage." [35]
Even the whale must undergo an ordeal by fire; after being cut
in pieces, he is at length "condemned to the pots, and, like
Shadrach, Meshach, and Abednego, his spermaceti, oil, and bone
pass unscathed through the fire. . . ." [36]

Most original of Melville's color schemes, however, is his
use of green. Since the conventional "color" for innocence,
white, represented to him something much more nearly ultimate,
it rarely has this meaning in his pages. But in contrast there
did exist in his imagination a connection between innocence or
experience or primitive or domestic life and the color green.
Truth is colorless, but the humanities are green.

The stages by which Melville arrived at this association are
well marked. Green is "the peculiar signet of all-fertile Nature
herself" [37] in contrast to the barren sea and the city, and therefore it is the emblem of the natural man in contrast to the restless inquirer after the universal secret. In moments when their
thought wanders from the white whale, Ishmael speaks of the
"grassy glades" and "ever vernal endless landscapes in the soul,"
and Ahab, swearing, "'By the green land; by the bright hearthstone!'" avers his life to have been "'the masoned, walled-town
of a captain's exclusiveness, which admits but small entrance
to any sympathy from the green country without. . . .'" [38] In
Pierre's early ignorance of his father's character he maintains
a white shrine for him in the "green bower" of his "fresh-foliaged
heart," and when in subsequent disillusion he dreams of Enceladus he sees growing side by side beneath the Delectable
Mountain the green, aromatic catnip and the colorless, inodor-
ous amaranth—man's earthly household peace, and the ever-
encroaching appetite for God." [39]

[35] Ibid., II, 279–280.
[36] Ibid., II, 184.
[37] Pierre, p. 9.
[38] Moby-Dick, II, 264, 328, 329.
[39] Pierre, pp. 93, 480. In Egypt Melville was struck with the same contrast:
"Line of desert & verdure, plain as line between good & evil. An instant collision
of alien elements. A long billow of desert forever hovers as in act of breaking,

The Biblical image which served Melville best in this connection was the image of Eden. He used it habitually to represent the life of innocence and felicity, and on occasion implied its color by calling the spot a greenwood, a glen, a garden, a neighborhood of "green Havilah."[40] How closely he associated it with domesticity, so important an aspect of the humanities to him, is evident from his coupling it with another favorite image: the hearth. Redburn confidently says of the new world: ". . . there is a future which shall see the estranged children of Adam restored as to the old hearthstone in Eden."[41]

Yet the earthly felicities which Melville often described in terms of greenness were to him less than the highest truth. Nostalgically dreaming of home, Ahab has a vision of the outworn scythe lying in the field—rusting "'amid greenness.'"[42] For all his love of Saddle Meadows, Pierre's first mature experience compels him to depart; following him Lucy must see the vine, "'the green heart-strings,'"[43] torn from her easel before it is transported with her. In the Biblical story the parallel continues: Adam, expelled from Eden, proceeds into the world with the knowledge of good and evil.

Since such symbolic values as these attach to so many of Melville's oft-repeated figures—ceaseless motion, ponderous bulk and intricate line, whiteness, fire, greenness—it is remarkable that his imagery has such strong sensuous properties as well. For the truth which he sought to represent was, he insisted, without body, color, odor, or sound; it could not be reached by the senses. Yet the movement, forms, and colors of his objects are among the richest and most memorable parts of his creation. In a characteristically Gothic method, he succeeded in defining reality by describing its masquerade.

III

Contrasted with Melville's fondness for experimentation elsewhere, the structure of his imagery is conventional. Meta-

---

upon the verdure of Egypt. Grass near the pyramids, but will not touch them, —as if in fear or awe of them" (*Journal up the Straits*, p. 59).

[40] *Clarel*, I, 230.
[41] *Redburn*, p. 217.
[42] *Moby-Dick*, II, 330.
[43] *Pierre*, p. 443.

phor, simile, and personification are his figures of speech, the catalogue and citation his other favorite devices. These forms are generally brief, loosely connected with the progress of the narrative, allusive rather than allegorical, pointing out a contrast at least as often as a comparison. Their simplicity insures their principal effect: the effect of the particular and the exalted rather than of the general and the common.

This desire to particularize, part of the Romanticism of his nature, accounts for the preponderance of proper names on Melville's pages, from scores of sources. The stomach of the whale does not resemble a cave, but the Kentucky Mammoth Cave; and whales swimming together in herds are like Hartz forest logs on the Rhine. Instead of referring to a gun, a grizzly bear, a miner, an elm, pebbles in the sun, a slave on an auction block, a king putting down a rebel, he speaks of a Colt revolver, a Missouri grizzly bear, a Cornwall miner, a Pittsfield elm, pebbles flashing in the Cuban sun, a slave up for auction in Charleston, King Richard overcoming Wat Tyler.

The same individualization is achieved by Biblical metaphor and metonomy. The conspicuously marked fin-back whale is the Cain of his race, and the albacore is the Nimrod of the seas. The continent of Africa in *Mardi* is represented by the island of Hamora. The sperm whale ordinarily produces but one of its kind at a time, but it has been known to give birth to an Esau and a Jacob. The priest Aleema is described aboard his barge: "Meantime, old Aaron . . . sat, and eyed us." [44] Occasionally the allusion is suggested by the context, rising from it with appropriateness, even with inevitability. Redburn, describing the predicament of small craft at the mercy of larger fleets in the fog, personifies them with the remark: "Their sad fate is frequently the result of their own remissness in keeping a good look-out by day, and not having their lamps trimmed, like the wise virgins, by night." [45]

Most of Melville's allusions, however, are deliberately random. For he aimed thereby to suggest that, since almost any comparison would do, the original could be matched not once but hundreds of times. True, his catalogues, which bear out his intention, are often extremely monotonous on this very ac-

[44] *Mardi*, I, 151.
[45] *Redburn*, p. 124.

count, but at his best, by cutting all associations, he achieved
a startling originality. The unusual and even the bizarre are no
small parts of his imagistic effect. So, after witnessing Cuticle's
amputation of the topman's leg, White Jacket declares that one
day "life runs through us like a thousand Niles; but to-morrow
we may collapse in death, and all our veins be dry as the brook
Kedron [*sic*] in a drought." [46] The uncle in "The Happy Failure"
thinks he spies a boy sitting like Zacchaeus in the tree across
the stream—a story, incidentally, which Melville marked in his
New Testament.

Of course, it must be remembered that such associations as
these are not always as capricious as they seem, and that connections not visible on the page existed in Melville's mind. In a
simile totally unprepared for, the sailors of the *Highlander*, de-
prived of their tobacco, are said to be as "inconsolable as the
Babylonish captives." [47] But the inspiration for the figure may
be contained in the second chapter thereafter, where Melville
returned to the story of the captivity with more appositeness:

> A sweet thing is a song; and though the Hebrew cap-
> tives hung their harps on the willows, that they could not
> sing the melodies of Palestine before the haughty beards of
> the Babylonians; yet, to themselves, those melodies of other
> times and a distant land were sweet as the June dew on
> Hermon.
>
> And poor Harry was as the Hebrews. He, too, had been
> carried away captive, though his chief captor and foe was
> himself; and he, too, many a night, was called upon to sing
> for those who through the day had insulted and derided
> him. [48]

Evidently the similarity which Melville saw between Harry and
the Babylonian captives cast its shadow before, causing him to
compare Harry's shipmates to the same group. The Psalm echoed
in the longer passage is among those marked in his Bible.

Melville's chief fault in these brief figures was to be sometimes obscure, often grotesque. With characteristic fondness
for the unusual he introduced unfamiliar verses without expla-

[46] *White Jacket,* p. 327.
[47] *Redburn,* pp. 353–354.
[48] *Redburn,* p. 358.

nation and referred cryptically to familiar ones. Often the spirit of facetious journalism predominates. A captain, he suggested, interrogating a Portuguese as a prospective seaman, should inquire: "His knees, any Belshazzar symptoms there?" [49] One of the bachelors in the Temple desires a little more wine, just for his stomach's sake, like Timothy. Having to pay instead of being paid is an infliction of the two orchard thieves, and hell is an idea first born on an undigested apple dumpling. Pierre tells Lucy they will be married to the accompaniment of Job's trumpeters. Omoo enjoys his cube of salt beef and his hard biscuit after subsisting on the Nebuchadnezzar fare of the valley.

On the whole, Melville's more fully developed figures of speech, of whatever source, reflect greater discrimination on his part than the brief ones. They, too, particularize his material. But they also enlarge and elevate it by imparting to essentially mundane persons and affairs significance far beyond that which they have in themselves. Thus, the common cock of Merrymusk, who was "more like the Emperor Charlemagne in his robes at Aix-la-Chapelle, than a cock" and whose evening crowing "went out of his mighty throat all over the land and inhabited it, like Xerxes from the East with his double-winged host," was also like "some overpowering angel in the Apocalypse. He seemed crowing over the fall of wicked Babylon, or crowing over the triumph of righteous Joshua in the vale of Askalon [sic]." He seemed to be saying, "'Glory to God in the highest!'" [50] Vivenza, the land of promise, is likened to

> St. John, feeding on locusts and wild honey, and with prophetic voice crying to the nations from the wilderness. Or, child-like, standing among the old robed kings and emperors of the Archipelago, Vivenza seemed a young Messiah, to whose discourse the bearded Rabbis bowed. [51]

The English sailor calls for a circle to be drawn about two quarreling sailors, but the Manxman, pointing to the horizon, exclaims: "'Ready formed. There! the ringed horizon. In that ring Cain struck Abel. Sweet work, right work! No? Why then,

[49] *Billy Budd and Other Prose Pieces*, p. 272.
[50] *Ibid.*, pp. 153, 164, 168–169. Melville must have meant Ajalon, to which he properly referred in *Clarel*, II, 247.
[51] *Mardi*, II, 175.

God, mad'st thou the ring?' "[52] A sailor watches from his piazza distant showers "which wrap old Greylock, like a Sinai, till one thinks swart Moses must be climbing among scathed hemlocks there. . . ."[53] The multitudes of sharks that swam round the sperm whale's body, as soon as his flesh was pierced, "rushed to the fresh blood that was spilled, thirstily drinking at every new gash, as the eager Israelites did at the new bursting fountains that poured from the smitten rock."[54] Viewing the unfortunate Bartleby's corpse, the lawyer quotes the words of Job to a by-stander:

> "Eh!—He's asleep, ain't he?"
> "With kings and counsellors," murmured I.[55]

In thus endowing his material with importance Melville was not above purposeful exaggeration and even burlesque. Addressing Duyckinck as "My Beloved," he implored him to "come out from among the Hittites & Hodites."[56] White Jacket's duff is as tough as the cock which crowed on the morning Peter told a lie, and the whale smoke "smells like the left wing of the day of judgment; it is an argument for the pit."[57] Observing that the whale has no proper face, Ishmael imagines his reply: "Thou shalt see my back parts, my tail, he seems to say, but my face shall not be seen."[58]

Nor did Melville forget the traditional method of giving his words authority by the device of Scriptural citation. Here again he sometimes parodied, but often he was in earnest. White Jacket, discussing the order for all sailors to cut their beards, refers to "the theocratical law laid down in the nineteenth chapter and twenty-seventh verse of Leviticus, where it is expressly ordained, *'Thou shalt not mar the corners of thy beard.'*"[59] And in defense of the custom of dining at noon, he compiles a cata-logue of Old Testament characters:

[52] *Moby-Dick*, I, 221.
[53] *The Piazza Tales*, p. 6.
[54] *Moby-Dick*, II, 54–55.
[55] *The Piazza Tales*, p. 64.
[56] Aug. 16, 1850 (*Representative Selections*, p. 380).
[57] *Moby-Dick*, II, 179.
[58] *Ibid.*, II, 123.
[59] *White Jacket*, p. 447.

> Doubtless, Adam and Eve dined at twelve; and the Patri-
> arch Abraham in the midst of his cattle; and old Job with
> his noon mowers and reapers, in that grand plantation of
> Uz; and old Noah himself, in the Ark, must have gone to
> dinner at precisely *eight bells* (noon), with all his floating
> families and farmyards.[60]

Of the Royal Mission Chapel of Papoar, which he calls "the
chapel of the Polynesian Solomon," Omoo declares: "The materials thus prepared being afterward secured together by thongs,
there was literally 'neither hammer, nor axe, nor any tool of iron
heard in the house while it was building.' " [61]

This last comparison, as a matter of fact, did not originate
with Melville, being contained in one of his chief sources for
Omoo: William Ellis's *Polynesian Researches.* Here Ellis wrote:

> It is probable, also, that, considering the Tahitians as a
> Christian people, he [the native king] had some desire to
> emulate the conduct of Solomon in building a temple, as
> well as surpassing in knowledge the kings and chieftains of
> the islands.[62]

The difference between this brief suggestion and Omoo's
equally brief but bolder metaphor and citation is significant.
Doubtless Melville found and duly appropriated a good deal of
Biblical imagery in his secular reading, and it would be difficult indeed to say how many of his allusions were inspired by
secondary sources. Certainly Stanley's *Sinai and Palestine* furnished some for *Clarel,* and the original Israel Potter document
suggested the general Biblical parallel for that yarn. In such
cases, however, Melville's method seems clear. It was to trans-
form what he borrowed, extending and enlivening the original
figure or substituting a more apt one.

To the Bible itself, in fact, Melville could be quite unfaithful, with the same simple artistic purpose. Sometimes it is his
own connotation regarding a verse rather than the verse itself
to which he alludes. A double image results: one perceives, in
addition to the immediate object, not only a Biblical scene but

[60] *Ibid.,* p. 35.
[61] *Omoo,* p. 199.
[62] London, 1833, II, 381. Quoted in Charles R. Anderson, *Melville in the South
Seas* (New York, 1939), p. 223.

one suggested by it which existed only in the author's mind. So the old man whom the Confidence-Man meets at the end of his tale had "a countenance like that which imagination ascribes to good Simeon, when, having at last beheld the Master of Faith, he blessed him and departed in peace."[63] Though there is nothing in the Bible to describe Paul's voice, Redburn vows upon hearing the great bell-buoy in the Liverpool harbor: "I thought I had never heard so boding a sound; a sound that seemed to speak of judgment and the resurrection, like belfry-mouthed Paul of Tarsus."[64] When the "Titan" boards the *Fidèle* he is "slanting his tall stature like a mainmast yielding to the gale, or Adam to the thunder."[65] The evening sun is likened to "the mild light from Abraham's tent"[66] and the fish following the *Chamois* are "tame and fearless . . . as the first fish that swam in Euphrates."[67]

The same kind of double image occurs when Melville referred to uncanonical variations on Biblical themes. He called by name the repentant thief—Dismas, and the three magi—Amerrian, Apelius, Damazon; and alluded to the Iron Crown of Lombardy, said to be made of a nail from the cross.[68] He cited the theory of the Rabbis that Jonah's whale was a female and that the devils as well as the sons of God intermarried with the daughters of men. In Ishmael's eyes the gentle rollings of the Pacific "seem to speak of some hidden soul beneath; like those fabled undulations of the Ephesian sod over the buried Evangelist St. John."[69]

IV

This predominantly artistic impulse behind all Melville's Biblical imagery is nowhere so clear as in *Clarel*, though in all his poetry that imagery is far less effective than in his prose. The shorter poems do not afford a very instructive comparison with the prose in this respect, since the imagery in both is intro-

[63] *The Confidence-Man*, p. 321.
[64] *Redburn*, p. 161.
[65] *The Confidence-Man*, p. 113.
[66] *The Piazza Tales*, p. 139.
[67] *Mardi*, I, 172–173.
[68] *Clarel*, I, 324; II, 155; *Moby-Dick*, I, 209.
[69] *Moby-Dick*, II, 252.

duced into generally similar contexts. But the content of *Clarel* is different. As the principal occurrence of the poem is a pilgrimage, undertaken by a man in the avowed hope of achieving a religious faith amid the scenes of that religion's birth, the imagery is largely predetermined. And since the poet's purpose is didactic, this imagery is never inappropriate or unelucidated, but it is often dull and obvious. There are fewer short, dramatic allusions to the Bible than there are in the prose, and more narratives are lengthily retold as the pilgrims come upon their original settings.

The fundamental contrast, in fact, which is necessary in all imagery is lacking in the use of Biblical allusion in *Clarel*. Underneath a superficial similarity there must be a permanent gulf, to be crossed by the imagination. In Melville's novels, tales, and shorter poems such a gulf exists between his secular or realistic material and the interspersed Biblical allusions, whereby an older, a weightier, and often a supernatural theme is suggested. In *Clarel* that contrast is not possible. Even if it be conceded that Melville's pessimism here is less religious than naturalistic, ethical, and political, and that it is the sins of all Western civilization which he has laid upon Christianity, the theme of the poem remains superficially religious, the setting deliberately Biblical. Images which in *Moby-Dick* or even in *Battle-Pieces* would be effective are obvious here. There is no element of surprise.

How fully Melville appreciated the value of contrast in imagery, however, is evident also in *Clarel*. Although the method he here pursued to achieve it differs from that employed elsewhere, it is an equally ingenious method, and had his purpose in writing been less argumentative it could have made the Biblical allusions in *Clarel* as effective as those in the main body of his work.

The contrasts achieved with Biblical imagery in *Clarel* are two. Biblical scenes are again compared with secular ones, but this time the immediate object is Biblical, the allusion secular. It is his earlier method reversed. Thus, Vine is pictured looking at

the Crag of Agonies.
Exceeding high (as Matthew saith)
It shows from skirt of that wild path

> Bare as an iceberg seamed by rain
> Toppling awash in foggy main
> Off Labrador.[70]

The primitive hunter is called "Moccasined Nimrod, belted Boone."[71] Joshua battled his foes in a country which is like green Vermont. Tahiti is said to be the proper place for Jesus to have appeared in advent. The vision appearing to the shepherds at the time of his birth is compared with a phenomenon of nature:

> So (might one reverently dare
> Terrene with heavenly to compare),
> So, oft in mid-watch on that sea
> Where the ridged Andes of Peru
> Are far seen by the coasting crew—
> Waves, sails and sailors in accord
> Illumed are in a mystery,
> Wonder and glory of the Lord,
> Though manifest in aspect minor—
> Phosphoric ocean in shekinah.[72]

The other way in which Melville used Biblical imagery for contrast in *Clarel* was by juxtaposing with pagan imagery, an economy in the pilgrims' lengthy discussions and a welcome dramatic relief. Especially Greek mythology is thus exploited. The flowers blossoming at the Sepulchre of Kings are

> Involved in dearth—to puzzle us—
> As 'twere thy line, Theocritus,
> Dark Joel's text of terror threading . . . .[73]

Celio, the crippled blond, has "Absalom's locks but Æsop's hump."[74] Ruth's is

> the grace
> Of Nature's dawn: an Eve-like face
> And Nereid eyes with virgin spell . . . .[75]

[70] *Clarel*, I, 229.
[71] *Ibid.*, II, 6.
[72] *Ibid.*, II, 190.
[73] *Ibid.*, I, 111.
[74] *Ibid.*, I, 47.
[75] *Ibid.*, I, 67.

The Hellenistic Jews are characterized:

> "Recall those Hebrews, which of old
> Sharing some doubts we moderns rue,
> Would fain Eclectic comfort fold
> By grafting slips from Plato's palm
> On Moses' melancholy yew . . . ."[76]

Clarel's imagination is fired by the sight of the Syrian doves:

> It charmed away half Clarel's care,
> And charmed the picture that he saw,
> To think how like that turtle pair
> Which Mary, to fulfil the law,
> From Bethlehem to temple brought
> For offering; these Saba doves
> Seemed natives—not of Venus' court
> Voluptuous with wanton wreath—
> But colonnades where Enoch roves,
> Or walks with God, as Scripture saith.[77]

A striking use of metonomy and personification and one of the most dramatic of these comparisons occurs when Nehemiah envisages the Lamb of God:

> Last, dearer than ere Jason found,
> A fleece—the Fleece upon a throne!
> And a great voice he hears which saith,
> *Pain is no more, no more is death* . . . .[78]

This interchange of symbols goes on also between Christianity and Egyptology, when Vine compares Jesus to Osiris; between Judaism and Zoroastrianism, when Cain and Abel are likened to Ormazd and Ahriman; between Judaism and paganism, when Clarel questions

> Whether the lesson Joel taught
> Confute what from the marble's caught
> In Sylvan sculpture . . . .[79]

---

[76] *Ibid.*, I, 259. At the end of the Wisdom of Solomon in his Bible Melville wrote: "This admirable [?] book seems partly Mosaic & partly Platonic in its tone. Who wrote it I know not. Some one to whom both Plato & Moses stood for godfather."

[77] *Ibid.*, II, 143–144.

[78] *Ibid.*, I, 325–326.

[79] *Ibid.*, II, 99.

The exception of such passages as these, with their philosophical content, makes all the more distinct the chief difference
between Melville's sacred and his secular imagery: it is the infrequent use of Scripture in his strictly metaphysical figures,
that is, in his embodiment of abstractions. For this purpose he
employed general images such as the loom, the cave or mine or
labyrinth, the isle, whereas he introduced most of his Biblical
allusions in a context not of speculation but of the observation
of specific physical phenomena.

Yet without exception they all serve his fundamental imagistic purpose, which was the expression of thought. It was, like
that of the metaphysical school, not merely to ornament or to
vindicate an idea but to give it form. If speculation about time
or truth or security was best conveyed by naturalistic images, the
appearance of the fleeting moment and of the changing scene was
captured above all else by legend and by myth. In either case,
to subtract Melville's image is largely to subtract his thought
as well. The image is the essence of the thought—the allegory,
the type, the emblem of its otherwise incommunicable nature.

MILLICENT BELL, a professor of English at Boston University, is the author
of *Hawthorne's View of the Artist* and *Edith Wharton and Henry James:
The Story of Their Friendship.*

From Pierre Bayle and *Moby Dick*

MILLICENT BELL

When Melville bought an English translation of Pierre Bayle's
Dictionnaire historique et critique[1] early in 1849, he obviously
anticipated—with mock alarm—an "influence." He wrote Evert

[1] He might have had one of three English editions: 1710 (London, Harper, etc.,
4 vols.), 1734–38 (London, Knapton, etc., 5 vols.), and 1734–41 (London,
Bettenham, etc., 10 vols.), all folio. All references to follow will be to the 2nd
ed. (1734–38), reputedly more accurate than the first and with fewer addi-
tions "in the spirit of Bayle" by the English editors, than the third.

Publications of the Modern Language Association, Vol. LXVI (September 1951)
626–36. (Reprinted by permission of the Modern Language Association.)

Duyckinck, in whose library he may have come across it earlier: "I bought a set of Bayle's Dictionary the other day, & on my return to New York I intend to lay the great old folios side by side & go to sleep on them thro' the summer, with the Phaedon in one hand & Tom Brown in the other."[2] It was, of course, a moment for influences, the most receptive and most productive period of Melville's life. That year, he saw *Mardi* and *Redburn* into print, and made the memorable trip to England with the MS. of *White Jacket*. A few months later he moved to the Berkshires, where he met Hawthorne and began work on a new book about a whaling voyage. Though we hear no more of Bayle's *Dictionary* we can feel sure that the program of summer reading was carried out. I shall show how pervasive were its effects on *Moby Dick*.

One of the knottiest problems in considering Melville's use of his reading will always be the question of how much he read in original sources and how much he derived at second-hand. How secondary sources might be used to give the appearance of a larger primary acquaintance is exhibited in the massive cetological display of *Moby Dick*, which, as has been amply shown,[3] draws references to numerous whaling authorities from a few basic texts; the scholarly citations of Scoresby, Beale, Bennett, and Browne enabled Melville to stuff his own discussion with mention of writers he himself had never read. He would have no inhibitions either about learning the history of thought from an encyclopedia. As a man who had barely finished high school, he developed an extraordinary ability to extract the essence of ideas from slight intimations, assimilating his reading with an imaginative intensity not often to be found among "trained minds." Hardly a Thoreau, moving with ease among classic texts, he did not even command the languages of modern philosophy—French and German. Yet much of what interested him was unavailable in translation—so important a writer as Spinoza could not be read in English. Only in a work like Bayle's could he find out what ancients and moderns had had to say about the great speculative questions. Then, having

---

[2] Willard Thorp, *Herman Melville: Representative Selections* (New York, 1938), p. 375.

[3] E.g., by Charles R. Anderson, *Melville in the South Seas* (New York, 1939), and Howard P. Vincent, *The Trying-Out of Moby Dick* (Boston, 1949).

developed the habit of such necessary recourse, he must have read further in this giant compendium, seizing odd fact and idea wherever they turned up. Merely by virtue of its encyclopedic nature, Bayle's biographical dictionary would have appealed to Melville's self-educative mind.

He might, of course, have found any encyclopedic work useful as a factual repository. In 1846, Herman Gansevoort gave him the two-volume *Cyclopaedia or Universal Dictionary of the Arts and Sciences* of Ephraim Chambers,[4] that eighteenth-century English precursor of the French encyclopedists. He may also have used John Kitto's *Cyclopaedia of Biblical Literature* for certain information.[5] But only Bayle could have provided him with a wealth of philosophic history, with theological argument and curious speculation garnered according to the bias of an enormously learned, enormously questioning mind.

It is a pity that we do not have Melville's set of Bayle's *Dictionary*, for he probably marked and annotated it as he read, leaving a valuable record of his reactions on the pages, just as he did with his copies of Shakespeare and of other writers who interested him. Melville's granddaughter, Mrs. Metcalf, states that when Mrs. Melville moved to smaller quarters in 1892, she disposed of a large portion of Herman's library. She particularly took pains to eliminate the larger, bulkier, volumes, we are told. There, presumably, went the "great folios" of Bayle.[6]

Our evidence for Melville's research in the *Dictionary* is thus entirely internal. But actual borrowing is probably the most trivial of its results, only the casual mark of Melville's eager assimilation. In the learned pondering of the first of the *philosophes*, Melville must have discovered a state of mind remark-

[4] The title page of this work, in the edition of 1728, alone survives. It is in the Metcalf Collection of the New York Public Library, bearing the inscription "Herman Gansevoort to Herman Melville."

[5] Vincent is to be credited with the discovery that Melville must have made some use of Kitto, even though there is no external evidence that he ever saw or read this two-volume work which was just newly issued in 1849.

[6] Merton M. Sealts, Jr., "Melville's Reading: A Check-List of Books Owned and Borrowed," *HLB*, II (1948), 141. A Brooklyn book dealer, A. F. Farnell, bought a cartload of these books from Mrs. Melville and Carl V. Wight, who purchased some of them, recalls that Farnell scrapped what he could not re-sell, for waste paper (Oscar Wegelin, "Herman Melville as I Recall Him," *Colophon*, n.s. I [1935], 22). If it was not destroyed then, perhaps Melville's Bayle will turn up one of these days.

ably like his own. Here was another who asked of the systematic philosophies of his times the unanswerable: "Why hath God wrought evil in the world?" The contradictions between life as it was and life as it was supposed to be were becoming rapidly more obvious to the American who had begun his observations in the forecastle. Formulated theologically, as, with his Calvinist background, Melville was bound to formulate it, his inquiry became the search for a theodicy. Exactly such a search was the obsessive preoccupation of Pierre Bayle.

Like Melville, who viewed with distaste the nineteenth-century transcendentalist denial of evil,[7] Bayle had directed his tallest scorn against the ancient and modern Platonists, and particularly against his contemporary Spinoza, whose "absurd and monstrous hypothesis" it was that "there is one Being and one Nature, and that Being produces in itself and by an immanent action, whatever goes by the name of creatures" (v, 211). Bayle thus provided Melville with an arsenal of destructive logic against the Goethe who would urge the "fellow with a raging toothache" to "Live in the All!"[8] or the Emerson who would opine that the true poet "reattaches things to Nature and the whole—reattaching even artificial things, and violations of nature, by a deeper insight."[9] For Bayle, in his attack upon the older examples of the same view, exploited the argumentative strength of the dualist philosophies such as Zoroastrianism and Manicheeism, which recognize the independent reality of ill.

It has been widely recognized that passages in *White Jacket* and *Mardi* as well as in *Moby Dick* and *Pierre* express Melville's rejection of the transcendental soporific. In *Moby Dick*, the episode of Tashtego's fall into "Plato's honey head" and the chapter called "The Mast Head" are the most conspicuous jibes at the pantheist daydream. It remains to be noted that these passages are part of a dialectic of ideas which Melville may have adopted from Bayle. For *Moby Dick*, as we shall see, makes

---

[7] For well-known statements of Melville's views on Emerson, see his letter to Evert Duyckinck, March 1849 (Thorp, *Representative Selections*, pp. 371–373), and later comments written into his copy of the *Essays* (W. Braswell, "Melville as a Critic of Emerson," *AL*, ix [1937–38], 317–333).

[8] So Melville expressed his disapproval of Goethe's pantheism, in a letter to Hawthorne in 1851 (Thorp, *Representative Selections*, p. 393).

[9] This sentence of Emerson's received scornful marginal comment from Melville in the 60's (Braswell, "Melville as a Critic of Emerson," p. 324).

central poetic use of the religious formula of a dual Godhead
and the philosophic hypothesis of a universe in which evil is
immanent and active.

When Melville opened his newly purchased copy of Bayle's
Dictionary he encountered the personality of a man who has
been called the "master of doubt." Few nineteenth-century
readers were very familiar with him. There had been no new
English editions of his work since the 1730's—indeed there still
are none. But the eighteenth century knew him well. Voltaire
called Bayle "le plus profond dialecticien qui ait jamais écrit" [10]
for Bayle was the first and most mordant of the sceptics—a
scholar, a rationalist, and one of the most lively controversialists
who ever lived. Though the modern memory relegates him to a
footnote to the story of Diderot, D'Alembert, Montesquieu, and
Voltaire, the *philosophes* were essentially popularizers; Bayle,
who died in 1706, belongs to an earlier moment, among the
seminal names of modernism—Descartes, Spinoza, Liebniz, Newton, and Locke.

Melville read none of these men; but three names have significance in his diagram of ideas—Descartes, Spinoza, and Locke
—and much of what he thought about them he got out of Bayle,
to whom Spinoza was a dangerous idealist and Descartes a more
dangerous empiric. Bayle was a man tossed between the will
to believe and the compulsion to doubt. He denied that he was
an atheist but, truly, one can say of him what Hawthorne was
to say of Melville one afternoon on the Southport dunes in 1856:
"He can neither believe nor be comfortable in his unbelief." [11]

Like Melville, Bayle was convinced that misery and wrong
were not to be pooh-poohed out of the sight of thoughtful men.
Yet what was God's responsibility in such a world? A French
Protestant, educated in Geneva, his is the essential Calvinist
dilemma which Melville later re-encountered. The anguish is
intense behind the words as he reviews the evil-doings of man
from Eden on, in the magnificent article on the Paulicians which
occupies a central place in his *Dictionary*. God's ambiguity was
conspicuous from the beginning: "God knew all the particulars
of the temptation, and he must needs have known a moment

[10] *Œuvres Completes de Voltaire* (Paris, 1819), x, 116.
[11] *The English Notebook by Nathaniel Hawthorne*, ed. Randall Stewart (New
York, 1941), p. 433.

before Eve yielded that she was going to ruin herself . . . there are no people of so little experience but without seeing what passes in the heart, and knowing the matter any otherwise than by signs, may be sure that a woman is ready to yield, if they see through a window how she defends herself when really her fall is near. . . . How much greater reason have we to think that God would perceive the yielding of Eve" (IV, 517).

From this there seemed only one logical recourse—that of the Manichees, the Paulicians, the Gnostics of the Second Century, the followers of Zoroaster—a dualism that admitted the dynamic power of the force of evil. Bayle's *Dictionary* can almost be said to be a treatise on this theme. It was not a truly inclusive biographical dictionary, really, for he chose only such subjects as afforded him opportunity for comment on his favorite topics, and his articles seem to be, in turn, merely occasions for the footnotes that crowd the text to the top of the long page. In these pages an intellectual struggle is waged against the traditional beliefs in a wholly-good cosmos. "Man alone," he wrote, "affords the greatest objection against the unity of God . . . it is the mixture of happiness and virtue with misery and vice which requires the hypothesis [of duality]" (IV, 94). And he holds for his contemporary, Spinoza, an enormous aversion, devoting more space to his "biography" than to any other, and taking every occasion to point out the fatuity of "the doctrine of the soul of the World," the doctrine which, holding that the universe is one substance, makes the infinite being responsible for "all the fancies, lewd and unjust practices of mankind" (v, 211).

The alternative to a belief in a world governed by evil as well as good, was, he knew, only the admission that the world was not governed at all. He is full of fearful respect for the deist instrument forged by Descartes. Speaking of the second-century Marcionites, he observes contemptuously that they did not realize the full power of their own theories, "from whence it came to pass that the Fathers easily confounded the Marcionites. . . . But if a man of abilities equal to those of Descartes had been to manage this affair, the system of the two principles could not have been overturned so easily as it was by the Fathers who had none to oppose but Cerdon, Maricon, Apelles and Manes" (IV, 112).

For a man with the will to believe, however, what Melville

was to call the "Descartian vortices" were as dangerous as the pantheist illusion. With faint conviction he forces himself to conclude: "Only in revelation we find what is sufficient to refute the hypothesis of the two principles" (IV, 96).

Gibbon, who greatly admired Bayle, characterized his value to himself by saying: "His critical Dictionary is a vast repository of facts and opinions; and he balances the false religions in his sceptical scales, till the opposite qualities annihilate each other." [12] Melville found Bayle similarly useful. To begin with, as we shall see, he culled facts and opinions from Bayle's collection (which sometimes reminds one of those early universal museums that were the receptacle for all things either rare or curious). But he also borrowed less tangibly from Bayle's fundamental philosophic discussion, making the argument we have described above an underlying preoccupation in *Moby Dick*. In addition, we may mention a stylistic device which Melville could have observed in Bayle. In such chapters as LV, LVI, LVII, LXV, LXXXIII, or CV of *Moby Dick*, Melville applies to various cetological questions what may be called the method of vulgar errors. Sir Thomas Browne, one of Melville's favorite writers, undoubtedly supplied models of this procedure, but in Bayle Melville witnessed its devastating effectiveness in the hands of a critic of faiths. Bayle cites authority against contradictory authority till the result is a house of cards, ready to fall at the first breath of disbelief, and in such a chapter of *Moby Dick* as LXXXIII, dealing with the Jonah story, both factual material and argumentative design are simultaneously coming through from Bayle.

In examining some prominent themes in *Moby Dick*, we shall see a correlation that is at times specific, at times philosophic, at times even stylistic, between Melville and Bayle. Taken together, they establish the depth of Melville's interest in the *Dictionary* and suggest the thoroughness with which he assimilated what he found there.

Jonah

Jonah appears in several guises in *Moby Dick*. He is, first, a sort of Ishmael, the mythic archetype of the man who is to

[12] *Miscellaneous Works* (London, 1837), p. 32.

come out alive from the belly of disaster, as does the single survivor of the *Pequod*. This Jonah appears in that extraordinary
tour-de-force, Father Mapple's Sermon, in the opening portion
of the book (Chapter IX). But Jonah is also the father of all
whale-fishermen, a folklore figure whose extraordinary experience has been of infinite vexation to Bible literalists.

Melville, with the help of Bayle, has fun with this second
Jonah in Chapter LXXXIII, "Jonah Historically Regarded," and in
both this and the preceding chapter, "The Honor and Glory of
Whaling," makes use of Bayle's critical reading of Bible material.[13] The Frenchman, of course, was one of the first great
Bible critics—his masterly chapter on David, in which he strips
that Biblical worthy of every dignity, helped to make certain
that the *Dictionary* would be banned from France during its
author's lifetime.

Giving Jonah a chapter to himself in his review of the heroic
followers of the whaleman's calling, Melville writes: "Now some
Nantucketers rather distrust this historical story of Jonah and the
whale. But then there were some sceptical Greeks and Romans,
who, standing out from the orthodox pagans of their times,
equally doubted the story of Hercules and the whale, and Arion
and the dolphin."[14] In the preceding chapter, Melville remarks
on the story of Perseus ("Prince of Whalemen") and Andromeda,
an event traditionally located at Joppa, adding, "What seems
singular and suggestively important is this: It was from Joppa
that Jonah set sail" (340). He mentions the tradition that Hercules was also swallowed by a whale, and then thrown up, observing: "But by the best contradictory authorities, this Grecian
story of Hercules and the whale is considered to be derived
from the still more ancient Hebrew of Jonah and the whale;
and vice versa" (341).

Now Bayle, who was forever applying the tests of historic
probability to Bible events, was fond of adding the Rabbinical

---

[13] Howard P. Vincent has discussed Melville's use of Bayle in these chapters in
The Trying-Out of Moby Dick, pp. 269–286. He does not include some pertinent comparisons given here, however. In particular, he omits the significant
bit of proof discussed below, Melville's translation of Bayle's supposition that
the shrewder ancients *would have* rejected all the fabulous whale stories, whether
Hebrew or Greek, into the flat statement that certain thinkers actually *did* so—
a slip that betrays the borrower more certainly than the most striking parallelism.
[14] *Moby-Dick or The Whale*, ed. Willard Thorp (New York, 1947), pp. 342–
343. All subsequent references to *Moby Dick* will be to this edition.

accretions to his portraits, thereby amusing himself by increasing their fabulous character, and attaching in addition, wherever possible, cognate stories of the heathens, which he treated with equal dignity. So he strews the essay on "Jonas" with such comparisons as these:

> The heathen poets have told a story of their Hercules somewhat resembling this. They stole it from the sacred story and falsified it, according to their fancy. . . . The fable of Arion was this, that in order to save his life, he was forced to cast himself out of the ship in which he was returning from Italy to Greece, and that he fell upon a dolphin, which carried him to shore. . . . Some confirm this conjecture by the fable of Andromeda, for they pretend that Jonas' adventure laid a foundation for the poetical accounts concerning Andromeda's being exposed to the fury of a sea-monster, which happened near Joppa. (III, 577–579)

It will be noted that Melville has kept a close eye on Bayle's text, for he has not merely used the same comparative method in selecting stories parallel to the Jonah narrative, but he has mentioned the same contradictory "historical" suppositions—that the Ancients took over the Jonah material in creating Hercules' adventure, and that the story of Jonah is confirmed by the myth of Perseus, whose dragon-slaying is somehow connected with Joppa, from which port Jonah set forth in his flight from God. But such parallels are not absolute proof of literary derivation. There is still better evidence, proof positive, in Melville's reference to "Greeks and Romans, who, standing out from the orthodox pagans of their times, equally doubted the story of Hercules and the whale and Arion and the dolphin." Now Bayle wrote:

> The ancient fathers thought it strange that the Heathens should reject this history of Jonas, after having adopted the fable of Hercules . . . [and he quotes the remark of St. Augustine that] "those who laughed at the story of Jonas did not question the truth of what is said of Arion." [To which Bayle rejoins:] The philosophers and learned men of Greece would have answered: we accept of your terms; you would either have us reject the story of Hercules, or adopt

that of Jonas, we reject them both . . . but a great many of the heathens would have condemned this alternative. (III, 578)

Melville's "some sceptical Greeks and Romans" are nothing more than suppositional supporters of Pierre Bayle, summoned by that wily philosopher who loved to stage imaginary debates in order to avoid the dangerous phrase "I believe . . ." [15] For Bayle has only said that the shrewder men of Greece "would have" scorned both fables if Augustine's challenge had been delivered to them. Nowhere else could Melville have found these non-existent classical sceptics save in the rhetoric of Pierre Bayle's chapter on Jonah.

Melville next undertakes to consider the objections put forward by "an old Sag-Harbor whaleman," who, among other things, [16] "urged for his want of faith in this matter of the prophet . . . something obscurely in reference to his incarcerated body and the whale's gastric juices" (343). Bayle had paraphrased Augustine's 49th Letter: "Is it easier to raise a dead man from the grave than to preserve a man alive in the body of a great fish? Will it be said that the digestive faculty of the stomach cannot be suspended" (III, 578)? Another of "Sag-Harbor's" cavils went as follows:

Jonah was swallowed by the whale in the Mediterranean Sea, and after three days, he was vomited up somewhere within three days' journey of Nineveh, a city on the Tigris.

But was there no other way for the whale to land the prophet within that short distance of Nineveh? Yes. He might have carried him round by the way of the Cape of Good Hope. But not to speak of the passage through the whole length of the Mediterranean, and another passage

[15] In the chapter on the Manichees, Bayle stages a discourse between Zoroaster and Melissus, Zoroaster producing telling arguments, while his creator sanctimoniously deplores his success; and in the chapter on Pyrrho, in which he deals with the perilous subject of Cartesian scepticism, the controversy is presented by another pair of puppets, two anonymous abbots.

[16] Vincent points out that a number of statements in this chapter as well as in Chapter XLV, "The Affadavit," owe something to Kitto's *Cyclopaedia of Biblical Literature*. Most of the material, however, stems from Bayle; Melville has taken along with this material something of the Frenchman's method and attitude, his very comic intent; and his use of other sources is merely incidental.

up the Persian Gulf and Red Sea, such a supposition would involve the complete circumnavigation of all Africa in three days, not to speak of the Tigris waters, near the site of Nineveh, being too shallow for any whale to swim in. (344)

Bayle had written:

> Those who say that his prophet came out of the fish's belly in the port of Nineveh are but little skilled in Geography; nor is it probable that he came out of it upon the coast of the Euxine or of the Red Sea. Note, that Nineveh was built upon the river Tigris, which has no immediate connection with the Mediterranean Sea. Besides there is not enough water for such a fish in the river at the port of Nineveh. This reason, together with the surprising miracle, we must suppose, if we say that the whale went into the ocean, and doubled the Cape of Good Hope, and entered into the mouth of the Tigris, and made that prodigious compass in three days, takes away all sorts of subterfuge from such as would excuse Sulpicius Severus. (III, 579)

Finally, Melville ends *his* exposition:

> But all these foolish arguments of old Sag-Harbor only evidenced his foolish pride of reason—a thing still more reprehensible in him, seeing that he had but little learning except what he had picked up from the sun and the sea. I say it only shows his foolish, impious pride, and abominable, devilish rebellion against the reverent clergy. For by a Portuguese Catholic priest, this very idea of Jonah's going to Nineveh via the Cape of Good Hope was advanced as a signal magnification of the general miracle. And so it was. Besides, to this day, the highly enlightened Turks devoutly believe in the historical story of Jonah. And some three centuries ago, an English traveller in old Harris' Voyages, speaks of a Turkish Mosque built in honor of Jonah in which mosque was a miraculous lamp that burnt without any oil. (344)

I have no idea where Melville picked up that Portuguese priest, but the accent of this paragraph is entire Bayle, with its sardonic pretense of censure for "the foolish pride of reason," its sardonic show of tenderness for the "reverent clergy." The last sentence derives not from Harris[17] but from Bayle, where it is even italicized:

> In St. Jerome's time the tomb of Jonas was still shown at the place of his birth. Mr. Simon [author of a *Dictionnaire de la Bible*] *affirms that the Turks have built a very fine mosque to the honor of Jonas in which there is a miraculous Lamp that burns, continually without any oil or other liquor.* (III, 579)

But let us pursue a more subtle parallelism of thinking which is also involved in Bayle's and Melville's concepts of Jonah. In his essay on Gregory of Rimini, Bayle considers the difficult problem presented by the episodes of the Bible which attribute false statements and dishonorable acts to God himself. Gregory had affirmed that God has shown Himself able to lie and cheat, for how else can we explain his intention when he hardened Pharoah's heart, when he sent "a lying spirit" into some prophets, when he commanded Jonah to preach in Nineveh that it would be destroyed in forty days, a prediction Jonah knew was bound to be false?

Gregory's arguments had seemed powerful to Descartes, Bayle observes, finding himself able to answer them only in this fashion:

> This great philosopher should at least have insisted more than he did on the nature of the expressions made use of by the holy writers, to accommodate themselves to the capacity of the people. Vulgar minds being not able to raise themselves to the most perfect being it was necessary that the Prophets should bring down God to man, and make him stammer with us as a nurse stammers with a child, whom she suckles. Hence it is that there are so many expressions in the Scripture, importing that God repents that he is angry, that he will inquire whether a thing has happened, that he will alter his mind if men obey, or do not obey him, and a thousand such things, that are inconsistent with infinite perfection. (IV, 876)

---

[17] John Harris' *Navigantum atque Itinerantum Biblotheca* (London, 1705) does contain a reference to a mosque near Tigris, but tells nothing about a perpetual lamp.

Now the problem of the inexplicable, seemingly immoral acts of God, His capacity to do evil, and our inability to rationalize His doing evil—this is pervasive in *Moby Dick*. We know that Melville marked in his own Bible passages illustrating Jehovah's evil-doing—his use of Necho the Egyptian to slay Josiah, and of Assyria to destroy Samaria. He checked such "dark" verses as "who can make that straight which He hath made crooked." [18] We can assume that Melville read the article on Gregory with particular attention, noting especially the two dramatic Bible instances employed—that of Jonah, and that of the prophets who spoke at the prompting of lying spirits, particularly the four hundred prophets who misled Ahab into launching a battle against the King of Damascus. Jonah and Ahab—these are the two dominant Bible protoypes in *Moby Dick*.

It will be recalled that in I Kings, the Bible story relates that Ahab's prophets had all promised him a victory in battle with the exception of Micaiah, who related that in a vision he had heard Jehovah inquiring among his angels for one who would persuade Ahab to engage in the battle and be killed. An angel volunteered: "I will go forth and I will be a lying spirit in the mouth of all his prophets." In the last chapter of the book of Jonah the prophet defends himself by maintaining that he had foreseen that Jehovah would rescind his decree of destruction if the wicked Ninevites were moved to repentance. To avoid seeing the revocation of his prophecy, he embarked for Tarshish. As he had expected, Jehovah pardons Nineveh.

Melville must have been aware of the implications of both of these stories. But while he uses all the ambiguous overtones of Ahab's relation to a dishonest God, even creating a false prophet in the person of Fedallah to give his hero the confidence which will destroy him, he suppresses the ironic sequel of the Jonah story. Father Mapple's sermon contains no criticism of God's harsh command. "As with all sinners among men, the sin of this son of Amitai was in his wilful disobedience of the command of God—never mind now what that command was or how conveyed" (40). There is nothing in the sermon either about the repentent city and God's pardon—as Nathalia Wright points out, Jonah's experiences in Father Mapple's narrative are actually closer to those of Jeremiah. Yet the fuller story did not

[18] Nathalia Wright, *Melville's Use of the Bible* (Durham, N.C., 1949), p. 186.

remain entirely repressed in Melville's mind; it coalesced with the symbolism of Ahab. The happier half of the story of Jonah remained like an isolated pillar of faith at the entrance gate of *Moby Dick.*

Both stories, as Melville was aware, are conspicuous Bible examples of divine arbitrariness in regard to human truth. And if God can lie and deceive kings and prophets, how can we regard his works as the expression of goodness and morality? Using the same Biblical examples as Bayle, Melville made them metaphorical examples of the paradox that plagued him also, the paradox of inexplicable evil in a divinely governed world. . . .

WILLIAM H. GILMAN [1911–   ] is professor of English at the University of Rochester and has coedited (with Merrell R. Davis) *The Letters of Herman Melville.* He is one of the editors of *The Journals and Miscellaneous Notebooks of Ralph Waldo Emerson* and of a forthcoming complete edition of Emerson.

Redburn

WILLIAM H. GILMAN

One reason for the power of Melville's characterization is the advance in style that with few lapses he achieves in *Redburn.* When he began the book he had developed two literary manners. In *Typee* and *Omoo,* written largely for entertainment, he was straightforward and pleasing enough but unable to make the most of his material. Despite a wealth of exact and rich detail, his images were scarce, his allusions commonplace and sparse. His sentences were often self-consciously formal, and sometimes his paragraphs sagged into anticlimax.[23] Frequently

[23] Consider the following: "There was a flavor and a relish to this small particle of food that, under other circumstances, it would have been impossible for the most delicate viands to have imparted. A copious draught of the pure water which flowed at our feet served to complete the meal, and after it we rose sensibly refreshed, and prepared for whatever might befall us" (*Typee,* pp. 61–62).

Melville's Early Life and Redburn (New York: New York University Press, 1951), pp. 220–27.

his diction was either inflated or stereotyped.[24] In the first part of *Mardi,* however, Melville graduated from his apprenticeship. His style had lost its debt to tradition. A vigorous freshness breathed through the narrative of the escape from the "Arcturion" and the encounter with Samoa and Annatoo. After these introductory chapters, Melville's other style emerged, Carlylean in its inversions and involutions, gorgeous in its multiplicity of allusions and images, and often rhapsodic in tone. Its very excesses burned with the fire of a genius who has just discovered his deeper powers. However, such an exalted manner was unsuitable for the pedestrian narrative of a boy's first voyage, and though Melville could not resist indulgence in it on two occasions in *Redburn,* it was to a different style that he turned when he sent his hero off to Liverpool on the "Highlander."

The dominant manner of Redburn imitates through the very structure of sentence and paragraph the rhythms of an adolescent's eager, spontaneous flow of feeling. Of the many passages in which the boy's mental processes come to life on the page, that on the glass ship, which had so much influence in directing Redburn's thoughts to the sea, is one of the best.

> In the first place, every bit of it was glass, and that was a great wonder of itself; because the masts, yards, and ropes were made to resemble exactly the corresponding parts of a real vessel that could go to sea. She carried two tiers of black guns all along her two decks; and often I used to try to peep in at the portholes to see what else was inside; but the holes were so small, and it looked so very dark indoors, that I could discover little or nothing; though, when I was very little, I made no doubt, that if I could but once pry open the hull, and break the glass all to pieces, I would infallibly light upon something wonderful, perhaps some gold guineas, of which I have always been in want, ever since I could remember. And often I used to feel a sort of insane desire to be the death of the glass ship, case and all, in order to come at the plunder; and one day, throwing out some hint of the kind to my sisters, they ran to my mother in a great clamor; and after that, the ship was placed on the

---

[24] Consider "adhesive matter" and "glutinous compound" to describe sticky food (*Typee,* p. 97); "communicate my appellation" for "tell my name" (*ibid.,* p. 95); "apply the olfactory organ" for "smell" (*ibid.,* p. 98).

mantelpiece for a time, beyond my reach, and until I should recover my reason.[25]

In a formal composition this hodgepodge would sound incoherent. The second sentence sets forth two sequent thoughts, followed by a contrasting statement, which in turn is qualified, and the qualification leads to a subject and a time situation quite different from those with which the sentence began. But in the reminiscences of Redburn, the paragraph is a triumph of artistic skill, reproducing with ease the natural digressiveness of a youthful mind. Through many artfully constructed ramblings like this, Melville mirrors not only a young boy's ideas but also their movement. The effect is a psychological realism that takes us into the inner nature of the hero. We know what he thinks, and we know the manner of his thinking.

This style predominates in *Redburn*, carrying the story for chapter after chapter, but it is not the only one. Often when Melville wants to relate a dramatic incident or scene, he records it not in terms of Redburn's adolescent observation but objectively, as the quality of the incident demands. Such are the descriptions of a starving woman and children in Liverpool and the death of Jackson, the account of the wreck that the "Highlander" passes at sea, the narrative of the cholera among the immigrants, and the horrible description of the burning corpse. Economy and a starkness in physical realism more plain than anything that marked Melville in his previous books are the stylistic qualities of these and many other scenes. The same element of terseness permeates the colloquial dialogue, as in the speech of the mate when Redburn fails to understand his order to slush down the topmast.

> "Green as grass! a regular cabbagehead! A fine time I'll have with such a greenhorn aboard. Look you, youngster. Look up to that long pole there—d'ye see it? that piece of a tree there, you timberhead—well—take this bucket here, and go up the rigging—that rope-ladder there—do you understand?—and dab this slush all over the mast, and look out for your head if one drop falls on deck. Be off now, Buttons." [26]

[25] *Redburn*, pp. 7–8.
[26] *Ibid.*, p. 37.

These are the unquestioned accents of a rough, uneducated man, irked at having to explain what is so obvious to himself but clear and earthily emphatic in his explanation. And all the other sailors talk with the same crisp forcefulness as the mate.

The simple diction of such passages echoes throughout the book. It is incomparably better than the innumerable contemporary reminiscences of old tars who manufacture dialogue by the page but tell less about the sailor than Melville does in a phrase or two.[27] It is also more convincing than the stage dialogue of Cooper, Captain Chamier, and Marryat, Melville's nearest rivals, for it rings truer and at the same time it is artistically selected and molded.

The simplicity of a boy and the terseness of a mariner, then, are the elements of style in *Redburn*. But Melville did not entirely forsake the grand manner he had developed in *Mardi*. He carried over, for example, the use of allusions, with which he had so liberally strewn his gigantic allegory. For a simple tale of a boy's first voyage, *Redburn* is surprisingly studded with a variety of decorative references, Biblical, geographical, literary, and philosophical. Melville's familiarity with Scripture supplies him with many a commonplace reference to Job, the wise virgins, Sodom and Gomorrah, and the lion and the lamb.[28] His personal experiences together with his reading enable him

[27] Melville's dialogue may be compared with H. J. Mercier's, who wrote better than any other contemporary ex-sailors: " 'Look here, Tubbs,' " cried Bradley, . . . " 'just clap a stopper on that *red rag* of yours; you are giving your opinion in this affair as if you were some old Nantucket whaler; and I know you hav'nt [*sic*] been many months from behind a *clam* cart; let somebody pass their remarks that know more about it than you do.' 'Do you think I hav'nt been whaling?' responded Tubbs—'I reckon if you ever fall in with Captain Seth Handy, of New Bedford, and ask him who pulled the after oar in his boat, I guess he'd mention my name. That was the man for turning up a fish; he made no more of *lancing* a whale in a *flurry* than others would of hooking a mackerel.' " (*Life in a Man-Of-War, or Scenes in Old Ironsides* [Boston: Houghton Mifflin Company, 1927; 1st ed.; Philadelphia, 1841], pp. 162–63. It may be noted that Melville borrowed scenes from this book for parts of *White-Jacket*. See Keith Huntress, "Melville's Use of a Source for White Jacket," *American Literature*, XVII [March 1945], 66–74.) Mercier's dialogue illustrates the common practice of underlining all nautical terms and sailor slang, a convention Melville follows in *Redburn*.

[28] Nathalia Wright counts fifty-one references in *Redburn* to the Bible, by far the most numerous group of allusions ("Biblical Allusion in Melville's Prose," *American Literature*, XII [May 1940], 185).

to exploit places as remote as Lima, Aroostook, the infamous North Corner in Plymouth, Pegu, and Nova Zembla. His literary allusions include a number of minor authors like Mrs. Ellis, Joel Barlow, Lavater, William Roscoe, and the sea poets Dibdin and Falconer, and writers of higher rank like Le Sage, Froissart, Johnson, Addison, Moore, Ossian, Smollett, Milton, and of course Shakespeare, whom he had been reading heavily just before writing *Redburn*. His recent reading of the classics furnished him with ready references to Homer, Livy, Martial, Petronius Arbiter, Seneca, Suetonius, Tacitus, Varro, and Tiberius at Capreae, while other references show his irrepressible interest in the lives or philosophies of Aristotle, Socrates, Paracelsus, Campanella, Hume, and Kant.

Despite the number and extent of these allusions, they give no evidence of extended indebtedness to any one author, nor even of any great amount of learning. Melville's knowledge was not deep but eclectic. Although he had acquired some familiarity with the classics, he was no more a scholar in his thirties than he had been in his teens. He was a wide reader with a brilliant memory who abstracted with rare perception the quintessence of what he read. Instinctively, he avoided mere window-dressing pedantry. His illustrations are almost always appropriate. Whole chapters go by without a single allusion, if the aim is physical realism and if decoration would be out of place. But he uses allusions liberally wherever they help to broaden or intensify the immediate meaning or supply color to an incident that requires it. Redburn's meditation on the old Liverpool guide-book, which he has suddenly discovered to be useless, is typical:

> Smell its old morocco binding, Wellingborough; does it not smell somewhat mummyish? Does it not remind you of Cheops and the Catacombs? I tell you it was written before the lost books of Livy, and is cousin-german to that irrecoverably departed volume entitled, *"The Wars of the Lord,"* quoted by Moses in the Pentateuch. Put it up, Wellingborough, . . . and hereafter follow your nose throughout Liverpool; it will stick to you through thick and thin: and be your ship's mainmast and St. George's spire your landmarks.[29]

[29] *Redburn*, p. 203.

The range of references here conveys exactly the intensity of the almost cynical disillusionment Redburn has just experienced.

In general, however, Melville is most allusive in those sections of *Redburn* that reflect his mature mind and interests rather than Redburn's impressions. His reference to Salvator Rosa's "lowering sea-pieces" and his catalogue of paintings in the gambling house parallel his interest in art awakened by George Duyckinck's circle and the exhibitions at the American Art Union. He writes of pictures like those in the Temple of Ammon in the Libyan oasis, in the shrine of Quetzalcoatl at Cholula, in the house of Pansa at Pompeii, in the private room of Tiberius, and in the secret side gallery of the Temple of Aphrodite in Corinth.[30] The inclusion of a blatantly pornographic picture is one measure of Melville's sophistication. If most of the allusions are to nonexistent works of art, they are further evidence that Melville could not confine himself to strict realism indefinitely.[31] He could not suppress the instinct for decorating his story with the strange and the wonderful, which he had indulged for many chapters in *Mardi*.

It was undoubtedly the need for satisfying this instinct that impelled Melville to write the chapter on Carlo, a fantastic, dreamlike effusion on music that bespeaks the love of opera and

---

[30] *Ibid.*, pp. 297–98.

[31] Melville refers to pictures which "the high priests, for a bribe, showed to Alexander in the innermost shrine of the white temple in the Libyan oasis." None of the ancient authorities on Alexander—Plutarch, Polybius, Diodorus Siculus, Arrian, or even the romantic Rufus Curtius—mentions any pictures in this temple, which was a shrine of Jupiter Ammon, nor is Alexander described as offering a bribe to the priests. Melville also refers to "such pictures as the pontiff of the sun strove to hide from Cortez, when, sword in hand, he burst open the sanctorum of the pyramid-fane at Cholula"; but neither Diaz nor Prescott nor Cortez himself describes any such incident. The house of Pansa in Pompeii is not known to have contained any pictures, nor does Varro, despite Melville's assertion, refer to the "central alcove" of Pansa's home as *"the hollow of the house."* It is true, as Melville says, that Suetonius mentions a picture which Tiberius kept in his private cabinet (it represented Atalanta performing a most unnatural service for Meleager), but Melville is wrong in declaring that Martial mentions the picture. Finally, no ancient traveler or historian mentions a "secret side gallery in the temple of Aphrodite in Corinth," nor pictures, as such, in the temple, though Pausanias does refer to the "images" of Aphrodite and of the Sun and of Love. It seems evident that Melville was inventing allusions in this passage, just as he had done ten years before in the second of the "Fragments from a Writing Desk."

symphony Melville had also developed through his association with the Duyckincks.[32] It is a dithyrambic, self-intoxicated piece of impressionism like the chapter on dreams in *Mardi*. Different kinds of music conjure up visions of Xerxes surrounded by his satraps, of the Fountain of Lions in the Alhambra, of "Medusa, Hecate, she of Endor, and all the Blocksberg's demons dire," and of "the inner palace of the Great Mogul."[33] Such stylistic extravagance, however artistically inappropriate in *Redburn,* is evidence of the poetic forces (many of its sentences scan perfectly) lying below the surface of Melville's consciousness and compelling him at times to jettison consistency.

In the prosaic story of Redburn, Melville's passion for allegorical or symbolical expression, which had blossomed suddenly in *Mardi*, is inevitably subdued. His figures are numerous but generally simple, in keeping with the character whose thoughts they are designed to convey. Occasionally, he contrives more arresting metaphors: a drowned sailor, with his uprolled sleeve exposing his tattooed name and birth date, "seemed his own headstone."[34] For the relation of sailors and other workers to society, he creates a memorable image:

> There are classes of men in the world who bear the same relation to society at large, that the wheels do to a coach; and are just as indispensable. But however easy and delectable the springs upon which the insiders pleasantly vibrate; however sumptuous the hammercloth and glossy the door-panels; yet, for all this, the wheels must still revolve in dusty, or muddy revolutions. No contrivance, no sagacity can lift *them* out of the mire; for upon something the coach must be bottomed; on something the insiders must roll.[35]

If such extended imagery is rare, Melville occasionally employs symbols in *Redburn* in a way that looks forward to *Moby-Dick* rather than backward to *Mardi*, where, as Matthiessen observes, abstractions unrooted in sense experience impair both understanding and imaginative stimulation. Confined as he was in *Redburn* to a framework of reality, he had to draw his illustra-

---

[32] Mansfield, "Herman Melville, Author and New Yorker," p. 94.
[33] *Redburn*, pp. 323–24.
[34] *Ibid.*, p. 230.
[35] *Ibid.*, p. 177.

tions largely from fact and, conversely, to make his ideas grow
out of real things. His technique varies. Sometimes he defines
the relationship and deduces a single specific meaning. About
an East Indian ship in Liverpool, where the English officers
hold services in the cabin while "the heathen at the other end
of the ship [are] left to their false gods and idols," Melville
comments:

> As if to symbolize this state of things, the *"fancy piece"*
> astern comprised, among numerous other carved decora-
> tions, a cross and a mitre; while forward . . . was a sort
> of devil for a figure-head . . . .[36]

Sometimes he merely suggests the relationship of a single physical fact and a single spiritual fact. On the very day that Redburn leaves home, the figurehead on the little glass ship falls
from its perch and "lies pitching head-foremost down into the
trough of a calamitous sea . . . ."[37] At other times, Melville
makes the physical object generate associations freely, giving
it multiple links in time and space. In the central strand, or
"heart," of an old piece of rope, he finds many "interesting,
mournful, and tragic suggestions."

> Who can say in what gales it may have been; in what re-
> mote seas it may have sailed? How many stout masts of
> seventy-fours and frigates it may have stayed in the tem-
> pest! . . . What outlandish fish may have nibbled at it
> in the water, and what uncatalogued sea-fowl may have
> pecked at it, when forming part of a lofty stay or shroud?[38]

Such a passage, though severely limited when compared with
the rich suggestiveness of chapters like "The Doubloon" in
Moby-Dick, differs in degree rather than in kind. In each Melville uses the same method, seizing upon a concrete object and
attaching to it as many associations as it can be made to suggest. Both here and elsewhere in *Redburn,* his technique of

[36] *Ibid.,* p. 220. In "Benito Cereno" Melville also uses the stern piece and the
figurehead (a real corpse) to symbolize conditions on a ship. He attaches more
significance to the objects, but the basic technique is the same as in *Redburn.*
(See *Piazza Tales,* p. 70.)

[37] *Redburn,* p. 9.

[38] *Ibid.,* pp. 352–53.

symbolism is proleptic, in that he elaborates his higher meaning from the foundation of real things.[39]

Taken as a whole, *Redburn* is stylistically an advance beyond Melville's first three books. His diction, stripped of the earlier artificiality and convention, is magnificently plain. Its range is small, but with apt choice and skillful manipulation it conveys a diversity of powerful impressions. Melville's sentences and paragraphs are also simpler and firmer than they had been, for his eye for the significant detail is more searching and he avoids the clutter of irrelevance. The movement is swifter and smoother, the digressions fewer and less remote from the immediate subject. Only occasionally does he let himself wander away from a manner consistent with his material to stylistic extravagance. The mingling of form and matter in *Redburn* is the most nearly perfect in all of Melville's early work.

No good book, however, is merely a mechanism of style, or of characterization or structure, or of artistic manipulation of experience. Undertones and overtones of feeling and thought, the chiaroscuro of mood and theme play through its pages to make up what may be called its personality. And *Redburn* has something of this inner quality of complexity, of diverse strains that will not, happily, submit to a formula. The fruits of Melville's manifold experience, both sensuous and intellectual, were ripening with tropical speed when he wrote *Redburn*, and every inspiration brought its plenteous windfall. This is why the book has more than one level of mood and more than one angle of vision. Both the inside world of emotion and spirit and the outside world of society spurred Melville's energies. They had driven him to the brilliant if not completely achieved ambitions of *Mardi*, and despite the demands of personal finances, which could be satisfied by a mere potboiler, they shared in the molding of *Redburn*.

[39] Despite Melville's constant reference to Redburn's shooting jacket as the badge of poverty and the source of humiliation and social rejection, I see no technique here that can properly be called symbolic. The jacket is never invested, openly or implicitly, with poetic or metaphysical or moral meaning. (Compare, however, Howard P. Vincent, "White Jacket: An Essay in Interpretation," *New England Quarterly*, XXII (September 1949), 306. Mr. Richard Chase's perception of mythological meanings in *Redburn* depends on such assumptions as that "[Redburn's] name is apparently meant to signify 'the Promethean fire' . . . ." (*Herman Melville, A Critical Study*, p. 7).

WALTER E. BEZANSON [1912–   ] is professor of American civilization at Rutgers University and the author of several influential Melville studies, including *"Moby-Dick:* Work of Art" in *Moby-Dick Centennial Essays* (reprinted in the Norton Critical Edition of *Moby-Dick*).

Introduction

WALTER E. BEZANSON

V

No reading can give the whole poem. The one above omits the multiplicity of incidents which both particularize and obscure the main effects. It skips lightly over the winding flow of discussion and debate, by-passing conceptualized argument and skirting dense thickets of historical allusion. It neglects that tone of the "picturesque" by which some of the lighter passages are colored. It merely types major characters whose intricacies of temperament are constantly unfolding. It ignores the parade of minor characters. And except through citations, it only hints at the language, images, and verse movements by which the poem exists. Yet perhaps the reading does give us what has proved so hard to come by—a sense of the primary design.

The characters and major images are so central to meaning that we shall soon want to look closely at them. But first we might ask how language, prosody, and formal structure relate to this primary design.

The language of the poem is in part genteel and weakly traditional. Where it is, it vitiates the sense of real crisis. In the first canto, for example, we encounter a series of dusty old words, the second-hand stock of a long run of English poets, at about the rate of one every ten lines: *anon, fro, boon, oft, lorn, paynims, Afric's, needs be, opes, lo, visage, thereat, e'en, flaw* (sudden gust of wind), *o'er, main* (sea), *portals* (ordinary doors), *wends.* Too often we meet with "Ah!"—that tedious Romantic-Victorian syllable from which Arnold drained all the poignancy. Again, words or phrases are abused to meet the tight line-and-rhyme pattern. We find *pard, wildered,* and *bide,* chopped-off substitutes for *leopard, bewildered,* and *abide.* We are often aware

Clarel (New York: Hendricks House, Inc., 1960), pp. lxiv–lxix.

that an article (*a, an,* or *the*) has been expunged to make the beat work—aware because both practices occur. On the other hand, to fatten lines, we find unfelt repetitions, unnecessary particles, or spread-out words like *bewrinkled, ungladsome, arborous, chanceful,* and *cascatelle.* One notes the archaic *sate* (for *sat*) in order to get rhymes with *gate, state, eight, late, fate,* and *mate.* These loppings and stretchings, this dredging up of what is needed, may be skillful or crude. One feels a poet who sensed the violence with which at times language must be ripped and cut and jammed into place, but who was not always able, like the good poet, to make one feel the rightness of the result. If one margin of the verse is softened by the worn-out language of the contemporary genteel tradition, the opposite margin is hardened by crudeness.

At the successful center there is a curious mixture of the archaic and the contemporary both in language and materials. Melville may well have had some notion that his ancient setting justified, even called for, a measure of antiquarianism. Thus we finds forms of *kern, scrip, carl, tilth, caitiff, dizzard, wynd, cruze, ken, wight, boon, gat, hap, fane, ingle,* and scores more like them. Clearly he relished the sound and weight of such words. One suspects, too, a good cut of willful pedantry, as if to say the light-minded *could* not, rather than would not, read on: the problems of the poem were to be denied those for whom the past was non-existent. Yet the poem also speaks for the contemporary crisis, the abrasive present: and so we find modern words, modern idiom, and modern referents for metaphor. Arvin's excellent analysis of the "powerfully prosaic vocabulary" of Melville's shorter poems, particularly *Battle-Pieces,* notes how they reflect the terminology of a new age, an age of business, technology, and professional services.[78] In *Clarel* we find words from shop and factory, from the laboratory, from trading, seafaring, and war. We encounter wires, tools, chemicals, business and law terms, an elaborate vocabulary of seamanship, Civil War lan-

[78] In the present section I am indebted to Arvin's highly original analysis of Melville's language, both in his *Herman Melville,* pp. 262–269, and in the somewhat ampler version, "Melville's Shorter Poems," *Partisan Review,* XVI (1949) 1034–1046. Another excellent piece on the manner of the short poems is Robert Penn Warren's "Melville the Poet," *Kenyon Review,* VIII (1946), 208–223. Laurence Barrett has commented more generally in "The Differences in Melville's Poetry," *PMLA,* LXX (1955), 606–623.

guage, etc. For example, the Elder, a fierce Scottish churchman
turned even fiercer positivist,

> bore
> A pruning-knife in belt; in vest
> A measuring-tape wound round a core;
> And field-glass slung athwart the chest;
> While peeped from holsters old and brown,
> Horse-pistols. . . .   (II.i.96)

Or we get a colloquial image of Mortmain in his conspiratorial,
pamphleteering days:

> Wear and tear and jar
> He met with coffee and cigar. . . .   (II.iv.46)

Such passages are meant to collide with the archaic world of
sepulchers and flamens through which the pilgrims move. The
same effect comes from words like *balloon, trombone, iron
plated, football;* or from half-slang words such as *pippin, Hog-
Latin, riff-raff, hullabaloo,* and *hee-haw,* often enough occurring
in the midst of passages of Biblical tone. A good example of this
wide variety of language, stepped up by a nervous dialogue of
fast give-and-take, may be examined in "The Fog" (II.xxviii).
Though Melville was unable to realize fully a style based on the
interplay of harmony and dissonance, he made a strong try for
it. As Robert Penn Warren suggests, even his failures are often
interesting and instructive.

The choice of an iambic tetrameter line, rhyming at irregular intervals, was odd for a poem of such length. What models
influenced Melville—Butler's *Hudibras,* Byron's oriental *The
Giaour,* or Arnold's short poem on faith-doubt, "Stanzas from
the Grande Chartreuse"—is less important than how the chosen
form operates in *Clarel.*[79] One can dislike the cramping effect of
endless octosyllabic lines inevitably linked one to the other, as a
good share of the critics do. But there can be no question of appropriateness. It is an essential part of the poem that the verse
form is constricting and bounded, that the basic movements are
tight, hard, constrained. This is an unbannered verse, without

---

[79] See my "Melville's Reading of Arnold's Poetry," pp. 388–390, for possible
specific indebtedness to the "Stanzas" in general theme, kinds of events, actual
vocabulary, technical devices, and rhythmic patterns.

processional possibilities. Only under high emotion (Celio at the Arch, Mortmain by Sodom, the narrator's Epilogue) do the lines flow forward with a sustained sense of destination. Typically the verse movements are short, exploratory, sometimes jerky. To wish that *Clarel* had been written in blank verse, for example, is simply to wish for a completely different poem. In earlier years Melville had often set Shakespearean rhythms echoing through his high-keyed prose with extraordinary effect. But now the bravura mood was gone. Melville did not propose a broad heroic drama in the Elizabethan manner. Pentameter—especially blank verse—was too ample and flowing for his present mood and theme. The tragedy of modern man, as Melville now viewed it, was one of constriction.

The tight rhyme-scheme of the poem hooks every line to one or more other lines. They may be bound in couplets, held in quatrain, or set in looser patterns; but the rhyme inevitably comes. No one could possibly have kept so tight a scheme interesting through thousands of lines, writing in English. Whenever the poetic metabolism sinks, the reader becomes overconscious of rhymes and meter and gets bored. But a quite different matter is the calculated effect, when poetic energies are high, whereby the reader gets uneasy and restless under the confining bonds of the short, rhymed lines. In one variety of successful passage there is a kind of internal ricochet along the hard walls of the end-rhymes. It is an attribute of the prosody as well as the psychology of the poem that all possibilities are locked in, that there is no broad release for either poetry or self. Variations from the basic prosodic pattern are so infrequent as to keep the movement along an insistently narrow corridor.[80]

Language, prosodic effects, and poetic imagination come together with startling force at regular intervals in this poem. Take, for example, the opening fifteen lines of "Night in Jericho" (II.xvi). They divide exactly in half to give two images: the

[80] The only notable and effective divergences occur in the varied forms of the short lyrics and in the expanded 5-beat line of the Epilogue. For the rest, one encounters an occasional 5-beat line at the end of a section of a canto (as in III.i.24 and IV.xii.85–86), or simply when the line gets out of hand (II.xxi.97). Such special effects as 2-beat lines in the middle of a section, for example, are rare (III.xix.64,68).

bandit crow and the lawless sheik; though the first is meant to serve the second, in fact each makes the other memorable. The "fires autumnal" are literal, and not a poeticism for fall foliage; the "luckless land" has been the site of a forest fire, say in New England. The analogy is part of an insistent metaphor (cf. the opening of II.xxix) about the Siddim Plain as a burnt-over region, a part of hell, and the mythic scene of the divine "blastment" (a beautifully archaic yet also technological word). From top of tower and pine, in ominous, lawless power, sheik and crow cry out. Repeated *l* sounds of the first line start a flow of liquid, incantatory tone that carries through to the weird climax of "Lord" and "wild hullabaloo." Against this plays a concatenation of *k* sounds, some thirteen in all. They begin with the peremptory opening word; rise to the haunting, mutinous "—killed, not overthrown" (the *c* of "gigantic" doubling the *k* sound); are reasserted in "captain-crow," which sets up the full onomatopoeia for "caws." Continuing, "scar" (placed for emphasis) echoes in "Crusaders'" and "sheik" and comes to the climax of the strophe—"Kings it"—a bold, cawing, homemade verb that summarizes all. This is one of several kinds of exciting poetry one encounters in *Clarel*.

The four-part structure of *Clarel* provides a firm, even rigid, base for the prosodic pattern. The 150 cantos are divided with sufficient evenness. Individual cantos vary somewhat in length but average out at three to four pages each.[81] Each canto ordinarily divides into several sections (they are not formal enough to be called stanzas) which mark slight shifts of subject matter, space the dialogue, or simply break the visual monotony. When the last line of one section is less than four beats, the first line of the next makes it up. Usually the form of one canto is like that of another; with each turn of the kaleidoscope, one more symmetrical pattern falls into view. Thus meter, rhyme, canto, and part, restrict the flow of experience, keeping it not only ordered, as all art does, but limited. Typically the cantos cluster in units of from two to five, giving a series of nine or ten movements to each Part. This internal rhythm of action is evident only

---

[81] The shortest canto is but 19 lines ("Dirge": IV.xxxi); the longest is one of 4 that exceed 300 lines ("Nathan": I.xvii). The term *canto*, by the way, is used by the narrator (IV.xxv.59).

after considerable familiarity with the poem, as some rhythms overlay others or are interrupted by diversions.

Several devices slightly relieve the prosodic and structural rigidity. The most notable divergence is the sizable number of short poems, or fragments of poems, which are sung, spoken, or read by one of the characters or the narrator in the course of events. If the count includes mere snatches of song, there are some forty-five such pieces in a variety of forms. Nineteen are lighthearted songs sung by the gay blades—Glaucon, the Cypriote, the Mytilene, the Lyonese; these are love lyrics, drinking songs, fragments after the Persian manner, mimic songs-from-the-dramatists. Yet their genuine levity never threatens the poem's center of gravity. Another group—about a third—are religious pieces, ranging from short hymns, invocations, or a bit of doggerel, to a four-voiced chant on the fall of Jerusalem (III.xvii) and a long masque on the Wandering Jew (III.xix).[82] In addition to the short poems there is a scattering of elaborate Homeric similes, which at intervals offer quick looks out the window at other times and places.[83] Thus the songs and similes give prosodic and thematic relief, or pictorial refreshment. Yet they are but pellets which scarcely dent the armor of rhyming tetrameters. Even the Epilogue, whose opened five-beat lines are a most welcome and effective coda, restates in close rhyme the fundamental complexity, the agnostic pro and con. This final counterpoint of major themes, rather than the concluding images of possible rebirth, is the final "summary."

To a meaningful degree, then, the language, prosody, and formal structure reflect the central tensions of the poem between what was and what is, between what might and what must be.

---

[82] Four of these religious "complaints" are especially effective: Hymn to the Slanted Cross (Mortmain), II.xxxi; Salt-Song (Beltha), II.xxxiv; Invocation (Rolfe), III.xxxii; Persian Rhyme (Rolfe), IV.xvi.

[83] The window is usually a porthole. Some examples of these brilliant sea similes begin at I.xli.70, III.ii.59; III.vii.58; III.xxix.11; IV.iv.42. Similes (or songs) often open cantos; they fracture reader complacency (as with II.xvi, analyzed above, or IV.vii).

WARNER BERTHOFF [1925–   ], professor of English at Bryn Mawr College, is the author of *The Ferment of Realism: American Literature 1884–1919.*

Words, Sentences, Paragraphs, Chapters

WARNER BERTHOFF

"His work is a whole and he is everywhere true to himself."—PASTERNAK, "Translating Shakespeare"

Between *Typee* and *Moby-Dick* Melville's signature distinctly emerges, out of the welter of the styles and expressive modes he was coincidentally learning to manage. This aspect of his achievement is unmistakable. We take it to be a sure mark of his literary mastery. But it is rather easier to recognize than to define. For by "signature" I mean something more at least than a certain pattern of mannerisms recurring with a certain frequency—as I mean something other, for example, than (in the case of Melville) that resourceful "idiosyncrasy" of diction itemized by Newton Arvin for *Moby-Dick.* I mean, rather, a consistent impress of consolidation that registers in every dimension of the writer's work and that compels our attention not because it produces this or that meritorious effect or serves this or that expressive task but because it contrives its own autonomous figures of statement and forces us to reckon with them on any spectrum of understanding we commit ourselves to at all seriously. For the writer this signature becomes part of the governing logic, perhaps the main part, of all the forms and conventions he employs. It justifies these forms and these conventions and renews the life in them; it becomes, in a way, their reason for being. Thus it results not so much in any specific tactics of expression as in a kind of fullness and finality of consideration—or so the reader has reason to feel. The matter in hand has been seen through to an end; we sense that we have come upon the last word.

In the writer's maturity his ordinary working idiom may continue to change and to change remarkably—as Melville's does

The Example of Melville (Princeton, N.J.: Princeton University Press, 1962), pp. 159–82. (Reprinted by permission of the Princeton University Press.)

with *Pierre* and again with the varied work of 1853–1856. He may contrive any number of new departures. Yet as his writing maintains some part of its mastered freedom and power of imagination, his signature will remain. It strikes us, once we are aware of it, as the essential instrument of his creative authority. It acts to complete the imaginative circuit, sealing the mechanism of the composed work into a certain uniformly directed energy of statement. Thus it will always seem as much a force of mind, a pressure of intelligence and imagination, as a perfection of craft or technique. But of course some steady competence of craft and technique is required for it to register at all, and for the contexts in which it can operate to be solidly established.

The assumption in this four-part chapter is that Melville is a master of expression, whose writing gives pleasure and secures its effects by a persistent variety and resourcefulness of technical performance, but whose greatness as a writer is in this further impress of consolidation, which is at once formal and intellectual. Precisely because this impress is felt at every significant point, however, what exactly it consists in can only be suggested rather abstractly. One can simply cite certain passages, the proper whole contexts of which are too long to be reproduced for demonstration. I apologize therefore for the fragmentariness of the argument that follows—which is scarcely more than a listing of admired examples—and must leave confirmation to the interested reader's own deliberated judgment.

I

The diction and idiom that gain for *Moby-Dick* its exceptional animation of style are sensitively analyzed in Newton Arvin's excellent study of the form of Melville's masterpiece.[1] Arvin describes two features in particular: first, that "verbal palette" of favorite words and epithets through which major themes are developed and an appropriate atmosphere conjured up; second, the coinages, the improvisations, the transpositions of parts of speech (verb-nouns and noun-adverbs, participial modifiers, pluralized substantives, adjective-compounds, and so on), by which Melville regularly quickens his presentation.

[1] *Herman Melville*, pp. 162–165. See also the essay by Jean-Jacques Mayoux, "La Langue et le Style de Melville," *Vivants Piliers: Le Roman Anglo-Saxon et les Symboles* (*Lettres Nouvelles* 6, Paris, 1960).

Arvin's efficient tabulation does not need to be repeated here. It may be considerably supplemented, however. The "dark" cluster of words Arvin noted as characteristic of the book's expressive vocabulary—"wild," "moody," "mystic," "subtle," "wondrous," "nameless," "intense," "malicious," and their cognates— is only a partial accounting. A quite different tone-cluster may quickly be identified, conveying an equally important set of impressions and themes: "calm," "fair," "mild," "serene," "tranquil," "cool" and "indifferent" (for behavior), "noble," "grand," "lovely," "heavenly," and so forth. Typically, such words appear in contrasted pairs—"joy" and "woe," "wolfish" and "soothing" —a practice helping to anchor the book's idealizing propensity in the ambiguities of actual feeling and actual experience.

But it is not just this kind of bold emotional coloring that Melville's epithets work toward. Words for states of feeling are matched in frequency by words for the generic forms and root conditions of things, or for the relations between things and their encounters with human perception. "Dim" and "indefinite" are two such (so the *Pequod* in its death-throes is seen "through dim, bewildering mediums"); indeed the commonest descriptive adjectives take on something of this generalizing power when used in support of categorical noun-abstractions. In the same vein we hear of a "desolate vacuity of life" or simply of "the half-known life"—the phrases seem to hint at some universal law in the particulars they speak for.[2] Certain other words in constant use neither describe nor categorize any specific objects or feelings. Rather, set out among the book's superabundant vocabulary for objects and feelings, they assert a defining frame within which these are to be felt as acting—thus, "world," "earth" and "earthly," "all," "mortal," and the like—or, like the emphatic modifiers "wilful" and "deliberate," they particularize certain ways of happening rooted both in human character and in the surrounding temper and habit of universal nature. It is Melville's genius to make these risky abstractions seem as concrete as his directly sensuous or kinesthetic language. And it is the co-

[2] Words of this sort, indicating whole categories and systems of phenomena, are among the principal instruments of Melville's expressive authority. Their definiteness, and their frequency, suggest that some prime effort of interrogation is irrepressibly going forward through the act of writing, and that nothing really significant is going to be slighted.

ordination of these two vocabularies, the sensuous and the categorical, involving the transposition of the values of each to the
other, that especially renews, in reading *Moby-Dick,* our confidence in the book's profoundest imaginative effort, its search
after some ideal apprehension of both the natural existence of
things and the active convulsions by which each thing partici-
pates in that existence.

The choice of words is primarily a function of the image-
making power, and thus too of the underlying sense, and conception, of reality. Their placing and timing, on the other hand,
is more strictly a matter of rhetoric, and in a prose writer of the
first rank will reveal at least an equal wit and inventiveness. The
narrative of *Moby-Dick* abounds in rhetorical manipulation of
the most provocative sort; and though the units of effectiveness
are more often the larger ones of sentence, paragraph, and
chapter, some instances of an essentially rhetorical use of the
single word or phrase deserve mention in this brief survey.
Exaggerated repetition of some otherwise unremarkable word
is a common enforcing device with Melville—for example, "old"
(with various synonyms) in the paragraph in Chapter 16 describing the *Pequod,* or "savage" in Chapter 57, concerning the
virtue of patient industry in men. Usually this kind of repetition,
as with Dickens and Carlyle, is for a comic or a polemical effect,
but it may also serve a graver expressive purpose, as in the
series "pitiable," "pity," "pitied," and "piteous" in the long account in Chapter 81 of running down an old, blind, stricken
bullwhale. There is frequent use, too, of archaism and of colloquial irregularity, carrying always a risk of affectation but
usually contributing some valid local emphasis. Unexpected ad-
jective-noun combinations are another typical device: in Chapter 26, the phrase, "concentrating brow," clinches a significant
premonition of the characteristic personal energy of Ahab, while
a few lines later the phrase, "immaculate manliness," intensifies
the idea of that common democratic heroism in Starbuck and
his kind which it will be the narrator's sorrowful task to show
overthrown.

But it is difficult to suggest out of context the effectiveness
of even these few and simple instances.[3] And it is next to im-

---

[3] The force and definiteness of language in *Moby-Dick* are so continuous that
to pick out a scattering of examples can misrepresent the actual running effec-

possible to do justice, in a hit-and-run fashion, to those verbal inventions in *Moby-Dick* which do not so much create yet another vivid picture or image as provide a stirring musical accompaniment for the ritual procession of all its pictures and images into our concentrated attention. To be led, in discussing a book's vocabulary, into consideration of effects of this kind is to begin to discover in just what way its style is inseparable from its general apprehension of things—at which point the most determined analysis of the writer's art falls hopelessly behind his actual inventiveness. One other characteristic operation of individual words in *Moby-Dick* should be mentioned, however, and that is Melville's way of calling attention through a single epithet to the whole sustaining form of his story and so of reinforcing, in the middle of some lively local context, the largest expectations already established. Typically his instrument for this effect is the participial modifier. "Preluding" is one such ("so still and subdued and yet somehow preluding was all the scene . . ."); "foreshadowing" is another ("In this foreshadowing interval . . ."); and both serve, like the corresponding series of epithets applied to the fatefully advancing ship, to support the whole precariously extended and delayed structure of the narrative.

A main part of our critical interest in Melville's books before *Moby-Dick* is in watching this expressive vocabulary forming and taking hold. So we pay special attention to the vivid, tensile language of certain passages in *Redburn* and *White-Jacket;* more than the rhapsodizing of *Mardi* these carry, we feel, the promise of their great sequel. A capacity for strong emotional coloring, an alertness to the resonance of the right names of things, a facility with metaphor, a natural command of prose cadence, and simply that plenitude and resourcefulness of diction which is Melville's least debatable merit as a writer—all are intermittently active in these two books just preceding *Moby-*

---

tiveness of the narrative style. The commonest descriptive sequence may also display this creative energy. Note the plain nouns and verbs and the one odd adverb in the following paragraph, showing us Ahab as in the intensity of his single purpose he impulsively forswears smoking: "He tossed the still lighted pipe into the sea. The fire hissed in the waves; the same instant the ship shot by the bubble the sinking pipe made. With slouched hat, Ahab lurchingly paced the planks."

Dick, and tend on the whole to gain in effective mass as each narrative goes forward. Following the ordinary romanticism of his era in prose, Melville started as primarily an expressionistic writer, a transmitter of salient aspects; and therefore it is less the affective energy of his language than its increasing solidity and explicitness that marks, for us, the emergent master. The first quality was in the contemporary romantic fashion; the second he had not only to achieve for himself but to learn to want to achieve.[4]

In the sparer style of Melville's prose after *Moby-Dick* and *Pierre,* individual words and phrases are less conspicuously thrust forward. They seem less exploratory, less (literally) provocative. We feel that Melville is no longer so consistently following their lead into the possible meanings and openings-out of the material in hand. Except as part of a general effort toward exact definition, the diction in this later work does not attract attention to itself. The distinction of the language is now a distinction of controlling intelligence, of right judgment and completed understanding. Single words are still potent—"penal" and "penitential" in "The Encantadas," along with the suggestive concreteness of "clinker" and "scar" as names for that blighted landscape; or the superb epithet "motionless" for the first appearance of Bartleby; or the whole rather stiff and angular vocabulary of specification in *The Confidence-Man* and *Billy Budd*—but they serve more to crystallize governing impressions than to search out new meanings. They function now like signals; like "apparitions," as Professor Mayoux nicely describes

---

[4] A practical sensitivity to the properties of particular words seems present in Melville's work from the first, and underlies all its further development. In *Typee* this virtue is applied pleasantly enough to the job of tone-coloring and picture-making. But it is *Omoo,* I think, with its more casually sufficient diction, that more distinctly presages the objective tact and competence of Melville's maturer style. One incidental sign of this is the liberal use of shipboard vernacular for ordinary exposition—though the author feels obliged to segregate it a little by means of quotation marks. In the opening pages we find "hove to," "ship" (as an intransitive verb), "bunk," "small stores," and "creating a sensation," all hedged typographically but not really apologized for.

We may note too how some of the "verbal palette" Arvin identifies in *Moby-Dick* is already in conscious use in *Omoo*—in the first chapter we find "melancholy" and "strangeness" pointedly focusing attention, and a moment later a fine spotting of participial modifiers in the phrase, "patched and blistered hull." But there is not yet the prolonged building up of complex tonal combinations in the service of a leading theme.

them; like standing mirrors of the realities they denote. The effort is simply to be precise, to give right names. A language of denomination, it might be called, and it has its own perils. When some right word or determinative name is not forthcoming, a kind of ponderous stuttering can set in—as in the first long paragraph of Chapter 5 of *The Confidence-Man*, with its proliferation of "may" and "might" and "seemed" and "appeared" and "perhaps" and "sometimes" and "not wholly" and "seldom very," without one firm verb or noun. Scrupulousness of that sort is likely to be self-defeating, even for a writer with great and grave things to say. There is always some use, stylistically speaking, in a capacity for small talk. But the instance is a freakish one; it is not for the most part in matters of language that *The Confidence-Man* falls short of its highest promise.

II

What Albert Thibaudet said of Proust—that the tide of his sentences indivisibly bears with it as it advances the creative élan that gives it life[5]—is true in some measure of every greatly original writer. The unit of the sentence is as a generative cell in which the writer's effort repeatedly renews its peculiar prerogative. And it is perhaps the making of successive sentences, the continuous syntactical propulsion of the writer's utterance, period upon period, that most insistently tests his working mettle and determines his acceptance with his readers.

What makes for good sentences is as hard to specify as any aspect of literary form. Here especially the ordinary separation of form and content, for convenience in argument and under cover of the truism that they are of course inseparable, breaks down entirely. No doubt various sound principles of evaluation can be formulated. At the least it will be agreed that no mere "ingenuity of varying structure"—as Robert Frost once put it— can hold attention for long, can "save prose from itself."[6] A test of fitness applies: fitness to the subject and to the whole expressive occasion (but the sentences themselves articulate the subject and compose the occasion); fitness also to the natural character

---

[5] "Marcel Proust et la Tradition Française," *Nouvelle Revue Française*, xx January 1923), 130–139.
[6] Preface to *A Way Out* (New York, 1929).

of the language (which lives only as such constant renewals keep it alive and in working order).

Can we say simply that those are good sentences, establishing a good style, which are most responsive to the nature of the performance they are a part of, as in their succession they build it up? For the Melville of *Moby-Dick*—a confident and effusive, yet restlessly speculative and interrogating writer, engaged upon a composition the whole grand design of which was apparently open to radical adjustment down almost to the completion of it —very different sentences, performing different local functions, will stand out, and not only those that most emphatically declare the book's major themes and accents. We are struck, in turn, by certain descriptive periods rich in sensuous and pictorial detail or vividly alert to the pressure and pace of physical events, by the teasingly conjectural aphorisms on the mysteriousness of phenomenal appearances, by the spectacular flourishes of completion with which various key paragraphs and chapters are wound up, and so on. Other general types of sentence may be identified; every reader of Melville will have his own favorite examples. But as in the case of individual words and phrases, to draw up a list of fine sentences in *Moby-Dick* is to misrepresent the nature of Melville's stylistic achievement, the real distinction of which is that it is nearly continuous throughout the long, packed narrative. The significant proof of his mastery of the sentence in this book, and in the best of his later writing, is that it operates at the level of ordinary workmanship.[7]

[7] Only with dialogue, in *Moby-Dick*, does it seriously falter, in misguided efforts at a theatrical excitement and sonority, or in attempts to communicate simultaneously a character's immediate passion and the objective condition of being that underlies it. Then we get the self-parody and plain awkwardness of a declaration like the following, spoken by Ahab: "What is best let alone, that accursed thing is not always what least allures." Or from pious Starbuck: "Let faith oust fact; let fancy oust memory; I look deep down and do believe." Or from Ahab again: "In the midst of the personified impersonal, a personality stands here." Such sentences usually, as it happens, are meant to convey important meanings, and regularly serve as cruxes of critical interpretation. But that of course does not justify them. Rather, it tends to cast some doubt back upon the writer's fundamental seriousness—not to speak of the critic's who builds his argument upon them.

It is not that Melville could not write dialogue, or could only write it for low or comic characters. The swift, serious exchange between Ahab and Captain Gardiner of the *Rachel*, for instance, is admirably done, and contributes solidly to the final tension of the chase. It is rather that for the high declamatory

A routine sentence opening Chapter 45, "The Affidavit," is a case in point. Characteristically it makes a full paragraph. It directly follows an intense and splendidly executed rhetorical climax in the chapter preceding and takes the form of a comment and apology about the whole shifting narrative enterprise as that now stands and is about to be renewed: "So far as what there may be of narrative in this book; and indeed, as indirectly touching one or two very interesting and curious particulars in the habits of sperm whales, the foregoing chapter, in its earlier part, is as important a one as will be found in this volume; but the leading matter of it [i.e., extraordinary evidences of the regular behavior of whales] requires to be still further and more familiarly enlarged upon, in order to be adequately understood, and moreover to take away any incredulity which a profound ignorance of the entire subject may induce in some minds, as to the natural verity of the main points of this affair." Sentences of this quality do not seem likely, on the face of it, to enhance a writer's reputation for style. The writing is audibly labored, as in the awkward terminal succession, "in this book," "in this volume," "of this affair." And though some flatness (irregular grammar apart) is expectable—given the job of resuming the exposition after the wrought-up passage just completed—it is not all to be explained away as a calculated effect or as something formally necessary. That this sentence has a more positive value, however, is not hard to show. It is clearly more than a mechanical connective—or, as Melville works it out, it presses to become so. It begins by acknowledging, and at an appropriate point, the peculiar design of this most peculiar book ("So far as what there may be of a narrative . . ."); it then directs attention to the relative importance of the matters immediately in view and to the manner ("indirectly touching") of their relationship to the suspense-shrouded main action; also, it keeps track of the reader's reactions, or that one reaction ("incredulity") which *must* be forestalled, and contributes to the fore-

---

soliloquies, mostly given to Ahab, he was unable to find, or to improvise, any viable prose convention—or else was kept from devising one by his temporary fascination with Shakespearean models—though his management of the same materials, same insights, same range of reference, same vocabulary of specification, in Ishmael's explanatory narrative is by contrast adroit, natural, and consistently graceful.

stalling by setting the narrator's promise to explain these matters "still further and more familiarly" over against the "profound
ignorance" of "some" hearers; finally, it specifies a standard
("natural verity") by which both matter and manner are properly to be judged. In short, it performs real work; and its modest
whole effect, launching us upon a new chapter, is at least momentarily to confirm our confidence in the general scheme of
the book and in the writer's readiness to carry it forward in an
intelligible and interesting way.

The test of such sentences is whether they do carry the
freightage packed into them without interrupting the sequences
they fill out. Melville's desire for thoroughness of treatment
seems on the whole to increase as his books accumulate, and
results eventually in the casual tortuousness and heaviness of
much of his later prose. The sentence-making in *The Confidence-Man* and *Billy Budd*, in particular, is of this nature.
Increasingly he seems to build each new syntactical period out
of the consciousness of a certain quantity of things to be got
into it—details, contingencies, cross-references, explanations,
analogues—without which his statement might be judged incomplete. Its job is more and more to *contain*, less and less to *discover* and *display*. The element of free inquiry and exploration
which gives his earlier writing much of its rare force and expan-
siveness tends to be replaced by static enumeration, in the
process losing for pace and momentum what may have been
gained for seriousness of consideration. The danger is not so
much of losing direction as simply of overloading. Each sentence still bears an intelligible relation to the governing ends
of the whole performance, but this relation is too often *over*-
elaborated. The consequence is to compound the danger of
overloading already present through Melville's commitment to
the Romantic virtues of richness of detail and exaggeration of
sentiment, and incidentally to dissipate the effects of colloquial
freshness and natural variety which his earlier use of first-person
narration had confirmed him in.

What especially carries Melville through these dangers in
his later work is the continuing seriousness and integrity of his
purposes as a writer. His "single-mindedness" (Roy Fuller's
phrase, apropos of *The Confidence-Man*) increases, without
lessening his extraordinary tactical inventiveness—though there

is also an increasing risk of monotony. Unity of apprehension gives him some margin for discontinuity and indirection, in prose syntax as in argument. It is one source, specifically, of that radical exactness of diction in *The Confidence-Man* and *Billy Budd* which continually gives point and emphasis to what would otherwise be a disabling contortion of ordinary statement.

From the first, Melville's sentences are units of definition as well as of expression; this is true even while, as still in *Moby-Dick,* they are preponderantly affective or pictorial. But after *Pierre* their characteristic behavior—what they count for and do as distinct from how they are constructed—noticeably alters. They no longer act *primarily* to thrust upon us the feelings, sensations, material densities, excitements, and felt intimations of the encountered things of "this world." The qualities that sustain *Moby-Dick,* the sensuous charm, the verbal music, the kinetic tension and urgency, seem relatively muted, even withheld, in the later stories. What the more remarkable sentences now appear to respond to are the whole conceived forms of the cycles of action and motive in the matters being presented. Not the intrinsic nature of the things we give names to but their phenomenal cadence and succession, the enacted logic of their known being, now direct Melville's concern and shape his gravest periods. The effort is to put us in contact with some latent rhythm of occurrence at the heart of existence, a rhythm of occurrence governing equally the participation in it and the attempt to know it. The prose that results from this effort is on the whole a serviceable instrument for the directing purposes of Melville's later fiction.

The prose of "Benito Cereno" is symptomatic. Almost nothing in it is detachable from context; it is steadily and admirably subordinated to the peculiar form of the story. As this long narrative-riddle moves tortuously forward to its single violent instant of unraveling, the sentences perform a double function. They must show and they must suspend, both at once; they must communicate tension but also damp it down, though only just so much. The device of very short, nearly discontinuous paragraphing (see above, pages 155–157) makes a contribution here, allowing for rapid shifts and contrasts of accent. But every now and then this taut, constricted prose opens out into something richer and fuller, capable of driving home a major emphasis of no little complexity; and we pass from the bare statement of Captain Delano's impressions to something like the following: "As his foot pressed the half-damp, half-dry sea-mosses matting the place, and a chance phantom cats-paw—an islet of breeze, unheralded, unfollowed—as this ghostly cats-paw came fanning his cheek; as his glance fell upon the row of small, round dead-lights—all closed like coppered eyes of the coffined—and the state-cabin door, once connecting with the gallery, even as the dead-lights had once looked out upon it, but now calked fast like a sarcophagus lid; and to a purple-black, tarred-over panel, threshold, and post; and he bethought him of the time, when that state-cabin and this state-balcony had heard the voices of the Spanish king's officers, and the forms of the Lima viceroy's daughters had perhaps leaned where he stood—as these and other images flitted through his mind, as the cats-paw through the calm, gradually he felt rising a dreamy inquietude, like that of one who alone on the prairie feels unrest from the repose of the noon." The sentence owes much, in carrying through its calculated effort of suspension, to Melville's ordinary descriptive powers, which never ceased to be of a high order. The whole form of it, however, is what I wish to stress here, in particular the rhythm of sensation and response it reproduces; for that rhythm is in miniature the rhythm of the whole action of "Benito Cereno" and correspondingly of its telling.[8]

III

"So paragraphing is a thing that anyone is enjoying. . . ."
—Gertrude Stein, *Narration*

The discipline of paragraphing we mostly take for granted in prose, except when it is missing or when it becomes extraordinarily irregular. The unit of the paragraph is a means, simply, of local organization and arrangement. In prose narrative especially, the pace and rhythm of presentation become as important as the primary naming of materials, and here the manner of paragraphing contributes substantially to the whole form of the composition. The paragraph unit both groups and divides. In

---

[8] Does not the unusual prevalence, in the sentence, of hyphenated compounds —"half-damp, half-dry sea-mosses," "cats-paw," "state-cabin," "dead-lights," "purple-black, tarred-over"—intensify this effect of suspension?

neither respect can it afford to appear automatic or perfunctory, a mere function of typography. Rhetorically it operates as the individual sentence operates, though on a broader scale: to place the local materials in the advancing context without smothering their potential suggestiveness, and to control the precise degree of consecutiveness in such a way as the dominant logic of the passage (a logic of action, of feeling, of thought, of persuasion) may direct.

A writer like Melville—who thought his way along as he wrote, and was often only roughly aware from one moment to the next of how he meant to carry through his general scheme—is likely to handle the business of paragraphing as he handles everything else in his craft, somewhat opportunistically. He will break off, and project a new start, as often to temper his own distractibleness and reaffirm some displaced emphasis as move ahead to a new one. As Melville's seriousness of intention increased, his practical job as a writer became more and more a matter of striking compromises between the broad narrative conception and the impulse to push every particular intimation through at once to its own speculative ending. The result is the distinctive *periodicity* of his writing. Often as his sentences grow longer and more loaded down, his paragraphs will grow shorter—until in fact the two coalesce in the one-sentence paragraphing characteristic of his later prose. Consider for example the superb first chapter of *The Confidence-Man*. Of fifteen paragraphs, seven consist of a single sentence, more or less elaborate in syntax, while four others contain only two, one of which does nearly all the work. The effect is at once of tightness or involution and yet of a radical casualness of development—an effect that corresponds to the disjointed coherence of the book as a whole.[9]

The same periodistic unwinding of the thread of exposition is evident in *Billy Budd* and makes, I think, a substantial contribution to the remarkable narrative economy of that work. A striking instance occurs in Chapter 13, at the climax of the patiently analytic characterization of Claggart (the last of the three principals to be so presented). The main argument of the

[9] Paragraphs of one sentence are as frequent in *Typee*, *Omoo*, and *Mardi*, but what they chiefly indicate in those haphazardly assembled books is short-windedness and a *lack* of consistent purpose.

chapter ends in a sentence that is a marvel of tact and controlled energy, that both denominates and dramatizes. The immediate point is Claggart's reaction to the "moral phenomenon" presented in Billy Budd. Mostly, Melville writes of him, he feels a "cynic disdain—disdain of innocence—to be nothing more than innocent!" "Yet in an aesthetic way he saw the charm of it, the courageous free-and-easy temper of it, and fain would have shared it, but he despaired of it." The immediate force of this is that it confirms in a highly specific précis the whole cumulative history of Claggart's association with Billy. It does so the more effectively by standing at the end of the chapter's long main paragraph; the rhetorical climax is ratified by the typographical division. That division equally affects, of course, what follows. A one-sentence paragraph now concludes the chapter, in a fine summary cadence that gains noticeably by being thus introduced and set apart: "With no power to annul the elemental evil in him, though readily enough he could hide it; apprehending the good, but powerless to be it; a nature like Claggart's surcharged with energy as such natures almost invariably are, what recourse is left to it, but to recoil upon itself and like the scorpion for which the Creator alone is responsible, act out to the end the part allotted it."

In Melville's later prose the forms of sentence and paragraph adapt themselves almost too submissively to the pressure of the thought. They give way a little too quickly to its multiplying qualifications. But at each step, in turn, the outward casualness of the construction and the seeming oddness of local emphasis are sustained by the steadiness of argumentative purpose. For the method of exposition Melville had come to favor as a storyteller such tactics served him fairly well. From the first, in the case of *Billy Budd,* the narrative voice holds the action at a remove and works by a kind of filtered and distilled recollection, issuing not so much in any continuous dramatic succession as in a series of vivid tableaux; and for this the periodism of the writing seems peculiarly in keeping, making itself a positive instrument of the narrative's developing statement.[10]

---

[10] A good case of the serviceability of these long and short paragraphs, and the short and long sentences within them, is the charming serio-comic sketch, "I and My Chimney." But in "The Bell-Tower," a rare (for Melville) exercise in the stricter Hawthornesque form of dramatic allegory and (to my taste) one

So in general this periodism—if I may be allowed the coinage; I mean to suggest something other than the rhetorical mechanism of periodic syntax—with its running rhythm of suspension, climax, and definition, is the effective means of the thoroughness and deliberation that characterize Melville's best work. Though its tendency is to break the ordinary narrative continuity, the instinct for consolidation and completeness of statement that it promotes will often turn an apparent interruption into an especially effective confirming flourish. There are paragraphs in *Moby-Dick* which we feel are drawn from the author's deepest penetration into his most challenging materials, but which oddly have the appearance—or so it seems as we begin them—of afterthoughts. The spring of the writer's imagination, coiled to its work, now pulses again as if under its own free power; and the mastered shape of the paragraph unit provides it a natural interval to move through. One fine instance of this effect is the paragraph in Chapter 41 (see above, page 110) developing the figure of the Hôtel de Cluny and the Roman ruins beneath it to represent all that must remain undefined in the character of Ahab. Another is the buoyantly Ishmaelian paragraph closing out Chapter 86, "The Tail," in which the tremendous mysteries of the sperm whale's behavior are compared finally with the invisibility, as told in Exodus, of the face of God. The virtuosity of these paragraphs and of others like them results in good part from their simultaneous compactness of form and free assembling of unanticipated further data. Their construction, their very existence in the text, appearing to some degree accidental, they are that much more able to push the argument ahead without constraint, and then to stop at a point of real strength.

IV

In all Melville's work through *Moby-Dick* the short chapter is the practical basis of the presentation. For the kind of documentary, episodic adventure-chronicle he was writing, it is the main ordering device. It becomes the simple means of piecing

---

of his few distinct failures, the writing seems cramped and obstructed; we feel for once a serious disparity between the form adopted and the writer's natural mode of elaboration.

out the narrative, of moving easily from one thing to the next or of building quickly but with a sufficient illusion of suspense to some short-run climax. The short chapter nicely suited Melville's raw talent in his first books, a talent principally for spot description and ruminative reporting. It served equally well the subsequent flaring of his ambition and competence as a writer. A unit of discourse is also a unit of conception; and for the eager, opportunistic, quick-opening bursts of Melville's expanding imagination, a better compositional scheme than the loose string of relatively self-contained chapters is hard to think of.

In *Typee* and *Omoo* there is already an attractive, a "magazinish," compactness to each successive chapter. Certain ones—the disquisition on breadfruit in *Typee,* the sketch of the sailor Rope-yarn in *Omoo*—have the simple efficiency of set-pieces; they are neatly turned, but also conscientiously detailed and informative. The risk incurred is fragmentation, and in the overblown structure of *Mardi* this shortness of narrative breath too exactly expresses the diffuseness of the whole. In the better-defined effort of *Redburn* and *White-Jacket,* on the other hand, the unit of the short chapter is felt more positively as an instrument of form, a means of concentrating impressions and themes and of running them through to their short-term limits; in fact, the general line of statement is now shaped to the measure of this unit—or so we think in observing how many chapters in these two lively chronicles rise to a distinct terminal flourish in a manner worthy of *Moby-Dick.*

After *Moby-Dick* individual chapters are less remarkable in themselves, and appear less determinative formally. With *Pierre* the strain of the effort to write "a regular romance, with a mysterious plot to it, & stirring passions at work"—as the author described the book to his English publisher—results in the odd formal compromise of "Books" sub-divided into short numbered sections, an arrangement that does, at least, help to salvage some degree of organization and pace from the chaos of Melville's purposes. Subsequently, in *Israel Potter* and *The Confidence-Man,* and also (not to be overlooked in this reckoning) *Clarel,* the unit of the chapter reappears to do its job of local division and emphasis. But only, perhaps, in *Billy Budd* does it once again play a vital part in the whole creative achievement. The sentence-making in *Billy Budd* gropes somewhat, but the chapters positively race in their succession, their juxtapositions of topics and of accents; and the free appositeness and taut grace of their joining, one to the next, produce no small part—so it seems to me—of the impression of completeness and irreversibility that distinguish that extraordinary work in the telling.[11]

With this as with most other phases of Melville's performance, *Moby-Dick* is the major instance. To look for the fullest development of a Melvillean signature, or indeed to think in general about the manner of his mastery as a writer, is (I find) to bring certain chapters and successions of chapters in *Moby-Dick* forcibly to mind. That is not to deny the book coherence as a whole. It is only to recognize certain facts about it: that its improvised practical structure is episodic and capitulatory, and that it finds its coherence not in the mechanism of its plot or in any other unitary (e.g., allegorical or speculative) scheme of presentation but in a continuous major harmony of apprehension—that is to say, in the sufficient assertion, each time anew, of a sufficient imaginative power to embrace, and so continue to create, the multiple connections it advances by. The chapter-episodes do, of course, have the advantage of a simple, stirring, naturally suspended main story; but without their continual reenactment of that story's manifold conditions we would not be held by it as we are. We do the author of *Moby-Dick* no disservice in remembering the grossness of the common fictional conventions—the melodrama, the mystification, the Gothic coloring and theatrical rant—by which he pieced out his grand conception; and then in considering why the book is not spoiled by them. Certainly the drama of Ahab arouses, excitingly enough, a sympathetic curiosity. Certainly the rendering of it appeals very artfully to our readiness to salve our ignorance of the ultimate reason of things with explanatory parables. But it may be, I think, in individual chapters like "The Ship" or "Brit" or "The Grand Armada," that the quick of our consent is touched most compellingly. There Melville gives us plain and full that "sheer

---

[11] The fine opening chapters of *Israel Potter* and *The Confidence-Man* might also be mentioned. Simply in their forwarding energy, their power to raise and fix our interest, they show Melville at the top of his form, though in both cases the initial momentum is rather wasted.

apprehension of the world," in D. H. Lawrence's fine words, which in one way or another particularly exacts from us (as we are capable) a "stillness in the soul, an awe."

Other chapters hardly less impressive might be named—and, properly, placed in context, quoted without abridgment, and delivered aloud in full voice like the eloquent recitatives and arias they function as. Certain ones cast in the book's best vein of genial hyperbole ("The Street," or "Nantucket," or—not everyone's choice—"Stubb's Supper," with its perhaps too easy footing in darky humor) would not go unmentioned; nor would those like "The Sermon," or "Moby-Dick" and "The Whiteness of the Whale," or "The Try-Works," that are most frequently appealed to for interpretation of the book as a whole; nor others, such as "The First Lowering" and the three chapters of the chase, in which the long narrative series bursts into its studied climaxes of tumultuous action; nor, finally, certain singularly vivid and moving short chapters as compact and resonant as great lyric poems—"The Albatross," "The Pacific," "The Symphony."

None of these, however, needs special pleading. Each has become a touchstone for appreciation of Melville's art and for explanation of his "meaning." For that reason it may be useful to look instead at one or two less spectacular chapters—chapters of the sort that, if accidentally left out in some reprinting, might not immediately be missed. One such is Chapter 110, "Queequeg in His Coffin." It comes just at the beginning of the final rush toward the meeting with Moby Dick, and shares in the renewal of dramatic excitement already underway. And it starts, efficiently, from an incident of some importance to the main action—Ahab's prudential yielding to Starbuck's request to heave to and investigate a leakage of oil in the hold. At once we are deep in technical detail—"tierces," "butts," "casks," "puncheons," "shooks of staves" and "iron bundles of hoops"—and just as quickly this objective data opens out into metaphor; the now topheavy *Pequod* herself bobs "like an air-freighted demijohn," or like "a dinnerless student with all Aristotle in his head." All this is by way of introduction to the main episode of the chapter, which is Queequeg's strange illness and stranger recovery. (I must leave to the reader's own observation the tact with which the chapter's transitions and enlargements are executed.) Typically this episode is launched in a one-sentence paragraph.

And that in turn, also typically, opens with an irregular cadence which in its slight artificiality delicately points up the overform of the telling; for in the borrowing of an accent from the style of legend, or of Scripture, the way is prepared for the fable-rounded interlude, the story-within-the-story, which the main narrative pauses here to present: "Now, at this time it was that my poor pagan companion, and fast bosom-friend, Queequeg, was seized with a fever, which brought him nigh to his endless end." The episode now moves along rapidly, but does not pass up its chances for underscoring. So Queequeg's falling ill after his sweated labor deep in the hold permits references, in quick succession, to the sea-going democracy of danger and job-responsibility, to the concrete severities of the ordinary chores of whaling, to the mysteries of body and soul in their joint course through life, and to all the further mysteries of life and death and of everything which, being "truly wondrous and fearful in man, never yet was put into words or books." Queequeg, wasting away into a strange, soft mildness, orders a boat-like coffin made in preparation for certain legendary pagan rites of death; he lies in it, with harpoons, idol-god, and provisions for the last journey; Pip and Starbuck gather to comment, each according to his lights; but then Queequeg, as if by his own "sovereign will and pleasure," decides that it is not really time to die yet, and promptly rallies—and upon his recovery sets about carving certain mystical hieroglyphs upon the coffin (now his sea-chest) which he himself cannot understand. So the chapter ends, but with a last emphasis—Ahab studying these hieroglyphs and crying out in anguish at the tantalizing mystery of them—which not only confirms the obvious correspondences between Queequeg's travail here and Ahab's in the main story but propels us violently back into that story; it is the momentous chapter, "The Pacific," that now follows.

My other example of Melville's ordinary chapter-making in *Moby-Dick*, Chapter 57, has no part at all in the main action. Its title suggests its place in the book, and also the problem of composition it presents: "Of Whales in Paint; in Teeth; in Wood; in Sheet-Iron; in Stone; in Mountains; in Stars." The last chapter in a group of three dealing with pictorial representations and images of the whale, it has the look of a repository for data that will not fit in anywhere else. The semicolons of the title almost flaunt its casualness. But in just this respect it puts us in mind of Melville's most general problems of organization in *Moby-Dick*, for it exemplifies the kind of itemizing of random materials that the whole central mass of the book advances by and that without a determined exertion of imaginative control would have stalled it entirely. There is some point in noting, therefore, that the actual life and charm of this chapter derive in good part from the more than usually emphatic assertion of the narrator's own interposed presence. The chapter is of negligible importance in the over-all design of *Moby-Dick;* nevertheless the same voice speaks in it as in the book's most intensely compelling passages, and speaks as boldly. A mere survey of instances—a painting, the art of skrim-shander, savage carvings, roadside emblems, geological formations, the *trompe d'oeil* of natural shapes—rapidly takes on both the thick topicality and the spaciousness of the whole. So in a brief space there is easy reference to Tower-Hill and Wapping, and to all Christendom; one hears of what can be observed "throughout the Pacific, and also in Nantucket, and New Bedford, and Sag Harbor"; a complex panorama of human types and conditions—Iroquois Indians, Hawaiian islanders, cannibals, Greek Achilles and Dutch Dürer, whaling forecastles and gable-roofed houses—is spread out, and succeeded by a complementary panorama of the whole physical earth, revealing fantastic rock-masses under grassy slopes, "amphitheatrical heights" of mountain, and remote and unknown island chains; until finally, "expandingly lifted by your subject," you discover that the tallying of this data has become one with the naming of stars and constellations—Cetus and Argo Navis and the Flying Fish—and so has merged into the mythological origins of all narrative and all experience. The ending (in yet another one-sentence paragraph) is precisely in keeping: "With a frigate's anchors for my bridle-bitts and fasces of harpoons for spurs, would I could mount that whale and leap the topmost skies, to see whether the fabled heavens with all their countless tents really lie encamped beyond my mortal sight." The mythical role Ishmael is roughly cast in being that of the free, versatile, curious, observant, adaptable, irrepressible, democratic everyman at home in all times, places, and conditions— the man born, in the words of the nineteenth-century song, "a hundred thousand years ago," whose report of all he has seen, and not seen, always shows him to be supremely the man upon whom nothing really discoverable has been lost—one cannot think of a fitter epitaph for him (of the kind he sympathetically devises for Bulkington) than this casually magnificent little chapter.

WALKER COWEN [1934–] cofounded a small press, Walker-deBerry, while a graduate student at Harvard. He has written an introduction to an edition of Howells' *Criticism and Fiction* and Norris' *Responsibilities of the Novelist* (published in one volume by Walker-deBerry). He is now assistant director of the University Press of Virginia and a member of the English Department of the University of Virginia.

Melville's "Discoveries": A Dialogue of the Mind with Itself

WALKER COWEN

The Houghton Library at Harvard has recently added to its Melville collection an octavo leather-bound volume marked on its spine CATALOGUE OF LIBRARY / H.M. The book is composed of the same kind of lined blue sheets bound in with the Chase *Narrative* but all of them are blank. Had Melville catalogued his library it would be possible to estimate just how comprehensive is this present collection of his marginalia. Professor Sealts' check list suggests, however, that the books examined for this study represent nearly all of the books it is certain were in his library.

Limitation is a condition of excellence. While Melville's collection of books was not over large, it is very high in quality and obviously selected with care. The present notes and markings are taken from over fifty different titles. Many of these, like the Byron and Shakespeare, are multivolume sets. There are books on subjects as varied as art, travel, gardening, and pottery.

Melville's Marginalia (1965), pp. 25–45.

Although there is little history, there are a number of biographies of personal and historical interest. The largest part of the marked books are works of literature and philosophy. But the quantity of narrative fiction is small in comparison with books of the drama, poetry, and essays. Most of the library is composed of classics like Homer, Shakespeare, and the Bible or the works of distinguished nineteenth-century writers, both American and foreign, like Balzac, Emerson, and Arnold.

If we do not have Melville's notes for every title we might hope for, the books with marginalia do, nevertheless, represent an unusually large and significant body of reading. The books establish a coherent and accurate impression of his intellectual life, his prejudices, and his enthusiasms. The notes provide abundant data about the complex process and development of his creative imagination and his own views of himself and his art.

Inquiry into these matters on the basis of the marginalia must be conducted with the knowledge of certain important qualifications. Because Melville did not mark his books with the intention of gratifying the researches of later scholars, we have the advantage of an intimacy and spontaneity in the marginalia, the recording of direct and unconsidered reactions, which is not present in his fiction or even in his letters. The marginalia provide a kind of road map or chart of his mind but, in part because of its unpremeditated nature, the information it conveys is not always complete.

In some instances Melville failed to mark passages he later incorporated into his writing. He neglected to distinguish in this way material, for example, that he found in Dryden, Emerson, and Spenser. Although there are a number of markings for Job 41, which describes the Leviathan, the story of Jonah and the whale, which he probably already knew by heart, is not marked in his Bible at all. Melville's copy of *The Life and Adventures of Israel Potter* is of an early date. Internal evidence strongly suggests that he may have drawn upon the poverty sections of this book for *Redburn* before he worked from the rest of the narrative later for his own *Israel Potter*. The absence of any markings in his own copy of the source volume points to the possibility that Melville may not have begun to mark his books in consistent fashion with the kinds of marks he used later until the onset, in 1849–1850, of his intensive study of the great writers.

Almost all the books which have survived date from these years onwards. Melville, of course, read widely during the 1840's and probably for most of his mature life. But it is well to remember that during the first part of his career he was much more a professional writer, in the sense of a man working up books to sell, than we tend now to remember. He implies in *Redburn* that much of his earlier reading was undertaken in order to augment the sense of his personal experience and to provide fact and detail for his stories. He describes those ropemakers who, "use odds and ends of old rigging called 'junk', the yarns of which are picked to pieces, and then twisted into new combinations, something as most books are manufactured." The discovery of sources for particular episodes in the earlier books, for example of the remarkable description of White Jacket's fall into the sea, appears to confirm this supposition. And we know how he sought specific detail in books like the Beale, Chase, and the Scoresby for *Moby Dick*. When he wrote to Bentley in England in June, 1850, describing that manuscript he went beyond matters of business to reveal something about his working methods. "Could you be positively put in possession of the copyright, it might be worth to you a larger sum—considering its great novelty; for I do not know that the subject treated of has ever been worked up by a romancer; or, indeed, by any writer, in any adequate manner."

But *Moby Dick* is different from the earlier novels. It is possible that at least part of the thematic richness of that narrative grew not only from a shift in the kinds of books Melville was reading but also from a change in his attitude toward them. Although he must have read in the Bible and Shakespeare before, the heavily marked and annotated copies were not acquired until 1849 and 1850. While he continued to read for factual matter and background materials he seems, about this time, to have initiated an intensive study of the great writers and the great themes. The impact of this reading has been discussed often and it can hardly be overestimated. The marginalia document the long process of intellectual development from its beginning at this point until the last month of his life. If we do not have earlier books with their evidence of first readings, it is at least possible that there might have been fewer of these than might be supposed. And it is probable that they were not marked from the point of view of the intelligence which guided the later reading. The writing after *Moby Dick* draws less upon the novelty of personal experience and the chronology suggests that Melville, confronted with the necessities of making a living by writing, had very little time during the first part of his career for the kind of study and meditation he enjoyed later.

It is not easy to pinpoint exactly changes in the processes of the imagination and shifts in points of view. But certain passages taken from books he acquired in 1849 and 1850 dramatize the sudden and remarkable deepening and broadening of Melville's intellect during these years. Among the lines that he marked, but later erased, in his copy of Ben Jonson's works which he purchased in London in November, 1849, is this paragraph from *Timber*.

> Imposture held up by credulity. All these are the Cobwebs of Learning, and to let them grow in us, is either sluttish or foolish. Nothing is more ridiculous, than to make an Author a *Dictator*, as the Schools have done Aristotle. The Damage is infinite, knowledge receives by it. For to many things a Man should owe but a Temporary Belief, and a Suspicion of his own Judgment, not an absolute Resignation of himself, or a perpetual Captivity. Let *Aristotle* and others have their dues; but if we can make farther Discoveries of Truth and Fitness than they, why are we envied?

The same emotions that led Melville to mark this passage also prompted the annotation he wrote in the copy of Chatterton's *Poetical Works* which he bought just four weeks later. Under,

> It is not unlikely that, had he lived, we might have had another Midsummer Night's Dream; and though Shakespeare must ever remain unapproachable, still we should have read the rich and exquisite faery poetry of his brother dreamer with delight, and returned to it again and again, as to a fountain of joy whose waters would well freshly and inexhaustibly.

Melville wrote

> Cant. No man "must ever remain unapproachable."

These ideas found a ready reception in Melville's mind because at just this time he was most keenly feeling the pressures of his own talent and the desire for some genuine recognition for the genius he realized he possessed. He found himself in greater sympathy than ever with magazine editors like O'Sullivan and Duyckinck who were seeking to establish, once and for all, our country's respect for its native writers and their works. When Melville sought to convey his deep and sincere admiration for Hawthorne in the essay he wrote the following summer for *The Literary World* he brought all these sources and emotions together.

> Some may start to read of Shakespeare and Hawthorne on the same page. They may say that if an illustration were needed, a lesser light might have sufficed to elucidate this Hawthorne, this small man of yesterday. But I am not willingly one of those who, as touching Shakespeare at least, exemplify the maxim of Rochefoucauld, that "we exalt the reputation of some, in order to depress that of others"—who, to teach all noble-souled aspirants that there is no hope for them, pronounce Shakespeare absolutely unapproachable. But Shakespeare has been approached. There are minds that have gone as far as Shakespeare into the universe. And hardly a mortal man, who, at some time or other, has not felt as great thoughts in him as any you will find in Hamlet. We must not inferentially malign mankind for the sake of any one man, who ever he may be. This is too cheap a purchase of contentment for conscious mediocrity to make. Besides, this absolute and unconditional adoration of Shakespeare has grown to be a part of our Anglo-Saxon superstitions. The Thirty-nine Articles are now forty. Intolerance has come to exist in this matter. You must believe in Shakespeare's unapproachability, or quit the country. But what sort of a belief is this for an American, a man who is bound to carry republican progressiveness into Literature as well as into Life? Believe me, my friends, that men not very much inferior to Shakespeare are this day being born on the banks of the Ohio.

But Melville's markings and annotations testify that he soon after emerged from a confrontation with Shakespeare's plays

which left no doubt in his mind about the greatness of the dramatist's genius. His increased respect brought with it complex
changes in his views about the nature of man. He marked, for
example, these lines in *The Tempest*.

> *Mira.*   O! wonder!
> How many goodly creatures are there here!
> How beautious mankind is! O brave new world,
> That has such people in't!
> *Pro.*   'Tis new to thee.

And Melville added these thoughts in his annotation by the
passage.

> Consider the character of the persons concerning whom
> Miranda says this—then Prospero's quiet words
> in comment—how terrible! In "Timon"
> itself there is nothing like it.

And here, the word 'terrible' has been written in over another
word that has been erased. The phrase he originally wrote was
very likely one he uses elsewhere in the marginalia—'how true.'
    Melville's feelings toward Hawthorne also altered in the
subsequent years. But it has not been possible to learn very
much about his reaction to the gradual estrangement of their
friendship. Clues may be hidden in the fiction, in the description of Pierre's attitudes toward Isabel, for example, or in the
China Aster fable in the *Confidence Man* where a Hawthorne
may be urging a Melville to continue writing great books which
will not sell. The marginalia contain other suggestive material.
It appears possible that Melville may have seen in the troubled
friendship of Byron and Shelley a reflection of scenes from his
own life. He studied both these writers at length and read
biographical works about them. And he marked passages like
this one from the *Shelley Memorials*.

> On the 1st of November, Byron arrived at Pisa, where
> he established himself. Leigh Hunt did not reach Italy until
> several months later. Shelley was now a good deal in the
> society of Byron; between whom and himself, however, a
> perfect cordiality seemed never to exist. The author of
> *Childe Harold* has confessed in one of his letters, that, much
> as he admired and esteemed Shelley, the feeling did not
> amount to entire friendship—an emotion which he could

realize only with regard to one of the companions of his childhood. And Shelley, in the presence of Byron, felt somewhat oppressed by the weight of what he conceived to be his Lordship's superior poetical powers; though on this point the world is rapidly reversing contemporary judgment. In writing to a friend, Shelley speaks of Byron's genius reducing him to despair; an excess of modesty to which, perhaps, may be attributed the comparatively small number of his compositions at this time.

If one thinks of Melville's dedication of *Moby Dick* to Hawthorne, one also recalls Melville's perception that "genius, all over the world, stands hand in hand, and one shock of recognition runs the whole world round." In his later years, perhaps because they shared so many of the demands and infirmities of genius, Melville undertook a study of Balzac. Among the many passages he marked is Balzac's letter of praise to Stendhal in the *Correspondence*. Here Melville found confirmation for an idea he had held for most of his life and one which made possible the kind of dialogue which he carried on with his books. Balzac wrote,

> Sir, — One must never put off giving pleasure to those who have given us pleasure. 'La Chartreuse' is a great and splendid book. I say this without flattery, without envy. And I should be incapable of writing it.

Along with the markings and annotations which offer biographical evidence are others which seem closely related but are much more enigmatic. One of the longest of Melville's annotations is what appears to be a description of a Solomon's temple together with a catalog of Masonic symbols which recall his use of this kind of material in "The Tail" chapter of *Moby Dick*. Whether or not these notes on the back flyleaves of his copy of Hawthorne's *Mosses* are related to his sketch for a story about the devil and the man at the Astor House, written in at the end of the Shakespeare, they do seem connected with the notes he wrote later in his copy of Madame de Staël's *Germany*.

> In knowledge there are paths which in their very nature are secret—such as have them in their possession, never found resolution to reveal them. But they are propagated in secret, and can not be made common.

Melville, of course, need not have been a Mason in order to have found an interest in their metaphors and attitudes towards knowledge. The references to dark and hidden truths in the Hawthorne essay and the determination to pierce through appearance so eloquently expressed in *Moby Dick* point to one of the most consistent themes in the marginalia. Part of Melville's reading was directed toward the problems of expression. Often he marked a telling phrase wherever he could find it and, in the case of Chapman's *Homer,* his annotations reveal he read this version along with Pope's in order to compare the different texts. But from first to last, Melville's inquiry was theological and philosophical. He described the toil of his own study in Babbalanja's fable of Mindi, the amiable scholar in *Mardi* who read at night by the light of glowworms, forever halting and stumbling through his books and obliged to wade through quagmires in search of a fresh glim.

The marginalia are the private journal of his discoveries, the documented history of Melville's half-century struggle with himself and his art. His acceptance and rejection and qualification of the truths others had wrung from the experience of their lives elevates these pages into something much greater than the sum of their biographical, critical, and literary parts. Each of the markings and annotations is the product of an exercise in discrimination. They are moral actions in the intellectual life of an artist who seeks, in the end, to discover himself.

The notebooks and journals of writers have always been highly valued, often as distinguished works in themselves and always for their accurate notes on the artist's attitude toward the development of his creative energies and his state of mind at given times throughout his career. We are especially indebted to the journals of Emerson and Thoreau and to Hawthorne's notebooks for much of what we now know about them and their relation to the forces that shaped the great classic period of American writing. Read in the same way, the marginalia offer much of the same kind of information about Melville. These notes and annotations are directed toward the ideas that were important to him and they demonstrate the direction and varying emphasis of his inquiry into them.

The direct and spontaneous character of the markings and notes differs from the more formal and calculated journals prepared by Melville's contemporaries. The Transcendentalists' journals were designed to provide a quarry from which to draw material for publication, and frequently men like Emerson and Alcott copied passages from each other's meditations and commented upon them. But Melville secured the privacy of his thoughts by his gradual withdrawal from the society of literary persons. He left the most complete and open record of his inmost thoughts scattered through the books on his shelves. He preferred to seek confirmation for his ideas in a private dialogue with the greatest and most demanding minds rather than among a circle of prejudiced friends. As he read he carried what he learned forward to confront each new idea with the accumulated resources of his earlier study. As the years pass, the markings become more demanding, and there is an increased compression and intensity in his epigrammatic annotations. What a man writes for himself will always be different from those things he prepares with the knowledge that others will see them.

Something of this process can be traced in a comparison of the two journals Melville kept of his trips to Europe and to the Near East. The account of the journey to London in 1849 is full of personal detail. "Came home, had a fire made, & wrote to Lizzie & Allan." Its chatty tone contrasts with the notes taken on his 1856 trip to the Holy Land, which seem much more the material of a writer's notebook. Here are the sights and sounds available only to a specialized point of view. There are outlines for projects and subtle judgments of art and other writers. At Oxford, Melville wrote, "In such a retreat old Burton sedately smiled at men." The first journal was done in the tradition of the American traveler's diary. Melville wrote it to be read, or knew it would be read, by his wife when he returned. The second was a notebook contrived for its own purposes and written, much like the marginalia, for the present and future reference of the author alone.

This travel journal along with the markings in Melville's guidebooks and in the works he read on the places he visited enable us to follow this journey very closely. Markings like this one in Stanley's *Sinai and Palestine* describing the approach to Petra designate the steps of Melville's physical progress on his travels but they also indicate the direction of his imagination.

after a mile or more through the defile—the cliffs over-
arching in their narrowest contraction—when, suddenly
through the narrow opening left beween the two dark walls
of another turn of the gorge, you see a pale pink front of
pillars and sculptured figures closing your view from top
to bottom. You rush towards it, and you find yourself at
the end of the defile, and in the presence of an excavated
temple.

With the hope that he might see more deeply into spiritual
mysteries, Melville brought himself in contact with physical
presences by climbing the pyramids and washing his hands in
the Red Sea. And he found a parable of the hopelessness of
worldly materialism at Petra. The desolation of that great city
seemed to confirm his traveler's self-trust and the spirit of indi-
vidualism he cherished all his life.

The journey and his reading provided, of course, most of
the material for *Clarel* and for much of the later poetry. In spite
of a heavy, oratorical manner, Melville unquestionably had the
splinters of a great poet in him. One of the great themes of the
later marginalia is his effort to study and master the principles
of poetic composition. Along with this study came an increased
interest in the problems of literary style marked by the patient
examination and rereading of essays like Arnold's on translating Homer. These concerns and the slow accumulation of references and thematic material from Marvell, FitzGerald, Southey,
and others coalesced, at the end, in *Billy Budd*.

The extraordinary abundance of later sources in the marginalia can lead to particular studies in identification as, for
example, the use of passages from Balzac's *The Two Brothers*
for *Timoleon*. Melville's attention to narrative masks in *Don
Quixote* and his own handling of similar techniques in the *Confidence Man* offer an opportunity to examine special aspects of
the imaginative organization of his fiction. The often-neglected
chapters on writing in the *Confidence Man* coupled with the
markings and annotations in the marginalia provide a remarkably comprehensive view of Melville's attitudes toward his own
and others' methods of composition.

The marginalia in works of other writers from other countries and other ages help to pry open some of the most difficult

questions associated with the romantic imagination. The problem of whether perception and the sources of the imagination lay in the external object or in the mind was made more difficult in America where writers were determined to be original and to draw upon the materials of their native environment. Crèvecoeur stated the ideal when he wrote, "The American is a new man who acts on new principles: he must therefore entertain new ideas and form new opinions." The wealth of marginalia here testifies that even our most imaginative native writer could not be wholly original. Almost in answer, he wrote, "Cursed be that mortal inter-indebtedness in . . . I would be as free as air; and I'm down in the whole world's books." But studies which help to isolate the contributions of Melville's reading and his visual experience to his writing serve to enable us to estimate more accurately the great power of what was truly original in his work.

Many of Melville's markings show an interest in and a ready sympathy for the efforts of others to meet similar problems of creativity. His library of art books and his notes reveal that he was eager to learn how plastic artists could, for example, impart a sense of movement to still forms with the play of color or light and darkness. These inquiries were accompanied by Johnsonian interest in the lives of the artists themselves. The struggles of other artists and writers with their craft and with the world and themselves always touched Melville's emotions. He responded with that charity which is won from the experience of one's own hopes and defeats. The eloquent phrase "poor Lamb" is penciled beneath the account of Lamb's shabby treatment by an editor of the *Quarterly Review.*

Annotations like these demonstrate the extraordinary intensity of Melville's involvement with what he read throughout his life. The vivid personal reaction and the sense of self-participation deepened with the years. After 1860 he began to enter more and more into the arena of the contested ideas of his own time. Through Arnold and others he followed the debate between science and religion, for example, but he always kept alive his conviction of the truths and insights of individual genius. In the increasing chaos, as he saw it, of heaven's truth and earth's truth, Melville held to the Renaissance convictions of pride, honor, and even revenge, and to a Christianity that looked back to the Old Testament virtues.

Whether we go to the marginalia for source material or for Melville's reaction to other writers and their ideas, we cannot help being caught up with the personality of this exceptional man and his sensitive responses to the pressures of a rapidly changing culture. These markings are not a disappointing collection of casual and random notes but a coherent record of a mind reaching out into time and space to amplify the depth and sense of its own experience. These passages exemplify what Arnold described with his phrase "a dialogue of the mind with itself." And so often, partly because of the texts but largely through intention, one has the sensation of hearing Melville himself speaking. In this checked and underlined section, for example, from Chamisso's *Peter Schlemihl:*

> Afterwards I became reconciled to myself. I learnt, in the first place to respect necessity, and those accidents which are yet more the result of necessity than any will of our own.

And Melville checked this reply of Benedict's in *Much Ado About Nothing* but it was later erased.

> *Bene.* O God, sir, here's a dish I love not; I cannot endure my lady Tongue.

This intimacy is reenforced by the constant, felt pressure in the marginalia of Melville's mind involved in process and always thrusting forward with great intellectual energy to add to the resources of a powerful memory. The cumulative reserves of past knowledge are here brought forward to confront the complex structures of large ideas or the telling evidence of detail. His quiet note, "the innocent hung," in FitzGerald's *Polonius* is charged with an imaginative power that was at once personal and universal. Melville may have read a translation of Anacreon in his set of Harper's Classical Library and certainly he noticed a reference to the grasshopper in Hawthorne's story, "The Virtuoso's Collection." Nearly a decade later he framed the memory into an annotation identifying the source of Emerson's poem when he saw it. He had read about the Kantian revolutionary, Adam Weishaupt, in Madame de Staël's *Germany* but it was nearly ten years later before he marked the passages he found which related to him when he studied Crabb Robinson's *Diary.* Details like these bring us near Melville and promote the belief

that, at last, we really "know" him, at least with that accuracy
Proust reminds us,

> which it is easier, often, to obtain when we are studying
> the lives of people who have been dead for centuries than
> when we are trying to chronicle those of our own most in-
> timate friends, an accuracy which it seems as impossible to
> obtain as it seemed impossible to speak from one town to
> another, before we learned of the contrivance by which that
> impossibility has been overcome.

Melville's reading gave him access to the great world community of ideas. His warm commendation, "Good old Sherry"
beside one of Sheridan's drinking songs illustrates his easy relation to that community. But this passage from Emerson's *Spiritual Laws,* beside which he wrote, "Bully for Emerson! Good,"
brings us nearer the humanistic motives for his study.

> We are always reasoning from the seen to the unseen.
> Hence the perfect intelligence that subsists between wise
> men of remote ages. A man cannot bury his meanings so
> deep in his book, but that time and like-minded men will
> find them. Plato had a secret doctrine, had he? What secret
> can he conceal from the eyes of Bacon? of Montaigne? of
> Kant? Therefore, Aristotle said of his works, "They are pub-
> lished and not published."

If we believe in an autobiographical reading of the opening of *Pierre,* Melville began his reading with Plato at hand. We
know that he ended his days still studying philosophy and still
encouraged by the belief, marked in his copy of Balzac's *Sera-
phita,* that

> The endless legacy of the past to the present is the secret
> source of human genius.

The marginalia demonstrate that the sense of genius and the
search for truth were always closely associated in Melville's
mind with the more immediate and personal problems of self-
realization and self-knowledge. The drama of this journal of his
most significant and most intimate quest lies in the comprehension and passion with which Melville conducted it. In *Mardi,*
if he noted—

> 'But, come now thou oracle, if all things are deceptive,
> tell us what is truth?

'The old interrogatory; did they not ask it when the world began? But ask it no more. As old Bardianna hath it, that question is more final than any answer.'

—the marginalia provide abundant evidence that Melville continued all his life to ask the great questions in his remarkable struggle to know himself. He expressed exactly what these markings and annotations meant to him when he wrote,

The higher the intelligence, the more faith, and the less credulity: Gabriel rejects more than we, but out-believes us all. The greatest marvels are first truths; and first truths the last unto which we attain. Things nearest are farthest off. Though your ear be next door to your brain, it is forever removed from your sight. Man has a more comprehensive view of the moon than the man in the moon himself. We know the moon is round; he only infers it. It is because we ourselves are in ourselves, that we know ourselves not. And it is only of our easy faith, that we are not infidels throughout; and only of our lack of faith, that we believe what we do.

In some universe-old truths, all mankind are disbelievers. Do you believe that you lived three thousand years ago? That you were at the taking of Tyre, were overwhelmed in Gomorrah? No. But for me, I was at the subsiding of the Deluge, and helped swab the ground, and build the first house. With the Israelites, I fainted in the wilderness; was in court when Solomon outdid all the judges before him. I, it was, who suppressed the lost work of Manetho, on Egyptian theology, as containing mysteries not to be revealed to posterity, and things at war with the canonical scriptures; I, who originated the conspiracy against that purple murderer, Domitian; I, who in the senate moved that great and good Aurelian be emperor. I instigated the abdication of Diocletian, and Charles the Fifth; I touched Isabella's heart that she hearkened to Columbus. I am he, that from the king's minions hid the Charter in the old oak at Hartford; I harboured Goffe and Whalley: I am the leader of the Mohawk masks, who in the old Commonwealth's harbour, overboard threw the East India Company's Souchong; I am the Veiled Persian Prophet; I, the man in the iron mask; I Junius.

JOHN D. SEELYE [1931–   ] is an associate professor of English at the University of Connecticut and the author of a number of articles on Melville. "The Ironic Diagram" is the Introduction to his book-length study of Melville's irony.

The Ironic Diagram

JOHN D. SEELYE

> Contiguity of desert & verdure,
> splendor & squalor, gloom & gayety.

I

According to Hawthorne, who knew him as well as any man ever did, it was Melville's curse never to rest "until he gets hold of a definite belief. It is strange how he persists—and has persisted ever since I knew him, and probably long before—in wandering to-and-fro over these deserts." An Ishmael in a wilderness of doubt, Melville could "neither believe, nor be comfortable in his unbelief; and [was] too honest and courageous not to try to do one or the other."[1] It is this uncertainty, compounded with Melville's deep desire to rid himself of it, which accounts for the ambiguity pervading his work.

It is not so much that Melville's art was hampered by his confusion, but rather that it was inspired by it: always a primitive artist in the sense that creation was for him an intense, sub-

---

[1] *The English Notebooks*, ed. Randall Stewart (New York: Russell & Russell, 1962), pp. 432–33. Though familiar, the full passage is herewith quoted: "He stayed with us [in Liverpool] from Tuesday till Thursday; and, on the intervening day, we took a pretty long walk together, and sat down in a hollow among the sand hills (sheltering ourselves from the high, cool wind) and smoked a cigar. Melville, as he always does, began to reason of Providence and futurity, and of everything that lies beyond human ken, and informed me that he had 'pretty much made up his mind to be annihilated'; but still he does not seem to rest in that anticipation; and, I think, will never rest until he gets hold of a definite belief. It is strange how he persists—and has persisted ever since I knew him, and probably long before—in wandering to-and-fro over these deserts, as dismal and monotonous as the sand hills amid which we were sitting. He can neither believe, nor be comfortable in his unbelief; and he is too honest and courageous not to try to do one or the other. If he were a religious man, he would be one of the most truly religious and reverential; he has a very high and noble nature, and better worth immortality than most of us."

jective investment in the materials of his art, Melville was impelled by his psychological and philosophical uncertainties to create forms which would encompass them. "Swayed to universality of thought," like his artist-hero, Pierre, Melville felt that "most grand productions of the best human intellects ever are built round a circle, as atolls . . . digestively including the whole range of all that can be known or dreamed" (p. 333).[2] He regarded a work of art as all-inclusive, like "Lombardo's 'Koztanza'" in *Mardi*, a unity of totalness, an organic composite given order by the artist's "crowned and sceptered instinct" (II, 320). Much that is baffling about his work becomes clear if the reader understands that Melville regarded his art as a system of tensions produced by diagrammatic contrasts, a paradoxical structure which would accommodate his search for belief and express his capacity for doubt.

Take, for example, the problem of the double-consciousness in *Moby-Dick*. There, two "voices" demand our attention: the heroic God-hatred of Ahab and the companionable, "cowardly" skepticism of Ishmael. The two attitudes meet on the common ground that there is a "wisdom that is woe," but whereas Ahab has carried his woe to an extreme, has hardened his heart against man, beast, and God, Ishmael realizes that there is also "a woe that is madness," and warns the reader against staring too long into the hell-fire of deepest doubt: "Give not thyself up, then, to fire, lest it invert thee, deaden thee" (p. 422). Fire is Ahab's portion, sunlight is Ishmael's. Both voices are invested with a deep weight of subjectiveness—the one through soliloquy, the other through a first-person address to the reader—and both have had their advocates among readers and critics who have imposed an absolute interpretation on Melville's ambiguities.

Writing to Hawthorne, Melville championed the man "who declares himself a sovereign nature (in himself) amid the powers of heaven, hell, and earth. He may perish; but so long as he exists, he insists upon treating with all Powers upon an equal basis. If any of those other Powers choose to withhold certain secrets, let them; that does not impair my sovereignty in myself, that does not make me tributary." This was written in 1851, as

---

[2] Page references to *Moby-Dick, Pierre,* and *The Confidence-Man* are to the Hendricks House editions and are given in parentheses in the text. Page references to *Mardi* are to the first American edition (1849).

Moby-Dick was being rushed towards completion, and it seems obvious that the Faustian "he" (Hawthorne) and "me" (Melville) reflect the "he-and-I" of Ahab, whose sovereign self dominates Melville's greatest book. But in another letter to Hawthorne, Melville noted that "what plays the mischief with the truth is that all men will insist upon the universal application of a temporary feeling or opinion." Ahab, plainly, is an absolutist, a "universal applicator," while Ishmael tempers his doubts with a saving skepticism. Both are important spokesmen for a troubled consciousness—both, moving in opposite directions, search for belief. Melville created in Ahab a figure to express his most profound doubts about the goodness of divine purpose; in Ishmael, he created a more complex vehicle, one which varies from sage appreciation of the wisdom of Solomon to a smug recommendation of home and hearth as Man's best felicity. Melville could not be completely an Ahab, nor could he subscribe to the excesses of Ishmael's kind regard for the sunnier aspects of life, but both voices serve as instruments to express his wanderings between those antipodes of light and shadow.

The problem of interpretation resulting from Melville's structural relativism, is made more difficult by his intermittent use of stylistic indirection, one aspect of which is the extremes to which Ahab and Ishmael go in expressing their opposing viewpoints. Disgusted by the censorious reception given *Typee* and *Omoo* by certain elements of his audience, and fortified by a sense of his burgeoning genius and his consequent responsibility to posterity, Melville attempted, from *Mardi* on, to emulate the Pyrrhonic essayists and satirists of the Renaissance, those sly encyclopedists, Burton, Bayle, and Rabelais.[3] The open, declamatory style of *Typee* and *Omoo* was discarded for the

---

[3] The rhetorical influence of the Elizabethan prose writers on Melville's work is well known and forms an important part of F. O. Matthiessen's discussion of Melville in *American Renaissance*. The Rabelaisan influence is discussed in Edward Rosenberry's *Melville and the Comic Spirit*, and the relevance to Melville's skeptical and ironical development of Pierre Bayle's *Dictionary* is treated in relation to *Moby-Dick*, in particular, by Howard P. Vincent in *The Trying-Out of Moby-Dick* (New York, 1949) and Millicent Bell in "Pierre Bayle and *Moby Dick*," *PMLA*, LXVI (1951), 626–48, and to Melville's work as a whole by Lawrance Thompson, in *Melville's Quarrel with God*. Robert Shulman's dissertation, "Toward Moby-Dick: Melville and Some Baroque Worthies" (Columbus, Ohio: Ohio State University, 1959), treats the influence upon Melville's style of (among others) Rabelais, Montaigne, and Sir Thomas Browne.

bewildering entanglements of the Baroque mode, with Truth passed off as a joke. Melville's movement towards indirection was given further impetus by his encounters with Shakespeare, whom he read through the eyes of Coleridge, and with Hawthorne, whom he saw as an American Shakespeare. The romantics' Shakespeare was a "tragic Titan," who provided one show for the populace, another for a select circle of intellects, aristocrats of genius who could understand what was meant by "those deep far-away things in him; those occasional flashings-forth of the intuitive Truth in him; those short, quick probings at the very axis of reality." It was, Melville felt, "through the mouths of the dark characters of Hamlet, Timon, Lear, and Iago," that Shakespeare "craftily says, or sometimes insinuates the things we feel to be so terrifically true, that it were all but madness for any good man, in his own proper character, to utter, or even hint of them." [4] It is this "infinite obscure" that Melville most prized in Shakespeare, the "mystical blackness" which he also found in Hawthorne—not behind any "popularizing noise and show of broad farce and blood-besmeared tragedy"—but lurking behind "the Indian-summer sunlight on the hither side of Hawthorne's soul." Shakespeare, Hawthorne, and Melville were three "masters of the great Art of Telling the Truth, —even though it be covertly and by snatches."

[4] This and the quotations following are taken from the text of " 'Hawthorne and His Mosses,' By a Virginian Spending July in Vermont," as edited by Willard Thorp, in *Herman Melville: Representative Selections* (New York, 1938), pp. 332–35. Cf. Coleridge on Shakespeare: "In thus placing these profound general truths in the mouths of such men as Cornwall, Edmund, Iago, &c. Shakspeare at once gives them utterance and yet shows how indefinite their application is. . . . Remark the use which Shakspeare always makes of his bold villains, as vehicles for expressing opinions and conjectures of a nature too hazardous for a wise man to put forth directly as his own, or from any sustained character" (*The Complete Works of Samuel Taylor Coleridge*, Shedd edition [New York, 1854], IV, 141; VI, 435). Compare also, with what follows, Coleridge's presentation of Shakespeare as a member of a select circle of genius, those "who will dare to force [their] way out of the crowd, —not of the mere vulgar, —but of the vain and banded aristocracy of intellect, and presume to join the almost supernatural beings that stand by themselves aloof" (IV, 43).

Melville's debt to Coleridge's Shakespearean criticism is discussed in Leon Howard's "Melville's Struggle with the Angel," *Modern Language Quarterly*, I (1940), 201–5. Howard stresses Coleridge's conception of the "morbid" and "diseased" tragic hero, an argument which is restated and modified somewhat in his *Herman Melville: A Biography* (Berkeley and Los Angeles, 1951), pp. 140, 165, 171–72.

It is this view of art, in which Lear is seen as speaking "the sane madness of vital truth," that suggests the reason for Ahab's insanity and warrants suspicion of Ishmael's frequent expression of sunny views. His jollity, like that of Burton or Rabelais, has something ambivalent about it. Like Stubb, he is "one of those odd sort of humorists, whose jollity is sometimes . . . curiously ambiguous" (p. 217). The madness of Ahab is a protective screen shielding Melville's periodic bouts of oracular pessimism, while Ishmael's hyena laugh is aimed, as Evert Duyckinck observed with distaste, at "the most sacred associations of life" (*Log*, 437). Ahab's vision is centered on one, obsessive goal, but Ishmael lets fly at a multitude of "sacred associations," insinuating his barbs (as well as a number of bawdy puns) into a flow of companionable chatter. Blinded by the glow of Ishmael's fraternal hearth, his readers (Melville hoped) would overlook the impudent faces in the flame.

This combination of "contraries" and contrariness reflects a sense of isolation as well as uncertainty of belief, for there is no absolute center in Melville's work to which one may refer, no moral standpoint against which to measure the declarations and actions of his characters. There is nothing but *tone* to go by, the facetious or declamatory extremes to which his voices mount, and this is a very unsure guide to intention. The only way to view a labyrinth is from a height, where the multitudinous paths resolve themselves into a plan. And so it is with Melville's work: any approach to his ambiguous structures should start by diagraming the main lines of construction, the articulations of opposing forces about which the confusing amalgam of digression and episode clings. Having done so, "it ought to fare with [the reader] something as with a stranger entering, map in hand, Boston town; the streets may be very crooked, he may often pause; but, thanks to his true map, he does not hopelessly lose his way" (*The Confidence-Man*, p. 78).

The problem is simplified by the sameness of Melville's structural devices, for each takes its form from the archetypal quest. This pattern is especially evident in *Mardi, Moby-Dick,* and *Pierre,* but it is also found, drastically modified, in what would seem unlikely places: *The Confidence-Man,* "Bartleby," and "Benito Cereno," among others. Considering Melville's Protestant heritage, his romantic pessimism, his love of the bur-

lesque and picaresque writers of the Renaissance and Enlighten-
ment, it is not strange that the quest pattern should have appealed to him. To a consciousness weaned on Bunyan and Spenser, nourished on Byron and Shelley, and satiated with Rabelais,
Voltaire, and Cervantes, the quest would be a mode of expression as easy to manage as his mother tongue, to say nothing of
its convenience as an instrument of his endless search for belief.

But the quest, because of its linear development, has absolute implications. It is, after all, a quest after or into *something*,
even if that something be nothing after all. For Spenser, the
veil of appearances conceals an absolute, Platonic reality; for
Bunyan, it merely clouds the true road to Paradise. For the
romantics, on the other hand, reality is a mist concealing an absolute void: *Childe Harold* and *Alastor* provide an impressive
heritage of futility. The skeptic satirists perhaps come closest
to Melville's vision, but their bitter laughter leaves no room for
the solemnity of Ahab's conception. Melville found no form
ready-made, and his lifetime was spent wrestling "with the angel
—Art." His chief problem in lending form to his brave schemes
was to adapt the quest pattern to his complexly relativistic
vision, to somehow modify the absolute implications of the outward voyage.

II

Melville's declaration to Hawthorne, that he had "'pretty
much made up his mind to be annihilated,'" suggests that his
wanderings between belief and unbelief tended, like a ship tack-
ing before the wind, to work their way towards increasing skepticism, darkening into pessimism. But by examining two of his
quest structures, one taken from his early (before *Mardi*) and
middle (before *The Confidence-Man*) periods, we can see that
the basis for all his work was nihilistic in implication, that Melville very early in his creative life was concerned with the possibilities of "annihilation." By comparing the two stories, moreover, we can obtain a reasonably fair idea of the uses, uniform
and varied, to which Melville put the quest pattern early and
late. Such an examination, finally, demonstrates the extent to
which he was indebted to other writers for the materials of
his art.

So far as scholarship can determine, Melville's first published fiction appeared in the *Lansingburgh Advertiser* for May 4 and 18, 1839. The second (and most important) of these "Fragments from a Writing Desk" is a tale about a young man who is handed a love letter by a mysterious, cloaked figure, and who follows the messenger into a deep forest grove in search of the anonymous admirer. The messenger leads him to an Arabian-Gothic palace, which the young man enters with great difficulty, to find a voluptuous "Andalusian" princess awaiting him. At first enraptured by his discovery, the youth recoils in horror when he realizes that the beautiful girl is deaf and dumb, and the story ends upon this note of ghastly disillusionment.[5]

"The Piazza," written late in 1855 as an introductory sketch to a collection of his short stories, seems representative in theme and technique to the work of that period. In this story, a land-locked sailor (clearly a projection of Melville's self) catches sight from his piazza of a gleam on a mountaintop. His curiosity aroused, he follows (like the knights of old) a mountain road towards the gleam, hoping to find "the queen of fairies." Instead, he finds a wretched mountain girl living in a miserable shack, whose only joy is dreaming about the King Charming who lives in the white palace below—that is, the sailor and his farmhouse. Disillusioned, the voyager returns to his piazza, and contents himself thereafter with accepting the theater of appearances without question, until "truth comes in with darkness."

Aside from the erotic motif (much stronger in the earlier sketch), these two short pieces share in common a landscape of deceptive scenery. The attitude towards that scenery, however, varies greatly between the early and late work. The first story is obviously influenced by the romantics—there is not much difference of intimation between it and, say, Shelley's *Alastor*. The oriental setting, the enthusiastic plunge, the luring cynosure—

[5] See Appendix B, to William H. Gilman's *Melville's Early Life and REDBURN* (New York, 1951), pp. 264–71, where the "Fragment No. 2" is reprinted entire. Cf. with what follows below, Gilman's discussion of the relevance of the "Fragment" to Melville's subsequent work: "Melville's exposure of his hero to an abrupt reversal of his rosy anticipations reveals a significant early attraction toward ironic themes and situations. . . . Of profound significance is the fact that the 'Fragment' tells the story of a frustrated quest. . . . As early as his twentieth year Melville's mind had formulated, however crudely, the concept that pursuit of the ideal is foredoomed to disillusion and defeat" (pp. 114–20). Gilman also summarizes the romantic sources—chiefly Byronic—of the "Fragment."

all of these devices are basic to the romantic quest. The later story, which commences with a Spenserian motif—the search for the fairy queen—ends on a Quixotic note, the purposeful suspension of disbelief for the sake of the pleasure such surrender brings. The "Fragment," with its straightforward movement into mystery and its sudden, violent climax, clearly prefigures the structure of *Mardi, Moby-Dick,* and *Pierre,* while the slower pace of "The Piazza" (a third of which is devoted to establishing the eccentric character of the narrator), as well as its essentially comic ending, is more typical of the short stories and sketches of the middle period. The attitude of acceptance, moreover, is a pose which comes increasingly to dominate Melville's later work, modifying, if not replacing, the violence of his earlier nihilism.

Attitude, however, is a treacherous guide to Melville's intention—the sailor of "The Piazza" can be trusted no more than the sailor of *Moby-Dick.* The "meaning" of the story emerges from the structure—the futile quest—and from the pattern of images and illusions by which Melville builds up his ironic terrain, the landscape of deceptive scenery through which the quester passes. The playing off of this scenery against the attitude of the quester is, in both stories, the important structural fact. It is the character of the quester, viewed against the ironic scenery, which informs Melville's "meaning," rather than the attitude of the quester alone.

In the "Fragment," the quester is a bored student, who opens the story with a cry of impatience: " 'Confusion seize the Greek!' exclaimed I, as wrathfully rising from my chair, I flung my ancient Lexicon across the room, and seizing my hat and cane, and throwing on my cloak, I sallied out into the clear air of heaven." The mention of the Greek Lexicon is thematic, since most of the allusions to follow are classical. A mysterious circle-in-a-grove through which the youth is led on his way to the castle has a vaulted roof of trees which seem to him "to have canopied the triumphal feasts of the sylvan god," and the chamber in which he meets the maimed princess is decorated with paintings "illustrative of the loves of Jupiter and Semele, Psyche before the tribunal of Venus, and a variety of other scenes." The fair inhabitant is robed in white, with a "zone . . . of pink satin, on which were broidered figures of Cupid in the act of drawing his bow, while the ample folds of her Turkish sleeve were gathered at the wrist by a bracelet of immense rubies, each of which represented a heart pierced thro' by a golden shaft." That is, the dry contents of the Lexicon are balanced by pagan (chiefly Ovidian) allusions, and the boredom of the student is replaced by the ecstacy of the lover.

The shock of discovery which numbs this ecstacy does not come without warning, however. The room is also furnished with "mirrors of unusual magnitude, multiplying in all directions the gorgeous objects," mirrors which "deceived the eye by their reflections, and mocked the vision with long perspective." "Deceived" and "mocked" are the key words, a hint of the deceptive appearances which lure the youth into the assurance of a bliss he is never to attain. Emphasizing artifice, the machinery of deception is patently Spenserian, adapted to the purposes of romantic disenchantment. The room is a Victorian version of Acrasia's bower.

The Spenserian hints are a minor element in the "Fragment." The eager, forward movement of the student is virtually unqualified until, with the springing of a trap, he is dropped into disillusionment. In "The Piazza," on the other hand, the fabric of the narrative is heavily interwoven with images and allusions which hint at the futile implications of the quest. In the first paragraph, for instance, the countryside surrounding the farmhouse is described as highly picturesque—"a very paradise of painters"—suggesting the artificiality of the scene and the ultimate illusoriness of beauty. Further illusion is provided by the view from the house: "The circle of the stars [is] cut by the circle of the mountains. At least, so looks it from the house; though, once upon the mountains, no circle of them can you see. Had the site been chosen five rods off, this charmed ring would not have been."

Underlying this motif of false appearances is a suggestion of threat: the farmhouse is perched upon "a long land-slide of sleeping meadow, sloping away off from my poppy bed," a situation described in terms suggesting disaster and a narcotic-induced sleep. The site of the house was wrested from "the Trogdolytes of those subterranean parts," and located where Orion (type of the blind quester) "flashed down his Damocles' sword" (token of impending doom) and commanded " 'Build there.' " It is from this house that the old sailor first catches a glimpse of the object of his quest, and it is into the maze-like range of mountains that he voyages in search of it, blissfully unaware of the dire implications of the landscape through which he must pass.

Forbidding also are the conditions under which the "uncertain object" is first seen on the mountain: it is snuggled among a range of mountains whose perspective baffles, and is "so situated as to be only visible, and then but vaguely, under certain conditions of light and shadow." The theme of enchantment suggested here, an essential part of the "inland voyage of fairyland," dominates the succeeding passages, enforcing the pattern of illusoriness. When the distant object is first sighted, it is on a "wizard afternoon in autumn," when the maple woods, "having lost their first vermilion tint, dully smoked, like smouldering towns, when flames expire upon their prey." By this process of accumulation, the themes of illusion, enchantment, and threat are joined: the sky is compared to a witches' cauldron, and "two sportsmen, crossing a red stubble buck-wheat field, seemed guilty Macbeth and foreboding Banquo." The allusion to the witches of *Macbeth* connotes an evil omen, but the threatening portent means nothing to the narrator: viewing the "one spot of radiance, where all else was shade," he can only conclude that it marks "some haunted ring where fairies dance."

The contrast between the threatening ambivalence of the scenery and the benign belief in fairies on the part of the old sailor provides the main tension of the sketch, and is broken only with his eventual discovery of the pauper maiden. The illusoriness of the landscape, the imagery of enchantment, and the idea of the search for the queen of fairies is borrowed explicitly from Spenser ("How to get to fairy-land, by what road, I did not know; nor could any one inform me; not even one Edmund Spenser, who had been there—so he wrote me—further than that to reach fairy-land, it must be voyaged to, and with faith"), while the old sailor's attitude towards the enchanted landscape is patently Quixotic ("Don Quixote, that sagest sage that ever lived"). He puts his faith in the good signs, such as the golden promise of a rainbow, and ignores the bad. The memory of the view from his piazza on an August noon, when the "vastness and the lonesomeness are so . . . oceanic; and the silence and the sameness, too, that the first peep of a strange house, rising beyond the trees, is for all the world like spying, on the Barbary coast, an unknown sail," turns his thoughts, not to the pirates one would normally associate with such a sail, but to "my inland voyage to fairyland."

Most potent of the many forbidding tokens is a Chinese creeper which climbs the post of the piazza, a "starry bloom" containing "millions of strange, cankerous worms, which, feeding upon those blossoms, so shared their blessed hue, as to make it unblessed evermore." But this, instead of discouraging the old sailor's faith in appearances, only makes him impatient with a long convalescence, and when once again the golden window gleams, he decides to "push away for fairy-land—for rainbow's end, in fairy-land." Throughout his journey his Quixotism prevails, and none of the ominous signs which he encounters qualifies his enthusiasm: "Fairy-land not yet, though the morning is here before me."

Like the landscape through which the sailor passes, the clearing in which he finds the object of his search—a little, gray-colored cottage—is emblematic. Neither threatening or promising, the mountaintop is a vortex of the natural world: "No fence was seen, no inclosure. Near by—ferns, ferns, ferns; further—woods, woods, woods; beyond—mountains, mountains, mountains; then—sky, sky, sky. Turned out in aerial commons, pasture for the mountain moon. Nature, and but nature, the house and all." Center of everything, center of nothing, the cottage is "set down on the summit, in a pass between the two worlds, participant of neither," and its centrality is symbolized by its roof, one half of which is shiny with new shingles, the other weather-stained and mossy. This pairing of lights and darks suggests the balance of opposing forces, the mystical chiaroscuro, that animates all Nature.

A similar balance informs the conclusion of the sketch. Although the narrator decides to "stick to the piazza," to accept Nature as a theater of beautiful illusion, "every night, when the curtain falls, truth comes in with darkness. No light shows from the mountain." Fairyland is the gift of sunlight; darkness, in dimming the golden window, brings back thoughts of "the weary face behind it." Despite the old sailor's continued faith in sunlight, once it is removed he walks "the piazza deck, haunted by Marianna's face, and many as real a story." It is his realization of the truth of darkness that gives point to the sailor's tale, for it is the same truth which has revealed itself in imagery and allusion throughout the narrative, hints of the blackness that underlies nature's bright gildings.

It is these cluelike devices which, along with the use of the optimistic character of the old man as a medium of indirection, distinguish the late sketch from the early. These are the techniques we associate with Melville's ironic masterpieces, *Moby-Dick*, "Bartleby," and *The Confidence-Man*, and any study of Melville's art must come to terms with their development and implication. But if we descend to the "little lower layer," we see that there is a structure shared in common by the two sketches: aroused by mystery, inspired by discontent, each quester moves through a magical terrain (in both cases a wood) and comes upon an ambiguous structure which houses disillusionment. The first story, written before Melville went to sea, couches the quest in typical romantic terms, while the later relies heavily on maritime imagery, but these are matters of style rather than ontology. In both sketches it is structure which tells, which provides a diagram of disillusionment. This structure remains remarkably consistent throughout the development of Melville's art, supplying a common denominator to which matters of style may be related.

The implications of this structure are nihilistic, hinting at the final annihilation whose possibility so tormented Melville: "perhaps, after all," he wrote to Hawthorne, "there is *no* secret," no ultimate meaning to the mystery of being: "We incline to think that the Problem of the Universe is like the Freemason's mighty secret, so terrible to all children. It turns out, at last, to consist in a triangle, a mallet, and an apron,—nothing more!" The world is a trap, a trick, a hoax, in which appearances mask a void, but—and it is here that Melville's will to believe somehow keeps him from complete denial—we ultimately must confront the rock-hard fact of our personal existence, the active being whose essence gives the quester validity: "it is this *Being* of the matter," he declared to Hawthorne, "there lies the knot with which we choke ourselves. As soon as you say *Me*, a *God*, a *Nature*, so soon you jump off from your stool and hang from the beam." It is a knot much like this which puts an end to Ahab's quest, which has, like that of the young student and the old sailor, progressed through ambiguous territory into a void of annihilatory implications.

If Melville's questers are all persistent in their settings-forth, their journeys expressing his own desire to believe, that persistence rests on Quixotic foundations, and all of them are ultimately baffled by the confusing contradictoriness of a world which has "no secret," no absolute basis. Empathizing with his outward-moving heroes, yet aware of their essential fallibility, Melville uses them to explore the shifting, relativistic territory of Truth, a journey which necessarily leads into the void of ultimate mystery. In the end, always, it is that final mystery which is the important thing, and it is toward the expression of that mystery that Melville's art is aimed. Thus it is that as his craft matured, its enigmatic quality increased, the irony of style merging with the irony of structure until, after *Pierre*, with the disappearance of the dynamic quester, the reader is presented with an alternativeless pattern of enigmas. We may view this final stage as evidence of Melville's increasing bitterness, but if we consider the implications of even his most dynamic quests, there is not much difference, ultimately, between *Moby-Dick* and *The Confidence-Man*. The forward thrust of the voyage out is only half of Melville's ironic diagram: equally important to it is a system of ironic contrasts, a paradoxical terrain that baffles, overwhelms, or destroys the expectant quester. In the later works, the forward thrust looses its impetus, and the system of ironic contrasts becomes more important, but the strategic balance—with all that it implies—remains to the very end:

> There is no steady unretracing progress in this life; we do not advance through fixed gradations, and at the last one pause: —through infancy's unconscious spell, boyhood's thoughtless faith, adolescence' doubt (the common doom), then scepticism, then disbelief, resting at last in manhood's pondering repose of If. But once gone through, we trace the round again; and are infants, boys, and men, and Ifs eternally.

III

We may regard Melville's ironic diagram as having two dimensions: a linear dimension, associated with the sequential or "story" element, and given shape by the hero's absolutist quest; and a circular dimension, associated with the relativistic maze within which that quest founders. I say "circle," because of the importance to his diagram of the return trip of wisdom as opposed to the voyage out of initiation, a roundness of total experience which corresponds to the wholeness of matched contraries that is the world. Many of Melville's quests, moreover, contain a meaningful use of circular images or devices: in "The Piazza," for example, the object of the quest is associated with the illusory circles of stars and mountains as well as with a "fairy ring," images whose roundness suggests the relativity of appearances. This circular element assumes more complex forms in the longer works: in *Mardi* and *Moby-Dick* it is the relativistic roundness of the globe which brings the quester back to the point from which he started.

There are times when Melville hints that the circle is a *discordia concors,* a binding together of the disparate elements of the world in a harmonious whole that seems to mock the straightforward, absolute intention (cheery or dark) of the quester. But a harmonious whole suggests an ultimate affirmation that Melville was never able to achieve, and there is found in these configurations, always, a saving image or allusion which calls the harmony to question. A good example is the episode in *Moby-Dick* in which Ishmael's boat glides through a circle of gallied whales into the calm of the inner circle, where "the storms in the roaring glens between the outermost whales were heard but not felt. Yes, we were now in that enchanted calm which they say lurks at the heart of every commotion." Gazing down through the transparent waters within the circle, Ishmael sees a vision of motherhood and love protected from the stormy violence beyond the barrier: "though surrounded by circle upon circle of consternations and affrights, did these inscrutable creatures at the centre freely and fearlessly indulge in dalliance and delight."

This mystic circle of quietude bordered by strife seems to approximate the "All" that was Nature for the Transcendentalists, a union of disparates that has its counterpart in the soul of man: "amid the tornadoed Atlantic of my being, do I myself still for ever centrally disport in mute calm; and while ponderous planets of unwaning woe revolve round me, deep down and deep inland there I still bathe me in eternal mildness of joy" (p. 387). But Melville also believed that there is "an immense deal of flummery" in the "*all* feeling," and the harmony of the whale circle is broken when a lone animal, maimed and in agony, dashes "among the revolving circles." Like the masthead philosopher who tumbles into a Pantheistic sea, the invading, wounded whale breaks the illusory contentment of the inner lake, the "entire host of whales . . . tumbling upon their inner centre." Flux, not stasis, is the true condition of Nature, and doubts, similarly, invade the serenity of the deepest soul. However peaceful may be the inner garden of contentment, no man may abide there forever.

Expressive of Melville's diagrammatic circle is the roof of Marianna's cottage in "The Piazza." Though not a literal circle, it contains in its imagery of matched halves an idea essential to the circular view, an apparent harmony of matched opposites qualified by the absolute misery of the girl who dwells within. A similar configuration is contained in the upper and lower shells of the Galapagos tortoise in "The Encantadas": "yet even the tortoise, dark and melancholy as it is upon the back, still possesses a bright side; its calipee or breast-plate being sometimes of a faint yellowish or golden tinge." Moving from the position that "the tortoise is both black and bright," the narrator goes on to describe a creature of unending woe, of "dateless, indefinite endurance," a description which would seem to give meaning to the fact that the creature's natural position is on its belly, the "bright side" perpetually hidden.

This endless process of qualification is intrinsic to the relative implications of the circle, the ceaseless flux that qualifies (in turn) the absolute implications of the quest. That it is the dark half which is emphasized gives warrant to Ahab's convictions, which are an extreme expression of Melville's own pessimism, but though the darkness dominates it is not the whole, and though the sunlight but gilds, the gilding must be accounted for: Marianna's illusions save her from the needless pain of Truth, and the soil on the mountain top is richest around the base of the ruined cottage. Perhaps, Melville hints, the gilding is only the thin covering of a pitfall, the smiling surface of a shark-ridden sea, the pleasant manner of a profound villain. Certain it is that he has nothing but contempt for those who are willing to accept surfaces for what they seem. And yet he appears unwilling to let go completely, to deny the validity of the bright side of the sphere, the fleshly joys of home and hearth.

The examples I have chosen above, particularly "The Piazza," are aimed against the easy optimism of Melville's contemporaries, and are tricky structures designed to trap the unwary reader. In the "Enceladus" episode in *Pierre*, however, we are provided with an example of almost unremitting darkness, a mountain tour like "The Piazza," but which ends with a description of the Ahab-like Titan "who despairing of any other mode of wreaking his immitigable hate, turned his vast trunk into a battering-ram, and hurled his own arched-out ribs again and yet again against the invulnerable steep." Apparently a gloss on Pierre's nihilistic self-assertion, the episode is introduced by a passage which expresses an idea central to Melville's ontology, and which modifies the extent to which we may accept Pierre's dark vision as "Truth": "Say what some poets will, Nature is not so much her own ever-sweet interpreter, as the mere supplier of that cunning alphabet, whereby selecting and combining as he pleases, each man reads his own peculiar lesson according to his peculiar mind and mood" (p. 402). Called Mount of the Titans and Delectable Mountain alike, the mountain puts forth an ambiguous face to the valley below. At a distance, "viewed from the piazza of a soft haze-canopied summer's noon," it presents "a long and beautiful, but not entirely inaccessible-looking purple precipice . . . on each hand sideways sloping down to lofty terraces of pastures." The traveler who attempts to climb this height discovers "horrible glimpses of dark-dripping rocks, and mysterious mouths of wolfish caves," and finally encounters "an impregnable redoubt, where he had fancied . . . a practicable vault to his courageous thews. Cunningly masked hitherto, by the green tapestry of the interlacing leaves, a terrific towering palisade of dark mossy massiness confronted you; and trickling with unevaporable moisture, distilled upon you from its beetling brow slow thunder-showers of water-drops, chill as the last dews of death." This revelation, like the fury which erupts from Moby Dick's gliding snow-hill of repose, would seem to substantiate Pierre's (and Ahab's) vision of malignity at the heart of benign appearances.

But the subjectiveness of appearances works both ways: if the prospect from the valley is illusory, casting a "cunning purpleness" over the hidden life on the mountain side, so also is that "stark desolation, ruin, merciless and ceaseless" in some way a mirage also. On this same height "the misanthropic hill-scaling goat nibbled his sweetest food; for the rocks, so barren in themselves, distilled a subtile moisture, which fed with greenness all things that grew about their igneous marge." Some hint of the meaningfulness of these proportions is given by Melville's description of the warfare between the evergreen amaranth and the deciduous catnip which grow on the mountainside: "every spring the amaranthine and celestial flower gained on the mortal household herb; for every autumn the catnip died, but never an autumn made the amaranth to wane. The catnip and the amaranth!—man's earthly household peace, and the ever-encroaching appetite for God." Amaranth and catnip, carapace and plastron, moss and shingle, outer and inner circles—these are the contraries from which Melville's complex mazes are built, for the "mingled, mingling threads of life are woven by warp and woof: calms crossed by storms, a storm for every calm."

It cannot be denied, however, that Melville's emphasis is generally on the outer circle—the circle of storms—and that he uses light in patterns of chiaroscuro dominated by darkness. Never a symbol of unqualified harmony, the circle can become a vortex of perfect emptiness, like the spreading ring of foam that marks the grave of the questing *Pequod.* The coefficient of that white ring is the massive whiteness of the Whale, who is, in turn, the coefficient of the Mount of Titans in *Pierre* and the hidden castle in the "Fragment." Whale, mountain, and castle are the equivalent of mystery, cynosures which draw the quester on to death or disillusionment, from puzzlement to obsession to madness. Mystery becomes Mystery, as the massive bulk of the Whale is resolved into a spreading circle of nothingness, as the arms of the maiden open into a void of silence, as the landscape of the mountain reveals its many changes, as the golden window fades into the darkness of truth.

For Melville, always, darkness, whiteness, and silence—in combination or alone—are tokens of mystery which suggest the possibility of ultimate nothingness, the grand hoax of the universe. It may be a coincidence that the youth in the "Fragment" hurries through a dark wood to an encounter with a silent maiden dressed in white, but it is not a coincidence that these three motifs appear again and again at important junctures in his many quests. Of the three, perhaps Silence is the most important symbol. Melville knew that silence was for the ancient Greeks "the vestibule to the higher mysteries," and he was deeply affected by the phenomenon himself, regarding it as "a strange thing," a correlative of the presence of emptiness, the inexpressible implication of infinitude.[6] "'The last wisdom is dumb,'" declares Babbalanja, and at the Beginning there was an "Ineffable Silence, proceeding from its unimaginable remoteness" (*Mardi:* II, 348; I, 268). From the mute maiden to the silence of the Typee valley, from there to the hush surrounding the swimming snow-hill bulk of Moby Dick and the deathly stillness following the execution of Billy Budd, one may trace a pattern of silences that gives a uniformity of meaning to those diverse works.

This Silence, like the Darkness on the mountain and the Whiteness of the great Whale, suggests that infinity may be a void, that there is no secret, that all meaning emerges from the mind of the beholder: "'for all things visible are but conceits of the eye: things imaginative, conceits of the fancy. If duped by one, we are equally duped by the other.'" To the "'old interrogatory . . . what is truth?'" there is no answer not in the question (*Mardi*, I, 327). But it is the urgent necessity of that question and the possibility of that answer which dictate the dimensions of Melville's ironic diagram. An awareness of that diagram does not provide the reader with a key to Melville's work, but it does serve to give some idea of the extent to which his many stories, novels, and poems have a common basis. The basis itself is in no way original with Melville, but in observing his particular adaptions of the quest, in particular the modifications which occur after *Pierre,* we can clarify somewhat the apparently puzzling contradictions which characterize his mind and art.

---

[6] *Journal of a Visit to London and the Continent, 1849–1850,* Ed. Eleanor Melville Metcalf (Cambridge, Mass., 1948, p. 48).